A CASEBOOK ON EXISTENTIALISM

A CASEBOOK ON

Existentialism

William V. Spanos

HARPUR COLLEGE

THOMAS Y. CROWELL COMPANY

Established 1834

New York

TO THE MEMORY OF MY FATHER, VAIOS,
A MAN OF FLESH AND BONE

 Library of Congress Catalog Card Number: 66-10926. Designed by Judith Woracek Barry. Manufactured in the United States of America. First Printing, January, 1966. Second Printing, May, 1966. Third Printing, May, 1967. Fourth Printing, March, 1968. Fifth Printing, January, 1969.

PREFACE

When the term existentialism became current in Europe after World War II, only the name of Jean-Paul Sartre was associated with it. Since then it has become clear that the body of existential thought constitutes an authentic philosophical movement embracing (despite their diversity) a large group of contemporary Western thinkers: Camus and Marcel, as well as Sartre, in France; Jaspers and Heidegger in Germany; Unamuno and Ortega y Gasset in Spain; Berdyaev and Shestov in Russia; Bultmann and Barth in Switzerland; Buber in Israel; and Tillich in the United States. But existentialism is more than a philosophical movement. It has become *the* perspective from which the sensitive and concerned modern man looks at his world. Indeed, one can scarcely understand in any deep sense the general direction of literature and theology today or the form and content of many contemporary works without some understanding of the existential attitude.

As a literary movement, existentialism has its antecedents in the nineteenth century, in such philosophers as Kierkegaard and Nietzsche, and in such writers as Dostoevsky, Tolstoy, and even Dickens. It includes, besides avowed existentialist writers like Sartre, Camus, and Unamuno, such early moderns as Kafka and Hemingway and such significant figures of the present as Auden, Beckett, Ionesco, and Pinter. Indeed, it might well be argued that the form and content of most of the important literature since World War I (the disaster, according to Tillich, that brought the innocent and optimistic Victorian Age to a sudden end), from "The Love Song of J. Alfred Prufrock" and *Ulysses* to "Howl" and *Herzog*, reflect aspects of the existential diagnosis of contemporary life. Certainly for the American writers of the 1950's and 60's, whose work as a whole is justly referred to as the Literature of Revolt—Salinger, Ginsberg, Kerouac, Corso, Styron, Mailer, Ellison, Albee, and Bellow, to name the best known—the influence of the existential outlook has become central.

This book introduces the student to existentialism. The opening essay, essentially a definition of the existentialist attitude, sets in broad perspective the readings that follow. From the vast body of modern existential literature, Part I presents selections that seem to illustrate especially well the various modes of the existential imagination. Part II contains general commentary on the content and forms of existential literature (including articles that allude to or debate the significant issues of Sartre's *littérature engagée*) and detailed analyses of specific works—analyses useful, I believe, in sharpening the student's own critical perceptions as he confronts the literature of existentialism. Part III presents characteristic statements by the major existential philosophers and theologians of the nineteenth and twentieth centuries. The order of the three parts is arbitrary, of course.

In choosing the material, I have aimed at (1) focusing on the basic categories of the existential attitude (such as dread, alienation, objectification, and freedom); thus (2) suggesting the spectrum from humanistic through theistic existentialism, both in the literature and in the essays; and (3) presenting statements characteristic yet accessible to undergraduate students by the major spokesmen of existentialism. This has not been an easy task; the aims have often cut across each other. I believe, however, that this modest collection will prove a sound introduction to an extremely complex subject and that it will yield more than ample material for discussion and composition. For those who wish to pursue issues still further, a bibliography appears at the end of the volume. In the texts of the selections, bracketed superscript numbers indicate the pagination of the original source. If a page of the original ended with part of a word, the bracketed page number follows the whole word.

The people to whom I became indebted in the process of bringing this book into print are more numerous than can be thanked individually. I must content myself with a general expression of gratitude. I feel obligated to give special thanks, however, to Richard Arber and Novello Grano of the Thomas Y. Crowell Company, for their interest and generous editorial advice; to Dr. Fred Newman of the Philosophy Department of the City College of New York, for his *presence;* to Ardena Henrichsen, for her efficient secretarial assistance; to Knox College, for the research grant that helped to defray the cost of manuscript preparation; and to my wife Margaret, for her uncanny ability to make minute discriminations. To all these people I owe most of whatever is valuable in this book. I claim all its faults.

W.V.S.

Galesburg, Illinois
October, 1965

CONTENTS

PHILOSOPHY AND THEOLOGY

APPENDICES

WILLIAM V. SPANOS

Abraham, Sisyphus, and the Furies: Some Introductory Notes on Existentialism

There are countless places of refuge, there is only one place of salvation; but the possibilities of salvation, again, are as numerous as all the places of refuge.

—FRANZ KAFKA

The roots of existentialism extend deeply into western history, even beyond St. Augustine to the pre-Socratic philosophers and the author of the Book of Job. But at no time in the past did the existential attitude (a term more appropriate, perhaps, than "philosophy") have the kind of relevance it has for modern man. In the past—as recently as Søren Kierkegaard's day—the existentialist philosopher or artist was an isolated voice asserting the precariousness of human life in the face of a community that largely ignored or refused to listen to him. As long as the community believed, or thought it believed, in the existence of a god who offered the reward of eternity as compensation for the suffering and anguish of temporal life, his warning went more or less unheard and the existential attitude thus remained marginal and undefined.

In the middle of the nineteenth century, however, after a long and inexorable process of secularization, God—at least the traditional image of God—expired and man was left naked to confront, in T. S. Eliot's great existential metaphor, "a heap of broken images." The proclamation by Nietzsche's madman of the death of God was the annunciation of the age of anxiety. After this, philosophers could no longer spin verbal webs in remote corners of the house of life without at least confronting the reality of Nothingness; nor could theologians build paper Gothic religious systems without confronting the absence of God; nor for that matter, could artists project rational microcosms without confronting the irrational macrocosm.

Since Nietzsche, philosophy, religion, and the arts (especially on the European continent, but increasingly in England and America) have reflected in one way or another the existential crisis of unaccommodated man. Whether atheistic or theistic, the philosophy and art of the twentieth century constitutes largely an encounter with Nothingness and the effort to transcend the threat that it poses to man's existence as man. Thus what was the attitude of an occasional outsider is now that of a generation.

II

What specifically, then, is the existential attitude? Ultimately it is undefinable. Like the unicorn, whom legend endows with wondrous attributes, but whom the empirical eye has never calibrated, existentialism is a kind of poetry of the philosophical imagination, defying rational systematization. Unlike traditional philosophies, existentialism is not a philosophy of essences, defining nature—including human nature—and imposing abstract structures upon it. It is, rather, a philosophy of existence, which attempts to view man in his relationship to the universe in all its concrete plenitude—and problematic complexity. Thus no two existentialists would have the same vision of the human condition. Nevertheless the contemporary philosophical and literary existentialists, both atheistic (or humanistic) and theistic, address themselves to two broad alternatives facing man in a world in which God is dead: (1) the institutionalized and collectivized life on the analogy of the machinery of technology toward which modern man is drifting and (2) the agonizingly difficult authentic existence of the individual who insists upon maintaining his unique consciousness in the face of the overwhelming pressures to conform.

Both humanistic and theistic existentialists recognize the threat of anonymity posed by the development of a mass technological society. They see the ultimate source of this threat, however, in man's real, if unconscious, obsession with order, which in the modern world has driven him into constructing rationally derived systems to replace the discredited Christian cosmology. Although the German idealist Hegel (whose "system" Kierkegaard felt it his life's mission to demolish) and, behind Hegel, the whole tradition of essentialist philosophy going back to Plato and Aristotle, come under the attack of existentialists, their more immediate philosophical *bête noire* is the scientific rationalism of nineteenth century utilitarian philosophers and their twentieth century counterparts, the logical positivists.[1] For in the eyes of the existentialists this

[1] Positivism is essentially a theory of meaning which holds that the meaningful is ultimately linked to the empirically verifiable—that which can be ex-

"scientism" stands as the fountainhead of the technological revolution which, in turn, has generated the worship of progress and consequently a materialistic utopianism that provides modern man with comfort and security but at the price of his freedom, his existential humanity, thus reducing the human community to the level of an ant colony.

According to the existentialists, scientific rationalism and its counterpart in practical life, the technological society, locate reality in the objective realm of measurable matter, and value in the production and utilization of objects. In so doing, they subordinate man to the tool, consciousness to efficiency, and the individual to the social and productive organizations (including educational institutions). By the inescapable logic of this system of valuation, the individual becomes dehumanized. Defined according to his function and evaluated by the degree of his utility, he is reduced to the status of an object like other objects in nature, or, to use Martin Buber's term, a manipulable *It* (Jean-Paul Sartre's *l'en soi,* or the in-itself). Thus stripped of his subjectivity (his *Thou*ness) he is alienated from his authentic self and, like Ulrich in Robert Musil's novel *Der Mann ohne Eigenschaften,* becomes a "man without qualities," and thus an easy, indeed willing, victim of a vast and efficient collective modelled after mass production processes, and often, as in the case of Nazi Germany, a brutalized weapon in the arsenal of such a collective in its effort to achieve universality.

Following Kierkegaard's violent denunciation of the crowd as "the untruth, by reason of the fact that it . . . weakens [the individual's] sense of responsibility by reducing it to a fraction," the condemnation of collectivism becomes a central preoccupation of existential philosophy and theology. From Nietzsche to Jaspers (though Sartre's Marxism constitutes a curious ambiguity in his thought) existentialists have passionately expressed their horror of both the unconscious drift of democracies and the planned advance of totalitarian societies toward the achievement of massive materialistic utopias. Perhaps no one, however, has put it so dramatically as Nicholas Berdyaev in *The End of Our Time:*

> Utopias appear to be far more possible than it was formerly thought. And we find ourselves confronting . . . a dreadful question: How to avoid their ultimate realization? . . . Utopias are possible. Life marches toward utopias. And perhaps a new century begins, a century in which

perienced by the senses. Unlike existentialism, positivism maintains that evaluative statements are not verifiable, and therefore are cognitively meaningless, though they do express attitude.

the intellectuals and the cultivated class will imagine ways of avoiding utopias and of returning to a non-utopian society, less "perfect" and more free.

In the literature of existentialism this criticism of modern man's obsession with materialistic progress has taken the form of the anti-utopian novel, which mercilessly satirizes his eagerness to relinquish the burden of his freedom to the collectivist state in return for the comforts and security of the easy life. Like its philosophical expression, the literary presentation of the theme of anti-utopianism is first encountered in the nineteenth century, in fiction such as Dostoevsky's *Notes from Underground* and "The Legend of the Grand Inquisitor," and in Dickens' *Hard Times.* But it was not until the mechanized brutality of World War I shook the modern artist into authentic awareness of the appallingly destructive potential of scientism that the form was fully defined in Eugene Zamiatin's novel *We* (1924). After this, the form achieved the status of something like a genre, a fact attested to by the successive appearance of such well-known anti-utopian novels as Aldous Huxley's *Brave New World* (which, incidentally, as the epigraph from Berdyaev and the Dostoevskian echoes suggest, is more "existential" than hitherto realized), George Orwell's *1984,* and Virgil Gheorghiu's *The Twenty-fifth Hour.* Projecting a horribly "perfected" society into the future, that is, a society that represents a rigorously logical fulfillment of the present abdication of freedom implicit in the worship of technological progress, this form has become a deadly satirical weapon in the existential assault upon contemporary utopianism, whether it be totalitarian, communist, or capitalistic in design.

It is primarily in their positive assertions about man and his relationship to the cosmos that humanistic and theistic existentialists differ. Nevertheless, there is considerable agreement even in this area to warrant grouping them together. The acknowledgement of the death of God implies that man has no preordained purpose to fulfill in the universe. (For atheists such as Sartre and the early Heidegger, the death of God means literally what it says, or, at any rate, implies radical uncertainty about his existence, whereas for theists, as Paul Tillich's concept of the God above God suggests, it means the death of the conventional gods of Christianity, above all, of the God who is the source of deterministic or idealistic theologies and the God "worshipped" on Sunday mornings by the complacent and self-satisfied middle class.) Thus his demise opens up to the individual the frightening need to choose between two broad alternative modes of existence. He can accept the definition of man posited by the rationalistic behavioral sciences, which views him as another object among the objects and things in the universe, and thus submit to the same natural laws that govern stones. Or he can revolt against his predicament.

As a self-conscious, that is, free, creature, man constitutes a minority in a cosmos governed by natural law. From a rational point of view, then, he is by virtue of his consciousness an anomaly. As Zeus tells Orestes in Sartre's play *The Flies,* "You are not in your own home, intruder, you are a foreign body in the world, like a splinter in flesh, or a poacher in his lordship's forest." All the empirical evidence (objects) in the universe leads to the logical conclusion that man ought to commit literal or at least spiritual suicide (i.e., negate his consciousness) and thus become one with—a rationally understandable part of—the universe. This, without being aware of it, is what mass man does. But the existentialist, who passionately insists on the dignity and worth of man, refuses to capitulate to the pressures of reason and the dehumanizing systems to which it gives rise. Despite the absence of rational justification, he irrationally affirms life against death. In this revolt against the cosmos, he becomes the absurd man. For the humanistic existentialist the mythic symbol of this man, according to Albert Camus, is Sisyphus, who, despite his being condemned to ceaselessly roll a rock to the top of a mountain only to have it fall back of its own weight, nevertheless not only endures but also finds joy in this task. For the theistic existentialist the mythic symbol of the absurd man, according to Kierkegaard, is the biblical Abraham, who although he cannot perceive God rationally, nevertheless obeys—"by virtue of the absurd"—His terrible command to kill his beloved son Isaac, and discovers joy in the very agony of not knowing that he has decided rightly.

Put philosophically, the existential affirmation of man as opposed to the universe of things becomes the well-known formula of Jean-Paul Sartre, "Existence precedes essence," which means simply that a man, as opposed to a thing, *becomes* rather than merely *is;* he is a live creature rather than a dead object. As such, he does not have a universal and thus permanent *nature,* as, for example, a stone has (its 'stoneness'). Unlike the stone, therefore, man cannot be abstracted and quantified, in other words, measured, classified, and placed in a system that can accurately predict his behavior. To attempt to universalize man into Mankind, to posit that essence precedes existence, as essentialist philosophies and collectivist states do, is to reduce a unique and vital being to the level of an inert thing and to render the abstract whole greater than the sum of its concrete parts. Put positively, "existence" refers to man and ultimately means that he is free, that, unlike objects, which merely *are* and thus are at the mercy of their pre-established essences, man alone is capable of choosing his own future, that is, of determining his own essence.

The concept of freedom, therefore, is the root principle of existential thought. But existential freedom has little to do with the rugged individualism of *laissez faire,* the right of economic man to pursue without constraint the pleasure principle or the profit motive, which is posited and defended by the capitalistic democracies of the West. On the contrary, existential freedom is grounded in the awareness of universal contingency and of the radical finality of man's middle state and, therefore, of his agonizing responsibility for choosing between complex alternatives concerning his existence. Stripped of the ethical guides deduced from theological or rational systems, the individual is left naked and alone to face in fear and trembling the great void and, to adapt King Lear's words, to decide whether to make something out of nothing.

Thus the existentialists refuse to allow man to take freedom for granted as he usually does. They reject the vague notion that it is a privilege that somehow renders life easier and happier. Rather, they assert its difficulty. As Sartre says, man "is *condemned* to freedom." Comfort and freedom are incompatible. The easy life, in fact, is the privilege of slaves, for whom all the painful decisions are made by others. The life of a truly free man is measured by the degree of his suffering. In short, freedom, as the existentialists understand it, is, in the words of Dostoevsky's Grand Inquisitor, "a terrible gift."

The existentialists (who are as much moralists as they are philosophers) attempt to activate a genuine awareness of the difficult burden of freedom by means of their analysis of the fact of death. In their view, death is the one certain reality in man's life. Nevertheless, because it opens up the terrible possibility of the existence of the irrational, the possibility that life ends meaninglessly and is absorbed into the void of Nothingness, most men obsessively refuse to acknowledge the reality of death. The conventionally religious man uses the promise of eternal life made by traditional Christian theology to anesthetize the personal sting of death. In a similar way, the modern mass man immersed in the secular life evades the implications of death by a process of self-deception which takes the form of domesticating its terrible irrationality. As Heidegger, following Kierkegaard, puts it in *Being and Time:*

> . . . death is 'known' as a mishap which is constantly occurring—as a 'case of death.' . . . The 'they' has already stowed away an interpretation for this event. It talks of it in a 'fugitive' manner, either expressly or else in a way which is mostly inhibited, as if to say, 'One of these days one will die too, in the end; but right now it has nothing to do with us.'
>
> . . . The expression 'one dies' spreads abroad the opinion that what gets reached, as it were, by death, is the 'they.' . . . 'Dying' is levelled off to an occurrence which reaches *Dasein* [being there; i.e., human existence], to be sure, but belongs to nobody in particular. . . . Dying, which is essentially mine in such a way that no one can be my representative, is perverted into an event of public occurrence which the 'they' encounters. . . . [Death's] character as a possibility gets concealed, and so are the other two items that belong to it—the fact that it is non-relational and that it is not to be outstripped.

The effort to socialize and thus to "outstrip" death, however, is inevitably unsuccessful. For the "fugitive" manner of speaking about death is a tacit awareness of the threat of personal annihilation. Eventually this uneasy awareness which, in T. S. Eliot's term, "flickers in the corner of [one's] eye,"—this anxiety or dread of death and Nothingness—*Angst,* as the existentialists call it—drives the fugitive into a corner where there are no further avenues of escape. Here in "the precincts of his last evasions," as Stanley Romaine Hopper puts it in *The Crisis of Faith,* he must encounter death, the absurd, and the possibility of the palpable reality of Nothingness, and then, as a unique and solitary individual stripped of his protective social garments, make a genuinely committed decision about his relationship to himself and to the universe.

Thus, as Wallace Stevens says in his poem "Sunday Morning,"

> Death is the mother of beauty; hence from her,
> Alone, shall come fulfillment to our dreams
> And our desires.[2]

As terrible as the threat of annihilation is, for the existentialist it often becomes a paradoxically benign agent. For the face to face

[2] From "Sunday Morning" by Wallace Stevens. Reprinted from *The Collected Poems of Wallace Stevens* by permission of Random House, Inc.

encounter with death clarifies the absurdity of the human condition and thus activates what Heidegger calls "concern" (*Sorge*), or what might be called the interrogative mood—the mood that distinguishes man from beast and stone. In other words, the confrontation *humanizes* the being who, like the biblical Job, becomes perilously like the dead objects in the universe of things in his effort to escape death and the absurd. Thus Jaspers, echoing the Book of Job, writes in *The Way of Wisdom* that the authentic life can only spring from "the darkness in which the individual finds himself . . . from his sense of forlornness when he stares without love into the void, from his self-forgetfulness when he feels that he is being consumed by the busy-ness of the world, when suddenly he wakes up in terror and asks himself: What am I failing to do? What should I do?"

It is precisely at this point in the analysis of the human predicament—the moment of the individual's confrontation with Nothingness—that the most significant difference between humanistic and theistic existentialists emerges. For the atheist, as we have seen, the alternative to physical or spiritual suicide is that of Sisyphus: a fully conscious, if agonized, acknowledgement of the irreconcilable nature of man's alienation from the universe and a rebellious, if precarious, assertion of the existential self against the discontinuities of the human predicament.[3] This is, as Paul Tillich puts it, the "courage of despair." For the theist, on the other hand, the alternative is that of Abraham: a leap of faith—not a rejection of the concrete world—a wager, to use Pascal's metaphor, concerning the truth of the existence of the absent God, or more specifically, the truth of the Incarnation, which reconciles time and eternity and thus infuses meaning into the apparently chaotic and fragmented temporal world.

As we have seen, the atheistic existentialist takes the death of God literally. Thus man is absolutely free to create his own essence. He becomes—from a Christian point of view at any rate—something like his own deity, and, along with the burden of responsibilities and risks, he also assumes the awesome creative potentialities generated by this situation. For the Christian, on the other hand, God is not dead; He is rationally incomprehensible; that is, He is absent. Thus man's freedom becomes the dreadful awareness of the

[3] In the literature of atheistic existentialism, the rebellious affirmation is often nothing more positive than the stoic endurance of Nothingness. Occasionally, as in some of the dramas of the absurd, there is no suggestion of affirmation at all.

necessity to choose between a life of despair in the realm of Nothingness and a life of precarious joy in the realm which to the empirical eye appears meaningless, but to the eye of faith constitutes on the microcosmic level a reconciliation between existence and essence and on the macrocosmic level (in the words of T. S. Eliot's *Four Quartets*) an "intersection of the timeless with time," when "the past and future / Are conquered and reconciled." For the Christian existentialist, in other words, existence precedes essence only in the sense that man cannot know his divine essence and achieve an I-Thou relationship with God without immersion into the destructive element of existence.[4]

For both atheistic and theistic existentialists, then, the royal way of "salvation" lies in the heart of darkness which is this world. Thus Camus, after taking his readers to the edge of the void, writes, "This hell of the present is [man's] Kingdom at last." And echoing him, the Christian poet W. H. Auden concludes his Christmas oratorio *For the Time Being:*

> He is the Truth
> Seek Him in the Kingdom of Anxiety;
> You will come to a great city that has expected your
> return for years.
>
> He is the Life
> Love Him in the World of the Flesh;
> And at your marriage all its occasions shall dance for joy. [5]

But there remains the crucial difference. For Camus, as for other humanistic existentialists, salvation is the humanizing awareness of the irreconcilable divorce between man and the world; for Auden, as for other theistic existentialists, it is a marriage of the individual and Christ, and, through this, a reconciliation between man and the universe.

III

The existential literary imagination is as various as its philosophical counterpart. It employs all the genres of creative literature—auto-

[4] Occasionally, however, as in some of the writings of Kierkegaard and especially in the existential theology of Karl Barth, Christian existentialism interprets the leap of faith as a rejection of the things of this world for eternity.

[5] From "For the Time Being" by W. H. Auden. Copyright 1944 by W. H. Auden. Reprinted from *The Collected Poetry of W. H. Auden* by permission of Random House, Inc.

biography, short and long fiction, drama, and poetry—and within each, a great variety of forms. Thus, for example, the forms of the drama of existentialism range from the traditional realism of Sartre's *Dirty Hands,* through the drama of ideas of Camus' *Caligula,* to the surrealist drama of the absurd of Eugène Ionesco. Like the thought of existentialist philosophers, therefore, the literature of existentialism is virtually impossible to classify in formal terms.

On the other hand, the metaphorical vehicles or myths that embody the existential predicament of modern man reveal a striking, and often illuminating, consistency. In *Modern Literature and the Religious Frontier* Nathan Scott distinguishes four such pervasive myths or patterns of symbolic statement: The Myth of the Isolato, which presents the theme of isolation and estrangement (for example, Franz Kafka's novels *The Trial* and *The Castle*); the Myth of Hell, which embodies the theme of Nothingness, the disintegration of meaning in the modern world (William Faulkner's *The Sound and the Fury* and T. S. Eliot's *The Waste Land*); the Myth of Voyage, which projects the painful journey through the irrational self or world (James Joyce's *Ulysses* and Jean-Paul Sartre's *The Age of Reason*); and, finally, the Myth of Sanctity, which depicts the theme of reconciliation and salvation (T. S. Eliot's *The Family Reunion* and Graham Greene's *The End of the Affair*). These categories constitute a brilliant insight into the ways in which myth has been appropriated by the contemporary existential writer, but Scott's hint that the four myths, taken as a unit, resemble Dante's journey in *The Divine Comedy* through the Inferno and the Purgatorio to the Paradiso, coupled with Heidegger's analysis of death and Nothingness, suggests a more inclusive symbolic pattern to stand as the archetypal myth of the existential imagination: the flight from a dark, threatening agent who pursues the fugitive protagonist into an isolated corner (often, the underground), where he must confront his relentless pursuer, whereupon, in a blinding moment of illumination he discovers the paradoxically benevolent aspect of his persecutor. This symbolic pattern, of course, is the Greek myth of the Furies, in which the protagonist's (Orestes') face-to-face encounter with the pursuing Erinyes (the Angry Ones) activates their transfiguration into the Eumenides (the Kindly Ones).[6]

[6] See William Barrett, "The Place of the Furies," *Irrational Man: A Study of Existential Philosophy* (Garden City, N.Y., 1958), pp. 237–248, in which he uses Aeschylus' symbol of the Furies to define the existential diagnosis of modern man's flight from the irrational (including death) and to present the existen-

This, for example, is precisely the symbolic pattern that underlies Tolstoy's "The Death of Ivan Ilych," a story William Barrett has called "something of a basic scripture for existential thought." The death that Ivan, the archetypal functionary, is trying desperately to evade is personified by Tolstoy in the image of something closely resembling the Erinyes. Despite his bad faith—his effort to re-establish the old current of thought ("that had once screened the thought of death from him") by taking up again his duties in the law courts—the pain in his side

> would begin its own gnawing work. Ivan Ilych would turn his attention to it and try to drive the thought of it away, but without success. *It* would come and stand before him and look at him, and he would be petrified and the light would die out of his eyes, and he would again begin asking himself whether *It* alone was true. . . . He would shake himself, try to pull himself together, manage somehow to bring the sitting to a close, and return home with the sorrowful consciousness that his judicial labours would not as formerly hide from him what he wanted them to hide, and could not deliver him from *It*. And what was worst of all was that *It* drew his attention to itself not in order to make him take some action but only that he should look at *It*, look it straight in the face: look at it and without doing anything, suffer inexpressibly.[7]

His flight away from death is presented as a paradoxical motion toward it: "What had happened to him was like the sensation one sometimes experiences in a railway carriage when one thinks one is going backwards while one is really going forward and suddenly becomes aware of the real direction." And finally, upon Ivan's authentic confrontation with his pursuer, death becomes a benign agent, or more precisely, a midwife who presides over a spiritual birth that Ivan perceives as his falling through the darkness of the

---

tial demand for authenticity. For the Christian existentialist, the figure of the pursuer takes the symbolic form of the hound of heaven, the archetypal projection of which occurs in that other ancient work which has been adopted by existentialists as a mythical construct of the human predicament: the Book of Job. The Old Testament myth can be interpreted as an analogy of the myth of the Furies presented by Aeschylus in *The Oresteia*. Just as the Furies pursue Orestes into perception of a different cosmos and thus of the positive side of his pursuers, so Satan, the symbol of the fallen world (i.e., the world in which death holds sway) from which Job wishes to escape, drives Job into acceptance of its fallenness and thus into awareness of his pursuer as an agent of God.

[7] The references to the gnawing in his side become pervasive after his accident, but only achieve a total identification with the *It*, the Fury figure, at the end of this section, when Ivan says to himself: "*It* sits there as before, gnawing just the same!"

womb into light ("In place of death there was light") and expresses in words that allude to Christ's final labor ("Death is finished").

In the literature of existentialism, the image of the pursuer often symbolizes something more than death. Nevertheless, its focal meaning is invariably a form or extension of death—the absurd, Nothingness, the fallen world, for example—and the pattern is invariably, if broadly, similar to that of "Ivan Ilych." Thus, in Jean-Paul Sartre's *The Flies,* the flies, which symbolize the agonizing remorse, or rather a view of death that demands remorse from the individual who breaks the dehumanizing eternal order of the gods and the political order of the world's Grand Inquisitors, become in the end the humanizing burden of anguish that Orestes assumes when he rejects Zeus and the eternal order for death and freedom. Thus also, in T. S. Eliot's *The Family Reunion,* the Furies, symbolizing the nauseous meaninglessness of the fallen world—the world of death—become Harry's "bright angels" after they have pursued him into "the precincts of his last evasions."

There is, of course, in line with the philosophical distinction, a significant difference between the humanistic existentialist's treatment of the Furies and that of the Christian existentialist. For the former, the Furies activate an authenticity which is characterized by the protagonist's existential awareness of his freedom and of the abyss that separates him from the world, and which manifests itself in the courage to be in the face of despair. The humanistic Furies, in other words, symbolize things as they are in the natural world. They may appear to be demonic to the protagonist, but in reality there is no supernatural significance associated with them. For the Christian, on the other hand, the Furies activate an authenticity characterized by the protagonist's existential awareness of the possibility of a ground of Being that gives order and worth to the world. They constitute, that is, the incarnational principle, the hound of heaven, pursuing the protagonist, undermining his self-sufficient legalistic, or at best ethical, vision and driving him finally, through anguish and despair, to a recognition of at least the possibility of the coherent nature of existence, in which even death (or evil) itself is an organic part of the larger rhythm of creation. As the Skeleton or *figura rerum* (another Fury symbol) puts it in Charles Williams' play *Thomas Cranmer of Canterbury,* this principle is "Christ's back" or again, "the Judas who betrays men to God." The difference, in other words, resides in the Christian existentialist's redemptive resolution. The journey activated by the Furies, which takes the protagonist to the edge of the abyss where the choice must be made, is fundamentally the same.

There are, of course, other myths and symbols that express the existential vision of the human predicament: the Underground Man (for example, in Dostoevsky's *Notes from Underground* and Ralph Ellison's *The Invisible Man*), the Metamorphosis (in Franz Kafka's "Metamorphosis" and Eugène Ionesco's *Rhinoceros*), the Eternal Return (in Ionesco's *The Bald Soprano* and *The Lesson*), and the Grand Inquisitor (in such anti-utopian novels as those of Aldous Huxley, George Orwell, and Virgil Gheorghiu). But none, it seems to me, is so pervasive and inclusive of the various facets of existentialism as the myth of the Furies. It is discoverable in a great many other works besides those already mentioned. It can be seen in humanistic existential works such as Albert Camus' *The Fall*, Archibald MacLeish's *J. B.*, and Harold Pinter's *The Room* and *The Birthday Party*. It also informs such Christian existential works as Dostoevsky's *Crime and Punishment*, Graham Greene's *The Power and the Glory*, T. S. Eliot's *The Waste Land* and *The Elder Statesman*, and Charles Williams' *Cranmer of Canterbury*, *Seed of Adam*, *Judgement at Chelmsford*, and *The House of the Octopus*.

This list could easily be extended, but these titles should be amply sufficient to suggest that the myth of the Furies (whether in the form given it by Aeschylus or the author of the Book of Job) constitutes something of an archetype in the literature of contemporary existentialism. This, however, should not be surprising. For more than any other aspect of the human condition, the phenomenon of death, as the existentialists observe, has always been the closest intimate of mankind. No matter how obsessively men have striven to outstrip death, the effort has been futile. Death demands that each individual face and come to terms with his mortality. It is, therefore, not difficult to understand why the human imagination has always, especially in times of crisis like the present, mythologized, that is, has made *something* of this terrible negation.

LITERATURE

ERNEST HEMINGWAY

A Clean, Well-Lighted Place

It was late and every one had left the café except an old man who sat in the shadow the leaves of the tree made against the electric light. In the daytime the street was dusty, but at night the dew settled the dust and the old man liked to sit late because he was deaf and now at night it was quiet and he felt the difference. The two waiters inside the café knew that the old man was a little drunk, and while he was a good client they knew that if he became too drunk he would leave without paying, so they kept watch on him.

"Last week he tried to commit suicide," one waiter said.

"Why?"

"He was in despair."

"What about?"

"Nothing."

"How do you know it was nothing?"

"He has plenty of money."

They sat together at a table that was close against the wall near the door of the café and looked at the terrace where the tables were all [17] empty except where the old man sat in the shadow of the leaves of the tree that moved slightly in the wind. A girl and a soldier went by in the street. The street light shone on the brass number on his collar. The girl wore no head covering and hurried beside him.

"The guard will pick him up," one waiter said.

"What does it matter if he gets what he's after?"

"He had better get off the street now. The guard will get him. They went by five minutes ago."

The old man sitting in the shadow rapped on his saucer with his glass. The younger waiter went over to him.

"What do you want?"

The old man looked at him. "Another brandy," he said.

"You'll be drunk," the waiter said. The old man looked at him. The waiter went away.

"He'll stay all night," he said to his colleague. "I'm sleepy now. I never get into bed before three o'clock. He should have killed himself last week."

The waiter took the brandy bottle and another [18] saucer from the counter inside the café and marched out to the old man's table. He put down the saucer and poured the glass full of brandy.

"You should have killed yourself last week," he said to the deaf man. The old man motioned with his finger. "A little more," he said. The waiter poured on into the glass so that the brandy slopped over and ran down the stem into the top saucer of the pile. "Thank you," the old man said. The waiter took the bottle back inside the café. He sat down at the table with his colleague again.

"He's drunk now," he said.

"He's drunk every night."

"What did he want to kill himself for?"

"How should I know."

"How did he do it?"

"He hung himself with a rope."

"Who cut him down?"

"His niece."

"Why did they do it?"

"Fear for his soul."

"How much money has he got?"

"He's got plenty."

"He must be eighty years old." [19]

"Anyway I should say he was eighty."

"I wish he would go home. I never get to bed before three o'clock. What kind of hour is that to go to bed?"

"He stays up because he likes it."

"He's lonely. I'm not lonely. I have a wife waiting in bed for me."

"He had a wife once too."

"A wife would be no good to him now."

"You can't tell. He might be better with a wife."

"His niece looks after him." *

"I know. You said she cut him down."

* The speaker of this line ought, it would seem, to be the older waiter, not the younger one. This confusion has been noted by several scholars, for example, F. P. Kroeger, "The Dialogue in A Clean, Well-Lighted Place," *College English* (February, 1959), pp. 240–41; and William E. Colburn, "Confusion in A Clean, Well-Lighted Place," *College English* (February, 1959), pp. 241–42 —ED.

"I wouldn't want to be that old. An old man is a nasty thing."

"Not always. This old man is clean. He drinks without spilling. Even now, drunk. Look at him."

"I don't want to look at him. I wish he would go home. He has no regard for those who must work."

The old man looked from his glass across the square, then over at the waiters.

"Another brandy," he said, pointing to his glass. The waiter who was in a hurry came over.[20]

"Finished," he said, speaking with that omission of syntax stupid people employ when talking to drunken people or foreigners. "No more tonight. Close now."

"Another," said the old man.

"No. Finished." The waiter wiped the edge of the table with a towel and shook his head.

The old man stood up, slowly counted the saucers, took a leather coin purse from his pocket and paid for the drinks, leaving half a peseta tip.

The waiter watched him go down the street, a very old man walking unsteadily but with dignity.

"Why didn't you let him stay and drink?" the unhurried waiter asked. They were putting up the shutters. "It is not half-past two."

"I want to go home to bed."

"What is an hour?"

"More to me than to him."

"An hour is the same."

"You talk like an old man yourself. He can buy a bottle and drink at home."

"It's not the same."

"No, it is not," agreed the waiter with a wife. He did not wish to be unjust. He was only in a hurry.[21]

"And you? You have no fear of going home before your usual hour?"

"Are you trying to insult me?"

"No, hombre, only to make a joke."

"No," the waiter who was in a hurry said, rising from pulling down the metal shutters. "I have confidence. I am all confidence."

"You have youth, confidence, and a job," the older waiter said. "You have everything."

"And what do you lack?"

"Everything but work."

"You have everything I have."

"No. I have never had confidence and I am not young."

"Come on. Stop talking nonsense and lock up."

"I am of those who like to stay late at the café," the older waiter said. "With all those who do not want to go to bed. With all those who need a light for the night."

"I want to go home and into bed."

"We are of two different kinds," the older waiter said. He was now dressed to go home. "It is not only a question of youth and confidence although those things are very beautiful. Each night I am reluctant to close up because there may be some one who needs the café." [22]

"Hombre, there are bodegas open all night long."

"You do not understand. This is a clean and pleasant café. It is well lighted. The light is very good and also, now, there are shadows of the leaves."

"Good night," said the younger waiter.

"Good night," the other said. Turning off the electric light he continued the conversation with himself. It is the light of course but it is necessary that the place be clean and pleasant. You do not want music. Certainly you do not want music. Nor can you stand before a bar with dignity although that is all that is provided for these hours. What did he fear? It was not fear or dread. It was a nothing that he knew too well. It was all a nothing and a man was nothing too. It was only that and light was all it needed and a certain cleanness and order. Some lived in it and never felt it but he knew it all was nada y pues nada y nada y pues nada. Our nada who art in nada, nada be thy name thy kingdom nada thy will be nada in nada as it is in nada. Give us this nada our daily nada and nada us our nada as we nada our nadas and nada us not into nada but deliver us from nada; pues [23] nada. Hail nothing full of nothing, nothing is with thee. He smiled and stood before a bar with a shining steam pressure coffee machine.

"What's yours?" asked the barman.

"Nada."

"Otro loco mas," said the barman and turned away.

"A little cup," said the waiter.

The barman poured it for him.

"The light is very bright and pleasant but the bar is unpolished," the waiter said.

The barman looked at him but did not answer. It was too late at night for conversation.

"You want another copita?" the barman asked.

"No, thank you," said the waiter and went out. He disliked bars and bodegas. A clean, well-lighted café was a very different thing. Now, without thinking further, he would go home to his room. He would lie in the bed and finally, with daylight, he would go to sleep. After all, he said to himself, it is probably only insomnia. Many must have it.[24]

FRANZ KAFKA

A Country Doctor

I was in great perplexity; I had to start on an urgent journey; a seriously ill patient was waiting for me in a village ten miles off; a thick blizzard of snow filled all the wide spaces between him and me; I had a gig, a light gig with big wheels, exactly right for our country roads; muffled in furs, my bag of instruments in my hand, I was in the courtyard all ready for the journey; but there was no horse to be had, no horse. My own horse had died in the night, worn out by the fatigues of this icy winter; my servant girl was now running round the village trying to borrow a horse; but it was hopeless, I knew it, and I stood there forlornly, with the snow gathering more and more thickly upon me, more and more unable to move. In the gateway the girl appeared, alone, and waved the lantern; of course, who would lend a horse at this time for such a journey? I strode through the courtyard once more; I could see no way out; in my confused distress I kicked at the dilapidated door of the yearlong uninhabited pigsty.[136] It flew open and flapped to and fro on its hinges. A steam and smell as of horses came out from it. A dim stable lantern was swinging inside from a rope. A man, crouching on his hams in that low space, showed an open blue-eyed face. "Shall I yoke up?" he asked, crawling out on all fours. I did not know what to say and merely stooped down to see what else was in the sty. The servant girl was standing beside me. "You never know what you're going to find in your own house," she said, and we both laughed. "Hey there, Brother, hey there, Sister!" called the groom, and two horses, enormous creatures with powerful flanks, one after the other, their legs tucked close to their bodies, each well-shaped head lowered like a camel's, by sheer strength of buttocking squeezed out through the door hole which they filled entirely. But at once they were standing up, their legs long and their bodies steaming thickly. "Give him a hand," I said, and the willing girl hurried to help the groom with the harnessing. Yet hardly was she beside him when the groom clipped hold of her and pushed his face against hers. She screamed and fled back to me; on her cheek stood out in red the marks of two rows of teeth. "You brute," I yelled in fury, "do you want a whipping?" but in the same moment reflected that the man was a stranger; that I did not know where he came from, and that of his own free will he was helping me out when everyone else had failed me. As if he knew my thoughts he took no offense at my threat but, still busied with the horses, only turned round once towards me. "Get in," he said then, and indeed: everything was ready. A magnificent pair of horses, I observed, such as I had never sat behind, and I climbed in happily. "But I'll drive, you don't know the way," I [137] said. "Of course," said he, "I'm not coming with you anyway, I'm staying with Rose." "No," shrieked Rose, fleeing into the house with a justified presentiment that her fate was inescapable; I heard the door chain rattle as she put it up; I heard the key turn in the lock; I could see, moreover, how she put out the lights in the entrance hall and in further flight all through the rooms to keep herself from being discovered. "You're coming with me," I said to the groom, "or I won't go, urgent as my journey is. I'm not thinking of paying for it by handing the girl over to you." "Gee up!" he said; clapped his hands; the gig whirled off like a log in a freshet; I could just hear the door of my house splitting and bursting as the groom charged at it and then I was deafened and blinded by a storming rush that steadily buffeted all my senses. But this only for a moment, since, as if my patient's farmyard had opened out just before my courtyard gate, I was already there; the horses had come quietly to a standstill; the blizzard had stopped; moonlight all around; my patient's parents hurried out of the house, his sister behind them; I was almost lifted out of the gig; from their confused ejaculations I gathered not a word; in the sickroom the air was almost unbreathable; the neglected stove was smoking; I wanted to push open a window; but first I had to look at my patient. Gaunt, without any fever, not cold, not warm, with vacant eyes, without a shirt, the youngster heaved himself up from under the feather bedding, threw his arms around my neck, and whispered in my ear: "Doctor, let me die." I glanced round the room; no one had heard it; the parents were leaning forward in silence waiting for my verdict; the sister had set a chair for my handbag; I opened the bag and hunted [138] among my instruments; the boy kept clutching at me from his bed to remind me of his entreaty; I picked up a pair of tweezers, examined them in the candlelight and laid them down again. "Yes," I thought blasphemously, "in cases like this the gods are helpful, send the missing horse, add to it a second because of the urgency, and to crown everything bestow even a groom—" And only now did I remember Rose again; what was I to do, how could I rescue her, how could I pull her away from under that groom at ten miles' distance, with a team of horses I couldn't control. These horses, now, they had somehow slipped the reins loose, pushed the windows open from outside, I did not know how; each of them had stuck a head in at a window and, quite unmoved by the startled cries of the family, stood eyeing the patient. "Better go back at once," I thought, as if the horses were summoning me to the return journey, yet I permitted the patient's sister, who fancied that I was dazed by the heat, to take my fur coat from me. A glass of rum was poured out for me, the old man clapped me on the shoulder, a familiarity justified by this offer of his treasure. I shook my head; in the narrow confines of the old man's thoughts I felt ill; that was my only reason for refusing the drink. The mother stood by the bedside and cajoled me towards it; I yielded, and, while one of the horses whinnied loudly to the ceiling, laid my head to the boy's breast, which shivered under my wet beard. I confirmed what I already knew; the boy was quite sound, something a little wrong with his circulation, saturated with coffee by his solicitous mother, but sound and best turned out of bed with one shove. I am no world reformer and so I let him lie. I was the district doctor and did my duty [139] to the uttermost, to the point where it became almost too much. I was badly paid and yet generous and helpful to the poor. I had still to see that Rose was all right, and then the boy might have his way and I wanted to die too. What was I doing there in that endless winter! My horse was dead, and not a single person in the village would lend me another. I had to get my team out of the pigsty; if they hadn't chanced to be horses I should have had to travel with swine. That was how it was. And I nodded to the family. They knew nothing about it, and, had they known, would not have believed it. To write prescriptions is easy, but to come to an understanding with people is hard. Well, this should be the end of my visit, I had once more been called out needlessly, I was used to that, the whole district made my life a torment with my night bell, but that I should have to sacrifice Rose this time as well, the pretty girl who had lived in my house for years almost without my noticing her—that sacrifice was too much to ask, and I had somehow to get it reasoned out in my head with the help of what craft I could muster, in order not to let fly at this family, which with the best will in the world could not restore Rose to me. But as I shut my bag and put an arm out for my fur coat, the family meanwhile standing together, the father sniffing at the glass of rum in his hand, the mother, apparently disappointed in me—why, what do people expect?—biting her lips with tears in her eyes, the sister fluttering a blood-soaked towel, I was somehow ready to admit conditionally that the boy might be ill after all. I went towards him, he welcomed me smiling as if I were bringing him the most nourishing invalid broth—ah, now both horses were whinnying together; the noise, I suppose, was ordained [140] by heaven to assist my examination of the patient—and this time I discovered that the boy was indeed ill. In his right side, near the hip, was an open wound as big as the palm of my hand. Rose-red, in many variations of shade, dark in the hollows, lighter at the edges, softly granulated, with irregular clots of blood, open as a surface mine to the daylight. That was how it looked from a distance. But on a closer inspection there was another complication. I could not help a low whistle of surprise. Worms, as thick and as long as my little finger, themselves rose-red and blood-spotted as well, were wriggling from their fastness in the interior of the wound towards the light, with small white heads and many little legs. Poor boy, you were past helping. I had discovered your great wound; this blossom in your side was destroying you. The family was pleased; they saw me busying myself; the sister told the mother, the mother the father, the father told several guests who were coming in, through the moonlight at the open door, walking on tiptoe, keeping their balance with outstretched arms. "Will you save me?" whispered the boy with a sob, quite blinded by the life within his wound. That is what people are like in my district. Always expecting the impossible from the doctor. They have lost their ancient beliefs; the parson sits at home and unravels his vestments, one after another; but the doctor is supposed to be omnipotent with his merciful surgeon's hand. Well, as it pleases them; I have not thrust my services on them; if they misuse me for sacred ends, I let that happen to me too; what better do I want, old country doctor that I am, bereft of my servant girl! And so they came, the family and the village elders, and stripped my clothes off me; a school [141] choir with the teacher at the head of it stood before the house and sang these words to an utterly simple tune:

> Strip his clothes off, then he'll heal us,
> If he doesn't, kill him dead!
> Only a doctor, only a doctor.

Then my clothes were off and I looked at the people quietly, my fingers in my beard and my head cocked to one side. I was altogether composed and equal to the situation and remained so, although it was no help to me, since they now took me by the head and feet and carried me to the bed. They laid me down in it next to the wall, on the side of the wound. Then they all left the room; the door was shut; the singing stopped; clouds covered the moon; the bedding was warm around me; the horses' heads in the open windows wavered like shadows. "Do you know," said a voice in my ear, "I have very little confidence in you. Why, you were only blown in here, you didn't come on your own feet. Instead of helping me, you're cramping me on my deathbed. What I'd like best is to scratch your eyes out." "Right," I said, "it is a shame. And yet I am a doctor. What am I to do? Believe me, it is not too easy for me either." "Am I supposed to be content with this apology? Oh, I must be, I can't help it. I always have to put up with things. A fine wound is all I brought into the world; that was my sole endowment." "My young friend," said I, "your mistake is: you have not a wide enough view. I have been in all the sickrooms, far and wide, and I tell you: your wound is not so bad. Done in a tight corner with two strokes of the ax. Many a one proffers his side and can hardly hear the ax in the forest, far less that it is coming nearer to him." "Is that really so, or are you deluding me in my [142] fever?" "It is really so, take the word of honor of an official doctor." And he took it and lay still. But now it was time for me to think of escaping. The horses were still standing faithfully in their places. My clothes, my fur coat, my bag were quickly collected; I didn't want to waste time dressing; if the horses raced home as they had come, I should only be springing, as it were, out of this bed into my own. Obediently a horse backed away from the window; I threw my bundle into the gig; the fur coat missed its mark and was caught on a hook only by the sleeve. Good enough. I swung myself on to the horse. With the reins loosely trailing, one horse barely fastened to the other, the gig swaying behind, my fur coat last of all in the snow. "Gee up!" I said, but there was no galloping; slowly, like old men, we crawled through the snowy wastes; a long time echoed behind us the new but faulty song of the children:

O be joyful, all you patients,
The doctor's laid in bed beside you!

Never shall I reach home at this rate; my flourishing practice is done for; my successor is robbing me, but in vain, for he cannot take my place; in my house the disgusting groom is raging; Rose is his victim; I do not want to think about it any more. Naked, exposed to the frost of this most unhappy of ages, with an earthly vehicle, unearthly horses, old man that I am, I wander astray. My fur coat is hanging from the back of the gig, but I cannot reach it, and none of my limber pack of patients lifts a finger. Betrayed! Betrayed! A false alarm on the night bell once answered—it cannot be made good, not ever.[143]

ALBERT CAMUS

The Guest

The schoolmaster was watching the two men climb toward him. One was on horseback, the other on foot. They had not yet tackled the abrupt rise leading to the schoolhouse built on the hillside. They were toiling onward, making slow progress in the snow, among the stones, on the vast expanse of the high, deserted plateau. From time to time the horse stumbled. Without hearing anything yet, he could see the breath issuing from the horse's nostrils. One of the men, at least, knew the region. They were following the trail although it had disappeared days ago under a layer of dirty white snow. The schoolmaster calculated that it would take them half an hour to get onto the hill.[85] It was cold; he went back into the school to get a sweater.

He crossed the empty, frigid classroom. On the blackboard the four rivers of France, drawn with four different colored chalks, had been flowing toward their estuaries for the past three days. Snow had suddenly fallen in mid-October after eight months of drought without the transition of rain, and the twenty pupils, more or less, who lived in the villages scattered over the plateau had stopped coming. With fair weather they would return. Daru now heated only the single room that was his lodging, adjoining the classroom and giving also onto the plateau to the east. Like the class windows, his window looked to the south too. On that side the school was a few kilometers from the point where the plateau began to slope toward the south. In clear weather could be seen the purple mass of the mountain range where the gap opened onto the desert.

Somewhat warmed, Daru returned to the window from which he had first seen the two men. They were no longer visible. Hence they must have tackled the rise. The sky was not so dark, for the snow had stopped falling during the night. The morning had opened with a dirty light which had [86] scarcely become brighter as the ceiling of clouds lifted. At two in the afternoon it seemed as if the day were merely beginning. But still this was better than those three days when the thick snow was falling amidst unbroken darkness with little gusts of wind that rattled the double door of the classroom. Then Daru had spent long hours in his room, leaving it only to go to the shed and feed the chickens or get some coal. Fortunately the delivery truck from Tadjid, the nearest village to the north, had brought his supplies two days before the blizzard. It would return in forty-eight hours.

Besides, he had enough to resist a siege, for the little room was cluttered with bags of wheat that the administration left as a stock to distribute to those of his pupils whose families had suffered from the drought. Actually they had all been victims because they were all poor. Every day Daru would distribute a ration to the children. They had missed it, he knew, during these bad days. Possibly one of the fathers or big brothers would come this afternoon and he could supply them with grain. It was just a matter of carrying them over to the next harvest. Now shiploads of wheat were arriving from France and the worst was over. But it would be hard to forget that poverty, that army of [87] ragged ghosts wandering in the sunlight, the plateaus burned to a cinder month after month, the earth shriveled up little by little, literally scorched, every stone bursting into dust under one's foot. The sheep had died then by thousands and even a few men, here and there, sometimes without anyone's knowing.

In contrast with such poverty, he who lived almost like a monk in his remote schoolhouse, nonetheless satisfied with the little he had and with the rough life, had felt like a lord with his whitewashed walls, his narrow couch, his unpainted shelves, his well, and his weekly provision of water and food. And suddenly this snow, without warning, without the foretaste of rain. This is the way the region was, cruel to live in, even without men—who didn't help matters either. But Daru had been born here. Everywhere else, he felt exiled.

He stepped out onto the terrace in front of the schoolhouse. The two men were now halfway up the slope. He recognized the horseman as Balducci, the old gendarme he had known for a long time. Balducci was holding on the end of a rope an Arab who was walking behind him with hands bound and head lowered. The gendarme waved a greeting to which Daru did not reply, lost as he was in contemplation [88] of the Arab dressed in a faded blue jellaba, his feet in sandals but covered with socks of heavy raw wool, his head surmounted by a narrow, short *chèche*. They were approaching. Balducci was holding back his horse in order not to hurt the Arab, and the group was advancing slowly.

Within earshot, Balducci shouted: "One hour to do the three kilometers from El Ameur!" Daru did not answer. Short and square in his thick sweater, he watched them climb. Not once had the Arab raised his head. "Hello," said Daru when they got up onto the terrace. "Come in and warm up." Balducci painfully got down from his horse without letting go the rope. From under his bristling mustache he smiled at the schoolmaster. His little dark eyes, deep-set under a tanned forehead, and his mouth surrounded with wrinkles made him look attentive and studious. Daru took the bridle, led the horse to the shed, and came back to the two men, who were now waiting for him in the school. He led them into his room. "I am going to heat up the classroom," he said. "We'll be more comfortable there." When he entered the room again, Balducci was on the couch. He had undone the rope tying him to the

Arab, who had squatted near the stove.[89] His hands still bound, the *chèche* pushed back on his head, he was looking toward the window. At first Daru noticed only his huge lips, fat, smooth, almost Negroid; yet his nose was straight, his eyes were dark and full of fever. The *chèche* revealed an obstinate forehead and, under the weathered skin now rather discolored by the cold, the whole face had a restless and rebellious look that struck Daru when the Arab, turning his face toward him, looked him straight in the eyes. "Go into the other room," said the schoolmaster, "and I'll make you some mint tea." "Thanks," Balducci said. "What a chore! How I long for retirement." And addressing his prisoner in Arabic: "Come on, you." The Arab got up and, slowly, holding his bound wrists in front of him, went into the classroom.

With the tea, Daru brought a chair. But Balducci was already enthroned on the nearest pupil's desk and the Arab had squatted against the teacher's platform facing the stove, which stood between the desk and the window. When he held out the glass of tea to the prisoner, Daru hesitated at the sight of his bound hands. "He might perhaps be untied." "Sure," said Balducci. "That was for the trip." He started to get to his feet. But Daru, setting the glass on the floor, had knelt beside the Arab.[90] Without saying anything, the Arab watched him with his feverish eyes. Once his hands were free, he rubbed his swollen wrists against each other, took the glass of tea, and sucked up the burning liquid in swift little sips.

"Good," said Daru. "And where are you headed?"

Balducci withdrew his mustache from the tea. "Here, son."

"Odd pupils! And you're spending the night?"

"No. I'm going back to El Ameur. And you will deliver this fellow to Tinguit. He is expected at police headquarters."

Balducci was looking at Daru with a friendly little smile.

"What's this story?" asked the schoolmaster. "Are you pulling my leg?"

"No, son. Those are the orders."

"The orders? I'm not . . ." Daru hesitated, not wanting to hurt the old Corsican. "I mean, that's not my job."

"What! What's the meaning of that? In wartime people do all kinds of jobs."

"Then I'll wait for the declaration of war!"

Balducci nodded.

"O.K. But the orders exist and they concern you [91] too. Things are brewing, it appears. There is talk of a forthcoming revolt. We are mobilized, in a way."

Daru still had his obstinate look.

"Listen, son," Balducci said. "I like you and you must understand. There's only a dozen of us at El Ameur to patrol throughout the whole territory of a small department and I must get back in a hurry. I was told to hand this guy over to you and return without delay. He couldn't be kept there. His village was beginning to stir; they wanted to take him back. You must take him to Tinguit tomorrow before the day is over. Twenty kilometers shouldn't faze a husky fellow like you. After that, all will be over. You'll come back to your pupils and your comfortable life."

Behind the wall the horse could be heard snorting and pawing the earth. Daru was looking out the window. Decidedly, the weather was clearing and the light was increasing over the snowy plateau. When all the snow was melted, the sun would take over again and once more would burn the fields of stone. For days, still, the unchanging sky would shed its dry light on the solitary expanse where nothing had any connection with man.

"After all," he said turning around toward Balducci,[92] "what did he do?" And, before the gendarme had opened his mouth, he asked: "Does he speak French?"

"No, not a word. We had been looking for him for a month, but they were hiding him. He killed his cousin."

"Is he against us?"

"I don't think so. But you can never be sure."

"Why did he kill?"

"A family squabble, I think. One owed the other grain, it seems. It's not at all clear. In short, he killed his cousin with a billhook. You know, like a sheep, *kreezk!*"

Balducci made the gesture of drawing a blade across his throat and the Arab, his attention attracted, watched him with a sort of anxiety. Daru felt a sudden wrath against the man, against all men with their rotten spite, their tireless hates, their blood lust.

But the kettle was singing on the stove. He served Balducci more tea, hesitated, then served the Arab again, who, a second time, drank avidly. His raised arms made the jellaba fall open and the schoolmaster saw his thin, muscular chest.

"Thanks, kid," Balducci said. "And now, I'm off." [93]

He got up and went toward the Arab, taking a small rope from his pocket.

"What are you doing?" Daru asked dryly.

Balducci, disconcerted, showed him the rope.

"Don't bother."

The old gendarme hesitated. "It's up to you. Of course, you are armed?"

"I have my shotgun."

"Where?"

"In the trunk."

"You ought to have it near your bed."

"Why? I have nothing to fear."

"You're crazy, son. If there's an uprising, no one is safe, we're all in the same boat."

"I'll defend myself. I'll have time to see them coming."

Balducci began to laugh, then suddenly the mustache covered the white teeth.

"You'll have time? O.K. That's just what I was saying. You have always been a little cracked. That's why I like you, my son was like that."

At the same time he took out his revolver and put it on the desk.

"Keep it; I don't need two weapons from here to El Ameur."

The revolver shone against the black paint of [94] the table. When the gendarme turned toward him, the schoolmaster caught the smell of leather and horseflesh.

"Listen, Balducci," Daru said suddenly, "every bit of this disgusts me, and first of all your fellow here. But I won't hand him over. Fight, yes, if I have to. But not that."

The old gendarme stood in front of him and looked at him severely.

"You're being a fool," he said slowly. "I don't like it either. You don't get used to putting a rope on a man even after years of it, and you're even ashamed—yes, ashamed. But you can't let them have their way."

"I won't hand him over," Daru said again.

"It's an order, son, and I repeat it."

"That's right. Repeat to them what I've said to you: I won't hand him over."

Balducci made a visible effort to reflect. He looked at the Arab and at Daru. At last he decided.

"No, I won't tell them anything. If you want to drop us, go ahead; I'll not denounce you. I have an order to deliver the prisoner and I'm doing so. And now you'll just sign this paper for me."

"There's no need. I'll not deny that you left him with me." [95]

"Don't be mean with me. I know you'll tell the truth. You're from hereabouts and you are a man. But you must sign, that's the rule."

Daru opened his drawer, took out a little square bottle of purple ink, the red wooden penholder with the "sergeant-major" pen he used for making models of penmanship, and signed. The gendarme carefully folded the paper and put it into his wallet. Then he moved toward the door.

"I'll see you off," Daru said.

"No," said Balducci. "There's no use being polite. You insulted me."

He looked at the Arab, motionless in the same spot, sniffed peevishly, and turned away toward the door. "Good-by, son," he said. The door shut behind him. Balducci appeared suddenly outside the window and then disappeared. His footsteps were muffled by the snow. The horse stirred on the other side of the wall and several chickens fluttered in fright. A moment later Balducci reappeared outside the window leading the horse by the bridle. He walked toward the little rise without turning around and disappeared from sight with the horse following him. A big stone could be heard bouncing down. Daru walked back toward the prisoner, who, without stirring, never took his eyes off him.[96] "Wait," the schoolmaster said in Arabic and went toward the bedroom. As he was going through the door, he had a second thought, went to the desk, took the revolver, and stuck it in his pocket. Then, without looking back, he went into his room.

For some time he lay on his couch watching the sky gradually close over, listening to the silence. It was this silence that had seemed painful to him during the first days here, after the war. He had requested a post in the little town at the base of the foothills separating the upper plateaus from the desert. There, rocky walls, green and black to the north, pink and lavender to the south, marked the frontier of eternal summer. He had been named to a post farther north, on the plateau itself. In the beginning, the solitude and the silence had been hard for him on these wastelands peopled only by stones. Occasionally, furrows suggested cultivation, but they had been dug to uncover a certain kind of stone good for building. The only plowing here was to harvest rocks. Elsewhere a thin layer of soil accumulated in the hollows would be scraped out to enrich paltry village gardens. This is the way it was: bare rock covered three quarters of the region. Towns sprang up, flourished, then disappeared; men came by, loved one another or fought [97] bitterly, then died. No one in this desert, neither he nor his guest, mattered. And yet, outside this desert neither of them, Daru knew, could have really lived.

When he got up, no noise came from the classroom. He was amazed at the unmixed joy he derived from the mere thought that the Arab might have fled and that he would be alone with no decision to make. But the prisoner was there. He had merely stretched out between the stove and the desk. With eyes open, he was staring at the ceiling. In that position, his thick lips were particularly noticeable, giving him a pouting look. "Come," said Daru. The Arab got up and followed him. In the bedroom, the schoolmaster pointed to a chair near the table under the window. The Arab sat down without taking his eyes off Daru.

"Are you hungry?"

"Yes," the prisoner said.

Daru set the table for two. He took flour and oil, shaped a cake in a frying-pan, and lighted the little stove that functioned on bottled gas. While the cake was cooking, he went out to the shed to get cheese, eggs, dates, and condensed milk. When the cake was done he set it on the window sill to cool, heated some condensed milk diluted with water,[98] and beat up the eggs into an omelette. In one of his motions he knocked against the revolver stuck in his right pocket. He set the bowl down, went into the classroom, and put the revolver in his desk drawer. When he came back to the room, night was falling. He put on the light and served the Arab. "Eat," he said. The Arab took a piece of the cake, lifted it eagerly to his mouth, and stopped short.

"And you?" he asked.

"After you. I'll eat too."

The thick lips opened slightly. The Arab hesitated, then bit into the cake determinedly.

The meal over, the Arab looked at the schoolmaster. "Are you the judge?"

"No, I'm simply keeping you until tomorrow."

"Why do you eat with me?"

"I'm hungry."

The Arab fell silent. Daru got up and went out. He brought back a folding bed from the shed, set it up between the table and the stove, perpendicular to his own bed. From a large suitcase which, upright in a corner, served as a shelf for papers, he took two blankets and arranged them on the camp bed. Then he stopped, felt useless, and sat down on his bed. There was nothing more to do or to get [99] ready. He had to look at this man. He looked at him, therefore, trying to imagine his face bursting with rage. He couldn't do so. He could see nothing but the dark yet shining eyes and the animal mouth.

"Why did you kill him?" he asked in a voice whose hostile tone surprised him.

The Arab looked away.

"He ran away. I ran after him."

He raised his eyes to Daru again and they were full of a sort of woeful interrogation. "Now what will they do to me?"

"Are you afraid?"

He stiffened, turning his eyes away.

"Are you sorry?"

The Arab stared at him openmouthed. Obviously he did not understand. Daru's annoyance was growing. At the same time he felt awkward and self-conscious with his big body wedged between the two beds.

"Lie down there," he said impatiently. "That's your bed."

The Arab didn't move. He called to Daru:

"Tell me!"

The schoolmaster looked at him.

"Is the gendarme coming back tomorrow?"

"I don't know." [100]

"Are you coming with us?"

"I don't know. Why?"

The prisoner got up and stretched out on top of the blankets, his feet toward the window. The light from the electric bulb shone straight into his eyes and he closed them at once.

"Why?" Daru repeated, standing beside the bed.

The Arab opened his eyes under the blinding light and looked at him, trying not to blink.

"Come with us," he said.

In the middle of the night, Daru was still not asleep. He had gone to bed after undressing completely; he generally slept naked. But when he suddenly realized that he had nothing on, he hesitated. He felt vulnerable and the temptation came to him to put his clothes back on. Then he shrugged his shoulders; after all, he wasn't a child and, if need be, he could break his adversary in two. From his bed he could observe him, lying on his back, still motionless with his eyes closed under the harsh light. When Daru turned out the light, the darkness seemed to coagulate all of a sudden. Little by little, the night came back to life in the window where the starless sky was stirring gently. The schoolmaster soon made out the body lying at his [101] feet. The Arab still did not move, but his eyes seemed open. A faint wind was prowling around the schoolhouse. Perhaps it would drive away the clouds and the sun would reappear.

During the night the wind increased. The hens fluttered a little and then were silent. The Arab turned over on his side with his back to Daru, who thought he heard him moan. Then he listened for his guest's breathing, become heavier and more regular. He listened to that breath so close to him and mused without being able to go to sleep. In this room where he had been sleeping alone for a year, this presence bothered him. But it bothered him also by imposing on him a sort of brotherhood he knew well but refused to accept in the present circumstances. Men who share the same rooms, soldiers or prisoners, develop a strange alliance as if, having cast off their armor with their clothing, they fraternized every evening, over and above their differences, in the ancient community of dream and fatigue. But Daru shook himself; he didn't like such musings, and it was essential to sleep.

A little later, however, when the Arab stirred slightly, the schoolmaster was still not asleep. When the prisoner made a second move, he stiffened, on [102] the alert. The Arab was lifting himself slowly on his arms with almost the motion of a sleepwalker. Seated upright in bed, he waited motionless without turning his head toward Daru, as if he were listening attentively. Daru did not stir; it had just occurred to him that the revolver was still in the drawer of his desk. It was better to act at once. Yet he continued to observe the prisoner, who, with the same slithery motion, put his feet on the ground, waited again, then began to stand up slowly. Daru was about to call out to him when the Arab began to walk, in a quite natural but extraordinarily silent way. He was heading toward the door at the end of the room that opened into the shed. He lifted the latch with precaution and went out, pushing the door behind him but without shutting it. Daru had not stirred. "He is running away," he merely thought. "Good riddance!" Yet he listened attentively. The hens were not fluttering; the guest must be on the plateau. A faint sound of water reached him, and he didn't know what it was until the Arab again stood framed in the doorway, closed the door carefully, and came back to bed without a sound. Then Daru turned his back on him and fell asleep. Still later he seemed, from the depths of his sleep, to hear furtive steps around the schoolhouse.[103] "I'm dreaming! I'm dreaming!" he repeated to himself. And he went on sleeping.

When he awoke, the sky was clear; the loose window let in a cold, pure air. The Arab was asleep, hunched up under the blankets now, his mouth open, utterly relaxed. But when Daru shook him, he started dreadfully, staring at Daru with wild eyes as if he had never seen him and such a frightened expression that the schoolmaster stepped back. "Don't be afraid. It's me. You must eat." The Arab nodded his head and said yes. Calm had returned to his face, but his expression was vacant and listless.

The coffee was ready. They drank it seated together on the folding bed as they munched their pieces of the cake. Then Daru led the Arab under the shed and showed him the faucet where he washed. He went back into the room, folded the blankets and the bed, made his own bed and put the room in order. Then he went through the classroom and out onto the terrace. The sun was already rising in the blue sky; a soft, bright light was bathing the deserted plateau. On the ridge the snow was melting in spots. The stones were about to reappear. Crouched on the edge of the plateau, the schoolmaster looked at the deserted expanse.[104] He thought of Balducci. He had hurt him, for he had sent him off in a way as if he didn't want to be associated with him. He could still hear the gendarme's farewell and, without knowing why, he felt strangely empty and vulnerable. At that moment, from the other side of the schoolhouse, the prisoner coughed. Daru listened to him almost despite himself and then, furious, threw a pebble that whistled through the air before sinking into the snow. That man's stupid crime revolted him, but to hand him over was contrary to honor. Merely thinking of it made him smart with humiliation. And he cursed at one and the same time his own people who had sent him this Arab and the Arab too who had dared to kill and not managed to get away. Daru got up, walked in a circle on the terrace, waited motionless, and then went back into the schoolhouse.

The Arab, leaning over the cement floor of the shed, was washing his teeth with two fingers. Daru looked at him and said: "Come." He went back into the room ahead of the prisoner. He slipped a hunting-jacket on over his sweater and put on walking-shoes. Standing, he waited until the Arab had put on his *chèche* and sandals.

They went into the classroom and the schoolmaster pointed to the exit,[105] saying: "Go ahead." The fellow didn't budge. "I'm coming," said Daru. The Arab went out. Daru went back into the room and made a package of pieces of rusk, dates, and sugar. In the classroom, before going out, he hesitated a second in front of his desk, then crossed the threshold and locked the door. "That's the way," he said. He started toward the east, followed by the prisoner. But, a short distance from the schoolhouse, he thought he heard a slight sound behind them. He retraced his steps and examined the surroundings of the house; there was no one there. The Arab watched him without seeming to understand. "Come on," said Daru.

They walked for an hour and rested beside a sharp peak of limestone. The snow was melting faster and faster and the sun was drinking up the puddles at once, rapidly cleaning the plateau, which gradually dried and vibrated like the air itself. When they resumed walking, the ground rang under their feet. From time to time a bird rent the space in front of them with a joyful cry. Daru breathed in deeply the fresh morning light. He felt a sort of rapture before the vast familiar expanse, now almost entirely yellow under its dome of blue sky. They walked an hour more, descending toward the south. They reached a level height made [106] up of crumbly rocks. From there on, the plateau sloped down, eastward, toward a low plain where there were a few spindly trees and, to the south, toward outcroppings of rock that gave the landscape a chaotic look.

Daru surveyed the two directions. There was nothing but the sky on the horizon. Not a man could be seen. He turned toward the Arab, who was looking at him blankly. Daru held out the package to him. "Take it," he said. "There are dates, bread, and sugar. You can hold out for two days. Here are a thousand francs too." The Arab took the package and the money but kept his full hands at chest level as if he didn't know what to do with what was being given him. "Now look," the schoolmaster said as he pointed in the direction of the east, "there's the way to Tinguit. You have a two-hour walk. At Tinguit you'll find the administration and the police. They are expecting you." The Arab looked toward the east, still holding the package and the money against his chest. Daru took his elbow and turned him rather roughly toward the south. At the foot of the height on which they stood could be seen a faint path. "That's the trail across the plateau. In a day's walk from here you'll find pasturelands and the first nomads.[107] They'll take you in and shelter you according to their law." The Arab had now turned toward Daru and a sort of panic was visible in his expression.

"Listen," he said. Daru shook his head: "No, be quiet. Now I'm leaving you." He turned his back on him, took two long steps in the direction of the school, looked hesitantly at the motionless Arab, and started off again. For a few minutes he heard nothing but his own step resounding on the cold ground and did not turn his head. A moment later, however, he turned around. The Arab was still there on the edge of the hill, his arms hanging now, and he was looking at the schoolmaster. Daru felt something rise in his throat. But he swore with impatience, waved vaguely, and started off again. He had already gone some distance when he again stopped and looked. There was no longer anyone on the hill.

Daru hesitated. The sun was now rather high in the sky and was beginning to beat down on his head. The schoolmaster retraced his steps, at first somewhat uncertainly, then with decision. When he reached the little hill, he was bathed in sweat. He climbed it as fast as he could and stopped, out of breath, at the top. The rock-fields to the south stood out sharply against the blue sky, but on the [108] plain to the east a steamy heat was already rising. And in that slight haze, Daru, with heavy heart, made out the Arab walking slowly on the road to prison.

A little later, standing before the window of the classroom, the schoolmaster was watching the clear light bathing the whole surface of the plateau, but he hardly saw it. Behind him on the blackboard, among the winding French rivers, sprawled the clumsily, chalked-up words he had just read: "You handed over our brother. You will pay for this." Daru looked at the sky, the plateau, and, beyond, the invisible lands stretching all the way to the sea. In this vast landscape he had loved so much, he was alone.[109]

JEAN-PAUL SARTRE

The Flies

Jean-Paul Sartre's play The Flies *is a contemporary existential version of the myth of Orestes' murder of his mother, Clytemnestra, and his consequent pursuit by the Furies, which has its classic dramatization in Aeschylus' trilogy* The Oresteia. *Accompanied by his tutor, whose rationalistic philosophy has rendered his pupil a disinterested and uncommitted observer of the human scene, Orestes returns from exile to Argos to find the citizens of his native city virtually enslaved by the guilt they feel (symbolized by the plague of flies) for the murder of Agamemnon, Orestes' father, fifteen years before. Despite his objectivity, Orestes' concern is activated by what he sees and by the story a stranger (Zeus) tells him, and when he encounters a rebellious young girl (Electra) who refuses to participate in the annual rites of remorse, his concern becomes an unnamable dissatisfaction with his rootlessness and a desire for a kind of engagement which will fill the void in him with an identity (Act I).*

Following the ceremony, during which Electra performs a sacrilegious dance of joy in a vain act of defiance intended to arouse the people against the tyrannies under which they suffer, Orestes reveals his identity to Electra. In the ensuing discussion, he makes the terrible and irrevocable decision to kill the king and queen (Aegistheus and Clytemnestra), that is, to commit himself, against the wishes of both his tutor and the demand of the gods, to the human community ("I must go down into the depths, among you") and to assume the burden of their remorse (Act II, scene 1). In the meantime, Zeus warns Aegistheus, his minister on earth, that Orestes plans to murder him. When Aegistheus asks why Agamemnon was not warned years ago, Zeus' reply distinguishes between two kinds of crimes: that which, like Aegistheus', pays, i.e., is accompanied by a remorse that enslaves the criminal to the laws of the gods; and that which, like the crime Orestes is about to commit, does not pay, i.e., leaves the perpetrator utterly free from remorse and universal laws. Finally, Zeus reveals the secret that both gods and kings share: "the bitterness of knowing men are free," which means that gods are powerless over man once "freedom lights its beacon in [his] heart." Following Zeus' departure Orestes enters the throne room and kills first Aegistheus and then (off stage) Clytemnestra. Conscious now of his unique identity, Orestes assumes the responsibility of his free and irrevocable act: "The heavier it is to carry the better pleased I shall be; for that burden is my freedom." As the act closes Electra, terrified by the horror of Orestes' act, perceives that the flies, "the Furies . . . the goddesses of remorse," have gathered around them ready to give pursuit.

ACT III

The temple of Apollo. Twilight. A statue of Apollo in the center of the stage. ELECTRA *and* ORESTES *are sleeping at the foot of the statue, their arms clasped round its legs. The* FURIES *ring them round; they sleep standing, like cranes.*

At the back is a huge bronze door.

FIRST FURY [*stretching herself*]: Aaaah! I slept the night out standing, stiff with rage, and my sleep was glorious with angry dreams. Ah, how lovely is the power of anger, the red flower in my heart! [*She circles round* ORESTES *and* ELECTRA.] Still sleeping. How white and soft they are! I'll roll on their breasts and bellies, like a torrent over stones. And I shall polish hour by hour their tender flesh; rub it, scour it, wear it to the bone. [*She comes a few steps forward.*] Oh clear, bright dawn of hate! A superb awakening. They're sleeping, sweating, a smell of fever rises from them. But I am awake; cool and hard and gemlike. My soul is adamant—and I feel my sanctity.

ELECTRA [*sighing in her sleep*]: No! No!

FIRST FURY: She's sighing. Wait, my pretty one, wait till you feel our teeth. Soon you'll be screaming with the agony of our caresses. I'll woo you like a man, for you're my bride, and you shall feel my love crushing your life out. You, Electra, are more beautiful than I; but you'll see how my kisses age you. Within six months I'll have you raddled like an old hag; but I stay young forever. [*She bends over* ORESTES *and* ELECTRA.] Ah, this lovely human carrion, what a tasty meal we have in store! As I gaze down at them and breathe their breath, I choke with rage. Nothing is sweeter, nothing, than to feel a dawn of hatred [110] spreading like quickfire in one's veins; teeth and talons ready for their task. Hatred is flooding through me, welling up in my breasts like milk. Awake, sisters, awake! The day has come.

SECOND FURY: I dreamt I was biting them.

FIRST FURY: Be patient. Today they are protected by a god, but soon hunger and thirst will drive them out of sanctuary. And then you shall bite them to your heart's content.

THIRD FURY: Aaah! How I want to claw them!

FIRST FURY: Your turn will come. In a little while your iron talons will be ribboning the flesh of those young criminals with angry red. Come closer, sisters, come and look at them.

A FURY: How young they are!

ANOTHER FURY: And how beautiful!

FIRST FURY: Yes, we are favored. Only too often criminals are old and ugly. Too seldom do we have the joy, the exquisite delight, of ruining what's beautiful.

THE FURIES: Heiah! Heiahah!

THIRD FURY: Orestes is almost a child. I shall mother him, oh so tenderly, with my hatred; I shall take his pale head on my knees and stroke his hair.

FIRST FURY: And then?

THIRD FURY: Then, when he least expects it, I shall dig these two fingers into his eyes.

[*All laugh.*]

FIRST FURY: See, they're stretching, sighing, on the brink of waking. And now, my sisters, flies my sisters, let's sing the sinners from their sleep.

THE FURIES [*together*]: Bzz. Bzz. Bzz. Bzz.
We shall settle on your rotten hearts like flies on butter;
Rotten hearts, juicy, luscious hearts.
Like bees we'll suck the pus and matter from your hearts,
And we'll turn it into honey, rich, green honey.
What love could ravish us as hatred does? [111]
Bzz. Bzz. Bzz. Bzz.
We shall be the staring eyes of the houses,
The growls of the kenneled mastiff baring his fangs as you go by,
A drone of wings pulsing in high air,
Sounds of the forest,
Whistlings, whinings, creakings, hissings, howlings.
We shall be the darkness,
The clotted darkness of your souls.
Bzz. Bzz. Bzz. Bzz.
Heiah, heiah, heiahah!
Bzz. Bzz. Bzz. Bzz.
We are the flies, the suckers of pus,
We shall have open house with you,
We shall gather our food from your mouths,
And our light from the depths of your eyes.

All your life we will be with you,
Until we make you over to the worms.
[*They dance.*]

ELECTRA [*still half asleep*]: Was someone speaking? Who—who are you?

THE FURIES: Bzz. Bzz. Bzz.

ELECTRA: Ah, yes. There you are. Well? Have we really killed them?

ORESTES [*waking*]: Electra!

ELECTRA: You, who are you? Ah, yes. Orestes. Go away.

ORESTES: But—what's wrong, Electra?

ELECTRA: You frighten me. I had a dream. I saw our mother lying on her back. Blood was pouring from her, gushing under the doors. A dream. . . . Feel my hands. They're icy. No, don't. Don't touch me. Did she really bleed much?

ORESTES: Don't!

ELECTRA [*waking up completely*]: Let me look at you. You killed them. It was you, you who killed them. You are here beside me, you have just waked up, there's nothing written on your face, no brand. . . . And yet you killed them.

ORESTES: Why, yes. I killed them. [*A short silence.*] [112] You, too, make me afraid. Yesterday you were so beautiful. And now you look as if some wild beast had clawed your face.

ELECTRA: No beast. Your crime. It's tearing off my cheeks and eyelids; I feel as if my eyes and teeth were naked. . . . But what are those creatures?

ORESTES: Take no notice of them. They can do you no harm.

FIRST FURY: No harm? Let her dare to come among us and you'll see if we can do no harm!

ORESTES: Keep quiet. Back to your kennel, bitches! [*The* FURIES *growl.*] Is it possible that the girl who only yesterday was dancing in a white dress on the temple steps—is it possible you were that girl?

ELECTRA: I've grown old. In a single night.

ORESTES: You have not lost your beauty, but— Where, now, have I seen dead eyes like those? Electra—you are like *her*. Like Clytemnestra. What use, then, was it killing her? When I see my crime in those eyes, it revolts me.

FIRST FURY: That is because *you* revolt *her*.

ORESTES: Is that true, Electra? Do I revolt you?

ELECTRA: Oh, let me be!

FIRST FURY: Well? Can you still have any doubt? How should she not hate you? She lived in peace, dreaming her dreams; and then you came, bringing murder and impiety upon her. So now she has to share your guilt and hug that pedestal, the only scrap of earth remaining to her.

ORESTES: Do not listen.

FIRST FURY: Away! Away! Make him go, Electra; don't let him touch you! He's a butcher. He reeks of fresh, warm blood. He used the poor old woman very foully, you know; he killed her piecemeal.

ELECTRA: Oh no! That's a lie, surely?

FIRST FURY: You can believe me; I was there all the time, buzzing in the air around them.

ELECTRA: So he struck her several times?

FIRST FURY: Ten times at least. And each time the sword [113] squelched in the wound. She tried to shield her face and belly with her hands, and he carved her hands to ribbons.

ELECTRA: So it wasn't a quick death. Did she suffer much?

ORESTES: Put your fingers in your ears, do not look at them, and, above all, ask no questions. If you question them, you're lost.

FIRST FURY: Yes, she suffered—horribly.

ELECTRA [*covering her face with her hands*]: Oh!

ORESTES: She wants to part us, she is building up a wall of solitude around you. But beware; once you are alone, alone and helpless, they will fling themselves upon you. Electra, we planned this crime together and we should bear its brunt together.

ELECTRA: You dare to say I planned it with you?

ORESTES: Can you deny it?

ELECTRA: Of course I deny it. Wait! Well, perhaps—in a way. . . . Oh, I don't know. I dreamt the crime, but you carried it out, you murdered your own mother.

THE FURIES [*shrieking and laughing*]: Murderer! Murderer! Butcher!

ORESTES: Electra, behind that door is the outside world. A world of dawn. Out there the sun is rising, lighting up the roads. Soon we shall leave this place, we shall walk those sunlit roads, and these hags of darkness will lose their power. The sunbeams will cut through them like swords.

ELECTRA: The sun—

FIRST FURY: You will never see the sun again, Electra. We shall mass between you and the sun like a swarm of locusts; you will carry darkness round your head wherever you go.

ELECTRA: Oh, let me be! Stop torturing me!

ORESTES: It's your weakness gives them their strength. Mark how they dare not speak to me. A nameless horror has descended on you, keeping us apart. And yet why should this be? What have you lived through that I have not shared? Do you imagine that my mother's cries will ever cease ringing in my ears? Or that my [114] eyes will ever cease to see her great sad eyes, lakes of lambent darkness in the pallor of her face? And the anguish that consumes you—do you think it will ever cease ravaging my heart? But what matter? I am free. Beyond anguish, beyond remorse. Free. And at one with myself. No, you must not loathe yourself, Electra. Give me your hand. I shall never forsake you.

ELECTRA: Let go of my hand! Those hell-hounds frighten me, but you frighten me more.

FIRST FURY: You see! You see! . . . That's quite true, little doll; you're less afraid of us than of that man. Because you need us, Electra. You are our child, our little girl. You need our nails to score your skin, our teeth to bite your breast, and all our savage love to save you from your hatred of yourself. Only the suffering of your body can take your mind off your suffering soul. So come and let us hurt you. You have only those two steps to come down, and we will take you in our arms. And when our kisses sear your tender flesh, you'll forget all in the cleansing fires of pain.

THE FURIES: Come down to us! Come down!

[*Slowly they dance round her, weaving their spell.* ELECTRA *rises to her feet.*]

ORESTES [*gripping her arm*]: No, no, for pity's sake. Don't go to them. Once they get you, all is lost.

ELECTRA [*freeing herself violently*]: Let go! Oh, how I hate you! [*She goes down the steps, and the* FURIES *fling themselves on her.*] Help!

[ZEUS *enters.*]

ZEUS: Kennel up!

FIRST FURY: The master!

[*The* FURIES *slink off reluctantly, leaving* ELECTRA *lying on the ground.*]

ZEUS: Poor children. [*He goes up to* ELECTRA.] So to this you've come, unhappy pair? My heart is torn between anger and compassion. Get up, Electra. So long as I am here, my Furies will not hurt you. [*He helps her to rise and gazes at her face.*] Ah, what a cruel change! In a night, a single night, all the wild-rose [115] bloom has left your cheeks. In one night your body has gone to ruin, lungs, gall, and liver all burnt out. The pride of headstrong youth—see what it has brought you to, poor child.

ORESTES: Stop talking in that tone, fellow. It is unbecoming for the king of the gods.

ZEUS: And you, my lad, drop that haughty tone. It's unbecoming for a criminal atoning for his crime.

ORESTES: I am no criminal, and you have no power to make me atone for an act I don't regard as a crime.

ZEUS: So you may think, but wait awhile. I shall cure you of that error before long.

ORESTES: Torture me to your heart's content; I regret nothing.

ZEUS: Not even the doom you have brought upon your sister?

ORESTES: Not even that.

ZEUS: Do you hear, Electra? And this man professed to love you!

ORESTES: She is dearer to me than life. But her suffering comes from within, and only she can rid herself of it. For she is free.

ZEUS: And you? You, too, are free, no doubt?

ORESTES: Yes, and well you know it.

ZEUS: A pity you can't see yourself as you are now, you fool, for all your boasting! What a heroic figure you cut there, cowering between the legs of a protecting god, with a pack of hungry vixen keeping guard on you! If you *can* brag of freedom, why not praise the freedom of a prisoner languishing in fetters, or a slave nailed to the cross?

ORESTES: Certainly. Why not?

ZEUS: Take care. You play the braggart now because Apollo is protecting you. But Apollo is my most obedient servant. I have but to lift a finger and he will abandon you.

ORESTES: Then do so. Lift a finger, lift your whole hand while you are about it.

ZEUS: No, that is not my way. Haven't I told you that I [116] take no pleasure in punishment? I have come to save you both.

ELECTRA: To save us? No, it is too cruel to make sport of us. You are the lord of vengeance and of death, but, god though you are, you have no right to delude your victims with false hopes.

ZEUS: Within a quarter of an hour you can be outside that door.

ELECTRA: Safe and sound?

ZEUS: You have my word for it.

ELECTRA: And what do you want from me in return?

ZEUS: Nothing, my child. Nothing.

ELECTRA: Nothing? Did I hear right? Then you are a kind god, a lovable god.

ZEUS: Or next to nothing. A mere trifle. What you can give most easily—a little penitence.

ORESTES: Take care, Electra. That trifle will weigh like a millstone on your soul.

ZEUS [*to* ELECTRA]: Don't listen to him. Answer me, instead. Why hesitate to disavow that crime? It was committed by someone else; one could hardly say even that you were his accomplice.

ORESTES: Electra! Are you going to go back on fifteen years of hope and hatred?

ZEUS: What has she to go back on? Never did she really wish that impious deed to be accomplished.

ELECTRA: If only that were true!

ZEUS: Come now! Surely you can trust my word. Do I not read in men's hearts?

ELECTRA [*incredulously*]: And you read in mine that I never really desired that crime? Though for fifteen years I dreamt of murder and revenge?

ZEUS: Bah! I know you nursed bloodthirsty dreams—but there was a sort of innocence about them. They made you forget your servitude, they healed your wounded pride. But you never really thought of making them come true. Well, am I mistaken?

ELECTRA: Ah, Zeus, dear Zeus, how I long to think you are not mistaken! [117]

ZEUS: You're a little girl, Electra. A mere child. Most little girls dream of becoming the richest or the loveliest woman on earth. But you were haunted by the cruel destiny of your race, you dreamt of becoming the saddest, most criminal of women. You never willed to do evil; you willed your own misfortune. At an age when most children are playing hopscotch or with their dolls, you, poor child, who had no friends or toys, you toyed with dreams of murder, because that's a game to play alone.

ELECTRA: Yes, yes! I'm beginning to understand.

ORESTES: Listen, Electra! It's *now* you are bringing guilt upon you. For who except yourself can know what you really wanted? Will you let another decide that for you? Why distort a past that can no longer stand up for itself? And why disown the firebrand that you were, that glorious young goddess, vivid with hatred, that I loved so much? Can't you see this cruel god is fooling you?

ZEUS: No, Electra, I'm not fooling you. And now hear what I offer.

If you repudiate your crime, I'll see that you two occupy the throne of Argos.

ORESTES: Taking the places of our victims?

ZEUS: How else?

ORESTES: And I shall put on the royal robe, still warm from the dead King's wearing?

ZEUS: That or another. What can it matter?

ORESTES: Nothing of course—provided that it's black.

ZEUS: Are you not in mourning?

ORESTES: Yes, I was forgetting; in mourning for my mother. And my subjects—must I have them, too, wear black?

ZEUS: They wear it already.

ORESTES: True. We can give them time to wear out their old clothes. . . . Well, Electra, have you understood? If you shed some tears, you'll be given Clytemnestra's shifts and petticoats—those dirty, stinking ones you had to wash for fifteen years. And the part she played is yours for the asking. Now that you have come to [118] look so much like her, you will play the part superbly; everyone will take you for your mother. But I—I fear I am more squeamish —I refuse to wear the breeches of the clown I killed.

ZEUS: You talk big, my boy. You butchered a defenseless man and an old woman who begged for mercy. But, to hear you speak, one would think you'd bravely fought, one against a crowd, and were the savior of your city.

ORESTES: Perhaps I was.

ZEUS: You a savior! Do you know what's afoot behind that door? All the good folk of Argos are waiting there. Waiting to greet you with stones and pikes and pitchforks. Oh, they are very grateful to their savior! . . . You are lonely as a leper.

ORESTES: Yes.

ZEUS: So you take pride in being an outcast, do you? But the solitude you're doomed to, most cowardly of murderers, is the solitude of scorn and loathing.

ORESTES: The most cowardly of murderers is he who feels remorse.

ZEUS: Orestes, I created you, and I created all things. Now see! [*The walls of the temple draw apart, revealing the firmament, spangled with wheeling stars.* ZEUS *is standing in the background. His voice becomes huge—amplified by loud-speakers—but his form is shadowy.*] See those planets wheeling on their appointed ways, never swerving, never clashing. It was I who ordained their courses, according to the law of justice. Hear the music of the spheres,

Freedom & god

that vast, mineral hymn of praise, sounding and resounding to the limits of the firmament. [*Sounds of music.*] It is my work that living things increase and multiply, each according to his kind. I have ordained that man shall always beget man, and dog give birth to dog. It is my work that the tides with their innumerable tongues creep up to lap the sand and draw back at the appointed hour. I make the plants grow, and my breath fans round the earth the yellow clouds of pollen. You are not in your own [119] home, intruder; you are a foreign body in the world, like a splinter in flesh, or a poacher in his lordship's forest. For the world is good; I made it according to my will, and I am Goodness. But you, Orestes, you have done evil, the very rocks and stones cry out against you. The Good is everywhere, it is the coolness of the wellspring, the pith of the reed, the grain of flint, the weight of stone. Yes, you will find it even in the heart of fire and light; even your own body plays you false, for it abides perforce by my law. Good is everywhere, in you and about you; sweeping through you like a scythe, crushing you like a mountain. Like an ocean it buoys you up and rocks you to and fro, and it enabled the success of your evil plan, for it was in the brightness of the torches, the temper of your blade, the strength of your right arm. And that of which you are so vain, the Evil that you think is your creation, what is it but a reflection in a mocking mirror, a phantom thing that would have no being but for Goodness. No, Orestes, return to your saner self; the universe refutes you, you are a mite in the scheme of things. Return to Nature, Nature's thankless son. Know your sin, abhor it, and tear it from you as one tears out a rotten, noisome tooth. Or else—beware lest the very seas shrink back at your approach, springs dry up when you pass by, stones and rocks roll from your path, and the earth crumbles under your feet.

ORESTES: Let it crumble! Let the rocks revile me, and flowers wilt at my coming. Your whole universe is not enough to prove me wrong. You are the king of gods, king of stones and stars, king of the waves of the sea. But you are not the king of man.

[*The walls draw together.* ZEUS *comes into view, tired and dejected, and he now speaks in his normal voice.*]

ZEUS: Impudent spawn! So I am not your king? Who, then, made you?

ORESTES: You. But you blundered; you should not have made me free.

ZEUS: I gave you freedom so that you might serve me.[120]

ORESTES: Perhaps. But now it has turned against its giver. And neither you nor I can undo what has been done.

ZEUS: Ah, at last! So this is your excuse?

ORESTES: I am not excusing myself.

ZEUS: No? Let me tell you it sounds much like an excuse, this freedom whose slave you claim to be.

ORESTES: Neither slave nor master. I *am* my freedom. No sooner had you created me than I ceased to be yours.

ELECTRA: Oh, Orestes! By all you hold most holy, by our father's memory, I beg you do not add blasphemy to your crime!

ZEUS: Mark her words, young man. And hope no more to win her back by arguments like these. Such language is somewhat new to her ears—and somewhat shocking.

ORESTES: To my ears, too. And to my lungs, which breathe the words, and to my tongue, which shapes them. In fact, I can hardly understand myself. Only yesterday you were still a veil on my eyes, a clot of wax in my ears; yesterday, indeed, I had an excuse. *You* were my excuse for being alive, for you had put me in the world to fulfill your purpose, and the world was an old pandar prating to me about your goodness, day in, day out. And then you forsook me.

ZEUS: *I* forsook you? How?

ORESTES: Yesterday, when I was with Electra, I felt at one with Nature, this Nature of your making. It sang the praises of the Good—*your* Good—in siren tones, and lavished intimations. To lull me into gentleness, the fierce light mellowed and grew tender as a lover's eyes. And, to teach me the forgiveness of offenses, the sky grew bland as a pardoner's face. Obedient to your will, my youth rose up before me and pleaded with me like a girl who fears her lover will forsake her. That was the last time, the last, I saw my youth. Suddenly, out of the blue, freedom crashed down on me and swept me off my feet. Nature sprang back, my youth went with the wind, and I knew myself alone, utterly alone in the midst of this well-meaning little universe of [121] yours. I was like a man who's lost his shadow. And there was nothing left in heaven, no right or wrong, nor anyone to give me orders.

ZEUS: What of it? Do you want me to admire a scabby sheep that has to be kept apart; or the leper mewed in a lazar-house? Remember, Orestes, you once were of my flock, you fed in my pastures among my sheep. Your vaunted freedom isolates you from the fold; it means exile.

ORESTES: Yes, exile.

ZEUS: But the disease can't be deeply rooted yet; it began only yesterday. Come back to the fold. Think of your loneliness; even your sister is forsaking you. Your eyes are big with anguish, your face is pale and drawn. The disease you're suffering from is inhuman, foreign to my nature, foreign to yourself. Come back. I am forgetfulness, I am peace.

ORESTES: Foreign to myself—I know it. Outside nature, against nature, without excuse, beyond remedy, except what remedy I find within myself. But I shall not return under your law; I am doomed to have no other law but mine. Nor shall I come back to nature, the nature you found good; in it are a thousand beaten paths all leading up to you—but I must blaze my trail. For I, Zeus, am a man, and every man must find out his own way. Nature abhors man, and you too, god of gods, abhor mankind.

ZEUS: That is true; men like you I hold in abhorrence.

ORESTES: Take care; those words were a confession of your weakness. As for me, I do not hate you. What have I to do with you, or you with me? We shall glide past each other, like ships in a river, without touching. You are God and I am free; each of us is alone, and our anguish is akin. How can you know I did not try to feel remorse in the long night that has gone by? And to sleep? But no longer can I feel remorse, and I can sleep no more.
[*A short silence.*]

ZEUS: What do you propose to do? [122]

ORESTES: The folk of Argos are my folk. I must open their eyes.

ZEUS: Poor people! Your gift to them will be a sad one; of loneliness and shame. You will tear from their eyes the veils I had laid on them, and they will see their lives as they are, foul and futile, a barren boon.

ORESTES: Why, since it is their lot, should I deny them the despair I have in me?

ZEUS: What will they make of it?

ORESTES: What they choose. They're free; and human life begins on the far side of despair.
[*A short silence.*]

ZEUS: Well, Orestes, all this was foreknown. In the fullness of time a man was to come, to announce my decline. And you're that man, it seems. But seeing you yesterday—you with your girlish face—who'd have believed it?

ORESTES: Could I myself have believed it? . . . The words I speak are too big for my mouth, they tear it; the load of destiny I bear is too heavy for my youth and has shattered it.

ZEUS: I have little love for you, yet I am sorry for you.

ORESTES: And I, too, am sorry for *you.*

ZEUS: Good-by, Orestes. [*He takes some steps forward.*] As for you, Electra, bear this in mind. My reign is not yet over—far from it! —and I shall not give up the struggle. So choose if you are with me or against me. Farewell.

ORESTES: Farewell. [ZEUS *goes out.* ELECTRA *slowly rises to her feet.*] Where are you going?

ELECTRA: Leave me alone. I'm done with you.

ORESTES: I have known you only for a day, and must I lose you now forever?

ELECTRA: Would to God that I had never known you!

ORESTES: Electra! My sister, dear Electra! My only love, the one joy of my life, do not leave me. Stay with me.

ELECTRA: Thief! I had so little, so very little to call mine; only a few weak dreams, a morsel of peace.[123] And now you've taken my all; you've robbed a pauper of her mite! You were my brother, the head of our house, and it was your duty to protect me. But no, you needs must drag me into carnage; I am red as a flayed ox, these loathsome flies are swarming after me, and my heart is buzzing like an angry hive.

ORESTES: Yes, my beloved, it's true, I have taken all from you, and I have nothing to offer in return; nothing but my crime. But think how vast a gift that is! Believe me, it weighs on my heart like lead. We were too light, Electra; now our feet sink into the soil, like chariot-wheels in turf. So come with me; we will tread heavily on our way, bowed beneath our precious load. You shall give me your hand, and we will go—

ELECTRA: Where?

ORESTES: I don't know. Towards ourselves. Beyond the rivers and mountains are an Orestes and an Electra waiting for us, and we must make our patient way towards them.

ELECTRA: I won't hear any more from you. All you have to offer me is misery and squalor. [*She rushes out into the center of the stage. The* FURIES *slowly close in on her.*] Help! Zeus, king of gods and men, my king, take me in your arms, carry me from this place, and shelter me. I will obey your law, I will be your creature and your slave, I will embrace your knees. Save me from the flies, from my brother, from myself! Do not leave me lonely and I will give up my whole life to atonement. I repent, Zeus. I bitterly repent.

[*She runs off the stage. The* FURIES *make as if to follow her, but the* FIRST FURY *holds them back.*]

FIRST FURY: Let her be, sisters. She is not for us. But that man is ours, and ours, I think, for many a day. His little soul is stubborn. He will suffer for two.

[*Buzzing, the* FURIES *approach* ORESTES.]

ORESTES: I am alone, alone.

FIRST FURY: No, no, my sweet little murderer, I'm staying with you, and you'll see what merry games I'll think up to entertain you.[124]

ORESTES: Alone until I die. And after that—?

FIRST FURY: Take heart, sisters, he is weakening. See how his eyes dilate. Soon his nerves will be throbbing like harp-strings, in exquisite arpeggios of terror.

SECOND FURY: And hunger will drive him from his sanctuary before long. Before nightfall we shall know how his blood tastes.

ORESTES: Poor Electra!

[*The* TUTOR *enters.*]

THE TUTOR: Master! Young master! Where are you? It's so dark one can't see a thing. I'm bringing you some food. The townspeople have surrounded the temple; there's no hope of escape by daylight. We shall have to try our chance when night comes. Meanwhile, eat this food to keep your strength up. [*The* FURIES *bar his way.*] Hey! Who are these? More of those primitive myths! Ah, how I regret that pleasant land of Attica, where reason's always right.

ORESTES: Do not try to approach me, or they will tear you in pieces.

THE TUTOR: Gently now, my lovelies. See what I've brought you, some nice meat and fruit. Here you are! Let's hope it will calm you down.

ORESTES: So the people of Argos have gathered outside the temple, have they?

THE TUTOR: Indeed they have, and I can't say which are the fiercer, the thirstier for your blood: these charming young creatures here, or your worthy subjects.

ORESTES: Good. [*A short silence.*] Open that door.

THE TUTOR: Have you lost your wits? They're waiting behind it, and they're armed.

ORESTES: Do as I told you.

THE TUTOR: For once permit me, sir, to disobey your orders. I tell you, they will stone you. It's madness.

ORESTES: Old man, I am your master, and I order you to unbar that door.

[THE TUTOR *opens one leaf of the double doors a few inches.*]

THE TUTOR: Oh dear! Oh dear! [125]

ORESTES: Open both leaves.

[THE TUTOR *half opens both leaves of the door and takes cover behind one of them. The* CROWD *surges forward, thrusting the doors wide open; then stops, bewildered, on the threshold. The stage is flooded with bright light. Shouts rise from the* CROWD: "Away with him!" "Kill him!" "Stone him!" "Tear him in pieces!"]

ORESTES [*who has not heard them*]: The sun!

THE CROWD: Murderer! Butcher! Blasphemer! We'll tear you limb from limb. We'll pour molten lead into your veins.

A WOMAN: I'll pluck out your eyes.

A MAN: I'll eat your gizzard!

ORESTES [*drawing himself up to his full height*]: So here you are, my true and loyal subjects? I am Orestes, your King, son of Agamemnon, and this is my coronation day. [*Exclamations of amazement, mutterings among the* CROWD.] Ah, you are lowering your tone? [*Complete silence.*] I know; you fear me. Fifteen years ago to the day, another murderer showed himself to you, his arms red to the elbows, gloved in blood. But him you did not fear; you read in his eyes that he was of your kind, he had not the courage of his crimes. A crime that its doer disowns becomes ownerless—no man's crime; that's how you see it, isn't it? More like an accident than a crime?

So you welcomed the criminal as your King, and that crime without an owner started prowling round the city, whimpering like a dog that has lost its master. You see me, men of Argos, you understand that my crime is wholly mine; I claim it as my own, for all to know; it is my glory, my life's work, and you can neither punish me nor pity me. That is why I fill you with fear.

And yet, my people, I love you, and it was for your sake that I killed. For your sake. I had come to claim my kingdom, and you would have none of me because I was not of your kind. Now I am of your kind, my subjects; there is a bond of blood between us, and I have earned my kingship over you.

As for your sins and your remorse, your night-fears, [126] and the crime Ægistheus committed—all are mine, I take them all upon me. Fear your dead no longer; they are *my* dead. And, see, your faithful flies have left you and come to me. But have no fear, people of Argos. I shall not sit on my victim's throne or take the scepter in my blood-stained hands. A god offered it to me, and I said no. I wish to be a king without a kingdom, without subjects.

Farewell, my people. Try to reshape your lives. All here is new, all must begin anew. And for me, too, a new life is beginning. A strange life. . . .

Listen now to this tale. One summer there was a plague of rats in Scyros. It was like a foul disease; they soiled and nibbled everything, and the people of the city were at their wits' end. But one day a flute-player came to the city. He took his stand in the market-place. Like this. [ORESTES *rises to his feet.*] He began playing on his flute and all the rats came out and crowded round him. Then he started off, taking long strides—like this. [*He comes down from the pedestal.*] And he called to the people of Scyros: "Make way!" [*The* CROWD *makes way for him.*] And all the rats raised their heads and hesitated—as the flies are doing. Look! Look at the flies! Then all of sudden they followed in his train. And the flute-player, with his rats, vanished forever. Thus.

[*He strides out into the light. Shrieking, the* FURIES *fling themselves after him.*]

Curtain [127]

FRIEDRICH DÜRRENMATT

The Tunnel

The young man who boarded his usual train that Sunday afternoon was twenty-four years old and fat. He was fat in order to protect himself, for anything he perceived out of the ordinary terrified him. Indeed, this clarity of vision was probably the only real ability he possessed, and even this was a burden to him. Although his fat

SOURCE: Reprinted from *Evergreen Review* by permission of the author's agent.

gave a general protection to his body, he found it necessary to stuff every sort of hole in his body through which the terrifying influences might reach him. He smoked cigars (Ormond Brazil 10). He wore a pair of sunglasses over his ordinary glasses. He even stuffed his ears with wads of cotton wool. At twenty-four he was still dependent on his parents, a consequence of rather nebulous studies at the University. And the University was two hours away from home by train. Departure time five-fifty. Arrival at seven twenty-seven.

And so this student, fat and twenty-four years old, boarded his usual Sunday train to attend a seminar the following day. The fact that he had already decided to skip class was irrelevant. As he left his home town the afternoon sun shone from a cloudless summer sky. It was pleasant weather for a trip he knew almost by heart. The train's route lay between the Alps and the Juras, past rich villages and towns, over a river and, after some twenty minutes further travel, into a little tunnel just beyond Burgdorf. The train was overcrowded and he had entered at one of the front cars. With considerable difficulty he worked his way toward the rear. Perspiring, and with two pairs of glasses, he offered an oafish appearance. All the travellers were sitting closely packed, some even on suitcases. All the second-class compartments were occupied, and only the first-class compartments were relatively empty. The young man fought through the melee of families and recruits, students and lovers, falling against this one or that one as the train swayed, stumbling against stomachs and breasts until he came to a seat in the last car. At last he had [32] found space enough to have a bench to himself, a pleasant surprise, since third-class coaches are seldom divided into compartments with benches. Opposite him, playing a solitary game of chess, he noted a man even fatter than himself, and on the same bench, near the corridor, sat a red-haired girl reading a novel. The young man gratefully chose the window seat on the empty bench. He had just lit an Ormond Brazil 10 when the train entered the little tunnel. Of course he had travelled this stretch many times before, almost every Saturday and Sunday throughout the past year, but he had never found the opportunity to examine the tunnel closely. He had, in fact, been only vaguely aware of it. Several times he had intended to give it his full attention, but each time he had been thinking of other matters, and each time the brief plunge into darkness had passed unnoticed, so fast was the train and so brief its plunge into the darkness of the little tunnel.

And even this time he had not been thinking of the tunnel and so had forgotten to take off his sunglasses. Outside the tunnel the sun had been shining with all its force, flooding the hills and woods and the distant chain of the Juras with golden evening light. Even the little houses of the town through which they had just passed had seemed built of gold. This abrupt passage from light to darkness must then be the reason why the tunnel seemed so much longer than usual. He waited patiently in the dark compartment for the return to daylight. At any moment the first pale shimmer of daylight would gleam on his window-pane, widen as quickly as a flash of lightning, then close in powerfully with its full yellow brightness. Nevertheless, the darkness lasted. He took off his sunglasses. At about the same time the girl lit a cigarette. As her match flared orange he thought he detected a grim annoyance in her face. No doubt she resented the interruption in her perusal of her novel. He looked at his wrist watch. The luminous dial said six-ten.

He leaned back, settling himself in the corner between window and compartment wall, and directed his thoughts to the complications of his studies. No one really believed he was studying at all. He thought of the seminar he had to attend the next day, and which he would not attend. Each of his activities seemed a pretext designed to achieve order behind the facade [33] of routine pursuits. Perhaps what he sought was not order itself, but only a semblance of order. The art of an actor who used his fat, his cigars and his cotton wool as make-up for a genteel comedy, while all the while he knew himself to be a part of some monstrous farce. When he next looked at his watch the time was six-fifteen. The train was still in the tunnel. He felt confused. At last the light bulbs flickered and the compartment brightened. The red-haired girl returned to her novel and the fat gentleman resumed his solitary chess game. The whole compartment now appeared reflected in the window. But outside, on the other side of the window, the tunnel was still there.

He stepped into the corridor in which a tall man was walking up and down restlessly. He observed the light raincoat and the black scarf around the gentleman's neck. Surely there was no need for a scarf in this weather? A black scarf? He peered into the other compartments in the rear coach. The passengers were reading their newspapers or chatting. Normal. He returned to his corner and sat down. The tunnel must come to an end any minute now. At any second? His wrist watch read six-twenty. He felt an obscure annoyance with himself for not having paid more attention to the tunnel on previous trips. They had been in the tunnel for a quarter of an hour now. And surely, allowing for the speed of the train, it must be one of the longest tunnels in Switzerland. Or perhaps he had taken the wrong train. But he could recall no other tunnel of such length and importance within twenty minutes of his home. On impulse he asked the fat chess player if the train were indeed bound for Zurich. The man confirmed this. The student ventured again that he hadn't known that there was such a long tunnel on this part of the journey. The chess player was more than a little annoyed to have his difficult considerations interrupted a second time. He replied testily that in Switzerland there were a great many tunnels, in fact, an extraordinary number of tunnels, that he was actually travelling in Switzerland for the first time, but that an affluence of tunnels was the first thing one noticed about Switzerland, and indeed, his statistical almanac confirmed the fact that no country possessed such a positive abundance of tunnels as Switzerland! And he added that now he must excuse himself; he was [34] very sorry, really, but a most difficult chess problem in regard to the Nimzowitsch Defence occupied his mind and he could afford no further diversions. The last remark was polite, but firm. It was evident that no further conversation could be expected from the chess player and, in any event, he could be of little use, since the route was new to him.

At that moment the conductor appeared, and the student had high hopes that his ticket would be refused. The official was pale and scrawny. He gave an impression of nervousness as he remarked to the girl near the door that she would have to change trains at Olten. Although Olten was also a regular stop on the Zurich run, the young man did not give up hope of being on the wrong train, so complete was his conviction that he had mistaken trains in boarding. He didn't doubt that he would have to pay extra fare, but he accepted the expense with equanimity. The return to daylight would be cheap at the price. He therefore handed his ticket to the conductor and said that his destination was Zurich. He accomplished the speech without once removing the Ormond Brazil 10 from his mouth.

"But the gentleman is on the right train," replied the conductor as he inspected the ticket.

"But we're going through a tunnel!" The young man had spoken with considerable anger. He was determined to put an end to the confusion. The official replied that they had just passed Herzogenbuchsee and would soon approach Langenthal where the train was due at six-twenty. The young man looked at his watch. Six-twenty. But they had been travelling through the tunnel for the past twenty minutes, he persisted. The conductor raised his brows.

"This is the Zurich train," he said, now looking for the first time toward the window. "Six-twenty," he said again, uneasily. "We'll be in Olten soon. Arrival time six thirty-seven. We must have gone into some bad weather suddenly. A storm. Yes. That's why it's dark."

The gentleman with the Nimzowitsch Defence problem entered the conversation now. He had been holding out his ticket (and holding up his game) for some time, but the conductor had not yet noticed him. "Nonsense," he interjected. "Nonsense! [35] We're travelling through a tunnel. I can see the rock clearly. Looks like granite. Switzerland has more tunnels than all the rest of the world put together. Read it in a statistical almanac."

The conductor relieved him of his ticket, and repeated pleadingly that this was truly the Zurich train. Unmollified, the young man demanded to speak to the Chief Conductor. The ticket collector now felt his dignity to have been abused. He directed the student to the front of the train, but reiterated huffily that the train was going to Zurich, that the time was now six twenty-five, that in twelve minutes time (according to the summer schedule) the train would arrive in Olten, and that the young man should have no further doubts on that point. *He* travelled this train at least twelve times a month.

Nevertheless the young scholar set off to find the Chief Conductor. Movement through the crowded train now seemed even more difficult than before. The train must be travelling exceedingly fast. In any event, it was making a frightful racket. He stuffed the wads of cotton a little more firmly into his ears, for he had loosened them in order to speak to the ticket collector. The passengers were behaving calmly. This train was no different from any other Sunday afternoon train, and no one appeared worried. In the second-class compartments he came upon an Englishman standing by the corridor window. "Simplon," he was saying, as he tapped the pane with his pipe and beamed inanely.

Things were very much as usual in the dining car too. No seats were vacant, and neither waiters nor diners, occupied with Wiener Schnitzel and rice, made any comment on the tunnel. But there, near the exit of the dining car, he recognized the red bag of the Chief Conductor.

"What can I do for you, sir?" The Chief Conductor was a tall man, quiet behind a carefully groomed black mustache and neat rimless glasses.

"We have been in a tunnel for twenty-five minutes."

The Conductor did not look toward the windows, as the young man might have expected, but turned to a nearby waiter. "Give me a packet of Ormond 10," he said. "I smoke the same brand as the gentleman here." The waiter, however, indicated that the brand was not in stock, and the young man, glad of an opportunity for further conversation, proffered a Brazil.[36]

"Thank you," returned the Conductor. "In Olten I shall hardly have time to buy any. You are doing me a great favor. Smoking is a most important business. Will you come this way, please?"

Mystified, the young man followed him into the freight car ahead of the diner.

"The next car is the locomotive," offered the official. "This is the front of the train."

A sickly yellow light burned amid the baggage. Most of the car lay in total darkness. The side doors were barred, as was the small window beside them, and through its irons the greater blackness of the tunnel seeped in. The trunks, many decorated with hotel stickers, the bicycles and the baby carriage that composed the cargo of the coach seemed haphazardly arranged. The Chief Conductor, an obviously precise man, hung his red bag on a nearby hook.

"What can I do for you?" he asked again, without, however, looking at the student. Instead, he began to enter neat columns in a book he had taken from his pocket.

"We have been in a tunnel since Burgdorf," answered the young man with determination. "There is no such enormous tunnel on this line. I know. I travel back and forth every week on this train."

The Chief Conductor continued to write. "Sir," he said, stepping close to his inquisitor, so close that their bodies almost touched, "sir, I have little to tell you. I have no idea how we got into this tunnel. I have no explanation for it. But I ask you to consider this. We are moving along on tracks: therefore this tunnel leads somewhere. We have no reason whatever to believe that anything is wrong with this tunnel, except, of course, that there seems to be no end to it." The Chief Conductor still held the unlit Ormond Brazil 10 between his lips. He had spoken extremely quietly, yet with such dignity and clarity, and with such assurance, that his words were audible despite the increased noise of the baggage car.

"Then I must ask you to stop the train," said the young man impatiently. "I really don't understand you. If there's something wrong with this tunnel—and it seems you can't explain even its existence—then your duty is to stop this train at once."

"Stop the train?" returned the older man slowly. It seemed [37] he had already thought of that, but, as he informed his companion, it was a serious matter to stop a train. With this, he shut the book and laid it in the red bag which was swaying to and fro on its hook. Then he carefully lit the Ormond 10. The young man offered to pull the emergency brake overhead, and was on the point of releasing the lever, when suddenly he staggered forwards and was sent crashing against the wall. At the same moment, the baby carriage rolled toward him and several trunks slid by. The Chief Conductor swayed strangely and began to move, hands outstretched, through the freight car.

"We are going downhill!" he announced as he joined the young man now leaning against the wall. But the expected crash of hurtling train against granite tunnel did not occur. There was no shattering of telescoped coaches. Once again the train seemed to be running on a level. The door opened at the other end of the car. In the bright light of the diner, until the door swung to again, they could see the passengers merrily toasting one another's health.

"Come into the locomotive." At this point the Chief Conductor was peering thoughtfully, almost menacingly at the student. He opened the door nearby. As he did so a rush of tempestuous heat-laden air struck the pair with such force that they were driven back against the wall. At the same moment a frightful clatter resounded through the almost empty freight car.

"We'll have to climb over to the engine," he cried into the younger man's ear. Despite his shouting, his voice was hardly audible. He then disappeared through the right-angle of the open doorway. The student followed cautiously in the direction of the swaying and brightly lit engine. He didn't know why he was climbing, but at this point determination had overcome reason. He found himself on a pitching platform between the two cars, and clung desperately to the iron rails on both sides. Although the terrific draught moderated but slightly as he inched his way up to the locomotive, he dreaded the wind less than the immediate nearness of the tunnel walls. They were hidden from him in the blackness, but were nevertheless frighteningly close. It was necessary to focus all his attention on the engine ahead, yet the pounding of the wheels and the hissing vibrating push [38] of air against him gave him the feeling of careening, at the speed of a falling star, into a world of stone.

A board just wide enough to walk on crossed the gap between the cars and ran the length of the engine. Above and parallel to it, a curving metal rod served as railing. To reach the plank he would have to make a jump of nearly a yard. He braced himself, leapt, and pushed himself along the board. His progress was slow, since he had to press close to the outside of the engine to keep his foothold. It was not until he reached the long side of the engine and was fully exposed to the roaring hurricane of wind and to the menacing cliff walls now brilliantly illuminated by the engine lights that he began to realize his fear. But just then he was rescued by the Chief Conductor who pulled him through a small door into the engine. Exhausted, the young man lay against the wall. He was grateful for the sudden quiet. With the engine door shut, the steel walls of the giant locomotive deadened the noise almost completely.

"Well, we've lost the Ormond Brazil too," said the Conductor. "It wasn't a very sensible idea to light one before starting the climb, but they break so easily in one's pocket. It's their unusual length."

The young man was delighted to converse normally again. The close and terrifying rock walls had reminded him uncomfortably of his everyday world, of its ever similar days and years. The thought occurred to him that their boring similitude had perhaps been only a preparation for the present moment: that this was a moment of initiation, of truth, this departure from the surface of the earth and precipitous descent into the womb of the earth. He took another brown package from his right coat pocket and offered the Chief Conductor a new cigar. He took one himself, and carefully they lit their Brazils from the Conductor's lighter.

"I am very fond of these Ormonds," said the older man, "but one must pull very hard on them. Otherwise they go out so easily."

For some reason these words made the student suspicious. Was the Conductor as uncomfortable as he about the tunnel? For the tunnel still ran on interminably, and his mind persisted [39] in the thought that surely the tunnel must stop, even as a dream can end, all of a sudden.

"Six-forty," he said, consulting his watch. "We should be in Olten now." Even as he spoke, he thought of the hills and woods radiant only a short while ago in the late golden sun. The thought could have been present in both their minds. Nevertheless, the two men stood and smoked and leaned against their wall.

"Keller is my name," announced the Conductor as he puffed at his Brazil.

The student refused to change the topic of conversation.

"The climb to the engine was very dangerous, didn't you think? At least it was for me. I'm not used to that sort of thing. Anyway, I'd like to know why you've brought me here."

"I don't know," said Keller. "I wanted time to consider."

"Time to consider?"

"Yes," returned the Chief Conductor. "That's right." And he went on smoking. Just then the engine reeled over at a still steeper angle.

"We could go into the engineer's cabin," suggested Keller. He did not, however, leave his position against the wall. Annoyed by his companion's indecisiveness, the young man stepped briskly along the corridor to the driver's cabin, then abruptly stopped.

"Empty!" he said to the Conductor who had now moved up behind him. "The driver's seat is empty!" They went into the cabin. It was swaying too, for the engine was still tearing through the tunnel at enormous speed, bearing the train along with it, as though the weight of the coaches behind no longer counted.

"Allow me," said the Chief Conductor. He pressed some levers and pulled the emergency brake. There was no change. "We tried to stop the engine earlier. As soon as we noticed the alteration in the tracks. It didn't stop then either."

"It certainly isn't stopping now," said the other. He pointed to the speed indicator. "A hundred. Has the engine ever done a hundred before?"

"Good heavens! It has never gone so fast. Sixty-five at the most." [40]

"Exactly. And the speed is increasing. Now the speedometer says a hundred and five. We must be falling." He went up to the window, but he couldn't keep his balance. He was pressed with his face against the glass, so fantastic was their speed. "The engine driver?" he shouted as he stared at the rock masses streaking towards him in the glare of the arc lights, disappearing above him and below him on either side of the engineer's cabin.

"He jumped off," Keller yelled back. He was now sitting on the floor, his back against the controls.

"When?" The student pursued the matter obstinately. Keller hesitated a while. He decided to relight his Ormond, an awkward task, for his legs were then at the same height as his head while the train continued its roll to one side.

"Five minutes after the switch. No use thinking to save him. Freight car man abandoned the train too."

"And you?" asked the student.

"I am in charge of this train. I, too, have always lived without hope."

"Without hope," repeated the young man. By then he was lying on the glass pane, face pressed against glass. Glass and engine and human flesh were pressed together above the abyss. "Back in the compartment," he thought, "we had entered the tunnel, but we didn't know that even then everything was already lost. We didn't think that anything had changed, and yet the shaft of the depths had already received us, and we had entered our abyss."

"I'll have to go to the rear," shouted the Chief Conductor. "The coaches will be in a panic. Everyone will be trying to get to the rear of the train."

"That's true." The student thought of the chessplayer and of the red-haired girl with her novel. He handed Keller his remaining packages of Ormond Brazil. "Take them. You'll lose your cigar again when you climb over."

"Aren't you coming?" The Conductor was once more on his feet and with difficulty he had begun to clamber up the funnel of the corridor. The student gazed at the useless instruments, at the useless ridiculous levers and switches shining silver-like in the glare of the cabin lights.[11]

"A hundred and thirty," he called. "I don't think you'll be able to get to the coaches above us at this speed."

"It's my duty," shouted Keller over his shoulder.

"Certainly," returned the young man. He didn't bother turning his head to watch the other's senseless efforts.

"At least I have to try," yelled the Conductor. He was already far over the head of the fat young man. He braced elbows and thighs against slippery walls and seemed, indeed, to be making some progress. But just then the engine took a further turn downwards. It hurtled towards the interior of the earth, goal of all things, in its terrible plunge. Keller now was directly over his friend who lay face downwards on the silver gleaming window at the bottom of the driver's cabin. His strength gave. Suddenly he fell, crashed against the control panel and came to rest on the window beside his companion.

"What are we to do?" he cried, clinging to the young man's shoulders and shouting into his ear. The very fact that it was now necessary to shout alarmed him. The noise of the onrushing walls had destroyed even the quiet of the engine.

The younger man lay motionless on the pane of glass which

separated him from the depths below. His fat body and weighty flesh were of no further use to him, no protection now.

"What are we to do?" persisted the Chief Conductor.

"Nothing," came the merciless reply. Merciless, yet not without a certain ghostly cheerfulness. Now, for the first time, his glasses were gone and his eyes were wide open. Greedily he sucked in the abyss through those wide-open eyes. Glass and metal splinters from the shattered control panel now studded his body. And still he refused to tear his thirsting eyes from the deadly spectacle below. As the first crack widened in the window beneath them, a current of air whistled into the cabin. It seized his two wads of cotton wool and swept them upwards like arrows into the corridor shaft overhead. He watched them briefly and spoke once more.

"Nothing. God let us fall. And now we'll come upon him." [42]

EUGÈNE IONESCO

The Future Is in Eggs or It Takes All Sorts to Make a World

Characters

JACQUES
FATHER-JACQUES
MOTHER-JACQUES
JACQUELINE
GRANDMOTHER-JACQUES
GRANDFATHER-JACQUES
ROBERTA
FATHER-ROBERT
MOTHER-ROBERT

This play constitutes a kind of sequel to *Jacques or obedience*

As the curtain rises, JACQUES *and* ROBERTA *are embracing, squatting in the same position as at the end of* 'JACQUES'; *the change of decor is of no importance.*

Up-stage left there is now a large piece of furniture, a sort of long table or a kind of divan which serves as a hatching apparatus. The picture, 'expressing nothing' on the up-stage wall is replaced in the present scene by a large frame containing a portrait of GRANDFATHER-JACQUES, *which is to say,* GRANDFATHER-JACQUES *himself. There are chairs around the hatching apparatus. There is a sound of rain.*

FATHER- *and* MOTHER-JACQUES, FATHER- *and* MOTHER-ROBERT, JACQUELINE, *and* GRANDMOTHER-JACQUES *are standing round* JACQUES *and* ROBERTA, *looking first at them, then at* [119] *each other, shaking their heads, shrugging their shoulders and murmuring: 'It's a bit much!'*

Engrossed in each other, JACQUES *and* ROBERTA *do not even see them.*

ROBERTA: Puss . . . Puss . . .
JACQUES: Puss . . . Puss . . .
ROBERTA: Puss . . . Puss . . .
JACQUES: Puss . . . Puss . . .
ROBERTA: Puss . . . Puuusss . . .
JACQUES: Puuuss . . . Puuuuuuuuss! . . .
[ROBERTA *and* JACQUES *purr. The four parents, the* GRANDMOTHER *and* JACQUELINE *are not at all pleased. They are heard to say*]:
FATHER-JACQUES: They go too far . . .
GRANDMOTHER-JACQUES: All this wasn't necessary in my day . . .
FATHER-ROBERT: They really do exaggerate.
MOTHER-ROBERT [*to her husband*]: It all comes from Jacques, of course.
MOTHER-JACQUES [*to her husband*]: Of course it's all Roberta's fault.
JACQUES [*absorbed in his love*]: Pusspusspusspusspuuuuusss . . . Pusspusspusspusspuuuuusss . . .
ROBERTA and JACQUES: Pusspusspussss . . . [*They purr.*] Pussy-pussy . . .
FATHER-JACQUES: They're making a proper spectacle of themselves!
JACQUELINE: But, father, you only have to look in the street, and at the bus-stops—nowadays young people don't seem to care.
MOTHER-ROBERT: Roberta would never dream of making a spectacle of herself.
MOTHER-JACQUES: It would never cross my son's mind . . .

JACQUES and ROBERTA: Pusspusspuss . . . Purr . . . purr . . . purr . . .

FATHER-JACQUES: Spectacle or no spectacle, it's the result that counts . . . And all this is leading nowhere!

MOTHER-JACQUES [*to* FATHER-JACQUES]: Come now, you must have a little patience, papa . . .[120]

GRANDMOTHER-JACQUES: Be practical!

MOTHER-JACQUES [*to* FATHER-JACQUES]: You're in too much of a rush —remember, it was the same with us, we didn't get results straightaway.

ROBERTA and JACQUES [*embracing*]: Pusspusspusspuuusss . . . Purr . . . purr . . . purr . . .

FATHER-JACQUES: You don't need to stick up for them.

GRANDMOTHER-JACQUES: She doesn't take after them at all.

FATHER-ROBERT [*to his wife*]: I never would have stood for it!

MOTHER-ROBERT [*to her husband*]: Now you calm down!

FATHER-JACQUES: Quiet!

MOTHER-JACQUES: Oh, you're always being nasty . . . yet you're always so good!

FATHER-ROBERT [*to his wife*]: Old Mother-Jacques's always bleating about something. Nobody's interested in what she thinks.

MOTHER-ROBERT [*to her husband*]: She ought to keep her mouth shut.

JACQUELINE [*to the* ROBERT-COUPLE]: What did you say?

FATHER-ROBERT: Nothing—that is, we were just saying something nice about you, my dear . . .

ROBERTA and JACQUES [*still squatting in an embrace*]: Puuuussss . . . purrpurrpurr . . .

MOTHER-ROBERT: I think they're rather sweet, the two of them.

FATHER-JACQUES: That's just what I blame them for, in the name of tradition . . . They've been sweet enough, they're far too sweet . . .

JACQUELINE: It's about all they are!

JACQUES and ROBERTA: Pusspuuuuss . . . Purrpurrpurr . . .

FATHER-JACQUES [*to* FATHER-ROBERT]: It's three years now since we arranged this marriage. And they've been stuck there ever since caterwauling, with us watching them. And nothing happens.

MOTHER-JACQUES: In spite of all our good wishes and encouragement.

FATHER-JACQUES: Nothing happens, nothing at all! We must get some results quickly! [121]

FATHER-ROBERT [*to* FATHER-JACQUES]: I'll say again. It's not my daughter's fault.

FATHER-JACQUES [*to* FATHER-ROBERT]: Are you suggesting it's the fault of my son? Is that what you're insinuating?

MOTHER-ROBERT [*to* FATHER-JACQUES]: Now, don't take it like that!

JACQUES and ROBERTA: Puuuuss . . . ! Purrpurrpurr . . .

FATHER-JACQUES: We must come to a decision! Come on, Jacqueline, show some initiative . . .

JACQUES and ROBERTA: Pusspusspussssss! Purrpurrpurr . . .

JACQUELINE: Why always me! . . . Why can't you all peave me in leace!

FATHER-JACQUES [*threateningly*]: Jacqueline! Jacqueline!! Jacqueline!!! . . .

JACQUELINE [*with bowed head*]: Sorry, papa.

MOTHER-ROBERT [*to her husband*]: And now they're getting on their high horses!

JACQUELINE [*to* FATHER-JACQUES]: I understand, papa. Very well, papa. Whatever you say, papa.

GRANDMOTHER-JACQUES: There's a good child!

MOTHER-JACQUES: My little girl . . . She's my big consolidation.

MOTHER-ROBERT [*to her husband*]: That's true enough!

FATHER-ROBERT
MOTHER-ROBERT
FATHER-JACQUES
GRANDMOTHER-JACQUES } [*holding out their arms to* JACQUELINE, *whilst the portrait of* GRANDFATHER *stays motionless and quiet*]: What a good child! What a good child! What a good child!

JACQUELINE: Let's first try and separate them . . . so we can unite them closer afterwards!

[*The parents withdraw slightly. All, including* GRANDFATHER, *follow* JACQUELINE *with their eyes.*]

JACQUELINE [*to the loving couple*]: Glet up!

JACQUES and ROBERTA: Pusspusspuuussss . . . pusspusspuss . . . purrpurrpurr purr . . . purrpurrpurr . . .

JACQUELINE [*claps her hands.* JACQUES *and* ROBERTA *still fail to hear and continue to purr tenderly in their embrace*]: That's enough, do [122] you hear? Enough!!! [*She shakes the couple vigorously.*] Now then! Come on!

[JACQUES *and* ROBERTA *stop their purring, and, as if waking from a deep sleep, look at* JACQUELINE *with surprise, having difficulty in recognizing her in their sleepy state; they get up painfully, looking haggard, still in an embrace.*]

JACQUELINE [*aside*]: Oh, look at her, with her three noses running!

[*Then, with great energy and some sharp taps, she frees their arms and separates them.*]

JACQUELINE: There . . . like that . . . Straighten yourselves up! . . .

[*Murmurs of satisfaction from* JACQUES' *and* ROBERTA's *parents.*]

JACQUES: I'm hungry.

ROBERTA: I'm hungry.

JACQUELINE: You're wet through.

JACQUES: I'm cold. Brrr! I'm trempling!

ROBERTA: I'm cold. Brrr! I'm trempling!

[*They both tremble with cold.*]

JACQUELINE: Serves you right!

FATHER-JACQUES: Serves you right!

JACQUES and ROBERTA: I'm hungry!

MOTHER-ROBERT: Poor things!

FATHER-ROBERT [*to his wife*]: They don't get anything to eat in this house.

JACQUELINE: All you think about is our stomach. You're neglecting production! Why don't you get on with it? After all, it is your main duty.

FATHER-JACQUES
MOTHER-JACQUES
GRANDMOTHER-JACQUES
MOTHER-ROBERT
FATHER-ROBERT } It's your duty!

TOG. { JACQUES [*to* ROBERTA]: That's true, my dear . . .
ROBERTA [*to* JACQUES]: That's true, my dear . . .

JACQUES and ROBERTA: It's our duty!

FATHER-JACQUES [*to* JACQUES *and* ROBERTA]: So what about it? [123]

JACQUES: I'm hungry.

ROBERTA: I'm hungry.

MOTHER-JACQUES: Oh, poor darlings [*Moved*] they're hungry! . . . Oh, my poor little sweets, my little darlings . . .

MOTHER-ROBERT [*to her husband*]: She's good-hearted.

FATHER-ROBERT [*to his wife*]: Don't you start climbing down! The Roberts have their pride, too, you know.

GRANDMOTHER-JACQUES [*handing a dish to* JACQUES *and* ROBERTA *into which they can dip with their fingers as she holds it*]: Here you are, dears, old granny's potatoes and bacon!

[JACQUES *and* ROBERTA, *famished, dive into the potatoes.*]

GRANDMOTHER-JACQUES: Eat them up! Eat them up!

MOTHER-JACQUES: Eat them up!

JACQUES [*suddenly the victim of an old qualm, timidly interrupts his gesture towards the potatoes*]: No . . . I . . .

JACQUELINE [*to* JACQUES]: Aren't you hungry any more?

MOTHER-ROBERT [*to* JACQUES]: You need to eat something!

ROBERTA [*to* JACQUES]: Pussssy . . . yes, eat something . . . pussss! like me!

JACQUES: I'm hungry.

[*He dives into the food.*]

ROBERTA: A bit more potato.

FATHER-JACQUES [*to* MOTHER-JACQUES]: She's got an appetite like a horse.

[GRANDMOTHER-JACQUES *gives some potatoes and bacon to* ROBERTA.]

JACQUES [*to* GRANDMOTHER-JACQUES]: Give him some, bacon is good for the stock.

[GRANDMOTHER-JACQUES *gives* JACQUES *some bacon.*]

ROBERTA: A bit more bacon.

[*She is given some.*]

JACQUES: A bit more potato.

[*He is given some.*]

FATHER-JACQUES: That's enough.

MOTHER-JACQUES: Oh! . . .

FATHER-JACQUES: I said, enough! [124]

[GRANDMOTHER-JACQUES *takes the dish and sets it down somewhere.*]

FATHER-ROBERT [*to his wife*]: That's through meanness rather than principles!

MOTHER-ROBERT [*to her husband*]: Perhaps it's through principles as well!

JACQUELINE [*to* JACQUES *and* ROBERTA]: Make up your minds . . . From now on production must be your constant thought.

FATHER-JACQUES: I see that I've got to bring all my authority to bear on this.

MOTHER-JACQUES: You do, my dear, if you feel you want to, of course . . . but with care and kindness, please!

MOTHER-ROBERT: We've got the right to bring some of our authority to bear on it, too.

FATHER-ROBERT: If it doesn't work, it's not our daughter's fault, it's certainly not our daughter's fault. Just because she's our only daughter, it doesn't mean she's sterile.

MOTHER-ROBERT [*to her husband*]: That's right. Don't let yourself be put upon.

FATHER-ROBERT: I would like to say . . .

FATHER-JACQUES: We must each impose our authority where it is called for.

FATHER-ROBERT: I agree.

FATHER-JACQUES [*to his son*]: Jacques. . . . I have something very serious to say to you.

[*They form two groups.* JACQUES's *parents,* GRANDMOTHER-JACQUES *and* JACQUELINE *surround* JACQUES; ROBERTA's *parents stay with* ROBERTA *withdrawing her slightly from the others.* FATHER-ROBERT *and* MOTHER-ROBERT *speak to their daughter;* ROBERTA *is heard to say docilely from time to time: 'Yes, papa, yes mamma, yes papa, yes mamma, yes papa, yes mamma.'*]

FATHER-JACQUES [*to his son*]: Jacques! I have some cruel news for you.

MOTHER-JACQUES [*weeping*]: Beuh! Beuh! Beuh!

JACQUES: What is it, father? [125]

FATHER-JACQUES: Look . . . you see your grandmother there. [JACQUELINE *puts a black veil on the* GRANDMOTHER's *head.*] Don't you notice anything?

JACQUES: No, papa. I don't notice anything.

JACQUELINE: Look harder. Make an effort.

JACQUES: I don't see anything at all.

MOTHER-JACQUES: My son . . . you don't understand! [*To her husband*]: He's at the carefree time of life! [*She weeps on her son's shoulder.*]

GRANDMOTHER-JACQUES: I'm in deep mourning . . .

JACQUES: What does that mean?

[*From her side of the stage, between her parents,* ROBERTA *repeats from time to time*]:

ROBERTA: Yes, papa, yes, mamma . . .

FATHER-JACQUES: A son like you—who for some time now has been a comfort to me, making up his youthful flollies, ought to understand . . .

JACQUELINE: Do you understand?

JACQUES: Understand what, papa, mamma?

FATHER-JACQUES: Well, in a word, this is the awful truth . . . Haven't you ever asked yourself why you don't hear your grandfather singing any longer?

MOTHER-JACQUES: Grandfather who loved you so much and who you adored?

JACQUELINE [*pointing to the frame*]: Or why he is up there? Instead of being here, in our midst?

[*From where he stands,* GRANDFATHER-JACQUES *makes a friendly movement with his head, and smiles.*]

JACQUES: No, I haven't asked myself that.

[*From her side of the stage,* ROBERTA *approves, and continues to say from time to time*]:

ROBERTA: Yes, papa, yes, mamma!

FATHER-JACQUES: If you've never asked yourself about it, now's the time to do so: ask yourself.

JACQUES: I'm asking myself.

JACQUELINE: And what do you answer yourself? [126]

JACQUES: I don't answer anything.

FATHER-JACQUES [*to his son*]: You're not asking yourself hard enough. Ask me.

JACQUES: Ask what?

FATHER-JACQUES: Why don't you hear your grandfather singing any more?

JACQUES: Why don't I hear my grandfather singing any more? Why?

FATHER-JACQUES: I leave it to your grandmother to tell you.

GRANDMOTHER-JACQUES: Because your grandfather is dead.

[JACQUES *makes no reaction of any sort.*]

JACQUELINE [*to* JACQUES]: Grandfather is dead.

[*She gives* JACQUES *a violent nudge.*]

FATHER-JACQUES: Your grandfather is dead.

[*She gives him another nudge.* JACQUES *still makes no reaction. From the* ROBERTS' *corner comes*]:

FATHER-ROBERT: His grandfather is dead.

MOTHER-ROBERT: His grandfather is dead.

ROBERTA: Yes, papa, yes, mamma.

FATHER-JACQUES [*to his son*]: Don't you understand that your grandfather is dead?

JACQUES: No. I don't understand that grandfather is dead.

MOTHER-JACQUES [*whining*]: Poor child. Your reflexes must have stopped working. We must get them going again.

[JACQUES *falls into* JACQUELINE'S *arms, who stands him up again. For a few moments his face remains expressionless. The parents, the grandmother and the sister search for a sign on their son's face. They appear to be very worried.* MOTHER-JACQUES *says*]:

MOTHER-JACQUES [*to her son*]: Cry! Let yourself go, my boy, and cry! [*Silence*] Cry! Come on then! [*Silence. Suddenly* JACQUES *starts to sob.*]

FATHER-JACQUES: There we are, at last! That's done it!

MOTHER-JACQUES and

GRANDMOTHER-JACQUES: That's done it! That's done it!

JACQUELINE: That's done it!

JACQUES: Oooh! Oooh! Poor grandfather! [127]

[*He stops and smiles.*]

MOTHER-JACQUES: Again!

JACQUES [*starting again*]: Oooh! Oooh! Poor grandpa!

[ROBERTA *in the* ROBERTS' *corner still repeats but at longer intervals: 'Yes, papa, yes, mamma.'*]

MOTHER-JACQUES [*embracing her weeping son*]: My poor baby . . . How he's suffering! . . .

JACQUES [*weeping*]: Hiii! Hiii! Hiii! Hiii! Hiii!

GRANDMOTHER-JACQUES: Yes, it's true, poor grandpa's passed away. [*She sobs.*]

FATHER-JACQUES: We must all console each other!

[*All the* JACQUES *weep. The* FATHER, *with dignity, wipes away his tears. From the* ROBERTS' *side is heard*]:

MOTHER-ROBERT: Go and offer your cordolences.

FATHER-ROBERT: We must all go; we're part of the family now.

ROBERTA: *Yes, papa, yes, mamma.*

[ROBERTA, *having moved across to the* JACQUES, *cries*]:

ROBERTA: Heartiest cordolences!

ALL THE JACQUES [*in chorus, with the exception of* GRANDFATHER-JACQUES]: Delighted.

[FATHER-ROBERT, MOTHER-ROBERT, *to* ROBERTA *who turns towards them.*]

MOTHER-ROBERT and

FATHER-ROBERT: Heartiest cordolences!

ROBERTA: Thank you very much. I'm so glad.

[*The three* ROBERTS *now turn to* FATHER-JACQUES.]

THE THREE ROBERTS [*to* FATHER-JACQUES]: Heartiest cordolences!

FATHER-JACQUES: Thank you, my dear friends, I accept them with joy.

THE THREE ROBERTS and

FATHER-JACQUES [*turning to* MOTHER-JACQUES *and saying, in chorus*]: We offer our heartiest cordolences, cordolences, cordolences, cordolences!!

MOTHER-JACQUES: Thank you, thank you, I'm so glad, thank you. [128]

THE THREE ROBERTS
FATHER-JACQUES
MOTHER-JACQUES } [*to* GRANDMOTHER-JACQUES]: Cordolences, cordolences, cordolences, heartiest cordolences!

GRANDMOTHER-JACQUES: Thank you so much! Thank you! Thank you! I shan't forget, thank you! So nice of you, thank you!

THE THREE ROBERTS and
THE THREE JACQUES [*to* JACQUELINE]: Heartiest cordolences! Cordolences! Cordolences!

JACQUELINE: Thank you! Thank you! Thank you! Thank you! And you, too!

[*Then, all—with the exception of* GRANDFATHER-JACQUES*—surround* JACQUES *who is the most moved of them all: 'Cordolences! Heartiest cordolences! Cordolences! Heartiest cordolences!'*]

JACQUES [*weeping*]: Hiiii! Hiiii! Hiiii! Thank you!

[*Then, when* FATHER-JACQUES *has said: 'We mustn't forget the departed'*]:

MOTHER-JACQUES
FATHER-JACQUES
GRANDMOTHER-JACQUES
JACQUES
JACQUELINE
MOTHER-ROBERT
FATHER-ROBERT
ROBERTA
[*in tone in chorus, turned towards the portrait of* GRANDFATHER-JACQUES *with their backs to the audience*]: Cordolences! Cordolences! Our heartiest, sincerest cordolences! Cordolences! Cordolences! Cordolences!

[*One must be able to discern the voice of* JACQUES, *weeping.*]

GRANDFATHER-JACQUES [*without leaving his frame, replies, with a wave of his hand*]: Cordolences! Cordolences! Cordolences!

[*Then all, including* GRANDFATHER-JACQUES *towards whom they are turned: 'Cordolences! Cordolences! Cordolences! Cordolences! Heartiest cordolences! Cordolences!'* GRANDFATHER-JACQUES *becomes once more motionless in his frame. All the characters—with the exception of* GRANDFATHER-JACQUES, *of course—turn to* JACQUES, *surrounding him and saying: 'Cordolences! Cordolences! Cordolences! Heartiest cordolences!'* [129] *Once or twice* JACQUES *replies: 'Cordolences!' then resumes his weeping with renewed energy. He collapses, as they continue to offer their cordolences. He is raised up, and installed in a chair.*]

JACQUES [*roaring*]: Hiii! Hiiii! Hiiii! Hiiii! Cor-dol-en-ces! Hiiii!

FATHER-JACQUES [*stopping his ears, and shouting to* MOTHER-JACQUES, *even louder than* JACQUES]: You've made his reflexes too sensitive. Desensitize them!

JACQUELINE [*shouting to* JACQUES]: Shut up, you're upsetting everybody!

MOTHER-ROBERT [*shouting*]: He's gone too far.

[MOTHER-JACQUES *gives* JACQUES *a powerful slap.* JACQUES *stops weeping abruptly. There is a general movement towards* MOTHER-JACQUES, *except for* FATHER-JACQUES. JACQUELINE, MOTHER-ROBERT, FATHER-ROBERT, ROBERTA, *in tone all together*]:

TOG. { THE ROBERT COUPLE: Oh, congratulations, Madame, warmest congratulations.
GRANDMOTHER-JACQUES and JACQUELINE: Bravo, Jacques dear! Bravo! Bravo! mamma! Bravo! }

FATHER-JACQUES: That's enough!

[*They all stop instantly. Silence. Everyone looks at* JACQUES.]

FATHER-JACQUES [*to* JACQUES]: It's your right, and your duty, to know in what circumstances your grandfather met his death! [GRANDFATHER-JACQUES *in his frame makes a sign.*]

JACQUELINE: Grandfather wants to say something! [GRANDFATHER-JACQUES *leaves his frame and comes towards the others.*] He speaks much better since he died.

FATHER-JACQUES [*to* JACQUES]: Here comes your grandfather, fit as a fiddle, to tell you himself how he met his death.

[*Respectful silence. As* GRANDFATHER-JACQUES *approaches, the others hold their noses.*]

GRANDFATHER-JACQUES [*very proud of being the centre of attention*]: Hmmm! Hmmm! It all passed off very well, passed away . . . I was in the middle of a song . . . [*He is about to sing.*] [130]

GRANDMOTHER-JACQUES: You're not going to start singing again . . . You're dead. You're in mourning.

GRANDFATHER-JACQUES: No . . . No . . . No . . . That doesn't matter. I feel like singing.

FATHER-JACQUES [*to* GRANDFATHER-JACQUES]: If you show no respect for your own grief, how do you expect others to? . . . Carry on with the story, only faster!

GRANDFATHER-JACQUES: I'll sing it!

GRANDMOTHER-JACQUES: You're not going to sing.

GRANDFATHER-JACQUES: Then I shan't say a word. Not another word. That's the last you'll see of me. There!

[GRANDFATHER-JACQUES *goes back to his frame.*]

GRANDMOTHER-JACQUES: Still as obstinate as ever! It hasn't taught him anything!

[*In his frame,* GRANDFATHER-JACQUES *looks sullen and moody in contrast to his air of gaiety at the beginning of the play. He will not move again until the end.*]

FATHER-JACQUES [*to his son*]: You see how it is, my boy, we all have to go! You're our one and only hope! It's essential, absolutely essential, that we replace those that pass away. Grandfather is dead, long live grandfather.

ALL TOGETHER [*except for* JACQUES, *who is nonplussed*]: Grandfather is dead, long live grandfather.

JACQUES: Why?

FATHER-JACQUES: We must assure the continuity of our race.

JACQUES: Why?

FATHER-JACQUES: The continuity of our race . . . the white race! Long live the white race!

[*All, except* JACQUES, *applaud and say together: 'Long live the white race! Long live the white race!'*]

FATHER-JACQUES [*to his son*]: The future of the white race is in your hands. It must go on, go on and extend its power more and more!

JACQUES: What can we do?

JACQUELINE: If it's to go on, we must stop it from going back.

JACQUES: Through what means? [131]

FATHER-JACQUES [*to his son*]: Through production. Whatever disappears must be replaced by new products, more numerous and varied than before. It's up to you to instigate production . . .

MOTHER-JACQUES [*to her son*]: My son, if you want me to be proud of you, try and instigate, instigate production . . .

[ROBERTA *looks embarrassed.*]

FATHER-ROBERT: My daughter is perfectly capable of it—as I've already officially declared.

[ROBERTA *looks more and more embarrassed.*]

FATHER-JACQUES: We shall soon see whether these last three years are going to yield good results. Up to now they don't seem to me to have been very remarkable!

[ROBERTA, *more and more embarrassed, assumes nevertheless extravagant poses.*]

MOTHER-ROBERT [*to* ROBERTA]: Now come on, dear, that's not very nice in front of everyone. Come with mamma, I'll teach you. All you need is a bit of training.

MOTHER-JACQUES [*to* MOTHER-ROBERT]: If my experience can be of any help to you. . . . Don't hesitate to ask.

MOTHER-ROBERT: With pleasure. We'd be only too happy.

GRANDMOTHER-JACQUES [*to* MOTHER-ROBERT]: I'll come as well. I'll sing her a lullaby . . .

MOTHER-ROBERT [*to* FATHER-ROBERT]: You stay here with your son-in-law. If we need you for the element, we'll call you. [*To* FATHER-

JACQUES]: We'll call you, too, if we find we need some element.

FATHER-JACQUES [*bowing*]: I'm here whenever you need me.

MOTHER-JACQUES: I've got some element, I've got some in reserve, if it's needed.

[ROBERTA, MOTHER-ROBERT, MOTHER-JACQUES *and* GRANDMOTHER-JACQUES *leave right.*] ROBERTA *exits making gestures and assuming more and more extravagant attitudes. As he sees her leaving,* JACQUES *makes a vague gesture with his arms towards her, pulls a grimace like a child who wants to cry, saying: 'Mm . . . Mm . . . Mm . . .'*] [132]

JACQUELINE [*watching* ROBERTA *and the others leaving*]: She already looks quite maternal. She's got an instinct for it.

[JACQUES *flops into a chair.*]

FATHER-ROBERT [*to* JACQUES]: We'll soon see what you're made of.

FATHER-JACQUES [*to* JACQUES]: Jacques, my son, pluck up your courage. Produce something! Be a man!

JACQUELINE: Come on, come on, where's your courage!

FATHER-ROBERT: Come on, come on, where's your courage! Get going!

JACQUELINE: Get going. Start pushing.

[JACQUES *grimaces. He settles in his chair.*]

JACQUELINE: Go on . . . Go on . . .

FATHER-ROBERT: Go on, go on, be a man. We've all had to go through it.

FATHER-JACQUES [*in a powerful voice, to his son*]: Hurry up, or you'll have me to deal with.

VOICE OF MOTHER-JACQUES: Is it working over there?

JACQUELINE [*to* JACQUES]: Get on with it, they're getting impatient. Push.

FATHER-ROBERT [*to* JACQUES]: Push.

JACQUES [*grimacing*]: It doesn't happen just like that . . . you can't do it to order . . . I don't feel any inspiration.

VOICE OF MOTHER-JACQUES: Jacques, Roberta is ready. Are you?

VOICE OF MOTHER-ROBERT: You won't be able to say it's my daughter's fault any more.

FATHER-JACQUES: Jacques, don't be so lazy.

JACQUELINE [*shouting so as to be heard on the other side*]: Just a minute, be patient for a moment . . .

JACQUES [*in his chair*]: It's coming . . . I feel it's going to come . . .

VOICE OF GRANDMOTHER-JACQUES: Jacques, my baby, get a move on, . . . Roberta's been ready for some time. She can't go on waiting.

JACQUES: I'm doing what I can.

FATHER-JACQUES: That's not amounting to much.

FATHER-ROBERT [*to* JACQUES]: Come on, show some grit.

JACQUELINE: Show some grit . . .[133]

FATHER-ROBERT [*to* FATHER-JACQUES]: Your son, it seems to me, is not worthy of my daughter.

FATHER-JACQUES: It seems to me, the die is not yet cast. We'll see about that later.

JACQUELINE [*to the portrait of* GRANDFATHER-JACQUES]: Do something, grandfather.

GRANDFATHER-JACQUES [*sardonic, motionless*]: Ah . . . ah . . . ah . . . I couldn't care less . . . I'm not in this world any longer . . . what's more, you wouldn't let me sing . . . that'll teach you . . . serves you right . . .

JACQUELINE [*to* GRANDFATHER-JACQUES]: Then keep your mouth shut.

GRANDFATHER-JACQUES [*very fast; furious*]: I'll keep my mouth shut if I feel like it, and if I don't, I won't, who do you think you are, what about the cult of the dead?

FATHER-ROBERT [*to* GRANDFATHER-JACQUES]: You shut up, Sir.

FATHER-JACQUES [*threateningly*]: Shut up!

[GRANDFATHER-JACQUES *does so.*]

VOICE OF MOTHER-ROBERT: Well, how's it going?

JACQUES [*clutching his stomach*]: Aie! Aie! Aie! Aie!

GRANDFATHER-JACQUES [*laughing in his frame*]: Hee! Hee! Hee!

FATHER-ROBERT [*to* GRANDFATHER-JACQUES]: Do I have to call for order?!

JACQUES [*hands on his stomach*]: Aie! Aie! Aie! Aie! Aie! Aie!

[*His cries get more and more shrill.*]

JACQUELINE [*calling to the others*]: Mamma, mamma, it's happened, he's having his labour pains!

FATHER-ROBERT [*shouting*]: Roberta . . . Roberta . . . you can let go now!

[*He goes out right.*]

JACQUES [*in agony*]: Aie! Aie! Aie! Aie!

VOICE OF MOTHER-ROBERT: Let go, my dear! . . . You can let go now . . .

VOICE OF ROBERTA [*very shrill*]: Co-co-codac! Co-co-codac! Co-co-codac! Co-co-codac! Co-co-codac! Co-co-codac! Co-co-codac! Co-co-codac! Co-co-codac! [134]

JACQUES: Aie! Aie! Aie! Aie!

[MOTHER-ROBERT, MOTHER-JACQUES, GRANDMOTHER-JACQUES *appear right.*]

VOICE OF ROBERTA: Co-co-co-co-co-codac!

[*The loud 'co-co-codacs!' of* ROBERTA *continue to be heard.* JACQUES *groans.* MOTHER-ROBERT *and* MOTHER-JACQUES *fall into each other's arms.*]

MOTHER-ROBERT: Jacques's dear little mother . . . our children! [*Tears*]

MOTHER-JACQUES: Roberta's dear little mother . . . our own little ones! [*In tears.*]

[*The 'co-co-codacs' get even louder.* JACQUES *makes a groaning 'Ah', and faints.*]

TOG. { MOTHER-JACQUES: Ah! My son! My son!
GRANDMOTHER-JACQUES: Now, now! It's no time for that!

FATHER-JACQUES: Jacqueline! Your brother's fainted!

[*All the characters rush to surround* JACQUES, *rubbing his temples, administering little slaps, during which time one hears*]:

VOICE OF FATHER-ROBERT: That's it now! Bring a basket!

FATHER-JACQUES: It's been too much for him! It's too much for him!

[*General feverish movement. Agitated fluttering round* JACQUES, *and also towards off-stage right whence the 'co-dacs' come.* JACQUELINE goes out right, carrying an empty basket, as JACQUES *recovers consciousness.*]

MOTHER-JACQUES: My boy! He's coming to!

JACQUES: Where am I?

MOTHER-JACQUES: At home, my dear, with your own loving parents!

MOTHER-ROBERT: In your darling Roberta's own castle!

JACQUES [*disqusted*]: Oh, I want to get away!

FATHER-ROBERT [*appears right, carrying the basket full of eggs*]: Here are the first eggs!

ALL [*except* JACQUES, *who is slumped in a chair, whilst* GRANDFATHER-JACQUES *watches him out of one eye*]: Aaah! Aaah! Bravo!

[*They applaud, embrace and congratulate each other.*] [135]

FATHER-JACQUES and

FATHER-ROBERT [*congratulating each other*]: Congratulations! Congratulations!

[*The two* MOTHERS *embrace, weeping, whilst* GRANDMOTHER-JACQUES, *having seized the basket of eggs, exclaims: 'Oh, aren't they pretty! They're so sweet! What a size! I do hope they're not addled!' The various characters now move and encircle* GRANDMOTHER-JACQUES; *they take the basket. This scene takes place down-stage.*]

FATHER-JACQUES: They're beautifully fresh, they must be worth twenty francs a piece. We could have them boiled.

MOTHER-ROBERT: They're my daughter's very first eggs! They look just like her!

GRANDMOTHER-JACQUES: Oh no, they're the spitting image of Jacques.

FATHER-ROBERT: I don't agree.

MOTHER-JACQUES: They haven't got three noses!

MOTHER-ROBERT: That's because they're too small. They'll grow later.

MOTHER-JACQUES: Nonsense, they look like both of them.

FATHER-JACQUES: Where is Jacqueline?

FATHER-ROBERT: She's with Roberta. Someone has to be there to help her.

MOTHER-JACQUES: I feel quite moved! It's a wonderful moment!

FATHER-JACQUES [*takes the basket, moves towards his son, with the others*]: Look, these are your own eggs!

JACQUES: Thank you.

FATHER-JACQUES: Now you must hatch them out.

MOTHER-JACQUES: He may be too tired at the moment.

FATHER-ROBERT: Our daughter can do her own hatching!

FATHER-JACQUES: In our family it's the man's job! [*To* JACQUES]: Come on, get up!

[*They all raise* JACQUES *up, who is exhausted, and bear him to the hatching table.*]

FATHER-JACQUES [*carrying his son*]: Carry him on to the hatching table! [136]

MOTHER-ROBERT [*carrying* JACQUES, *to her husband*]: You always let people get the better of you. You're not very smart.

GRANDMOTHER-JACQUES [*carrying* JACQUES]: You're married, I'm very happy about that. Now you've got to hatch!

[*They heave* JACQUES *on to the table.*]

MOTHER-JACQUES: Hatch well, my boy!

GRANDMOTHER-JACQUES: Like your forefathers did!

GRANDFATHER-JACQUES [*in his frame*]: Hee! Hee! Hee! [*It is a sardonic laugh.*]

FATHER-JACQUES: Hatch, hatch in the name of glory and for the greatness of nations, and for immortality.

[*The 'Co-co-codacs', which have stopped, now start up again with even greater force.*]

FATHER-ROBERT: We must hurry! The eggs will start piling up!

[JACQUES *is installed on, or in the middle of, his eggs.* JACQUELINE *appears, carrying a second basket of eggs.*]

ALL [*except for* JACQUES, *and* GRANDFATHER-JACQUES *who laughs silently*]: Bravo! Bravo! Oh, they're lovely!

FATHER-ROBERT: I'm going to get the others!

[He goes out right.]

JACQUELINE: There's still a lot more!

FATHER-JACQUES [*lifts up* JACQUES *who is lying flat on his stomach, takes a look, and says*]: You can bring some more! There's still room! Don't worry!

[He empties the contents of the basket on and around JACQUES.]

MOTHER-ROBERT: Bring them! Bring them here!

FATHER-JACQUES: Come on, come on, don't stop!

JACQUES: I'm hot . . .

MOTHER-JACQUES [*to* JACQUES]: That's what you need, my dear, to hatch . . . warmth, and a lot of love! . . .

[She sponges her son's brow.]

FATHER-JACQUES [*clapping his hands*]: Production! Production! Production!

GRANDMOTHER-JACQUES: Eggs! Eggs! Eggs! Eggs!

[She leaps and dances.]

MOTHER-JACQUES: Hatch, hatch, my son, hatch! [137]

[JACQUELINE *takes out the empty basket as* FATHER-ROBERT *comes in with a third full one. The 'Co-co-codacs' continue.*]

ALL: Bravo! Bravo!

FATHER-ROBERT: There's more still!

JACQUES [*puffing noisily like a steam engine*]: Tuff! Tuff! Tuff! Tuff! Tuff! Tuff!

[*The rhythm of his 'Tuff Tuffs' steadily accelerates and so do the 'Co-co-codacs', as well as the movements of* FATHER-ROBERT *and* JACQUELINE *as they dart ceaselessly to and fro, fetching and carrying the egg baskets; the action is so arranged that as one of them arrives the other leaves, and vice-versa.*]

FATHER-JACQUES: Long live production! Still more production! Produce! Produce!

JACQUES: Tuff! Tuff! Tuff! Tuff!

['Co-co-codacs' from the side.]

MOTHER-JACQUES [*sponging his brow*]: Bear up . . . bear up . . .

JACQUES: I'm very hot, mamma. Tuff! Tuff!

MOTHER-ROBERT: Keep going, don't stop!

FATHER-JACQUES [*tapping his hands together*]: Production! Production! Production! [*etc.*]

[*The general movement increases.* MOTHER-ROBERT *takes the egg baskets alternately from* FATHER-ROBERT *and* JACQUELINE, *and pours the contents on* JACQUES' *head and body, on the table and on the ground.* JACQUES *becomes quite covered in them; and* MOTHER-ROBERT, *handing back the empty baskets, says*]:

MOTHER-ROBERT: Production! Production! Production! [*etc.*]

[GRANDMOTHER-JACQUES, *in the centre of the stage, also claps her hands as she spins round, saying: 'Production! Production! Production!' etc. The movement and the noise continue: 'Co-co-codac!' 'Tuff! Tuff! Tuff!' 'Production! Production!' become a chorused refrain whilst, without interrupting the action and the comings and goings, one hears, in voices loud enough to surmount the tumult, the following speeches*]:

MOTHER-JACQUES: I keep thinking of the future of all these children!

MOTHER-ROBERT: What are we going to make of the offspring? [138]

FATHER-JACQUES: Sausage meat!

FATHER-ROBERT [*between his comings and goings*]: Cannon fodder!

GRANDMOTHER-JACQUES: We'll need some for omelettes.

JACQUELINE [*between her comings and goings*]: Some can be athletes!

MOTHER-JACQUES: We'll keep some back for reproduction.

MOTHER-ROBERT: And for modelling paste.

FATHER-ROBERT: And pastry paste.

FATHER-JACQUES: We'll make officers, officials, and officious people.

GRANDMOTHER-JACQUES: And we'll put some aside to eat ourselves.

JACQUELINE: Valets and masters!

FATHER-JACQUES: Diplomats.

MOTHER-JACQUES: Knitting wool.

[*In his frame,* GRANDFATHER-JACQUES *can direct the action, with a finger, like an orchestra leader.*]

MOTHER-ROBERT: Leeks and onions.

FATHER-ROBERT: Bankers and pigs.

FATHER-JACQUES: Citizens and country yokels.

MOTHER-JACQUES: Employers and employees!

JACQUELINE: Popes, kings and emperors.

FATHER-JACQUES: Policemen.

MOTHER-ROBERT: Solicitors and parsons.

GRANDMOTHER-JACQUES: Omelettes! Lots of omelettes!

JACQUELINE: Humanitarians and anti-humanitarians!

[*After this last remark, the refrain becomes: 'Yes, yes, yes!'; with only* FATHER-JACQUES *continuing with his former refrain of 'Production! Production! Production!' and still clapping his hands.*]

MOTHER-JACQUES: Opportunists!

MOTHER-ROBERT: Nationalists!

FATHER-ROBERT: Internationalists!
FATHER-JACQUES: Revolutionaries!
GRANDMOTHER-JACQUES: Anti-revolutionaries!
JACQUELINE: Radishes! Radicals! [139]
MOTHER-JACQUES: Proletarians!
FATHER-ROBERT: Householders!
FATHER-JACQUES: Housebreakers!
GRANDMOTHER-JACQUES: Chemists.
JACQUELINE: Firemen, teachers.
MOTHER-JACQUES: Jansenists.
MOTHER-ROBERT: Free thinkers.
FATHER-ROBERT: Marxists. Marquis, marks and counter-marks.
FATHER-JACQUES: Idealists. Relativists.
GRANDMOTHER-JACQUES: Existentialists.
JACQUELINE: Essentialists and materialists.
MOTHER-JACQUES: Federalists and spiritualists.
MOTHER-ROBERT: Intellectuals.
FATHER-ROBERT: Brothers, half-brothers!
FATHER-JACQUES: Friends and enemies!
GRANDMOTHER-JACQUES: Army cooks!
JACQUELINE: Customs officials, actors!
MOTHER-JACQUES: Drunkards and Catholics.
MOTHER-ROBERT: Protestants and Israelites!
FATHER-ROBERT: Stairs and shoes.
FATHER-JACQUES: Pencils and pen-holders.
MOTHER-ROBERT: Aspirins! Matches!
GRANDMOTHER-JACQUES: And omelettes! Above all, lots of omelettes!

[JACQUELINE *and* FATHER-ROBERT *are standing centre stage, empty baskets in their hands.*]

ALL TOGETHER IN CHORUS [*except for* JACQUES *and* GRANDFATHER-JACQUES]: Yes, yes, omelettes, lots of omelettes.

[*The movement and noise cease abruptly.* JACQUES *is heard to say in a feeble voice*]:

JACQUES: And pessimists!
ALL [*indignant*]: What? How dare he? What's the matter with him? Is he still going on? Never content!

[*They move towards him. Tense silence.*]

JACQUES: Anarchists. And nihilists.
FATHER-ROBERT: I said, we could never rely on him.[140]
FATHER-JACQUES [*to his son*]: Have you lost your faith?
MOTHER-ROBERT: He hasn't got any faith.
FATHER-JACQUES [*to his son*]: Then say what it is you want!

JACQUES: I want a fountain of light, incandescent water, fire of ice, snows of fire.

JACQUELINE [*to* JACQUES]: Don't forget your obligations.

GRANDFATHER-JACQUES [*in his frame, to* JACQUES]: Look after your eggs!

FATHER-ROBERT [*to* JACQUES]: You can always go to the firework displays.

MOTHER-ROBERT: He's certainly got some big ideas!

FATHER-ROBERT: Why not go to the Chateau of Merdailles?

ALL: Long live production! Long live the white race! Keep it up! Keep it up!

[*The cries of 'Production!' and 'Co-co-codac' start up again, the action speeds up even more in the general enthusiasm.* GRANDFATHER-JACQUES *in his frame also cries out: 'Produce! Produce!!' The others say 'Let's produce! Let's produce!'; they all give out 'Co-co-codacs', and applaud.*]

GRANDFATHER-JACQUES: As it was in the past, the future lies in eggs!

[*A trap-door may or may not open; or perhaps the stage may or may not slowly collapse, and the characters—all unwittingly—gently sink and disappear without interrupting their actions—or just quite simply carry on, according to the technical facilities available.*

Curtain [141]

MIGUEL de UNAMUNO

Saint Emmanuel the Good, Martyr

If with this life only in view we have had hope in Christ, we are of all men the most to be pitied.

SAINT PAUL: I COR. 15:19.

Now that the bishop of the diocese of Renada, to which this my beloved village of Valverde de Lucerna belongs, is seeking (according to rumor), to initiate the process of beatification of our

SOURCE: From *Abel Sanchez.* Copyright 1958. Henry Regnery Co.

Don Manuel, or more correctly, Saint Emmanuel the Good, who was parish priest here, I want to state in writing, by way of confession (although to what end only God, and not I can say), all that I can vouch for and remember of that matriarchal man who pervaded the most secret life of my soul, who was my true spiritual father, the father of my spirit, the spirit of myself, Angela Carballino.

The other, my flesh-and-blood temporal father, I scarcely knew, for he died when I was still a [207] very young girl. I know that he came to Valverde de Lucerna from the outside world—that he was a stranger—and that he settled here when he married my mother. He had brought a number of books with him: *Don Quixote,* some plays from the classic theatre, some novels, a few histories, the *Bertoldo,* everything all mixed together. From these books (practically the only ones in the entire village), I nurtured dreams as a young girl, dreams which in turn devoured me. My good mother gave me very little account either of the words or the deeds of my father. For the words and deeds of Don Manuel, whom she worshipped, of whom she was enamored, in common with all the rest of the village—in an exquisitely chaste manner, of course—had obliterated the memory of the words and deeds of her husband; him she commended to God, with full fervor, as she said her daily rosary.

Don Emmanuel I remember as if it were yesterday, from the time when I was a girl of ten, just before I was taken to the convent school in the cathedral city of Renada. At that time Don Emmanuel, our saint, must have been about thirty-seven years old. He was tall, slender, erect; he carried himself the way our Buitre Peak carries its crest, and his eyes had all the blue depth of our lake. As he walked he commanded all eyes, and not only the eyes but the hearts of all; gazing round at us he seemed to look through [208] our flesh as through glass and penetrate our hearts. We all of us loved him, especially the children. And the things he said to us! Not words, things! The villagers could scent the odor of sanctity, they were intoxicated with it.

It was at this time that my brother Lazarus, who was in America, from where he regularly sent us money with which we lived in decent leisure, had my mother send me to the convent school, so that my education might be completed outside the village; he suggested this move despite the fact that he had no special fondness for the nuns. "But since, as far as I know," he wrote us, "there are no lay schools there yet,—especially not for young ladies—we will have to make use of the ones that do exist. The important thing is for Angelita to receive some polish and not be forced to continue among village girls." And so I entered the convent school. At one point I even thought I would become a teacher; but pedagogy soon palled upon me.

At school I met girls from the city and I made friends with some of them. But I still kept in touch with people in our village, and I received frequent reports and sometimes a visit.

And the fame of the parish priest reached as far as the school, for he was beginning to be talked of in the cathedral city. The nuns never tired of asking me about him.[209]

Ever since early youth I had been endowed, I don't very well know from where, with a large degree of curiosity and restlessness, due at least in part to that jumble of books which my father had collected, and these qualities were stimulated at school, especially in the course of a relationship which I developed with a girl friend, who grew excessively attached to me. At times she proposed that we enter the same convent together, swearing to an everlasting "sisterhood"—and even that we seal the oath in blood. At other times she talked to me, with eyes half closed, of sweethearts and marriage adventures. Strangely enough, I have never heard of her since, or of what became of her, despite the fact that whenever our Don Manuel was spoken of, or when my mother wrote me something about him in her letters—which happened in almost every letter—and I read it to her, this girl would exclaim, as if in rapture: "What luck, my dear, to be able to live near a saint like that, a live saint, of flesh and blood, and to be able to kiss his hand; when you go back to your village write me everything, everything, and tell me about him."

Five years passed at school, five years which now have evanesced in memory like a dream at dawn, and when I became fifteen I returned to my own Valverde de Lucerna. By now everything revolved around Don Emmanuel: Don [210] Emmanuel, the lake and the mountain. I arrived home anxious to know him, to place myself under his protection, and hopeful he would set me on my path in life.

It was rumored that he had entered the seminary to become a priest so that he might thus look after the sons of a sister recently widowed and provide for them in place of their father; that in the seminary his keen mind and his talents had distinguished him and that he had subsequently turned down opportunities for a brilliant career in the church because he wanted to remain exclusively a part of his Valverde de Lucerna, of his remote village which lay like a brooch between the lake and the mountain reflected in it.

How he did love his people! His life consisted in salvaging wrecked marriages, in forcing unruly sons to submit to their parents, or reconciling parents to their sons, and, above all, of consoling the embittered and the weary in spirit; meanwhile he helped everyone to die well.

I recall, among other incidents, the occasion when the unfortunate daughter of old aunt Rabona returned to our town. She had been in the city and lost her virtue there; now she returned unmarried and castoff, and she brought back a little son. Don Emmanuel did not rest until he had persuaded an old sweetheart, Perote by name, to marry the poor girl and, moreover,[211] to legitimize the little creature with his own name. Don Emmanuel told Perote:

"Come now, give this poor waif a father, for he hasn't got one except in heaven."

"But, Don Emmanuel, it's not my fault . . . !"

"Who knows, my son, who knows . . . ! And besides, it's not a question of guilt."

And today, poor Perote, inspired on that occasion to saintliness by Don Emmanuel, and now a paralytic and invalid, has for staff and consolation of his life the son he accepted as his own when the boy was not his at all.

On Midsummer's Night, the shortest night of the year, it was a local custom here (and still is) for all the old crones, and a few old men, who thought they were possessed or bewitched (hysterics they were, for the most part, or in some cases epileptics) to flock to the lake. Don Emmanuel undertook to fulfill the same function as the lake, to serve as a pool of healing, to treat his charges and even, if possible, to cure them. And such was the effect of his presence, of his gaze, and above all of his voice—the miracle of his voice!—and the infinitely sweet authority of his words, that he actually did achieve some remarkable cures. Whereupon his fame increased, drawing all the sick of the environs to our lake and our priest. And yet once when a mother came to ask for a miracle in behalf of her son, he answered her with a sad smile: [212]

"Ah, but I don't have my bishop's permission to perform miracles."

He was particularly interested in seeing that all the villagers kept themselves clean. If he chanced upon someone with a torn garment he would send him to the church: "Go and see the sacristan, and let him mend that tear." The sacristan was a tailor, and when, on the first day of the year, everyone went to congratulate him on his saint's day—his holy patron was Our Lord Jesus Himself—it was by Don Emmanuel's wish that everyone appeared in a new shirt, and those that had none received the present of a new one from Don Emmanuel himself.

He treated everyone with the greatest kindness; if he favored anyone, it was the most unfortunate, and especially those who rebelled. There was a congenital idiot in the village, the fool Blasillo, and it was toward him that Don Emmanuel chose to show the greatest love and concern; as a consequence he succeeded in miraculously teaching him things which had appeared beyond the idiot's comprehension. The fact was that the embers of understanding feebly glowing in the idiot were kindled whenever, like a pitiable monkey, he imitated his Don Emmanuel.

The marvel of the man was his voice; a divine voice which brought one close to weeping. Whenever he officiated at Solemn High Mass and intoned [213] the prelude, a tremor ran through the congregation and all within sound of his voice were moved to the depths of their being. The sound of his chanting, overflowing the church, went on to float over the lake and settle at the foot of the mountain. And when on Good Friday he intoned "My God, my God, my God, why hast Thou forsaken me?" a profound shudder swept through the multitude, like the lash of a northeaster across the waters of the lake. It was as if these people heard the Lord Jesus Christ himself, as if the voice sprang from the ancient crucifix, at the foot of which generations of mothers had offered up their sorrows. And it happened that on one occasion his mother heard him and was unable to contain herself, and cried out to him right in the church, "My son!," calling her child. And the entire congregation was visibly affected. It was as if the mother's cry had issued from the half-open lips of the Mater Dolorosa—her heart transfixed by seven swords—which stood in one of the chapels of the nave. Afterwards, the fool Blasillo went about piteously repeating, as if he were an echo, "My God, my God, my God, why hast Thou forsaken me?" with such effect that everyone who heard him was moved to tears, to the great satisfaction of the fool, who prided himself on this triumph of imitation.

The priest's effect on people was such that no one ever dared to tell him a lie, and everyone [214] confessed themselves to him without need of a confessional. So true was this that on one occasion, when a revolting crime had been committed in a neighboring village, the judge—a dull fellow who badly misunderstood Don Emmanuel—called on the priest and said:

"Let us see, Don Manuel, if you can get this bandit to admit the truth."

"So that afterwards you may punish him?" asked the saintly man. "No, Judge, no; I will not extract from any man a truth which could be the death of him. That is a matter between him and his God. . . . Human justice is none of my affair. 'Judge not that ye be not judged,' said our Lord."

"But the fact is, Father, that I, a judge . . ."

"I understand. You, Judge, must render unto Caesar that which is Caesar's, while I shall render unto God that which is God's."

And, as Don Emmanuel departed, he gazed at the suspected criminal and said:

"Make sure, only, that God forgives you, for that is all that matters."

Everyone went to Mass in the Village, even if it were only to hear him and see him at the altar, where he appeared to be transfigured, his countenance lit from within. He introduced one holy practice to the popular cult; it consisted in assembling the whole town inside the church, men and women, ancients and youth, some thousand [215] persons; there we recited the Creed, in unison, so that it sounded like a single voice: "I believe in God, the Almighty Father, Creator of heaven and earth . . ." and all the rest. It was not a chorus, but a single voice, a simple united voice, all the voices based on one on which they formed a kind of mountain, whose peak, lost at times in the clouds, was Don Emmanuel. As we reached the section "I believe in the resurrection of the flesh and life everlasting," the voice of Don Emmanuel was submerged, drowned in the voice of the populace as in a lake. In truth, he was silent. And I could hear the bells of that city which is said hereabouts to be at the bottom of the lake—bells which are also said to be audible on Midsummer's Night—the bells of the city which is submerged in the spiritual lake of our populace; I was hearing the voice of our dead, resurrected in us by the communion of saints. Later, when I had learned the secret of our saint, I understood that it was as if a caravan crossing the desert lost its leader as they approached the goal of their trek, whereupon his people lifted him on their shoulders to bring his lifeless body into the promise land.

When it came to dying themselves, most of the villagers refused to die unless they were holding on to Don Emmanuel's hand, as if to an anchor chain.

In his sermons he never inveighed against unbelievers,[216] Masons, liberals or heretics. What for, when there were none in the village? Nor did it occur to him to speak against the wickedness of the press. On the other hand, one of his most frequent themes was gossip, against which he lashed out.

"Envy," he liked to repeat, "envy is nurtured by those who prefer to think they are envied, and most persecutions are the result of a persecution complex rather than of an impulse to persecute."

"But Don Emmanuel, just listen to what that fellow was trying to tell me . . ."

"We should concern ourselves less with what people are trying to tell us than with what they tell us without trying . . ."

His life was active rather than contemplative, and he constantly fled from idleness, even from leisure. Whenever he heard it said that idleness was the mother of all the vices, he added: "And also of the greatest vice of them all, which is to think idly." Once I asked him what he meant and he answered: "Thinking idly is thinking as a substitute for doing, or thinking too much about what is already done instead of about what must be done. What's done is done and over with, and one must go on to something else, for there is nothing worse than remorse without possible relief." Action! Action! Even in those early days I had already begun to realize that [217] Don Emmanuel fled from being left to think in solitude, and I guessed that some obsession haunted him.

And so it was that he was always occupied, sometimes even occupied in searching for occupations. He wrote very little on his own, so that he scarcely left us anything in writing, even notes; on the other hand, he acted as scrivener for everyone else, especially mothers, for whom he composed letters to their absent sons.

He also worked with his hands, pitching in to help with some of the village tasks. At threshing time he reported to the threshing floor to flair and winnow, meanwhile teaching and entertaining the workers by turn. Sometimes he took the place of a worker who had fallen sick. One day in the dead of winter he came upon a child, shivering with the bitter cold. The child's father had sent him into the woods to bring back a strayed calf.

"Listen," he said to the child, "you go home and get warm, and tell your father that I am bringing back the calf." On the way back with the animal he ran into the father, who had come out to meet him, thoroughly ashamed of himself.

In winter he chopped wood for the poor. When a certain magnificent walnut tree died—"that matriarchal walnut," he called it, a tree under whose shade he had played as a boy and whose fruit he had eaten for so many years—he [218] asked for the trunk, carried it to his house and, after he had cut six planks from it, which he put away at the foot of his bed, he made firewood of the rest to warm the poor. He also was in the habit of making handballs for the boys and a goodly number of toys for the younger children.

Often he used to accompany the doctor on his rounds, adding his presence and prestige to the doctor's prescriptions. Most of all he was interested in maternity cases and the care of children; it was his opinion that the old wives' saying "from the cradle to heaven" and the other one about "little angels belong in heaven" were nothing short of blasphemy.[1] The death of a child moved him deeply.

"A child stillborn," I once heard him say, "or one who dies soon after birth, is the most terrible of mysteries to me. It's as if it were a suicide. Or as if the child were crucified."

And once, when a man had taken his own life and the father of the suicide, an outsider, asked Don Emmanuel if his son could be buried in consecrated ground, the priest answered:

"Most certainly, for at the last moment, in the very last throes, he must certainly have repented. There is no doubt of it whatsoever in my mind."

From time to time he would visit the local school to help the teacher, to teach alongside [219] him—and not only the catechism. The simple truth was that he fled relentlessly from idleness and from solitude. He went so far in this desire of his to mingle with the villagers, especially the youth and the children, that he even attended the village dances. And more than once he played the drum to keep time for the young men and women dancing; this kind of activity, which in another priest would have seemed like a grotesque mockery of his calling, in him somehow took on the appearance of a holy and religious exercise. When the Angelus would ring out, he would put down the drum and sticks, take off his hat (all the others doing the same) and pray: "The angel of the Lord declared unto Mary: Hail Mary . . ." And afterwards: "Now, let us rest until tomorrow."

"First of all," he would say, "the village must be happy; every-

[1] "Teta y gloria" and "angelitos al cielo."

one must be happy to be alive. To be satisfied with life is of first importance. No one should want to die until it is God's will."

"I want to die now," a recently widowed woman once told him, "I want to be with my husband . . ."

"And why now?" he asked. "Stay here and pray God for his soul."

One of his well-loved remarks was made at a wedding: "Ah, if I could only change all the water in our lake into wine, into a dear little wine which, no matter how much of it one [220] drank, would always make one joyful without intoxicating . . . or, if intoxicating, would make one joyfully drunk."

Once upon a time a band of poor acrobats came through the village. The leader—who arrived on the scene with a gravely ill and pregnant wife and three sons to help him—played the clown. While he was in the village square making all the children, and even some of the adults, laugh with glee, his wife suddenly fell desperately ill and had to leave; she went off accompanied by a look of anguish from the clown and a howl of laughter from the children. Don Emmanuel hurried after, and, a little later, in a corner of the inn's stable, he helped her give up her soul in a state of grace. When the performance was over and the villagers and the clown learned of the tragedy, they came to the inn, and there the poor bereaved clown, in a voice choked with tears, told Don Emmanuel, as he took his hand and kissed it: "They are quite right, Father, when they say you are a saint." Don Emmanuel took the clown's hand in his and replied before everyone:

"It's you who are the saint, good clown. I watched you at your work and understood that you do it not only to provide bread for your children, but also to give joy to the children of others. And I tell you now that your wife, the mother of your children, whom I sent to God [221] while you worked to give joy, is at rest in the Lord, and that you will join her there, and that the angels, whom you will make laugh with happiness in heaven, will reward you with their laughter."

And everyone present wept, children and elders alike, as much from sorrow as from a mysterious joy in which all sorrow was drowned. Later, recalling that solemn hour, I have come to realize that the imperturbable joyousness of Don Emmanuel was merely the temporal, earthly form of an infinite, eternal sadness which the priest concealed from the eyes and ears of the world with heroic saintliness.

His constant activity, his ceaseless intervention in the tasks and diversions of everyone, had the appearance, in short, of a flight from himself, of a flight from solitude. He confirmed this suspicion: "I have a fear of solitude," he would say. And still, from time to time he would go off by himself, along the shores of the lake, to the ruins of the abbey where the souls of pious Cistercians seem still to repose, although history has long since buried them in oblivion. There, the cell of the so-called Father-Captain can still be found, and it is said that the drops of blood spattered on the walls as he flagellated himself can still be seen. What thoughts occupied our Don Emmanuel as he walked there? I remember a conversation we held once in which I asked [222] him, as he was speaking of the abbey, why it had never occurred to him to enter a monastery, and he answered me:

"It is not at all because of the fact that my sister is a widow and I have her children and herself to support—for God looks after the poor—but rather because I simply was not born to be a hermit, an anchorite; the solitude would crush my soul; and, as far as a monastery is concerned, my monastery is Valverde de Lucerna. I was not meant to live alone, or die alone. I was meant to live for my village, and die for it too. How should I save my soul if I were not to save the soul of my village as well?"

"But there have been saints who were hermits, solitaries . . ." I said.

"Yes, the Lord gave them the grace of solitude which He has denied me, and I must resign myself. I must not throw away my village to win my soul. God made me that way. I would not be able to resist the temptations of the desert. I would not be able, alone, to carry the cross of birth . . ."

I have summoned up all these recollections, from which my faith was fed, in order to portray our Don Emmanuel as he was when I, a young girl of sixteen, returned from the convent of Renada to our "monastery of Valverde de Lucerna," once more to kneel at the feet of our "abbot." [223]

"Well, here is the daughter of Simona," he said as soon as he saw me, "made into a young woman, and knowing French, and how to play the piano, and embroider, and heaven knows what else besides! Now you must get ready to give us a family. And your brother Lazarus; when does he return? Is he still in the New World?"

"Yes, Father, he is still in the New World."

"The New World! And we in the Old. Well then, when you

write him, tell him for me, on behalf of the parish priest, that I should like to know when he is returning from the New World to the Old, to bring us the latest from over there. And tell him that he will find the lake and the mountain as he left them."

When I first went to him for confession, I became so confused that I could not enunciate a word. I recited the "Forgive me, Father, for I have sinned," in a stammer, almost a sob. And he, observing this, said:

"Good heavens, my dear, what are you afraid of, or of whom are you afraid? Certainly you're not trembling now under the weight of your sins, nor in fear of God. No, you're trembling because of me, isn't that so?"

At this point I burst into tears.

"What have they been telling you about me? What fairy tales? Was it your mother, perhaps? [224] Come, come, please be calm; you must imagine you are talking to your brother . . ."

At this I plucked up courage and began to tell him of my anxieties, doubts and sorrows.

"Bah! Where did you read all this, Miss Intellectual. All this is literary nonsense. Don't succumb to everything you read just yet, not even to Saint Theresa. If you need to amuse yourself, read the *Bertoldo,* as your father before you did."

I came away from my first confession to that holy man deeply consoled. The initial fear—simple fright more than respect—with which I had approached him, turned into a profound pity. I was at that time a very young woman, almost a girl still; and yet, I was beginning to be a woman, in my innermost being I felt the juice and stirrings of maternity, and when I found myself in the confessional at the side of the saintly priest, I sensed a kind of unspoken confession on his part in the soft murmur of his voice. And I remembered how when he had intoned in the church the words of Jesus Christ: "My God, my God, why hast Thou forsaken me?" his own mother had cried out in the congregation: "My son!"; and I could hear the cry that had rent the silence of the temple. And I went to him again for confession—and to comfort him.[225]

Another time in the confessional I told him of a doubt which assailed me, and he responded:

"As to that, you know what the catechism says. Don't question me about it, for I am ignorant; in Holy Mother Church there are learned doctors of theology who will know how to answer you."

"But you are the learned doctor here."

"Me? A learned doctor? Not even in thought! I, my little doctress, am only a poor country priest. And those questions, . . . do you know who whispers them into your ear? Well . . . the Devil does!"

Then, making bold, I asked him point-blank:

"And suppose he were to whisper these questions to you?"

"Who? To me? The Devil? No, we don't even know each other, my daughter, we haven't met at all."

"But if he did whisper them? . . ."

"I wouldn't pay any attention. And that's enough of that; let's get on, for there are some people, really sick people, waiting for me."

I went away thinking, I don't know why, that our Don Emmanuel, so famous for curing the bedeviled, didn't really even believe in the Devil. As I started home, I ran into the fool Blasillo, who had probably been hovering around outside; as soon as he saw me, and by way of treating me to a display of his virtuosity, he [226] began the business of repeating—and in what a manner!—"My God, my God, why hast Thou forsaken me?" I arrived home utterly saddened and locked myself in my room to cry, until finally my mother arrived.

"With all these confessions, Angelita, you will end by going off to a nunnery."

"Don't worry, Mother," I answered her. "I have plenty to do here, in the village, and it will be my only convent."

"Until you marry."

"I don't intend to," I rejoined.

The next time I saw Don Emmanuel I asked him, looking straight into his eyes:

"Is there really a Hell, Don Emmanuel?"

And he, without altering his expression, answered:

"For you, my daughter, no."

"For others, then?"

"Does it matter to you, if you are not to go there?"

"It matters for the others, in any case. Is there a Hell?"

"Believe in Heaven, the Heaven we can see. Look at it there"—and he pointed to the heavens above the mountain, and then down into the lake, to the reflection.

"But we are supposed to believe in Hell as well as in Heaven," I said.

"That's true. We must believe everything believed [227] and

taught by our Holy Mother Church, Catholic, Apostolic, and Roman. And now, that will do!"

I thought I read a deep unknown sadness in his eyes, eyes which were as blue as the waters of the lake.

Those years passed as if in a dream. Within me, a reflected image of Don Emmanuel was unconsciously taking form. He was an ordinary enough man in many ways, of such daily use as the daily bread we asked for in our Paternoster. I helped him whenever I could with his tasks, visiting the sick, his sick, the girls at school, and helping, too, with the church linen and the vestments; I served in the role, as he said, of his deaconess. Once I was invited to the city for a few days by a school friend, but I had to hurry home, for the city stifled me—something was missing, I was thirsty for a sight of the waters of the lake, hungry for a sight of the peaks of the mountain; and even more, I missed my Don Emmanuel, as if his absence called to me, as if he were endangered by my being so far away, as if he were in need of me. I began to feel a kind of maternal affection for my spiritual father; I longed to help him bear the cross of birth.

My twenty-fourth birthday was approaching when my brother Lazarus came back from America with the small fortune he had saved [228] up. He came back to Valverde de Lucerna with the intention of taking me and my mother to live in a city, perhaps even Madrid.

"In the country," he said, "in these villages, a person becomes stupefied, brutalized and spiritually impoverished." And he added: "Civilization is the very opposite of everything countryfied. The idiocy of village life! No, that's not for us; I didn't have you sent away to school so that later you might spoil here, among these ignorant peasants."

I said nothing, though I was disposed to resist emigration. But our mother, already past sixty, took a firm stand from the start: "Change pastures at my age?" she demanded at once. A little later she made it quite clear that she could not live out of sight of her lake, her mountain, and, above all, of her Don Emmanuel.

"The two of you are like those cats that get attached to houses," my brother muttered.

When he realized the complete sway exercised over the entire village—especially over my mother and myself—by the saintly priest, my brother began to resent him. He saw in this situation an example of the obscurantist theocracy which, according to him, smothered Spain. And he commenced to spout the old anti-clerical commonplaces, to which he added anti-religious and "progressive" propaganda brought back from the New World.[229]

"In the Spain of sloth and flabby useless men, the priests manipulate the women, and the women manipulate the men. Not to mention the idiocy of the country, and this feudal backwater!"

"Feudal," to him, meant something frightful. "Feudal" and "medieval" were the epithets he employed to condemn something completely.

The failure of his diatribes to move us and their total lack of effect upon the village—where they were listened to with respectful indifference—disconcerted him no end. "The man does not exist who could move these clods." But, he soon began to understand—for he was an intelligent man, and therefore a good one—the kind of influence exercised over the village by Don Emmanuel, and he came to appreciate the effect of the priest's work in the village.

"This priest is not like the others," he announced. "He is, in fact, a saint."

"How do you know what the others are like," I asked. To which he answered:

"I can imagine."

In any case, he did not set foot inside the church nor did he miss an opportunity to parade his incredulity—though he always exempted Don Emmanuel from his scorning accusations. In the village, an unconscious expectancy began to build up, the anticipation of a kind of duel between my brother Lazarus and Don Emmanuel [230]—in short, it was expected that Don Emmanuel would convert my brother. No one doubted but that in the end the priest would bring him into the fold. On his side, Lazarus was eager (he told me so himself, later) to go and hear Don Emmanuel, to see and hear him in the church, to get to know him and to talk with him, so that he might learn the secret of his spiritual hold over our souls. And he let himself be coaxed to this end, so that finally—"out of curiosity," as he said—he went to hear the preacher.

"Now, this is something else again," he told me as soon as he came from hearing Don Emmanuel for the first time. "He's not like the others; still, he doesn't fool me, he's too intelligent to believe everything he must teach."

"You mean you think he's a hypocrite?"

"A hypocrite . . . no! But he has a job by which he must live."

As for me, my brother undertook to see that I read the books he brought me, and others which he urged me to buy.

"So your brother Lazarus wants you to read," Don Emmanuel queried. "Well, read, my daughter, read and make him happy by doing so. I know you will read only worthy books. Read even if only novels; they are as good as the books which deal with so-called 'reality.' You are better off reading than concerning yourself [231] with village gossip and old wives' tales. Above all, though, you will do well to read devotional books which will bring you contentment in life, a quiet, gentle contentment, and peace."

And he, did he enjoy such contentment?

It was about this time that our mother fell mortally sick and died. In her last days her one wish was that Don Emmanuel should convert Lazarus, whom she expected to see again in heaven, in some little corner among the stars from where they could see the lake and the mountain of Valverde de Lucerna. She felt she was going there now, to see God.

"You are not going anywhere," Don Emmanuel would tell her; "you are staying right here. Your body will remain here, in this land, and your soul also, in this house, watching and listening to your children though they do not see or hear you."

"But, Father," she said, "I am going to see God."

"God, my daughter, is all around us, and you will see Him from here, right from here. And all of us in Him, and He in all of us."

"God bless you," I whispered to him.

"The peace in which your mother dies will be her eternal life," he told me.

And, turning to my brother Lazarus: "Her heaven is to go on seeing you, and it is at this [232] moment that she must be saved. Tell her you will pray for her."

"But—"

"But what? . . . Tell her you will pray for her, to whom you owe your life. And I know that once you promise her, you *will* pray, and I know that once you pray . . ."

My brother, his eyes filled with tears, drew near our dying mother and gave her his solemn promise to pray for her.

"And I, in heaven, will pray for you, for all of you," my mother responded. And then, kissing the crucifix and fixing her eyes on Don Emmanuel, she gave up her soul to God.

"Into Thy hands I commend my spirit," prayed the priest.

My brother and I stayed on in the house alone. What had happened at the time of my mother's death had established a bond between Lazarus and Don Emmanuel. The latter seemed even to neglect some of his charges, his patients and his other needy to look after my brother. In the afternoons, they would go for a stroll together, walking along the lake or toward the ruins, overgrown with ivy, of the old Cistercian abbey.

"He's an extraordinary man," Lazarus told me. "You know the story they tell of how there is a city at the bottom of the lake, submerged [233] beneath the water, and that on Midsummer's Night at midnight the sound of its church bells can be heard . . ."

"Yes, a city 'feudal and medieval' . . ."

"And I believe," he went on, "that at the bottom of Don Emmanuel's soul there is a city, submerged and inundated, and that sometimes the sound of its bells can be heard . . ."

"Yes . . . And this city submerged in Don Emmanuel's soul, and perhaps—why not?—in yours as well, is certainly the cemetery of the souls of our ancestors, the ancestors of our Valverde de Lucerna . . . 'feudal and medieval'!"

In the end, my brother began going to Mass. He went regularly to hear Don Emmanuel. When it became known that he was prepared to comply with his annual duty of receiving Communion, that he would receive when the others received, an intimate joy ran through the town, which felt that by this act he was restored to his people. The rejoicing was of such nature, moreover, so openhanded and honest, that Lazarus never did feel that he had been "vanquished" or "overcome."

The day of his Communion arrived; of Communion before the entire village, with the entire village. When it came time for my brother's turn, I saw Don Emmanuel—white as January snow on the mountain, and moving like the surface of the lake when it is stirred by the northeast wind [234]—come up to him with the holy wafer in his hand, which trembled violently as it reached out to Lazarus's mouth; at that moment the priest had an instant of faintness and the wafer dropped to the ground. My brother himself recovered it and placed it in his mouth. The people saw the tears on Don Emmanuel's face, and everyone wept, saying: "What great love he bears!" And then, because it was dawn, a cock crowed.

On returning home I locked myself in with my brother; alone with him I put my arms around his neck and kissed him.

"Lazarus, Lazarus, what joy you have given us all today; the entire village, the living and the dead, and especially our mother.

Did you see how Don Emmanuel wept for joy? What joy you have given us all!"

"It was for that reason that I did what I did," he answered me.

"For what? To give us pleasure? Surely you did it for your own sake, first of all; because of your conversion."

And then Lazarus, my brother, grown as pale and tremulous as Don Emmanuel when he was giving Communion, bade me sit down, in the very chair where our mother used to sit. He took a deep breath, and, in the intimate tone of a familiar and domestic confession, he told me:

"Angelita, the time has come when I must tell [235] you the truth, the absolute truth, and I shall tell you because I must, because I cannot, I ought not, conceal it from you, and because, sooner or later, you are bound to intuit it anyway, if only halfway—which would be worse."

Thereupon, serenely and tranquilly, in a subdued voice, he recounted a tale that drowned me in a lake of sorrow. He told how Don Emmanuel had appealed to him, particularly during the walks to the ruins of the old Cistercian abbey, to set a good example, to avoid scandalizing the townspeople, to take part in the religious life of the community, to feign belief even if he did not feel any, to conceal his own ideas—all this without attempting in any way to catechize him, to instruct him in religion, or to effect a true conversion.

"But is it possible?" I asked in consternation.

"Possible and true. When I said to him: 'Is this you, the priest, who suggests I dissimulate?' he replied, hesitatingly: 'Dissimulate? Not at all! That is not dissimulation. "Dip your fingers in holy water, and you will end by believing," as someone said.' And I, gazing into his eyes, asked him: 'And you, celebrating the Mass, have you ended by believing?' He looked away and stared out at the lake, until his eyes filled with tears. And it was in this way that I came to understand his secret." [236]

"Lazarus!" I cried out, incapable of another word.

At that moment the fool Blasillo came along our street, crying out his: "My God, my God, why hast Thou forsaken me?" And Lazarus shuddered, as if he had heard the voice of Don Emmanuel, or of Christ.

"It was then," my brother at length continued, "that I really understood his motives and his saintliness; for a saint he is, Sister, a true saint. In trying to convert me to his holy cause—for it is a holy cause, a most holy cause—he was not attempting to score a triumph, but rather was doing it to protect the peace, the happiness, the illusions, perhaps, of his charges. I understood that if he thus deceives them—if it *is* deceit—it is not for his own advantage. I submitted to his logic,—and that was my conversion.

"I shall never forget the day on which I said to him: 'But, Don Emmanuel, the truth, the truth, above all!'; and he, all a-tremble, whispered in my ear—though we were all alone in the middle of the countryside—'The truth? The truth, Lazarus, is perhaps something so unbearable, so terrible, something so deadly, that simple people could not live with it!'

" 'And why do you show me a glimpse of it now, here, as if we were in the confessional?' I asked. And he said: 'Because if I did not, I [237] would be so tormented by it, so tormented, that I would finally shout it in the middle of the plaza, which I must never, never, never do . . . I am put here to give life to the souls of my charges, to make them happy, to make them dream they are immortal—and not to destroy them. The important thing is that they live sanely, in concord with each other,—and with the truth, with my truth, they could not live at all. Let them live. That is what the Church does, it lets them live. As for true religion, all religions are true as long as they give spiritual life to the people who profess them, as long as they console them for having been born only to die. And for each people the truest religion is their own, the religion that made them . . . And mine? Mine consists in consoling myself by consoling others, even though the consolation I give them is not ever mine.' I shall never forget his words."

"But then this Communion of yours has been a sacrilege," I dared interrupt, regretting my words as soon as I said them.

"Sacrilege? What about the priest who gave it to me? And his Masses?"

"What martyrdom!" I exclaimed.

"And now," said my brother, "there is one more person to console the people."

"To deceive them, you mean?" I said.[238]

"Not at all," he replied, "but rather to confirm them in their faith."

"And they, the people, do they really believe, do you think?"

"About that, I know nothing! . . . They probably believe without trying, from force of habit, tradition. The important thing is not to stir them up. To let them live from their thin sentiments, without acquiring the torments of luxury. Blessed are the poor in spirit!"

"That then is the sentiment you have learned from Don Emmanuel. . . . And tell me, do you feel you have carried out your promise to our mother on her deathbed, when you promised to pray for her?"

"Do you think I *could* fail her? What do you take me for, sister? Do you think I would go back on my word, my solemn promise made at the hour of death to a mother?"

"I don't know. . . . You might have wanted to deceive her so she could die in peace."

"The fact is, though, that if I had not lived up to my promise, I would be totally miserable."

"And . . ."

"I carried out my promise and I have not neglected for a single day to pray for her."

"Only for her?"

"Well, now, for whom else?"

"For yourself! And now, for Don Emmanuel." [239]

We parted and went to our separate rooms. I to weep through the night, praying for the conversion of my brother and of Don Emmanuel. And Lazarus, to what purpose, I know not.

From that day on I was fearful of finding myself alone with Don Emmanuel, whom I continued to aid in his pious works. And he seemed to sense my inner state and to guess at its cause. When at last I came to him in the confessional's penitential tribunal (who was the judge, and who the offender?) the two of us, he and I, bowed our heads in silence and began to cry. It was he, finally, Don Emmanuel, who broke the terrible silence, with a voice which seemed to issue from the tomb:

"Angelita, you have the same faith you had when you were ten, don't you? You believe, don't you?"

"I believe, Father."

"Then go on believing. And if doubts come to torment you, suppress them utterly, even to yourself. The main thing is to live . . ."

I summoned up courage, and dared to ask, trembling:

"But, Father, do you believe?"

For a brief moment he hesitated, and then, mastering himself, he said:

"I believe!"

"In what, Father, in what? Do you believe in [240] the after life? Do you believe that in dying we do not die in every way, completely? Do you believe that we will see each other again, that we will love each other in a world to come? Do you believe in another life?"

The poor saint was sobbing.

"My child, leave off, leave off!"

Now, when I come to write this memoir, I ask myself: Why did he not deceive me? Why did he not deceive me as he deceived the others? Why did he afflict himself? Why could he not deceive himself, or why could he not deceive me? And I want to believe that he was afflicted because he could not deceive himself into deceiving me.

"And now," he said, "pray for me, for your brother, and for yourself—for all of us. We must go on living. And giving life."

And, after a pause:

"Angelita, why don't you marry?"

"You know why I do not."

"No, no; you must marry. Lazarus and I will find you a suitor. For it would be good for you to marry, and rid yourself of these obsessions."

"Obsessions, Don Emmanuel?"

"I know well enough what I am saying. You should not torment yourself for the sake of others, for each of us has more than enough to do answering for himself."

"That it should be you, Don Emmanuel, who says this! That you should advise me to marry [241] and answer for myself alone and not suffer over others! That it should be you!"

"Yes, you are right, Angelita. I am no longer sure of what I say. I am no longer sure of what I say since I began to confess to you. Only, one must go on living. Yes! One must live!"

And when I rose to leave the church, he asked me:

"Now, Angelita, in the name of the people, do you absolve me?"

I felt pierced by a mysterious and priestly prompting and said:

"In the name of the Father, the Son and the Holy Ghost, I absolve you, Father."

We quitted the church, and as I went out I felt the quickening of maternity within me.

My brother, now totally devoted to the work of Don Emmanuel, had become his closest and most zealous collaborator and companion. They were bound together, moreover, by their common secret. Lazarus accompanied the priest on his visits to the sick, and to schools, and he placed his resources at the disposition of the saintly man. A little more zeal, and he would have learned to help celebrate Mass. All the while he was sounding deeper in the unfathomable soul of the priest.

"What manliness!" he exclaimed to me once.[242] "Yesterday, as we walked along the lake he said: 'There lies my direst temptation.' When I interrogated him with my eyes, he went on: 'My poor father, who was close to ninety when he died, was tormented all his life, as he confessed to me himself, by a temptation to suicide, by an instinct to self-destruction which had come to him from a time before memory—from birth, from his *nation,* as he said—and was forced to fight against it always. And this fight grew to be his life. So as not to succumb to this temptation he was forced to take precautions, to guard his life. He told me of terrible episodes. His urge was a form of madness,—and I have inherited it. How that water beckons me in its deep quiet! . . . an apparent quietude reflecting the sky like a mirror—and beneath it the hidden current! My life, Lazarus, is a kind of continual suicide, or a struggle against suicide, which is the same thing. . . . Just so long as our people go on living!' And then he added: 'Here the river eddies to form a lake, so that later, flowing down the plateau, it may form into cascades, waterfalls, and torrents, hurling itself through gorges and chasms. Thus does life eddy in the village; and the temptation to suicide is the greater beside the still waters which at night reflect the stars, than it is beside the crashing falls which drive one back in fear. Listen, Lazarus, I have helped [243] poor villagers to die well, ignorant, illiterate villagers, who had scarcely ever been out of their village, and I have learned from their own lips, or divined it when they were silent, the real cause of their sickness unto death, and there at the head of their deathbed I have been able to see into the black abyss of their life-weariness. A weariness a thousand times worse than hunger! For our part, Lazarus, let us go on with our kind of suicide of working for the people, and let them dream their life as the lake dreams the heavens.'

"Another time," said my brother, "as we were coming back, we spied a country girl, a goatherd, standing erect on a height of the mountain slope overlooking the lake and she was singing in a voice fresher than its waters. Don Emmanuel took hold of me, and pointing to her said: 'Look, it's as though time had stopped, as though this country girl had always been there just as she is, singing in the way she is, and as though she would always be there, as she was before my consciousness began, as she will be when it is past. That girl is a part of nature—not of history—along with the rocks, the clouds, the trees, and the waters.' He has such a subtle feeling for nature, he infuses it with spirit!

"I shall not forget the day when snow was falling and he asked me: 'Have you ever seen a [244] greater mystery, Lazarus, than the snow falling, and dying, in the lake, while a hood is laid upon the mountain?' "

Don Emmanuel had to moderate and temper my brother's zeal and his neophyte's rawness. As soon as he heard that Lazarus was going about inveighing against some of the popular superstitions he told him forcefully:

"Leave them alone! It's difficult enough making them understand where orthodox belief leaves off and where superstition begins. It's hard enough, especially for us. Leave them alone, then, as long as they get some comfort. . . . It's better for them to believe everything, even things that contradict one another, than to believe nothing. The idea that someone who believes too much ends by not believing in anything is a Protestant notion. Let us not protest! Protestation destroys contentment and peace."

My brother told me, too, about one moonlit night when they were returning to town along the lake (whose surface a mountain breeze was stirring, so that the moonbeams topped the whitecaps), Don Emmanuel turned to him and said:

"Look, the water is reciting the litany and saying: *ianua caeli, ora pro nobis;* gate of heaven, pray for us." [245]

Two evanescent tears fell from his lashes to the grass, where the light of the full moon shone upon them like dew.

And time went hurrying by, and my brother and I began to notice that Don Emmanuel's spirits were failing, that he could no longer control completely the deep rooted sadness which consumed him; perhaps some treacherous illness was undermining his body and soul. In an effort to rouse his interest, Lazarus spoke to him of the good effect the organization of a type of Catholic agrarian syndicate would have.

"A syndicate?" Don Emmanuel repeated sadly. "A syndicate? And what is that? The Church is the only syndicate I know. And you have certainly heard 'My kingdom is not of this world.' Our kingdom, Lazarus, is not of this world . . ."

"And of the other?"

Don Emmanuel bowed his head:

"The other is here. Two kingdoms exist in this world. Or rather, the other world. . . . Ah, I don't really know what I'm saying. But as for the syndicate, that's a vestige from your days of 'progressivism.' No, Lazarus, no; religion does not exist to resolve the economic or political conflicts of this world, which God handed over to men for their dsputes. Let men think and act as they will, let them console themselves for [246] having been born, let them live as happily as possible in the illusion that all this has a purpose. I don't propose to advise the poor to submit to the rich, nor to suggest to the rich that they subordinate themselves to the poor; but rather to preach resignation in everyone, and charity toward everyone. For even the rich man must resign himself—to his riches, and to life; and the poor man must show charity—even to the rich. The Social Question? Ignore it, for it is none of our business. So, a new society is on the way, in which there will be neither rich nor poor, in which wealth will be justly divided, in which everything will belong to everyone—and so, what then? Won't this general well-being and comfort lead to even greater tedium and weariness of life? I know well enough that one of those chiefs of what they call the Social Revolution has already said that religion is the opium of the people. Opium . . . Opium . . . Yes, opium it is. We should give them opium, and help them sleep, and dream. I, myself, with my mad activity, give myself opium. And still I don't manage to sleep well, let alone dream well. . . . What a fearful nightmare! . . . I, too, can say, with the Divine Master: 'My soul is weary unto death.' No, Lazarus, no; no syndicates for us. If *they* organize them, well and good—they would be distracting themselves in that way. Let [247] them play at syndicates, if that makes them happy."

The entire village began to realize that Don Emmanuel's spirit was weakening, that his strength was waning. His very voice—that miracle of a voice—acquired a kind of quaking. Tears came into his eyes for any reason whatever—or for no reason. Whenever he spoke to people about the other world, about the other life, he was compelled to pause at frequent intervals, and he would close his eyes. "It is a vision," people would say, "he has a vision of what lies ahead." At such moments the fool Blasillo was the first to break into tears. He wept copiously these days, crying now more than he laughed, and even his laughter had the sound of tears.

The last Easter Week which Don Emmanuel was to celebrate among us, in this world, in this village of ours, arrived, and all the village sensed the impending end of tragedy. And how the words did strike home when for the last time Don Emmanuel cried out before us: "My God, my God, why hast Thou forsaken me?"! And when he repeated the words of the Lord to the Good Thief ("All thieves are good," Don Emmanuel used to tell us): "Tomorrow shalt thou be with me in Paradise." . . . ! And then, the last general Communion which our saint was to give! When he came to my brother to give him [248] the Host—his hand steady this time—, just after the liturgical ". . . *in vitam aeternam,*" he bent down and whispered to him: "There is no other life but this, no life more eternal . . . let them dream it eternal . . . let it be eternal for a few years . . ."

And when he came to me he said: "Pray, my child, pray for us all." And then, something so extraordinary happened that I carry it now in my heart as the greatest of mysteries: he bent over and said, in a voice which seemed to belong to the other world: ". . . and pray, too, for our Lord Jesus Christ."

I stood up, going weak as I did so, like a somnambulist. Everything around me seemed dream-like. And I thought: "Am I to pray, too, for the lake and the mountain?" And next: "Am I bewitched, then?" Home at last, I took up the crucifix my mother had held in her hands when she had given up her soul to God, and, gazing at it through my tears and recalling the "My God, my God, why hast Thou forsaken me?" of our two Christs, the one of this earth and the other of this village, I prayed: "Thy will be done on earth as it is in heaven," and then, "And lead us not into temptation. Amen." After this I turned to the statue of the Mater Dolorosa—her heart transfixed by seven swords—which had been my poor mother's most sorrowful comfort, and I prayed again: "Holy Mary, Mother of [249] God, pray for us sinners, now and in the hour of our death. Amen." I had scarcely finished the prayer, when I asked myself: "Sinners? Sinners are we? And what is our sin, what is it?" And all day I brooded over the question.

The next day I presented myself before Don Emmanuel—Don Emmanuel now in the full sunset of his magnificent religiosity—and I said to him:

"Do you remember, my Father, years ago when I asked you a

certain question you answered: 'That question you must not ask me; for I am ignorant; there are learned doctors of the Holy Mother Church who will know how to answer you'?"

"Do I remember? . . . Of course. And I remember I told you those were questions put to you by the Devil."

"Well, then, Father, I have come again, bedeviled, to ask you another question put to me by my Guardian Devil."

"Ask it."

"Yesterday, when you gave me Communion, you asked me to pray for all of us, and even for . . ."

"That's enough! . . . Go on."

"I arrived home and began to pray; when I came to the part 'Pray for us sinners, now and at the hour of our death,' a voice in me asked: [250] Sinners? Sinners are we? And what is our sin?' What is our sin, Father?"

"Our sin?" he replied. "A great doctor of the Spanish Catholic Apostolic Church has already explained it; the great doctor of *Life is a Dream* has written 'The greatest sin of man is to have been born.' That, my child, is our sin; to have been born."

"Can it be atoned, Father?"

"Go and pray again. Pray once more for us sinners, now and at the hour of our death. . . . Yes, at length the dream is atoned . . . at length life is atoned . . . at length the cross of birth is expiated and atoned, and the drama comes to an end. . . . And as Calderón said, to have done good, to have feigned good, even in dreams, is something which is not lost."

The hour of his death arrived at last. The entire village saw it come. And he made it his finest lesson. For he would not die alone or at rest. He died preaching to his people in the church. But first, before being carried to the church (his paralysis made it impossible for him to move), he summoned Lazarus and me to his bedside. Alone there, the three of us together, he said:

"Listen to me: watch over these poor sheep; find some comfort for them in living, and let [251] them believe what I could not. And Lazarus, when your hour comes, die as I die, as Angela will die, in the arms of the Holy Mother Church, Catholic, Apostolic, and Roman; that is to say, of the Holy Mother Church of Valverde de Lucerna. And now, farewell; until we never meet again, for this dream of life is coming to an end . . ."

"Father, Father," I cried out.

"Do not grieve, Angela, only go on praying for all sinners, for all who have been born. Let them dream, let them dream . . . O, what a longing I have to sleep, to sleep, sleep without end, sleep for all eternity, and never dream! Forgetting this dream! . . . When they go to bury me, let it be in a box made from the six planks I cut from the old walnut tree—poor old tree!—in whose shade I played as a child, when I began the dream. . . . In those days, I did really believe in life everlasting. That is to say, it seems to me now that I believed. For a child, to believe is the same as to dream. And for a people, too. . . . You'll find those six planks I cut at the foot of the bed."

He was seized by a sudden fit of choking, and then, composing himself once more, he went on:

"You will recall that when we prayed together, animated by a common sentiment, a community of spirit, and we came to the final verse of the [252] Creed, you will remember that I would fall silent. . . . When the Israelites were coming to the end of their wandering in the desert, the Lord told Aaron and Moses that because they had not believed in Him they would not set foot in the Promised Land with their people; and he bade them climb the heights of Mount Hor, where Moses ordered Aaron stripped of his garments, so that Aaron died there, and then Moses went up from the plains of Moab to Mount Nebo, to the top of Pisgah, looking into Jericho, and the Lord showed him all of the land promised to His people, but said to him: 'You will not go there.' And there Moses died, and no one knew his grave. And he left Joshua to be chief in his place. You, Lazarus, must be my Joshua, and if you can make the sun stand still, make it stop, and never mind progress. Like Moses, I have seen the face of God—our supreme dream—face to face, and as you already know, and as the Scripture says, he who sees God's face, he who sees the eyes of the dream, the eyes with which He looks at us, will die inexorably and forever. And therefore, do not let our people, so long as they live, look into the face of God. Once dead, it will no longer matter, for then they will see nothing . . ."

"Father, Father, Father," I cried again.

And he said:

"Angela, you must pray always, so that all [253] sinners may go on dreaming, until they die, of the resurrection of the flesh and the life everlasting . . ."

I was expecting "and who knows it might be . . ." But instead, Don Emmanuel had another attack of coughing.

"And now," he finally went on, "and now, in the hour of my death, it is high time to have me brought, in this very chair, to the church, so that I may take leave there of my people, who await me."

He was carried to the church and brought, in his armchair, into the chancel, to the foot of the altar. In his hands he held a crucifix. My brother and I stood close to him, but the fool Blasillo wanted to stand even closer. He wanted to grasp Don Emmanuel by the hand, so that he could kiss it. When some of the people nearby tried to stop him, Don Emmanuel rebuked them and said:

"Let him come closer. . . . Come, Blasillo, give me your hand."

The fool cried for joy. And then Don Emmanuel spoke:

"I have very few words left, my children; I scarcely feel I have strength enough left to die. And then, I have nothing new to tell you, either. I have already said everything I have to say. Live with each other in peace and contentment,[251] in the hope that we will all see each other again some day, in that other Valverde de Lucerna up there among the nighttime stars, the stars which the lake reflects over the image of the reflected mountain. And pray, pray to the Most Blessed Mary, and to our Lord. Be good . . . that is enough. Forgive me whatever wrong I may have done you inadvertently or unknowingly. After I give you my blessing, let us pray together, let us say the Paternoster, the Ave Maria, the Salve, and the Creed."

Then he gave his blessing to the whole village, with the crucifix held in his hand, while the women and children cried and even some of the men wept softly. Almost at once the prayers were begun. Don Emmanuel listened to them in silence, his hand in the hand of Blasillo the fool, who began to fall asleep to the sound of the praying. First the Paternoster, with its "Thy will be done on earth as it is in heaven"; then the Ave Maria, with its "Pray for us sinners, now and in the hour of our death"; followed by the Salve, with its "mourning and weeping in this vale of tears"; and finally, the Creed. On reaching "The resurrection of the flesh and life everlasting" the people sensed that their saint had yielded up his soul to God. It was not necessary to close his eyes even, for he died with them closed. When an attempt was made to wake [255] Blasillo, it was found that he, too, had fallen asleep in the Lord forever. So that later there were two bodies to be buried.

The village immediately repaired en masse to the house of the saint to carry away holy relics, to divide up pieces of his garments among themselves, to carry off whatever they could find as a memento of the blessed martyr. My brother preserved his breviary, between the pages of which he discovered a carnation, dried as in a herbarium and mounted on a piece of paper, and upon the paper a cross and a certain date.

No one in the village seemed able to believe that Don Emmanuel was dead; everyone expected to see him—perhaps some of them did—taking his daily walk along the side of the lake, his figure mirrored in the water, or silhouetted against the background of the mountain. They continued to hear his voice, and they all visited his grave, around which a veritable cult sprang up, old women "possessed by devils" came to touch the cross of walnut, made with his own hands from the tree which had yielded the six planks of his casket.

The ones who least of all believed in his death were my brother and I. Lazarus carried on the tradition of the saint, and he began to compile a record of the priest's words. Some of the conversations [256] in this account of mine were made possible by his notes.

"It was he," said my brother, "who made me into a new man. I was a true Lazarus whom he raised from the dead. He gave me faith."

"Ah, faith . . ."

"Yes, faith, faith in the charity of life, in life's joy. It was he who cured me of my delusion of 'progress,' of my belief in its political implications. For there are, Angela, two types of dangerous and harmful men: those who, convinced of life beyond the grave, of the resurrection of the flesh, torment other people—like the inquisitors they are—so that they will despise this life as a transitory thing and work for the other life; and then, there are those who, believing only in this life . . ."

"Like you, perhaps . . ."

"Yes, and like Don Emmanuel. Believing only in this world, this second group looks forward to some vague future society and exerts every effort to prevent the populace finding consoling joy from belief in another world . . ."

"And so . . ."

"The people should be allowed to live with their illusion."

The poor priest who came to the parish to replace Don Emmanuel found himself overwhelmed [257] in Valverde de Lucerna by the memory of the saint, and he put himself in the hands of my brother and myself for guidance. He wanted only to follow in the footsteps of the saint. And my brother told him: "Very little theology, Father, very little theology. Religion, religion, religion." Listening to him, I smiled to myself, wondering if this was not a kind of theology, too.

I had by now begun to fear for my poor brother. From the time Don Emmanuel died it could scarcely be said that he lived. Daily he went to the priest's tomb; for hours on end he stood gazing into the lake. He was filled with nostalgia for deep, abiding peace.

"Don't stare into the lake so much," I begged him.

"Don't worry. It's not this lake which draws me, nor the mountain. Only, I cannot live without his help."

"And the joy of living, Lazarus, what about the joy of living?"

"That's for others. Not for those of us who have seen God's face, those of us on whom the Dream of Life has gazed with His eyes."

"What; are you preparing to go and see Don Emmanuel?"

"No, sister, no. Here at home now, between the two of us, the whole truth—bitter as it may be, bitter as the sea into which the sweet waters [258] of our lake flow—the whole truth for you, who are so set against it . . ."

"No, no, Lazarus. You are wrong. Your truth is not the truth."

"It's my truth."

"Yours, perhaps, but surely not . . ."

"His, too."

"No, Lazarus. Not now, it isn't. Now, he must believe otherwise; now he must believe . . ."

"Listen, Angela, once Don Emmanuel told me that there are truths which, though one reveals them to oneself, must be kept from others; and I told him that telling me was the same as telling himself. And then he said, he confessed to me, that he thought that more than one of the great saints, perhaps the very greatest himself, had died without believing in the other life."

"Is it possible?"

"All too possible! And now, sister, you must be careful that here, among the people, no one even suspects our secret . . ."

"Suspect it?" I cried in amazement. "Why even if I were to try, in a fit of madness, to explain it to them, they wouldn't understand it. The people do not understand your words, they understand your actions much better. To try and explain all this to them would be like reading some pages from Saint Thomas Aquinas to eight-year-old children, in Latin." [259]

"All the better. In any case, when I am gone, pray for me and for him and for all of us."

At length, his own time came. A sickness which had been

eating away at his robust nature seemed to flare with the death of Don Emmanuel.

"I don't so much mind dying," he said to me in his last days, "as the fact that with me another piece of Don Emmanuel dies too. The remainder of him must live on with you. Until, one day, even we dead will die forever."

When he lay in the throes of death, the people of the village came in to bid him farewell (as is customary in our towns) and they commended his soul to the care of Don Emmanuel the Good, Martyr. My brother said nothing to them; he had nothing more to say. He had already said everything there was to say. He had become a link between the two Valverde de Lucernas—the one at the bottom of the lake and the one reflected in its surface. He was already one more of us who had died of life, and, in his way, one more of our saints.

I was desolate, more than desolate; but I was, at least, among my own people, in my own village. Now, having lost my Saint Emmanuel, the father of my soul, and my own Lazarus, my more than carnal brother, my spiritual brother, now it is I realize that I have aged. But, have I [260] really lost them then? Have I grown old? Is my death approaching?

I must live! And he taught me to live, he taught us to live, to feel life, to feel the meaning of life, to merge with the soul of the mountain, with the soul of the lake, with the soul of the village, to lose ourselves in them so as to remain in them forever. He taught me by his life to lose myself in the life of the people of my village, and I no longer felt the passing of the hours, and the days, and the years, any more than I felt the passage of the water in the lake. It began to seem that my life would always be thus. I no longer felt myself growing old. I no longer lived in myself, but in my people, and my people lived in me. I tried to speak as they spoke, as they spoke without trying. I went into the street—it was the one highway—and, since I knew everyone, I lived in them and forgot myself (while, on the other hand, in Madrid, where I went once with my brother, I had felt a terrible loneliness, since I knew no one, and had been tortured by the sight of so many unknown people).

Now, as I write this memoir, this confession of my experience with saintliness, with a saint, I am of the opinion that Don Emmanuel the Good, my Don Emmanuel, and my brother, too, died believing they did not believe, but that, without believing in their belief, they actually believed, with resignation and in desolation.[261]

But why, I have asked myself repeatedly, did not Don Emmanuel attempt to convert my brother deceitfully, with a lie, pretending to be a believer himself without being one? And I have finally come to think that Don Emmanuel realized he would not be able to delude him, that with him a fraud would not do, that only through the truth, with his truth, would he be able to convert him; that he knew he would accomplish nothing if he attempted to enact the comedy—the tragedy, rather—which he played out for the benefit of the people. And thus did he win him over, in effect, to his pious fraud; thus did he win him over to the cause of life with the truth of death. And thus did he win me, who never permitted anyone to see through his divine, his most saintly, game. For I believed then, and I believe now, that God—as part of I know not what sacred and inscrutable purpose—caused them to believe they were unbelievers. And that at the moment of their passing, perhaps, the blindfold was removed.

And I, do I believe?

As I write this—here in my mother's old house, and I past my fiftieth year and my memories growing as dim and blanched as my hair—outside it is snowing, snowing upon the lake, snowing upon the mountain, upon the memory [262] of my father, the stranger, upon the memory of my mother, my brother Lazarus, my people, upon the memory of my Saint Emmanuel, and even on the memory of the poor fool Blasillo, my Saint Blasillo—and may he help me in heaven! The snow effaces corners and blots out shadows, for even in the night it shines and illuminates. Truly, I do not know what is true and what is false, nor what I saw and what I merely dreamt—or rather, what I dreamt and what I merely saw—, nor what I really knew or what I merely believed true. Neither do I know whether or not I am transferring to this paper, white as the snow outside, my consciousness, for it to remain in writing, leaving me without it. But why, any longer, cling to it?

Do I really understand any of it? Do I really believe in any of it? Did what I am writing about here actually take place, and did it take place in just the way I tell it? Is it possible for such things to happen? Is it possible that all this is more than a dream dreamed within another dream? Can it be that I, Angela Carballino, a woman in her fifties, am the only one in this village to be assailed by far-fetched thoughts, thoughts unknown to everyone else? And the others, those around me, do they believe? And what does it mean, to believe? At least they go on living. And now they believe in Saint Emmanuel the Good, Martyr, who, with no hope [263] of immortality for himself, preserved their hope in it.

It appears that our most illustrious bishop, who set in motion the process for beatifying our saint from Valverde de Lucerna, is intent on writing an account of Don Emmanuel's life, something which would serve as a guide for the perfect parish priest, and with this end in mind he is gathering information of every sort. He has repeatedly solicited information from me; more than once he has come to see me; and I have supplied him with all sorts of facts. But I have never revealed the tragic secret of Don Emmanuel and my brother. And it is curious that he never suspected. I trust that what I have set down here will never come to his knowledge. For, all temporal authorities are to be avoided; I fear all authorities on this earth—even when they are church authorities.

But this is an end to it. Let its fate be what it will . . .[264]

How, you ask, did this document, this memoir of Angela Carballino fall into my hands? That, reader, is something I must keep secret. I have transcribed it for you just as it is written, just as it came to me, with only a few, a very few editorial emendations. It recalls to you other things I have written? This fact does not gainsay its objectivity, its originality. Moreover, for all I know, perhaps I created real, actual beings, independent of me, beyond my control, characters with immortal souls. For all I know, Augusto Perez in my novel *Mist* [2] was right when he claimed to be more real, more objective than I myself, who had thought to have invented him. As for the reality of this Saint Emmanuel the Good, Martyr—as he is revealed to me by his disciple and spiritual daughter Angela Carballino—of his reality it has not occurred to me to doubt. I believe in it more than the saint himself did. I believe in it more than I do in my own reality.

[2] In the denouement of *Mist*, the protagonist Augusto Perez turns on Unamuno, and tells him that he, a creation of human thought and genius, is more real than his author, a product of blind animality.

And now, before I bring this epilogue to a close, I wish to recall to your mind, patient reader, the ninth verse of the Epistle of the forgotten Apostle, Saint Judas—what power in a name!—where we are told how my heavenly patron, St. Michael Archangel (Michael means [265] "Who such as God?" and archangel means archmessenger) disputed with the Devil (Devil means accuser, prosecutor) over the body of Moses, and would not allow him to carry it off as a prize, to damnation. Instead, he told the Devil: "May the Lord rebuke thee." And may he who wishes to understand, understand!

I would like also, since Angela Carballino injected her own feelings into her narrative—I don't know how it could have been otherwise—to comment on her statement to the effect that if Don Emmanuel and his disciple Lazarus had confessed their convictions to the people, they, the people, would not have understood. Nor, I should like to add, would they have believed the pair. They would have believed in their works and not their words. And works stand by themselves, and need no words to back them up. In a village like Valverde de Lucerna one makes one's confession by one's conduct.

And as for faith, the people scarce know what it is, and care less.

I am well aware of the fact that no action takes place in this narrative, this *novelistic* narrative, if you will—the novel is, after all, the most intimate, the truest history, so that I scarcely understand why some people are outraged to have the Bible called a novel, when such a designation actually sets it above some mere chronicle or other. In short, nothing happens.[266] But I hope that this is because everything that takes place happens, and, instead of coming to pass, and passing away, remains forever, like the lakes and the mountains and the blessed simple souls fixed firmly beyond faith and despair, the blessed souls who, in the lakes and the mountains, outside history, in their divine novel, take refuge.

Salamanca, 1930 [267]

FYODOR DOSTOEVSKY

The Legend of the Grand Inquisitor

The scene of this crucial selection from The Brothers Karamazov *is set in a screened-off section of a room in a Moscow tavern. Accompanied by the shouts for waiters, the popping of corks, the click of billiard balls, and the drone of an organ, Ivan Karamazov attempts to reveal his true self to his saintly brother Alyosha. Admitting the possibility of the existence of God, "the underlying order and meaning of life," and even the "eternal harmony" toward which existence is said to move, he nevertheless refuses to "accept this world of God's." For God's achievement of eternal harmony in the future is grounded on the senseless suffering of the innocent in the here and now. To Ivan the "higher harmony" is "not worth the tears of . . . one tortured child . . . because those tears are unatoned for." Nor will vengeance against the oppressors do, for that means greater suffering. He wants forgiveness, but "is there in the whole world a being who would have the right to forgive and could forgive?" Alyosha points to Christ, "who can forgive everything, all and for all, because He gave His innocent blood for all and everything." At this point Ivan recites his "poem in prose": The Legend of the Grand Inquisitor.*

"Even this must have a preface—that is, a literary preface," laughed Ivan, "and I am a poor hand at making one. You see, my action takes place in the sixteenth century, and at that time, as you probably learnt at school, it was customary in poetry to bring down heavenly powers on earth. Not to speak of Dante, in France, clerks, as [255] well as the monks in the monasteries, used to give regular performances in which the Madonna, the saints, the angels, Christ, and God himself were brought on the stage. In those days it was done in all simplicity. In Victor Hugo's 'Notre Dame de Paris' an

SOURCE: Reprinted from *The Brothers Karamazov,* trans. Constance Garnett, Modern Library edition (Random House, Inc.).

edifying and gratuitous spectacle was provided for the people in the Hotel de Ville of Paris in the reign of Louis XI. in honour of the birth of the dauphin. It was called *Le bon jugement de la très sainte et gracieuse Vierge Marie,* and she appears herself on the stage and pronounces her *bon jugement.* Similar plays, chiefly from the Old Testament, were occasionally performed in Moscow too, up to the times of Peter the Great. But besides plays there were all sorts of legends and ballads scattered about the world, in which the saints and angels and all the powers of Heaven took part when required. In our monasteries the monks busied themselves in translating, copying, and even composing such poems—and even under the Tatars. There is, for instance, one such poem (of course, from the Greek), 'The Wanderings of Our Lady through Hell,' with descriptions as bold as Dante's. Our Lady visits Hell, and the Archangel Michael leads her through the torments. She sees the sinners and their punishment. There she sees among others one noteworthy set of sinners in a burning lake; some of them sink to the bottom of the lake so that they can't swim out, and 'these God forgets'—an expression of extraordinary depth and force. And so Our Lady, shocked and weeping, falls before the throne of God and begs for mercy for all in Hell—for all she has seen there, and indiscriminately. Her conversation with God is immensely interesting. She beseeches Him, she will not desist, and when God points to the hands and feet of her Son, nailed to the Cross, and asks, 'How can I forgive His tormentors?' she bids all the saints, all the martyrs, all the angels and archangels to fall down with her and pray for mercy on all without distinction. It ends by her winning from God a respite of suffering every year from Good Friday till Trinity day, and the sinners at once raised a cry of thankfulness from Hell, chanting, 'Thou art just, O Lord, in this judgment.' Well, my poem would have been of that kind if it had appeared at that time. He comes on the scene in my poem, but He says nothing, only appears and passes on. Fifteen centuries have passed since He promised to come in His glory, fifteen centuries since His prophet wrote, 'Behold, I come quickly'; 'Of that day and that hour knoweth no man, neither the Son, but the Father,' as He Himself predicted on earth. But humanity awaits him with the same faith and with the same love. Oh, with greater faith, for it is fifteen centuries since man has ceased to see signs from Heaven.[256]

No signs from Heaven come to-day
To add to what the heart doth say.

There was nothing left but faith in what the heart doth say. It is true there were many miracles in those days. There were saints who performed miraculous cures; some holy people, according to their biographies, were visited by the Queen of Heaven herself. But the devil did not slumber, and doubts were already arising among men of the truth of these miracles. And just then there appeared in the north of Germany a terrible new heresy. 'A huge star like to a torch' (that is, to a church) 'fell on the sources of the waters and they became bitter.' These heretics began blasphemously denying miracles. But those who remained faithful were all the more ardent in their faith. The tears of humanity rose up to Him as before, awaiting His coming, loved Him, hoped for Him, yearned to suffer and die for Him as before. And so many ages mankind had prayed with faith and fervour, 'O Lord our God, hasten Thy coming,' so many ages called upon Him, that in His infinite mercy He deigned to come down to His servants. Before that day He had come down, He had visited some holy men, martyrs and hermits, as is written in their 'Lives.' Among us, Tyutchev, with absolute faith in the truth of his words, bore witness that

Bearing the Cross, in slavish dress
Weary and worn, the Heavenly King
Our mother, Russia, came to bless,
And through our land went wandering.

And that certainly was so, I assure you.

"And behold, He deigned to appear for a moment to the people, to the tortured, suffering people, sunk in iniquity, but loving Him like children. My story is laid in Spain, in Seville, in the most terrible time of the Inquisition, when fires were lighted every day to the glory of God, and 'in the splendid *auto da fé* the wicked heretics were burnt.' Oh, of course, this was not the coming in which He will appear according to His promise at the end of time in all His heavenly glory, and which will be sudden 'as lightning flashing from east to west.' No, He visited His children only for a moment, and there where the flames were crackling round the heretics. In His infinite mercy He came once more among men in that human shape in which He walked among men for three years fifteen centuries ago. He came down to the 'hot [257] pavement' of the southern town in which on the day before almost a hundred heretics had, *ad majorem gloriam Dei,* been burnt by the cardinal, the Grand Inquisitor, in a magnificent *auto da fé,* in the presence of the king, the court, the knights, the cardinals, the most charming ladies of the court, and the whole population of Seville.

"He came softly, unobserved, and yet, strange to say, every one recognised Him. That might be one of the best passages in the poem. I mean, why they recognised Him. The people are irresistibly drawn to Him, they surround Him, they flock about Him, follow Him. He moves silently in their midst with a gentle smile of infinite compassion. The sun of love burns in His heart, light and power shine from His eyes, and their radiance, shed on the people, stirs their hearts with responsive love. He holds out His hands to them, blesses them, and a healing virtue comes from contact with Him, even with His garments. An old man in the crowd, blind from childhood, cries out, 'O Lord, heal me and I shall see Thee!' and, as it were, scales fall from his eyes and the blind man sees Him. The crowd weeps and kisses the earth under His feet. Children throw flowers before Him, sing, and cry hosannah. 'It is He—it is He!' all repeat. 'It must be He, it can be no one but Him!' He stops at the steps of the Seville cathedral at the moment when the weeping mourners are bringing in a little open white coffin. In it lies a child of seven, the only daughter of a prominent citizen. The dead child lies hidden in flowers. 'He will raise your child,' the crowd shouts to the weeping mother. The priest, coming to meet the coffin, looks perplexed, and frowns, but the mother of the dead child throws herself at His feet with a wail. 'If it is Thou, raise my child!' she cries, holding out her hands to Him. The procession halts, the coffin is laid on the steps at His feet. He looks with compassion, and His lips once more softly pronounce, 'Maiden, arise!' and the maiden arises. The little girl sits up in the coffin and looks round, smiling with wide-open wondering eyes, holding a bunch of white roses they had put in her hand.

"There are cries, sobs, confusion among the people, and at that moment the cardinal himself, the Grand Inquisitor, passes by the cathedral. He is an old man, almost ninety, tall and erect, with a withered face and sunken eyes, in which there is still a gleam of light. He is not dressed in his gorgeous cardinal's robes, as he was the day before, when he was burning the enemies of the Roman Church—at that moment he was wearing his coarse, old, monk's cassock. At a distance behind him come his gloomy assistants and slaves and the 'holy guard.' He stops at the sight of the crowd and watches it from a distance. He sees everything; [258] he sees them set the coffin down at His feet, sees the child rise up, and his face darkens. He knits his thick grey brows and his eyes gleam with a sinister fire. He holds out his finger and bids the guards take Him. And such is his power, so completely are the people cowed into submission and trembling obedience to him, that the crowd immediately make way for the guards, and in the midst of deathlike silence they lay hands on Him and lead Him away. The crowd instantly bows down to the earth, like one man, before the old inquisitor. He blesses the people in silence and passes on. The guards lead their prisoner to the close, gloomy vaulted prison in the ancient palace of the Holy Inquisition and shut Him in it. The day passes and is followed by the dark, burning 'breathless' night of Seville. The air is 'fragrant with laurel and lemon.' In the pitch darkness the iron door of the prison is suddenly opened and the Grand Inquisitor himself comes in with a light in his hand. He is alone; the door is closed at once behind him. He stands in the doorway and for a minute or two gazes into His face. At last he goes up slowly, sets the light on the table and speaks.

"'Is it Thou? Thou?' but receiving no answer, he adds at once, 'Don't answer, be silent. What canst Thou say, indeed? I know too well what Thou wouldst say. And Thou hast no right to add anything to what Thou hadst said of old. Why, then, art Thou come to hinder us? For Thou hast come to hinder us, and Thou knowest that. But dost Thou know what will be to-morrow? I know not who Thou art and care not to know whether it is Thou or only a semblance of Him, but to-morrow I shall condemn Thee and burn Thee at the stake as the worst of heretics. And the very people who have to-day kissed Thy feet, to-morrow at the faintest sign from me will rush to heap up the embers of Thy fire. Knowest Thou that? Yes, maybe Thou knowest it,' he added with thoughtful penetration, never for a moment taking his eyes off the Prisoner."

"I don't quite understand, Ivan. What does it mean?" Alyosha, who had been listening in silence, said with a smile. "Is it simply a wild fantasy, or a mistake on the part of the old man—some impossible *qui pro quo*?"

"Take it as the last," said Ivan, laughing, "if you are so corrupted by modern realism and can't stand anything fantastic. If you like it to be a case of mistaken identity, let it be so. It is true," he went on, laughing, "the old man was ninety, and he might well be crazy over his set idea. He might have been struck by the appearance of the Prisoner. It might, in fact, be simply his ravings, the delusion of an old man of [259] ninety, over-excited by the *auto da fé* of a hundred heretics the day before. But does it matter to us after all whether it was a mistake of identity or a wild fantasy? All that matters is that the old man should speak out, should speak openly of what he has thought in silence for ninety years."

"And the Prisoner too is silent? Does He look at him and not say a word?"

"That's inevitable in any case," Ivan laughed again. "The old man has told Him He hasn't the right to add anything to what He has said of old. One may say it is the most fundamental feature of Roman Catholicism, in my opinion at least. 'All has been given by Thee to the Pope,' they say, 'and all, therefore, is still in the Pope's hands, and there is no need for Thee to come now at all. Thou must not meddle for the time, at least.' That's how they speak and write too—the Jesuits, at any rate. I have read it myself in the works of their theologians. 'Hast Thou the right to reveal to us one of the mysteries of that world from which Thou hast come?' my old man asks Him, and answers the question for Him. 'No, Thou hast not; that Thou mayest not add to what has been said of old, and mayest not take from men the freedom which Thou didst exalt when Thou wast on earth. Whatsoever Thou revealest anew will encroach on men's freedom of faith; for it will be manifest as a miracle, and the freedom of their faith was dearer to Thee than anything in those days fifteen hundred years ago. Didst Thou not often say then, "I will make you free"? But now Thou has seen these "free" men,' the old man adds suddenly, with a pensive smile. 'Yes, we've paid dearly for it,' he goes on, looking sternly at Him, 'but at last we have completed that work in Thy name. For fifteen centuries we have been wrestling with Thy freedom, but now it is ended and over for good. Dost Thou not believe that it's over for good? Thou lookest meekly at me and deignest not even to be wroth with me. But let me tell Thee that now, to-day, people are more persuaded than ever that they have perfect freedom, yet they have brought their freedom to us and laid it humbly at our feet. But that has been our doing. Was this what Thou didst? Was this Thy freedom?' "

"I don't understand again," Alyosha broke in. "Is he ironical, is he jesting?"

"Not a bit of it! He claims it as a merit for himself and his Church that at last they have vanquished freedom and have done so to make men happy. 'For now' (he is speaking of the Inquisition, of course) 'for the first time it has become possible to think of the happiness of men.[260] Man was created a rebel; and how can rebels be happy? Thou wast warned,' he says to Him. 'Thou hast had no lack of admonitions and warnings, but Thou didst not listen to those warnings; Thou didst reject the only way by which men might be made happy. But, fortunately, departing Thou didst hand on the work to us. Thou hast promised, Thou hast established by Thy word, Thou has given to us the right to bind and to unbind, and now, of course, Thou canst not think of taking it away. Why, then, hast Thou come to hinder us?' "

"And what's the meaning of 'no lack of admonitions and warnings'?" asked Alyosha.

"Why, that's the chief part of what the old man must say.

" 'The wise and dread Spirit, the spirit of self-destruction and nonexistence,' the old man goes on, 'the great spirit talked with Thee in the wilderness, and we are told in the books that he "tempted" Thee. Is that so? And could anything truer be said than what he revealed to Thee in three questions and what Thou didst reject, and what in the books is called "the temptation"? And yet if there has ever been on earth a real stupendous miracle, it took place on that day, on the day of the three temptations. The statement of those three questions was itself the miracle. If it were possible to imagine simply for the sake of argument that those three questions of the dread spirit had perished utterly from the books, and that we had to restore them and to invent them anew, and to do so had gathered together all the wise men of the earth—rulers, chief priests, learned men, philosophers, poets—and had set them the task to invent three questions, such as would not only fit the occasion, but express in three words, three human phrases, the whole future history of the world and of humanity—dost Thou believe that all the wisdom of the earth united could have invented anything in depth and force equal to the three questions which were actually put to Thee then by the wise and mighty spirit in the wilderness? From those questions alone, from the miracle of their statement, we can see that we have here to do not with the fleeting human intelligence, but with the absolute and eternal. For in those three questions the whole subsequent history of mankind is, as it were, brought together into one whole, and foretold, and in them are united all the unsolved historical contradictions of human nature. At the time it could not be so clear, since the future was unknown; but now that fifteen hundred years have passed, we see that everything in those three questions was so justly divined and foretold, and has been so truly fulfilled, that nothing can be added to them or taken from them.[261]

"'Judge Thyself who was right—Thou or he who questioned Thee then? Remember the first question; its meaning, in other words, was this: "Thou wouldst go into the world, and art going with empty hands, with some promise of freedom which men in their simplicity and their natural unruliness cannot even understand, which they fear and dread—for nothing has ever been more insupportable for a man and a human society than freedom. But seest Thou these stones in this parched and barren wilderness? Turn them into bread, and mankind will run after Thee like a flock of sheep, grateful and obedient, though for ever trembling, lest Thou withdraw Thy hand and deny them Thy bread." But Thou wouldst not deprive man of freedom and didst reject the offer, thinking, what is that freedom worth, if obedience is bought with bread? Thou didst reply that man lives not by bread alone. But dost Thou know that for the sake of that earthly bread the spirit of the earth will rise up against Thee and will strive with Thee and overcome Thee, and all will follow him, crying, "Who can compare with this beast? He has given us fire from heaven!" Dost Thou know that the ages will pass, and humanity will proclaim by the lips of their sages that there is no crime, and therefore no sin; there is only hunger? "Feed men, and then ask of them virtue!" that's what they'll write on the banner, which they will raise against Thee, and with which they will destroy Thy temple. Where Thy temple stood will rise a new building; the terrible tower of Babel will be built again, and though, like the one of old, it will not be finished, yet Thou mightest have prevented that new tower and have cut short the sufferings of men for a thousand years; for they will come back to us after a thousand years of agony with their tower. They will seek us again, hidden underground in the catacombs, for we shall be again persecuted and tortured. They will find us and cry to us, "Feed us, for those who have promised us fire from heaven haven't given it!" And then we shall finish building their tower, for he finishes the building who feeds them. And we alone shall feed them in Thy name, declaring falsely that it is in Thy name. Oh, never, never can they feed themselves without us! No science will give them bread so long as they remain free. In the end they will lay their freedom at our feet, and say to us, "Make us your slaves, but feed us." They will understand themselves, at last, that freedom and bread enough for all are inconceivable together, for never, never will they be able to share between them! They will be convinced, too, that they can never be free, for they are weak, vicious, worthless and rebellious. Thou didst promise them the bread of Heaven, but, I repeat again, can it compare with [262] earthly bread in the eyes of the weak, ever sinful and ignoble race of man? And if for the sake of the bread of Heaven thousands and tens of thousands shall follow Thee, what is to become of the millions and tens of thousands of millions of creatures who will not have the strength to forego the earthly bread for the sake of the heavenly? Or dost Thou care only for the tens of thousands of the great and strong, while the millions, numerous as the sands of the sea, who are weak but love Thee, must exist only for the sake of the great and strong? No, we care for the weak too. They are sinful and rebellious, but in the end they too will become obedient. They will marvel at us and look on us as gods, because we are ready to endure the freedom which they have found so dreadful and to rule over them—so awful it will seem to them to be free. But we shall tell them that we are Thy servants and rule them in Thy name. We shall deceive them again, for we will not let Thee come to us again. That deception will be our suffering, for we shall be forced to lie.

" 'This is the significance of the first question in the wilderness, and this is what Thou hast rejected for the sake of that freedom which Thou hast exalted above everything. Yet in this question lies hid the great secret of this world. Choosing "bread," Thou wouldst have satisfied the universal and everlasting craving of humanity—to find some one to worship. So long as man remains free he strives for nothing so incessantly and so painfully as to find some one to worship. But man seeks to worship what is established beyond dispute, so that all men would agree at once to worship it. For these pitiful creatures are concerned not only to find what one or the other can worship, but to find something that all would believe in and worship; what is essential is that all may be *together* in it. This craving for *community* of worship is the chief misery of every man individually and of all humanity from the beginning of time. For the sake of common worship they've slain each other with the sword. They have set up gods and challenged one another, "Put away your gods and come and worship ours, or we will kill you and your gods!" And so it will be to the end of the world, even when gods disappear from the earth; they will fall down before idols just the same. Thou didst know, Thou couldst not but have known, this fundamental secret of human nature, but Thou didst reject the one infallible banner which was offered Thee to make all men bow down to Thee alone—the banner of earthly bread; and Thou hast rejected it for the sake of freedom and the bread of Heaven. Behold what Thou didst further. And all again in the name of freedom! I tell Thee that [263] man is tormented by no greater anxiety than to find some one quickly to whom he can hand over that gift of freedom with which the ill-fated creature is born. But only one who can appease their conscience can take over their freedom. In bread there was offered Thee an invincible banner; give bread, and man will worship Thee, for nothing is more certain than bread. But if some one else gains possession of his conscience—oh! then he will cast away Thy bread and follow after him who has ensnared his conscience. In that Thou wast right. For the secret of man's being is not only to live but to have something to live for. Without a stable conception of the object of life, man would not consent to go on living, and would rather destroy himself than remain on earth, though he had bread in abundance. That is true. But what happened? Instead of taking men's freedom from them, Thou didst make it greater than ever! Didst Thou forget that man prefers peace, and even death, to freedom of choice in the knowledge of good and evil? Nothing is more seductive for man than his freedom of conscience, but nothing is a greater cause of suffering. And behold, instead of giving a firm foundation for setting the conscience of man at rest for ever, Thou didst choose all that is exceptional, vague and enigmatic; Thou didst chose what was utterly beyond the strength of men, acting as though Thou didst not love them at all—Thou who didst come to give Thy life for them! Instead of taking possession of men's freedom, Thou didst increase it, and burden the spiritual kingdom of mankind with its sufferings for ever. Thou didst desire man's free love, that he should follow Thee freely, enticed and taken captive by Thee. In place of the rigid ancient law, man must hereafter with free heart decide for himself what is good and what is evil, having only Thy image before him as his guide. But didst Thou not know he would at last reject even Thy image and Thy truth, if he is weighed down with the fearful burden of free choice? They will cry aloud at last that the truth is not in Thee, for they could not have been left in greater confusion and suffering than Thou hast caused, laying upon them so many cares and unanswerable problems.

"'So that, in truth, Thou didst Thyself lay the foundation for the destruction of Thy kingdom, and no one is more to blame for it. Yet what was offered Thee? There are three powers, three powers alone, able to conquer and to hold captive for ever the conscience of these impotent rebels for their happiness—those forces are miracle, mystery and authority. Thou hast rejected all three and hast set the example for doing so. When the wise and dread spirit set Thee on the pinnacle of the temple and said to Thee, "If Thou wouldst know whether Thou art [264] the Son of God then cast Thyself down, for it is written: the angels shall hold him up lest he fall and bruise himself, and Thou shalt know then whether Thou art the Son of God and shalt prove then how great is Thy faith in Thy Father." But Thou didst refuse and wouldst not cast Thyself down. Oh! of course, Thou didst proudly and well like God; but the weak, unruly race of men, are they gods? Oh, Thou didst know then that in taking one step, in making one movement to cast Thyself down, Thou wouldst be tempting God and have lost all Thy faith in Him, and wouldst have been dashed to pieces against that earth which Thou didst come to save. And the wise spirit that tempted Thee would have rejoiced. But I ask again, are there many like Thee? And couldst Thou believe for one moment that men, too, could face such a temptation? Is the nature of men such, that they can reject miracle, and at the great moments of their life, the moments of their deepest, most agonising spiritual difficulties, cling only to the free verdict of the heart? Oh, Thou didst know that Thy deed would be recorded in books, would be handed down to remote times and the utmost ends of the earth, and Thou didst hope that man, following Thee, would cling to God and not ask for a miracle. But Thou didst not know that when man rejects miracle he rejects God too; for man seeks not so much God as the miraculous. And as man cannot bear to be without the miraculous, he will create new miracles of his own for himself, and will worship deeds of sorcery and witchcraft, though he might be a hundred times over a rebel, heretic and infidel. Thou didst not come down from the Cross when they shouted to Thee, mocking and reviling Thee, "Come down from the cross and we will believe that Thou art He." Thou didst not come down, for again Thou wouldst not enslave man by a miracle, and didst crave faith given freely, not based on miracle. Thou didst crave for free love and not the base raptures of the slave before the might that has overawed him for ever. But Thou didst think too highly of men therein, for they are slaves, of course, though rebellious by nature. Look round and judge; fifteen centuries have passed, look upon them. Whom hast Thou raised up to Thyself? I swear, man is weaker and baser by nature than Thou hast believed him! Can he, can he do what Thou didst? By showing him so much respect, Thou didst, as it were, cease to feel for him, for Thou didst ask far too much from him—Thou who hast loved him more than Thyself! Respecting him less, Thou wouldst have asked less of him. That would have been more like love, for his burden would have been lighter. He is weak and vile. What though he is everywhere now rebelling against [265] our power, and proud of his rebellion? It is the pride of a child and a schoolboy. They are little children rioting and barring out the teacher at school. But their childish delight will end; it will cost them dear. They will cast down temples and drench the earth with blood. But they will see at last, the foolish children, that, though they are rebels, they are impotent rebels, unable to keep up their own rebellion. Bathed in their foolish tears, they will recognize at last that He who created them rebels must have meant to mock at them. They will say this in despair, and their utterance will be a blasphemy which will make them more unhappy still, for man's nature cannot bear blasphemy, and in the end always avenges it on itself. And so unrest, confusion and unhappiness—that is the present lot of man after Thou didst bear so much for their freedom! Thy great prophet tells in vision and in image, that he saw all those who took part in the first resurrection and that there were of each tribe twelve thousand. But if there were so many of them, they must have been not men but gods. They had borne Thy cross, they had endured scores of years in the barren, hungry wilderness, living upon locusts and roots—and Thou mayest indeed point with pride at those children of freedom, of free love, of free and splendid sacrifice for Thy name. But remember that they were only some thousands; and what of the rest? And how are the other weak ones to blame, because they could not endure what the strong have endured? How is the weak soul to blame that it is unable to receive such terrible gifts? Canst Thou have simply come to the elect and for the elect? But if so, it is a mystery and we cannot understand it. And if it is a mystery, we too have a right to preach a mystery, and to teach them that it's not the free judgment of their hearts, not love that matters, but a mystery which they must follow blindly, even against their conscience. So we have done. We have corrected Thy work and have founded it upon *miracle, mystery* and *authority*. And men rejoiced that they were again led like sheep, and that the terrible gift that had brought them such suffering, was, at last, lifted from their hearts. Were we right teaching them this? Speak! Did we not love mankind, so meekly acknowledging their feebleness, lovingly lightening their burden, and permitting their weak nature even sin with our sanction? Why hast Thou come now to hinder us? And why dost Thou look silently and searchingly at me with Thy mild eyes? Be angry. I don't want Thy love, for I love Thee not. And what use is it for me to hide anything from Thee? Don't I know to Whom I am speaking? All that I can say is known to Thee already. And is it for me to conceal from Thee our mystery? Perhaps it is Thy will to [266] hear it from my lips. Listen, then. We are not working with Thee, but with *him*—that is our mystery. It's long—eight centuries—since we have been on *his* side and not on Thine. Just eight centuries ago, we took from him what Thou didst reject with scorn, that last gift he offered Thee, showing Thee all the kingdoms of the earth. We took from him Rome and the sword of Cæsar, and proclaimed ourselves sole rulers of the earth, though hitherto we have not been able to complete our work. But whose fault is that? Oh, the work is only beginning, but it has begun. It has long to await completion and the earth has yet much to suffer, but we shall triumph and shall be Cæsars, and then we shall plan the universal happiness of man. But Thou mightest have taken even then the sword of Cæsar. Why didst Thou reject that last gift? Hadst Thou accepted that last counsel of the mighty spirit, Thou wouldst have accomplished all that man seeks on earth—that is, some one to worship, some one to keep his conscience, and some means of uniting all in one unanimous and harmonious ant-heap, for the craving for universal unity is the third and last anguish of men. Mankind as a whole has always striven to organise a universal state. There have been many great nations with great histories, but the more highly they were developed the more unhappy they were, for they felt more acutely than other people the craving for worldwide union. The great conquerors, Timours and Ghenghis-Khans, whirled like hurricanes over the face of the earth striving to subdue its people, and they too were but the unconscious expression of the same craving for universal unity. Hadst Thou taken the world and Cæsar's purple, Thou wouldst have founded the universal state and have given universal peace. For who can rule men if not he who holds their conscience and their bread in his hands. We have taken the sword of Cæsar, and in taking it, of course, have rejected Thee and followed *him*. Oh, ages are yet to come of the confusion of free thought, of their science and cannibalism. For having begun to build their tower of Babel without us, they will end, of course, with cannibalism. But then the beast will crawl to us and lick our feet and spatter them with tears of blood. And we shall sit upon the beast and raise the cup, and on it will be written, "Mystery." But then, and only then, the reign of peace and happiness will come for men. Thou art proud of Thine elect, but Thou hast only the elect, while we give rest to all. And besides, how many of those elect, those mighty ones who could become elect, have grown weary waiting for Thee, and have transferred and will transfer the powers of their spirit and the warmth of their heart to the other camp, and end by raising their *free* banner [267] against Thee. Thou didst Thyself lift up that banner. But with us all will be happy and will no more rebel nor destroy one another as under Thy freedom. Oh, we shall persuade them that they will only become free when they renounce their freedom to us and submit to us. And shall we be right or shall we be lying? They will be convinced that we are right, for they will remember the horrors of slavery and confusion to which Thy freedom brought them. Freedom, free thought and science, will lead them into such straits and will bring them face to face with such marvels and insoluble mysteries, that some of them, the fierce and rebellious, will destroy themselves, others, rebellious but weak, will destroy one another, while the rest, weak and unhappy, will crawl fawning to our feet and whine to us: "Yes, you were right, you alone possess His mystery, and we come back to you, save us from ourselves!"

" 'Receiving bread from us, they will see clearly that we take the bread made by their hands from them, to give it to them, without any miracle. They will see that we do not change the stones to bread, but in truth they will be more thankful for taking it from our hands than for the bread itself! For they will remember only too well that in old days, without our help, even the bread they made turned to stones in their hands, while since they have come back to us, the very stones have turned to bread in their hands. Too, too well they know the value of complete submission! And until men know that, they will be unhappy. Who is most to blame for their not knowing it, speak? Who scattered the flock and sent it astray on unknown paths? But the flock will come together again and will submit once more, and then it will be once for all. Then we shall give them the quiet humble happiness of weak creatures such as they are by nature. Oh, we shall persuade them at last not to be proud, for Thou didst lift them up and thereby taught them to be proud. We shall show them that they are weak, that they are only pitiful children, but that childlike happiness is the sweetest of all. They will become timid and will look to us and huddle close to us in fear, as chicks to the hen. They will marvel at us and will be awe-stricken before us, and will be proud at our being so powerful and clever, that we have been able to subdue such a turbulent flock of thousands of millions. They will tremble impotently before our wrath, their minds will grow fearful, they will be quick to shed tears like women and children, but they will be just as ready at a sign from us to pass to laughter and rejoicing, to happy mirth and childish song. Yes, we shall set them to work, but in their leisure hours we shall make their life like a child's game, with children's songs and innocent dance. Oh,[268] we shall allow them even sin, they are weak and helpless, and they will love us like children because we allow them to sin. We shall tell them that every sin will be expiated, if it is done with our permission, that we allow them to sin because we love them, and the punishment for these sins we take upon ourselves. And we shall take it upon ourselves, and they will adore us as their saviour who have taken on themselves their sins before God. And they will have no secrets from us. We shall allow or forbid them to live with their wives and mistresses, to have or not to have children—according to whether they have been obedient or disobedient—and they will submit to us gladly and cheerfully. The most painful secrets of their conscience, all, all they will bring to us, and we shall have an answer for all. And they will be glad to believe our answer, for it will save them from the great anxiety and terrible agony they endure at present in making a free decision for themselves. And all will be happy, all the millions of creatures except the hundred thousand who rule over them. For only we, we who guard the mystery, shall be unhappy. There will be thousands of millions of happy babes, and a hundred thousand sufferers who have taken upon themselves the curse of the knowledge of good and evil. Peacefully they will die, peacefully they will expire in Thy name, and beyond the grave they will find nothing but death. But we shall keep the secret, and for their happiness we shall allure them with the reward of heaven and eternity. Though if there were anything in the other world, it certainly would not be for such as they. It is prophesied that Thou wilt come again in victory, Thou wilt come with Thy chosen, the proud and strong, but we will say that they have only saved themselves, but we have saved all. We are told that the harlot who sits upon the beast, and holds in her hands the *mystery,* shall be put to shame, that the weak will rise up again, and will rend her royal purple and will strip naked her loathsome body. But then I will stand up and point out to Thee the thousand millions of happy children who have known no sin. And we who have taken their sins upon us for their happiness will stand up before Thee and say: "Judge us if Thou canst and darest." Know that I fear Thee not. Know that I too have been in the wilderness, I too have lived on roots and locusts, I too prized the freedom with which Thou hast blessed men, and I too was striving to stand among Thy elect, among the strong and powerful, thirsting "to make up the number." But I awakened and would not serve madness. I turned back and joined the ranks of those *who have corrected Thy work.* I left the proud and went back to the humble, for the happiness of the humble. What I say to Thee will come [269] to pass, and our dominion will be built up. I repeat, to-morrow Thou shalt see that obedient flock who at a sign from me will hasten to heap up the hot cinders about the pile on which I shall burn Thee for coming to hinder us. For if any one has ever deserved our fires, it is Thou. To-morrow I shall burn Thee. Dixi.' " [270]

. . . . .

". . . When the Inquisitor ceased speaking he waited some time for his Prisoner to answer him. His silence weighed down upon him. He saw that the Prisoner had listened intently all the time, looking gently in his face and evidently not wishing to reply. The old man longed for Him to say something, however bitter and terrible. But He suddenly approached the old man in silence and softly kissed him on his bloodless aged lips. That was all his answer. The old man shuddered. His lips moved. He went to the door, opened it, and said to Him: 'Go, and come no more. . . . Come not at all, never, never!' And he let Him out into the dark alleys of the town. The Prisoner went away."

"And the old man?"

"The kiss glows in his heart, but the old man adheres to his idea."

"And you with him, you too?" cried Alyosha, mournfully.

Ivan laughed.

"Why, it's all nonsense, Alyosha. It's only a senseless poem of a senseless student, who could never write two lines of verse. Why do you take it so seriously? Surely you don't suppose I am going straight off to the Jesuits, to join the men who are correcting His work? Good Lord, it's no business of mine. I told you, all I want is to live on to thirty, and then . . . dash the cup to the ground!"

"But the little sticky leaves, and the precious tombs, and the blue sky, and the woman you love! How will you live, how will you love them?" Alyosha cried sorrowfully. "With such a hell in your heart and your head, how can you? No, that's just what you are going away for, to join them . . . if not, you will kill yourself, you can't endure it!" [272]

"There is a strength to endure everything," Ivan said with a cold smile.

"What strength?"

"The strength of the Karamazovs—the strength of the Karamazov baseness."

"To sink into debauchery, to stifle your soul with corruption, yes?"

"Possibly even that . . . only perhaps till I am thirty I shall escape it, and then."

"How will you escape it? By what will you escape it? That's impossible with your ideas."

"In the Karamazov way, again."

" 'Everything is lawful,' you mean? Everything is lawful, is that it?"

Ivan scowled, and all at once turned strangely pale.

"Ah, you've caught up yesterday's phrase, which so offended Miüsov—and which Dmitri pounced upon so naïvely and paraphrased!" he smiled queerly. "Yes, if you like, 'everything is lawful' since the word has been said. I won't deny it. And Mitya's version isn't bad."

Alyosha looked at him in silence.

"I thought that going away from here I have you at least," Ivan said suddenly, with unexpected feeling; "but now I see that there is no place for me even in your heart, my dear hermit. The formula, 'all is lawful,' I won't renounce—will you renounce me for that, yes?"

Alyosha got up, went to him and softly kissed him on the lips.

"That's plagiarism," cried Ivan, highly delighted. "You stole that from my poem. Thank you though. Get up, Alyosha, it's time we were going, both of us." [273]

W. H. AUDEN

For the Time Being

The following two selections constitute the sixth and seventh sections of W. H. Auden's For the Time Being *(1942), a dramatic oratorio in eight parts celebrating the Nativity in both its universal and contemporary significance. Written during World War II, this poem clearly reveals the influence of Søren Kierkegaard and of the English religious poet Charles Williams, who, as an editor of Oxford University Press, was instrumental in introducing the Danish existentialist to the English-speaking world. Unlike most Christmas plays, which tend to project a pious and nostalgic image that implies an effort to escape from the evils or the discontinuities of the present into a remote and innocent past,* For the Time Being *creates an image that is devastatingly contemporary; that is, Auden takes his subject matter, the Incarnation, seriously. He presents the Nativity not merely as an event that happened in the remote past, but as an event that occurs every Christmas (and that requires of men a perpetually renewed decision). The characters retain their traditional names and functions, but they are, as their concerns and their manner of expressing them clearly indicate, contemporary men who are confronting the problem of belief in the context of their condition in a technological world. Thus, Simeon is not only the universal type of the Christian convert but also a symbol of the contemporary Christian existentialist. And Herod is not only the Herod of the Christian narrative but also an ironic portrait of the modern progressivist or utopian intellectual.*

THE MEDITATION OF SIMEON

SIMEON: As long as the apple had not been entirely digested, as long as there remained the least understanding between Adam and the stars, rivers and horses with whom he had once known complete intimacy, as long as Eve could share in any way with the moods of the rose or the ambitions of the swallow, there was still a hope that the effects of the poison would wear off, that the exile from Paradise was only a bad dream, that the Fall had not occurred in fact.

CHORUS: *When we woke, it was day; we went on weeping.*

SIMEON: As long as there were any roads to amnesia and anaesthesia still to be explored, any rare wine or curiosity of cuisine as yet untested, any erotic variation as yet unimagined or unrealised, any method of torture as yet undevised, any style of conspicuous waste as yet unindulged, any eccentricity of mania or disease as yet unrepresented, there was still a hope that man has not been poisoned but transformed, that Paradise was not an eternal state from which he had been forever expelled, but a childish state which he had permanently outgrown, that the Fall had occurred by necessity.

CHORUS: *We danced in the dark, but were not deceived.*

SIMEON: As long as there were any experiments still to be undertaken in restoring that order in which desire had once rejoiced to be reflected, any code of equity and obligation upon [448] which some society had not yet been founded, any species of property of which the value had not yet been appreciated, any talent that had not yet won private devotion and public honour, any rational concept of the Good or intuitive feeling for the Holy that had not yet found its precise and beautiful expression, any technique of contemplation or ritual of sacrifice and praise that had not yet been properly conducted, any faculty of mind or body that had not yet been thoroughly disciplined, there was still a hope that some antidote might be found, that the gates of Paradise had indeed slammed to, but with the exercise of a little patience and ingenuity would be unlocked, that the Fall had occurred by accident.

CHORUS: *Lions came loping into the lighted city.*

SIMEON: Before the Positive could manifest Itself specifically, it was necessary that nothing should be left that negation could remove; the emancipation of Time from Space had first to be complete, the Revolution of the Images, in which the memories rose up and cast into subjection the senses by Whom hitherto they had been enslaved, successful beyond their wildest dreams, the mirror in which the Soul expected to admire herself so perfectly polished that her natural consolation of vagueness should be utterly withdrawn.

CHORUS: *We looked at our Shadow, and, Lo, it was lame.*

SIMEON: Before the Infinite could manifest Itself in the finite, it was necessary that man should first have reached that point [449] along his road to Knowledge where, just as it rises from the swamps of Confusion onto the sunny slopes of Objectivity, it forks in opposite directions towards the One and the Many; where, therefore, in order to proceed at all, he must decide which is Real and which only Appearance, yet at the same time cannot escape the knowledge that his choice is arbitrary and subjective.

CHORUS: *Promising to meet, we parted forever.*

SIMEON: Before the Unconditional could manifest Itself under the conditions of existence, it was necessary that man should first have reached the ultimate frontier of consciousness, the secular limit of memory beyond which there remained but one thing for him to know, his Original Sin, but of this it is impossible for him to become conscious because it is itself what conditions his will to knowledge. For as long as he was in Paradise he could not sin by any conscious intention or act: his as yet unfallen will could only rebel against the truth by taking flight into an unconscious lie; he could only eat of the Tree of the Knowledge of Good and Evil by forgetting that its existence was a fiction of the Evil One, that there is only the Tree of Life.

CHORUS: *The bravest drew back on the brink of the Abyss.*

SIMEON: From the beginning until now God spoke through His prophets. The Word aroused the uncomprehending depths of their flesh to a witnessing fury, and their witness was this: [450] that the Word should be made Flesh. Yet their witness could only be received as long as it was vaguely misunderstood, as long as it seemed either to be neither impossible nor necessary, or necessary but not impossible, or impossible but not necessary; and the prophecy could not therefore be fulfilled. For it could only be fulfilled when it was no longer possible to receive, because it was clearly understood as absurd. The Word could not be made Flesh until men had reached a state of absolute contradiction between clarity and despair in which they would have no choice but either to accept absolutely or to reject absolutely, yet in their choice there should be no element of luck, for they would be fully conscious of what they were accepting or rejecting.

CHORUS: *The eternal spaces were congested and depraved.*

SIMEON: But here and now the Word which is implicit in the Beginning and in the End is become immediately explicit, and that which hitherto we could only passively fear as the incomprehensible I AM, henceforth we may actively love with comprehension that THOU ART. Wherefore, having seen Him, not in some prophetic vision of what might be, but with the eyes of our own weakness as to what actually is, we are bold to say that we have seen our salvation.

CHORUS: *Now and forever, we are not alone.*

SIMEON: By the event of this birth the true significance of all other events is defined, for of every other occasion it can be said that it could have been different, but of this birth it is the case that it could in no way be other than it is. And by the [451] existence of this Child, the proper value of all other existences is given, for of every other creature it can be said that it has extrinsic importance but of this Child it is the case that He is in no sense a symbol.

CHORUS: *We have right to believe that we really exist.*

SIMEON: By Him is dispelled the darkness wherein the fallen will cannot distinguish between temptation and sin, for in Him we become fully conscious of Necessity as our freedom to be tempted, and of Freedom as our necessity to have faith. And by Him is illuminated the time in which we execute those choices through which our freedom is realised or prevented, for the course of History is predictable in the degree to which all men love themselves, and spontaneous in the degree to which each man loves God and through Him his neighbour.

CHORUS: *The distresses of choice are our chance to be blessed.*

SIMEON: Because in Him the Flesh is united to the Word without magical transformation, Imagination is redeemed from promiscuous fornication with her own images. The tragic conflict of Virtue with Necessity is no longer confined to the Exceptional Hero; for disaster is not the impact of a curse upon a few great families, but issues continually from the hubris of every tainted will. Every invalid is Roland defending the narrow pass against hopeless odds, every stenographer Brunnhilde refusing to renounce her lover's ring which came into existence through the renunciation of love.[452]

Nor is the Ridiculous a species any longer of the Ugly; for since of themselves all men are without merit, all are ironically assisted to their comic bewilderment by the Grace of God. Every

Cabinet Minister is the woodcutter's simple-minded son to whom the fishes and the crows are always whispering the whereabouts of the Dancing Water or the Singing Branch, every heiress the washerwoman's butter-fingered daughter on whose pillow the fairy keeps laying the herb that could cure the Prince's mysterious illness.

Nor is there any situation which is essentially more or less interesting than another. Every tea-table is a battlefield littered with old catastrophes and haunted by the vague ghosts of vast issues, every martyrdom an occasion for flip cracks and sententious oratory.

Because in Him all passions find a logical In-Order-That, by Him is the perpetual recurrence of Art assured.

CHORUS: *Safe in His silence, our songs are at play.*

SIMEON: Because in Him the Word is united to the Flesh without loss of perfection, Reason is redeemed from incestuous fixation on her own Logic, for the One and the Many are simultaneously revealed as real. So that we may no longer, with the Barbarians, deny the Unity, asserting that there are as many gods as there are creatures, nor, with the philosophers, deny the Multiplicity, asserting that God is One who has no need of friends and is indifferent to a World of Time and Quantity and Horror which He did not create, nor, with Israel, may we limit the co-inherence of the One and the Many to a special case, asserting that God is only concerned with and of concern to that People whom out of all that He created He has chosen for His own.[453]

For the Truth is indeed One, without which is no salvation, but the possibilities of real knowledge are as many as are the creatures in the very real and most exciting universe that God creates with and for His love, and it is not Nature which is one public illusion, but we who have each our many private illusions about Nature.

Because in Him abstraction finds a passionate For-The-Sake-Of, by Him is the continuous development of Science assured.

CHORUS: *Our lost Appearances are saved by His love.*

SIMEON: And because of His visitation, we may no longer desire God as if He were lacking: our redemption is no longer a question of pursuit but of surrender to Him who is always and everywhere present. Therefore at every moment we pray that, following Him, we may depart from our anxiety into His peace.

CHORUS: *Its errors forgiven, may our Vision come home.*

THE MASSACRE OF THE INNOCENTS

I

HEROD: Because I am bewildered, because I must decide, because my decision must be in conformity with Nature and Necessity, let me honour those through whom my nature is by necessity what it is.[454]

To Fortune—that I have become Tetrarch, that I have escaped assassination, that at sixty my head is clear and my digestion sound.

To my Father—for the means to gratify my love of travel and study.

To my Mother—for a straight nose.

To Eva, my coloured nurse—for regular habits.

To my brother, Sandy, who married a trapeze-artist and died of drink—for so refuting the position of the Hedonists.

To Mr. Stewart, nicknamed The Carp, who instructed me in the elements of geometry through which I came to perceive the errors of the tragic poets.

To Professor Lighthouse—for his lectures on The Peloponnesian War.

To the stranger on the boat to Sicily—for recommending to me Brown on Resolution.

To my secretary, Miss Button—for admitting that my speeches were inaudible.

There is no visible disorder. No crime—what could be more innocent than the birth of an artisan's child? Today has been one of those perfect winter days, cold, brilliant, and utterly still, when the bark of a shepherd's dog carries for miles, and the great wild mountains come up quite close to the city walls, and the mind feels intensely awake, and this evening as I stand at this window high up in the citadel there is nothing in the whole magnificent panorama of plain and mountains to indicate that the Empire is threatened by a danger more dreadful than any invasion of Tartars on racing camels or conspiracy of the Praetorian Guard.

Barges are unloading soil fertiliser at the river wharves. Soft drinks and sandwiches may be had in the inns at reasonable prices. Allotment gardening has become popular.[455] The highway to the coast goes straight up over the mountains and the truck-drivers no longer carry guns. Things are beginning to take shape. It is a long time since anyone stole the park benches or murdered the swans. There are children in this province who have never seen a louse, shopkeepers who have never handled a counterfeit coin, women of forty who have never hidden in a ditch except for fun. Yes, in twenty years I have managed to do a little. Not enough, of course. There are villages only a few miles from here where they still believe in witches. There isn't a single town where a good bookshop would pay. One could count on the fingers of one hand the people capable of solving the problem of Achilles and the Tortoise. Still it is a beginning. In twenty years the darkness has been pushed back a few inches. And what, after all, is the whole Empire, with its few thousand square miles on which it is possible to lead the Rational Life, but a tiny patch of light compared with those immense areas of barbaric night that surround it on all sides, that incoherent wilderness of rage and terror, where Mongolian idiots are regarded as sacred and mothers who give birth to twins are instantly put to death, where malaria is treated by yelling, where warriors of superb courage obey the commands of hysterical female impersonators, where the best cuts of meat are reserved for the dead, where, if a white blackbird has been seen, no more work may be done that day, where it is firmly believed that the world was created by a giant with three heads or that the motions of the stars are controlled from the liver of a rogue elephant?

Yet even inside this little civilised patch itself, where, at the cost of heaven knows how much grief and bloodshed, it has been made unnecessary for anyone over the age of twelve to believe in fairies or that First Causes reside in mortal and finite objects, so many are still homesick for that disorder wherein every passion formerly enjoyed a frantic licence. Caesar flies to his hunting lodge pursued by ennui; [450] in the faubourgs of the Capital, Society grows savage, corrupted by silks and scents, softened by sugar and hot water, made insolent by theatres and attractive slaves; and everywhere, including this province, new prophets spring up every day to sound the old barbaric note.

I have tried everything. I have prohibited the sale of crystals and ouija-boards; I have slapped a heavy tax on playing cards; the courts are empowered to sentence alchemists to hard labour in the mines; it is a statutory offence to turn tables or feel bumps. But nothing is really effective. How can I expect the masses to be sensible when, for instance, to my certain knowledge, the captain of my own guard wears an amulet against the Evil Eye, and the richest merchant in the city consults a medium over every important transaction?

Legislation is helpless against the wild prayer of longing that rises, day in, day out, from all these households under my protection: "O God, put away justice and truth for we cannot understand them and do not want them. Eternity would bore us dreadfully. Leave Thy heavens and come down to our earth of waterclocks and hedges. Become our uncle. Look after Baby, amuse Grandfather, escort Madam to the Opera, help Willy with his home-work, introduce Muriel to a handsome naval officer. Be interesting and weak like us, and we will love you as we love ourselves."

Reason is helpless, and now even the Poetic Compromise no longer works, all those lovely fairy tales in which Zeus, disguising himself as a swan or a bull or a shower of rain or what-have-you, lay with some beautiful woman and begot a hero. For the Public has grown too sophisticated. Under all the charming metaphors and symbols, it detects the stern command, "Be and act heroically"; behind the myth of divine origin, it senses the real human excellence that is a reproach to its own baseness. So, with a bellow of rage, it [457] kicks Poetry downstairs and sends for Prophecy. "Your sister has just insulted me. I asked for a God who should be as like me as possible. What use to me is a God whose divinity consists in doing difficult things that I cannot do or saying clever things that I cannot understand? The God I want and intend to get must be someone I can recognise immediately without having to wait and see what he says or does. There must be nothing in the least extraordinary about him. Produce him at once, please. I'm sick of waiting."

Today, apparently, judging by the trio who came to see me this morning with an ecstatic grin on their scholarly faces, the job has been done. "God has been born," they cried, "we have seen him ourselves. The World is saved. Nothing else matters."

One needn't be much of a psychologist to realise that if this rumour is not stamped out now, in a few years it is capable of diseasing the whole Empire, and one doesn't have to be a prophet to predict the consequences if it should.

Reason will be replaced by Revelation. Instead of Rational Law, objective truths perceptible to any who will undergo the necessary intellectual discipline, and the same for all, Knowledge will degenerate into a riot of subjective visions—feelings in the solar plexus induced by undernourishment, angelic images generated by fevers or drugs, dream warnings inspired by the sound of falling water. Whole cosmogonies will be created out of some forgotten personal resentment, complete epics written in private languages, the daubs of school children ranked above the greatest masterpieces.

Idealism will be replaced by Materialism. Priapus will only have to move to a good address and call himself Eros to become the darling of middle-aged women. Life after death will be an eternal dinner party where all the guests are twenty years old. Diverted from its normal and wholesome outlet in patriotism and civic or family pride, the need [458] of the materialistic Masses for some visible Idol to worship will be driven into totally unsocial channels where no education can reach it. Divine honours will be paid to silver teapots, shallow depressions in the earth, names on maps, domestic pets, ruined windmills, even in extreme cases, which will become increasingly common, to headaches, or malignant tumours, or four o'clock in the afternoon.

Justice will be replaced by Pity as the cardinal human virtue, and all fear of retribution will vanish. Every corner-boy will congratulate himself: "I'm such a sinner that God had to come down in person to save me. I must be a devil of a fellow." Every crook will argue: "I like committing crimes. God likes forgiving them. Really the world is admirably arranged." And the ambition of every young cop will be to secure a death-bed repentance. The New Aristocracy will consist exclusively of hermits, bums, and permanent invalids. The Rough Diamond, the Consumptive Whore, the bandit who is good to his mother, the epileptic girl who has a way with animals will be the heroes and heroines of the New Tragedy when the general, the statesman, and the philosopher have become the butt of every farce and satire.

Naturally this cannot be allowed to happen. Civilisation must be saved even if this means sending for the military, as I suppose it does. How dreary. Why is it that in the end civilisation always has to call in these professional tidiers to whom it is all one whether it be Pythagoras or a homicidal lunatic that they are instructed to exterminate. O dear, Why couldn't this wretched infant be born somewhere else? Why can't people be sensible? I don't want to be horrid. Why can't they see that the notion of a finite God is absurd? Because it is. And suppose, just for the sake of argument, that it isn't, that this story is true, that this child is in some inexplicable manner both God and Man, that he grows up, lives, and dies, without committing a single sin? Would that [459] make life any better? On the contrary it would make it far, far worse. For it could only mean this; that once having shown them how, God would expect every man, whatever his fortune, to lead a sinless life in the flesh and on earth. Then indeed would the human race be plunged into madness and despair. And for me personally at this moment it would mean that God had given me the power to destroy Himself. I refuse to be taken in. He could not play such a horrible practical joke. Why should He dislike me so? I've worked like a slave. Ask anyone you like. I read all official dispatches without skipping. I've taken elocution lessons. I've hardly ever taken bribes. How dare He allow me to decide? I've tried to be good. I brush my teeth every night. I haven't had sex for a month. I object. I'm a liberal. I want everyone to be happy. I wish I had never been born.

II

SOLDIERS

When the Sex War ended with the slaughter of the Grandmothers,
They found a bachelor's baby suffocating under them;
Somebody called him George and that was the end of it:
  They hitched him up to the Army.
  George, you old debutante,
  How did you get in the Army?

In the Retreat from Reason he deserted on his rocking-horse
And lived on a fairy's kindness till he tired of kicking her;
He smashed her spectacles and stole her check-book and mackintosh
  Then cruised his way back to the Army.
  George, you old numero,
  How did you get in the Army? [460]

Before the Diet of Sugar he was using razor-blades
And exited soon after with an allergy to maidenheads;
He discovered a cure of his own, but no one would patent it,
  So he showed up again in the Army.
  George, you old flybynight,
  How did you get in the Army?

When the Vice Crusades were over he was hired by some Muscovites

Prospecting for deodorants among the Eskimos;
He was caught by a common cold and condemned to the whiskey mines,
But schemozzled back to the Army.
George, you old Emperor,
How did you get in the Army?

Since Peace was signed with Honour he's been minding his business;
But, whoops, here comes His Idleness, buttoning his uniform;
Just in tidy time to massacre the Innocents;
He's come home to roost in the Army.
George, you old matador,
Welcome back to the Army.

III

RACHEL

On the Left are grinning dogs, peering down into a solitude too deep to fill with roses.
On the Right are sensible sheep, gazing up at a pride where no dream can grow.
Somewhere in these unending wastes of delirium is a lost child, speaking of Long Ago in the language of wounds.
Tomorrow, perhaps, he will come to himself in Heaven.[461]
But here Grief turns her silence, neither in this direction, nor in that, nor for any reason.
And her coldness now is on the earth forever.[462]

COMMENTARY AND CRITICISM

JEAN-PAUL SARTRE

We Write for Our Own Time

We take our stand against certain critics and authors. We declare that salvation must be won upon this earth, that it must be won for the whole man by the whole man, and that art is a meditation on life, not on death. It is true that for history, only talent is important. But I have not yet entered history, and I do not know how I will enter it: perhaps alone, perhaps in an anonymous crowd, perhaps as one of those names that one finds in the notes of textbooks on literature. In any case, I shall not worry about the judgments that the future may pronounce upon my work, because there is nothing I can do about them. Art cannot be reduced to a dialogue with dead men and men as yet unborn: that would be both too hard and too easy. In my opinion, this idea constitutes the last trace of the Christian belief in immortality: just as the sojourn of man upon this earth is represented as a brief testing time between Limbo and Hell or Heaven, so a book is supposed to enjoy a transitory period that is approximately the same as that of its effectiveness; after that, disincarnated and free as a soul, it enters eternity. But at least for Christians our sojourn upon earth is the decisive factor and eternal beatitude is only a reward. Yet people seem to believe that the career our books have after we are no more should be justified by the life we once led. This is true from an objective point of view. Objectively, we are classified according to our talent. But the perspective our grandchildren will have upon us is not infallible, since others will come after them and judge them in their turn. It goes without saying that we all write out of need for the absolute; and a work of the spirit is, indeed, an absolute. However, people make a double mistake on this score. First, it is not true that a writer [236] raises his sufferings or his errors to the level of the absolute by writing about them; and it is not true that he redeems them. People say of the unhappily married man who writes well about marriage that he has made a good book *out of* his conjugal misery. That would be too easy. The bee makes honey *out of* the flower by causing *real*

SOURCE: *Virginia Quarterly Review*, Vol. 25, No. 1 (Spring 1947). Reprinted with the permission of the author, *Virginia Quarterly Review*, and Editions Gallimard.

transformations in the substance of the flower; the sculptor makes a statue *out of* marble. But the writer makes books out of words, not out of his sorrows. If he wants to stop his wife from behaving badly, he should not write about her; he should beat her. One cannot *put* one's misfortunes into a book, any more than one can put a model on a canvas; one draws inspiration from one's misfortunes—and they remain as they are. Perhaps one gets temporary consolation from placing oneself above them in order to describe them, but once the book is finished, one finds them again. Bad faith begins when the artist tries to give meaning, a sort of immanent finality, to his troubles and persuades himself that they are there *so that* he can talk about them. When he justifies his own sufferings by this deception, he makes himself ridiculous; but he is despicable if he tries to justify the sufferings of others in the same fashion. The most beautiful book in the world will not redeem the sufferings of a child. We cannot redeem evil, we must combat it. The most beautiful book in the world redeems itself and redeems the artist, but not the man; no more than the man can redeem the artist. We want the man and the artist to win salvation together; we want the work of art to be an act as well; we want it to be expressly conceived as an arm in man's struggle against evil.

The other mistake is equally serious: there is in every human heart such a hunger for the absolute, that people have often confused eternity, which would be a timeless absolute, with immortality which is only a perpetual delay of execution and a long series of vicissitudes. I understand this desire for the absolute very well. I desire it also. But need we go so far afield to look for it? It is there all around us, under our feet and in all our gestures. We make absolutes, just as M. Jourdain made prose.[237] You light your pipe and that is an absolute; you don't like oysters and that is an absolute; you join the Communist Party and that is an absolute. Whether the world is matter or spirit, whether God exists or does not exist, whether the judgment of future centuries is favorable or hostile to you, nothing will ever be able to negate the fact that you passionately loved such and such a picture, such and such a cause, and such and such a woman; that you lived that love from day to day: lived it, willed it, and undertook it; and that you engaged your whole being in it. Our grandfathers were perfectly right when they used to say as they drank their glass of wine: "One more that the Prussians won't have." Neither the Prussians nor anyone else. People may kill you or deprive you of wine for the rest of your life; but that last drop of Bordeaux that slipped over your palate, no God and no man can take away from you. No relativity; nor the "eternal course of history"; nor the dialectic of perception; nor the dissociations of psychoanalysis. That drop of wine is a pure event and we, too, in the very depths of historical relativity and our own insignificance are absolutes, inimitable and incomparable, and our choice of ourselves is an absolute. All the vital and passionate choices that we are and that we are perpetually making with or against other people, all the common undertakings into which we throw ourselves from birth until death, all the bonds of love and hate that unite us with each other and that exist only in so far as we feel them, the enormous complexes of movements that supplement or negate each other and that are lived, this whole discordant and harmonious life combines to create a new absolute which I like to call the *time*. The time is intersubjectivity, the living absolute, the dialectical wrong side of history. It is born in the pangs of events that historians will later stick labels on. Blindly, in fury, in fear, and in enthusiasm, it lives the meanings that they will later define by rational methods. In its own time, each word, before it is an historical slogan or the recognizable origin of a social process, is first an insult or a call or a confession. Economic phenomena themselves, before they are the theoretical causes of social upheavals,[238] are suffered in humiliation or despair. Ideas are tools or flights; facts are born of intersubjectivity and unsettle it as emotions unsettle the individual soul. Men make history out of dead times, because each time, upon its death, enters into relativity and takes its place in the line of the centuries with the other dead. Then people try to throw new light upon it, dispute its meaning with their new knowledge, resolve its problems, prove that its most ardent searchings were doomed to failure, that the great undertakings of which it was most proud had opposite results to those it hoped for; suddenly its limitations appear and its ignorance. But all this is *because that time is dead;* those limits and that ignorance did not exist "at the time": men do not live a lack; or rather, that time was a perpetual overstepping of its own limits toward a future which was *its* future and which is dead with it. It was *that* boldness, *that* imprudence, *that* ignorance of its own ignorance: to live means to make short-term provisions and to manage on one's margin. Perhaps our fathers, had they had a little more knowledge, would have understood that such and such a problem was insoluble and that such and such a question should not have been raised in those terms. But the human condition requires that we make our choice in ignorance; it is ignorance that makes morality possible. If we knew all the facters that condition events, if we could play our hand without uncertainty, risk would disappear; and with risk courage, fear, waiting, the final joy and effort; we would be languid gods, but certainly not men. The bitter quarrels of the Babylonians over the meaning of omens, the bloody and passionate heresies of the Albigensians and the Anabaptists today seem to us errors. At the time man engaged his whole being in them and in expressing them at the risk of his life let truth live through them, for truth never yields itself directly; it only appears through errors. The fate of human Reason was at stake in the quarrel of the Universals and in that of the Immaculate Conception or Transubstantiation. And at the time of the great lawsuits of certain American states against the professors who taught the theory of evolution, it was again the fate of Reason that was at stake. It is absolutely [239] at stake in every period in connection with doctrines that the next period will condemn as false. It is possible that some day the belief in evolution will seem the greatest folly of our century: yet, in supporting it against the churchmen, the American professors *lived* the truth, they lived it passionately and absolutely at great risk to themselves. Tomorrow they will be wrong, today they are absolutely right: the time is always wrong when it is dead, always right when it is alive. Let people condemn it after the fact, if they wish; nevertheless, it had its own passionate way of loving itself and tearing itself apart, against which future judgments will be of no avail; it had its own taste which it alone tasted and which was as incomparable, as irremediable as the taste of wine in our mouth.

A book has its absolute truth in its own time. It is lived like a riot or a famine, with much less intensity, of course, and by fewer people, but in the same way. It is an emanation of intersubjectivity, a living bond of rage, hatred, or love between those who have produced it and those who receive it. If it gains ground, thousands of people reject it and deny it: we all know very well that to read a book is to rewrite it. *At the time* it is first a panic, an escape, or a courageous affirmation; at the time it is a good or a bad *action*. Later, when the time has died, it will become relative; it will become a message. But the judgment of posterity will not invalidate the opinions men had of it during its lifetime. People have often said to me about dates and bananas: "You can't judge them: to know what they are really like, you have to eat them on the spot, just after they have been picked." And I have always considered bananas a dead fruit whose real taste escaped me. The books which pass from one period to another are dead fruits, too. In another time they had a different taste, sharp and tangy. We should have read "Emile" or the "Persian Letters" just after they were picked.

Thus we must write for our own time, as the great writers did. But this does not imply that we must shut ourselves up in it. To write for our time does not mean to reflect it passively. It means that we must will to maintain it or change it; therefore,[240] go beyond it toward the future; and it is this effort to change it which establishes us most deeply in it, for it can never be reduced to a dead mass of tools and customs. It is in flux, it perpetually goes beyond itself; in it the concrete present and the living future of all the men who compose it exactly coincide. If, among other characteristics, Newtonian physics and the theory of the noble savage help to define the first half of the eighteenth century, we must not forget that the former represented a consistent effort to wrest fragments of the truth from the fog of ignorance in order to reach, beyond the contemporary state of knowledge, an ideal science in which phenomena could be deduced mathematically from the principle of gravitation, and that the latter was an attempt to go beyond the vices of civilization and restore a state of nature. Both theories outlined a future; and if it is true that this future never became a present, that men later renounced the Golden Age and the idea of making science a strictly logical chain of reasons, it is nonetheless true that these profound and vital hopes sketched a future beyond men's daily cares and that in order to penetrate the meaning of our day-to-day existence we must approach it with the future as our point of departure. One cannot be a man or make oneself a writer without drawing a line on the horizon beyond oneself, but this going beyond oneself is in each case finite and unique. One does not go beyond *in general* and for the simple pride and pleasure of going beyond; Baudelairian dissatisfaction represents only the abstract scheme of transcendence and, since it is a dissatisfaction with everything, ends by being a dissatisfaction with nothing. Real transcendence requires that one wish to change certain definite aspects of the world and any going beyond is colored by and characterized by the concrete situation it seeks to modify. A man throws himself completely into his plan for freeing the Negroes or restoring the Hebrew language to the Jews of Palestine; he throws himself into it completely and at the same time expresses man's fate in all its universality, but it must always be through a unique and dated undertaking. And if people say to me, as does M. Schlumberger,[241] that one also goes beyond one's time when one strives for immortality, I shall answer that this is a false going beyond: instead of wishing to change an intolerable situation, one attempts to escape from it and seeks refuge in a future that is entirely strange to us, since it is not the future that we *make,* but the concrete present of our grandchildren. We have no way of affecting that present; they will live it for themselves and as they wish, situated in their own time as we in ours. If they make any use of our writings it will be for their own ends, ends which we did not foresee, just as one picks up stones on the road and hurls them in the face of an aggressor. It would be quite vain on our part to throw off on them our effort to prolong our own existence: they have neither the duty nor the desire to do so. And since we have no means of acting upon these strangers, we shall present ourselves to them like beggars and beg them to lend us the appearance of life by using us for any purpose whatsoever. If we are Christians, we shall accept our lot humbly, provided only that they still speak of us, even though they use us to show that faith is ineffectual; if we are atheists, we shall be very happy if they still concern themselves with our anguish and our errors, were it even to prove that man is miserable without God. Would you be satisfied, M. Schlumberger, if after the Revolution our grandsons saw in your writings the most obvious example of the conditioning of art by the economic structure? And if you do not have that literary destiny, you will have another that will be hardly any better: if you escape from dialectical materialism, it will only be to serve the ends of some psychoanalysis. In any case, our grandchildren will be impudent orphans, so why should we concern ourselves with them? Perhaps of all of us, only Céline will endure; it is theoretically possible, although highly improbable, that the twenty-first century will remember Drieu's name and forget Malraux'; in any case it will not espouse our quarrels, it will not mention what today we call the betrayal of certain writers, or if it mentions this, it will do so without anger or contempt. And what difference does it make to us? What Malraux and [242] Drieu are for us is an absolute. In certain hearts there is an absolute of contempt for Drieu and an absolute of friendship for Malraux that one hundred posthumous judgments will not be able to shake. There is a living Malraux, a lump of warm blood in the very heart of our time, and there will be a dead Malraux at the mercy of history. Why should the living man try to fix the image of the dead man he will one day be? Certainly he lives beyond himself; his gaze and his concerns go beyond the death of his flesh; the presence of a man and his weight are measured not by the fifty or sixty years of his organic life, nor by the borrowed life he will lead in future centuries in the minds of strangers: they are measured by his own choice of the temporal cause that goes beyond him. The story is told that the runner of Marathon was dead an hour before he reached Athens. He was dead, yet he still ran; he ran dead and as a dead man announced the victory of the Greeks. It is a beautiful myth and shows that the dead act for a little while as if they were still alive. A little while—one year, ten years, fifty years perhaps, in any case, a finite period; and then they are buried for the second time. This is the measure that we propose to the writer: as long as his books provoke anger, embarrassment, shame, hatred, love, he will live, even if he is only a shadow. After that, the deluge. We are for a finite morality and a finite art.[243]

KENNETH TYNAN

Ionesco and the Phantom

On June 22, 1958, the English drama critic Kenneth Tynan, one of Eugène Ionesco's earliest and strongest champions in England, reviewed a revival of The Chairs *and* The Lesson *in* The Observer. *Contrary to expectation, he attacked Ionesco's "anti-drama," his radical departure from the realistic tradition, observing that his theater, though exciting, was "diversion. It is not on the main road: and we do him no good, nor the drama at large, to pretend that it is." Detecting in this criticism an implicit equation between the realistic dramatic tradition and the embodiment of progressive political ideologies, Ionesco responded that such a definition by restricting reality to the social level made the "main road" a very narrow one. Rejecting the "realists"—Sartre, Osborne, Miller, Brecht—as "simply the new* auteurs du boulevard, *representatives of a left-wing conformism*

SOURCE: ***The Observer*** **(July 6, 1958). Reprinted with the permisson of the author. The article is also reprinted in *Notes and Counter Notes* by Eugène Ionesco (New York: Grove Press, 1964).**

which is just as lamentable as the right-wing sort," he went on to advocate a drama that imitates a "vaster and more complex" reality: the reality of the profoundly mysterious unique self. Thus began what came to be known as "The London Controversy," that raged for nearly a month in the pages of The Observer *and has become a point of departure for almost all discussion of the drama of the absurd. The two following articles constitute a fragment of this debate. Kenneth Tynan's article first appeared in* The Observer *on July 6, 1958, in answer to Ionesco's first response. Ionesco's article was written as a second reply to Tynan, but* The Observer *did not publish it. The complete text of "The London Controversy" is printed in Ionesco's* Notes and Counter Notes: Writings on the Theatre (*New York: Grove Press, 1964*).

M. Ionesco's article on "The Playwright's Role" is discussed elsewhere in these pages by Mr. Toynbee and several readers. I want to add what I hope will not be a postscript, for this is a debate that should continue.[93]

As I read the piece I felt first bewilderment, next admiration, and finally regret. Bewilderment at his assumption that I wanted drama to be forced to echo a particular political creed, when all I want is for drama to realize that it is a *part* of politics, in the sense that every human activity, even buying a pack of cigarettes, has social and political repercussions. Then, admiration: no one could help admiring the sincerity and skill with which, last Sunday, M. Ionesco marshaled prose for his purposes. And ultimately, regret: regret that a man so capable of stating a positive attitude toward art should deny that there was any positive attitude worth taking toward life. Or even (which is crucial) that there was an umbilical connection between the two.

The position toward which M. Ionesco is moving is that which regards art as if it were something different from and independent of everything else in the world; as if it not only did not but *should* not correspond to anything outside the mind of the artist. This position, as it happens, was reached some years ago by a French painter who declared that, since nothing in nature exactly resembled anything else, he proposed to burn all of his paintings which in any way resembled anything that already existed. The end of that line, of course, is action painting.

M. Ionesco has not yet gone so far. He is stuck, to pursue the analogy, in an earlier groove, the groove of cubism, which has fascinated him so much that he has begun to confuse ends and means. The cubists employed distortion to make discoveries about the nature of objective reality. M. Ionesco, I fear, is on the brink of believing that his distortions are more valid and important than the external world it is their proper function to interpret. To adapt Johnson, I am not yet so lost in drama criticism as to forget that plays are the daughters of earth, and that things are the sons of heaven. But M. Ionesco is in danger of forgetting; of locking himself up in that hall of mirrors which in philosophy is known as solipsism.[94]

Art is parasitic on life, just as criticism is parasitic on art. M. Ionesco and his followers are breaking the chain, applying the tourniquet, aspiring as writers to a condition of stasis. At their best, of course, they don't succeed: the alarming thing is that they try. As in physiology, note how quickly the brain, starved of blood, produces hallucinations and delusions of grandeur. "A work of art," says M. Ionesco, "is the source and the raw material of ideologies to come." O hubris! Art and ideology often interact on each other; but the plain fact is that both spring from a common source. Both draw on human experience to explain mankind to itself; both attempt, in very different ways, to assemble coherence from seemingly unrelated phenomena; both stand guard for us against chaos. They are brothers, not child and parent. To say, as M. Ionesco does, that Freud was inspired by Sophocles is serious nonsense. Freud merely found in Sophocles confirmation of a theory he had formed on a basis of empirical evidence. This does not make Sophocles a Freudian, or vice versa: it is simply a pleasing instance of fraternal corroboration.

You may wonder why M. Ionesco is so keen on this phantom notion of art as a world of its own, answerable to none but its own laws. Wonder no more: he is merely seeking to exempt himself from any kind of value judgment. His aim is to blind us to the fact that we are all in some sense critics, who bring to the theatre not only those "nostalgias and anxieties" by which, as he rightly says, world history has largely been governed, but also a whole series of new ideas—moral, social, psychological, political—through which we hope some day to free ourselves from the rusty hegemony of *Angst*. These fond ideas, M. Ionesco quickly assures us, do not belong in the theatre. Our job, as critics, is just to hear the play and "simply say whether it is true to its own nature." Not, you notice, whether it is true to ours; or even relevant; for we, as an audience, have forfeited our right to a hearing as conscious, sentient beings. "Clear evidence of cancer here,[95] sir." "Very well, leave it alone: it's being true to its own nature."

Whether M. Ionesco admits it or not, every play worth serious consideration is a statement. It is a statement addressed in the first person singular to the first person plural; and the latter must retain the right of dissent. I am rebuked in the current *Encounter* for having disagreed with the nihilistic philosophy expressed in Strindberg's *Dream Play:* "The important thing," says my interviewer, "seems to me to be not the rightness of Strindberg's belief, but rather how he has expressed it. . . ." Strindberg expressed it very vividly, but there are things more important than that. If a man tells me something I believe to be an untruth, am I forbidden to do more than congratulate him on the brilliance of his lying?

Cyril Connolly once said, once and wanly, that it was closing time in the gardens of the West; but I deny the rest of that suavely cadenced sentence, which asserts that "from now on an artist will be judged only by the resonance of his solitude or the quality of his despair." Not by me, he won't. I shall, I hope, respond to the honesty of such testimonies: but I shall be looking for something more, something harder; for evidence of the artist who is not content with the passive role of a symptom, but concerns himself, from time to time, with such things as healing. M. Ionesco correctly says that no ideology has yet abolished fear, pain or sadness. Nor has any work of art. But both are in the business of trying. What other business is there? [96]

EUGÈNE IONESCO

Hearts Are Not Worn on the Sleeve

For a brief discussion of the literary controversy of which this article is a part, see the introductory note to the previous article on page 153.

I cannot answer all the problems raised by my courteous enemy, Mr. Kenneth Tynan, in his last article (*Ionesco and the Phantom*). It would take too long and I cannot go on abusing the hospitality of *The Observer*. It would also, in a way, be a waste of time, for we would only succeed in repeating ourselves. That is what Mr. Kenneth Tynan is already beginning to do. So I shall above all try to put my views in greater detail and answer those questions which seem to me essential.

Mr. Tynan reproaches me for being so fascinated by the means of expressing "objective reality" (but it is another question to know what objective reality really is), that I forget objective reality in favor of the means of expressing it, which therefore becomes an end in itself. In other words, he is, I believe, accusing me of formalism. But what is the history of art or literature if it is not, first and foremost, the history of its expression, the history of its language or idiom? For me expression is form and content at one and the same time. To approach the problem of literature by studying its expression (and that, in my opinion, is what a critic should do) [101] is also to deal with its content and arrive at its essence. But to attack an idiom that is out of date, to try and hold it up to ridicule and reveal its limitations and its deficiencies; to try and shake it up, for every idiom wears out, gets hidebound and is drained of significance; to try and renew it or reinvent it or simply to amplify it is the function of every "creator," who in so doing, as I have just said, reaches the heart of things, of living and changing reality, always different and yet always the same. This process can take place consciously as well as instinctively, with humor, if you like, and in perfect freedom, with ideas but without ideology, if ideology means a closed system of thought, a system of slogans, good, bad or indifferent, far removed from life, which it quite fails to absorb, although it persists in trying to impose itself as though it were the expression of life itself. I am not the first to point out the divergency that exists, in art as well as in "political" life, between ideology and reality. I therefore consider art to be more concerned with an independent search for knowledge than with any system of morals, political or not. It is of course a way of knowing that involves the emotions, an exploration that is objective in its subjecitvity, testimony rather than teaching, evidence of how the world appears to the artist.

To renew one's idiom or one's language is to renew one's conception or one's vision of the world. A revolution is a change of mentality. Any new artistic expression enriches us by answering some spiritual need and broadens the frontiers of known reality; it is an adventure, it is a gamble, so it cannot be a repetition of some already classified ideology, it cannot serve any other kind of truth but its own (because a truth, once uttered, is already superseded). Any work that answers this requirement may seem strange at the outset, since it communicates what has not been communicated before in this particular way. And as everything is to be found in its expression, its structure or inner logic, it is the expression [102] that must be examined. In a reasoned argument one should see that the conclusion follows logically from the data; for it is a construction that seems (but only *seems*) to be independent, to stand alone—just as a play, for example, is a construction one has to describe in order to verify its internal unity. The data used in any reasoning process are of course verified by other reasoned arguments, which are also again constructions.

I do not believe there is any contradiction between creation and knowledge, for mental structures are probably a reflection of the structure of the universe.

What is the point of a temple, a church or a palace? Can we find any realism there? Certainly not. Yet architecture reveals the fundamental laws of construction; every building testifies to the *objective* reality of the principles of architecture. And what is the purpose of a building? Of a church? Apparently to accommodate people and shelter the faithful. But that is their least important use. Their principal purpose is to reveal and be the expression of these architectonic laws, and it is in order to study and admire these buildings that we visit abandoned temples, cathedrals, deserted palaces and old, uninhabitable houses. Is it then the purpose of all these buildings to improve the lot of man (which according to Mr. Tynan should be the essential aim of all thought and all works of art)? Certainly not. And what also is the purpose of music, unless it be to reveal its own different laws? In a sense one could therefore say that a column or a sonata is of no practical use at all. Their purpose is to be what they are. The one should just stand there, the other should be heard. And what is the point of the existence of the universe? Simply that it should exist. But whether it is of any use to existence to exist is a matter of opinion and a different question, an unthinkable one moreover, for existence cannot but exist.

When Mr. Tynan defends realist writers, because they express themselves in an idiom everyone can immediately [103] recognize, he is nevertheless defending a narrow realism—even if he denies it—

the kind of realism that no longer captures reality and must therefore be exploded. Once a thing is admitted by all, it is no longer admissible.

There was, at the beginning of this century, what is usually called a vast avant-garde in all realms of the spirit. A revolution, an upheaval in our mental habits. Exploration continues, of course, and intelligence perseveres in its research, which in turn transforms intelligence itself and completely alters our understanding of the world. In the West the renewal continues, particularly in music and painting. In literature and especially in the theatre this movement seems to have come to a halt, about 1925 perhaps. I should like to be allowed the hope that I may be considered one of the modest craftsmen who are trying to take it further. I have attempted, for example, to exteriorize, by using objects, the anguish (I hope Mr. Tynan will excuse my employing this word) of my characters, to make the set speak and the action on the stage more visual, to translate into concrete images terror, regret or remorse, and estrangement, to play with words (but not to send them packing) and even perhaps to deform them—which is generally accepted in the work of poets and humorists. I have thus thought to extend the idiom of the theatre. I believe I have to some degree succeeded in my aim. Is this to be condemned? I do not know. All I know is that I have not been judged on the merit of these plays, for this does not seem to be one of the considerations of a dramatic critic as important as Mr. Tynan, who is moreover far from blind.

But let us come back to realism for the last time. Quite recently I happened to see an international exhibition of painting. There were "abstract" pictures (which do not seem to appeal to Mr. Tynan) and representational pictures: impressionist, postimpressionist and "social realist." In the Soviet pavilion, of course, only the latter were in evidence.[104] These paintings were dead: portraits of heroes frozen into conventional and unreal poses; sailors and snipers in captured castles, so academic they were no longer credible; and non-political pictures too, a few frosty flowers; and a street scene with *abstract* city folk, and in the center a woman devoid of life, inexpressive though exact in detail, dehumanized. It was very curious. And what was even more curious was that the sturdy local bourgeois were lost in admiration. They said that this particular pavilion was the only one worth seeing; for even the fauves or the impressionists went over their heads. This was not the first time I had noticed that the reactions of Stalinist bourgeois realists and capitalist bourgeois realists are identical. By a still more curious trick of fate, it is clear that these social-realist painters were in fact formalist and academic, unable to emphasize content just because they neglected the requirements of form. The content had escaped them and formal technique had turned against them and taken revenge by extinguishing reality.

In the French pavilion, on the other hand, the pictures by Masson (a painter who is indeed exclusively concerned with the way he paints, his means of expression, his technique) gave evidence of a deeply moving truth, of an extraordinary pictorially dramatic quality. Dark night surrounds a dazzlingly brilliant throbbing light and struggles to overcome it. Curves trace a pattern, lines rear up violently and through a gap in the serried planes of composition we can glimpse infinite space. As Masson, the craftsman, had left human reality strictly alone, as he had not tried to track it down and thought of nothing but "the act of painting," human reality and the tragedy of it had for this very reason, truly and freely, been unveiled. So it was what Mr. Tynan calls anti-reality that had become real, the incommunicable was communicated; and it is there too, behind an apparent rejection of all concrete and moral human truth, that his living heart was hidden, whereas with the others, the anti-formalists,[105] there was nothing but dried-up forms, dead and empty: hearts are not worn on the sleeve.

Mr. Tynan agrees with me when he remarks that "no ideology has yet abolished fear, pain or sadness. Nor has any work of art. But both are in the business of trying. What other business is there?"

What other business? Painting, for example. Or having a sense of humor. No Englishman should be without that. I beg of you, Mr. Tynan, do not attempt, by means of art or any other means, to improve the lot of mankind. Please do not do it. We have had enough of civil wars already, enough of blood and tears and trials that are a mockery, enough of "righteous" executioners and "ignoble" martyrs, of disappointed hopes and penal servitude.

Do not improve the lot of mankind, if you really wish it well.

A few words for Mr. Philip Toynbee. I take back all the wicked things I said about Arthur Miller. Mr. Toynbee judges Mr. Arthur Miller's plays according to this dramatist's own ideas about writing drama. I did not think this could be anything but a presumption in his favor. No doubt I was wrong. So I am going to make a favorable judgment of his work too, according to something that lies outside the work itself. I shall therefore judge Mr. Arthur Miller's work according to the photograph of Mr. Miller published in *The Observer.* Mr. Miller does indeed look a very fine fellow. And so I admire his work.

On the other hand, I am rather amazed that Mr. Philip Toynbee should be amazed at the idea that man can be hampered in his movements by society or by the air he breathes. It seems to me it is not so easy to breathe and to live; I also think it possible for man not to be a social animal. A child has great difficulty in fitting into society, he struggles against it and finds it hard to adapt himself to it: those who [106] work with children will know what I am talking about. And if a child finds it hard to adapt himself to society, it is because there is in human nature something that has to escape the social order or be alienated by it. And even when a man becomes part of society, he does not always manage things very well. Social life, living with other people and what that can mean, has been shown to us by Sartre himself (Mr. Toynbee will not object to my quoting Sartre) in his play *No Exit.* Society is hell, hell is other people. We would be very pleased to do without them. And was it not Dostoevski who said that one could not live more than a few days with anyone before beginning to detest him? And does not the hero of *Homme pour homme* lose his soul and his name, and does he not lose his individuality to the point of becoming totally alienated when he joins in the collective irresponsibilty of the wearers of uniform?

I too have done my military service. My sergeant despised me because my boots were not well polished. How could I make him understand that there are other standards of judgment apart from polishing boots. And that shining my boots did not entirely exhaust my possibilities as a human being? At dances, girls did not want me as a partner because I was not a lieutenant. And yet, out of uniform, I was still a man. As for my general, he was so morally deformed that he thought of himself as nothing but a general, and used to go to bed in his uniform. Later on I worked as a clerk, yet I still had the feeling I was "something more" than a clerk. I believe I was really well aware of my estrangement from society, the kind of alienation that is denounced by the most Marxist of the Marxists and prevents a man from developing freely and finding fulfillment. When my play, *The Chairs,* was performed in Warsaw and a few other Polish towns my characters were immediately seen to be not mentally deranged but socially estranged. And yet they wore the working clothes of the proletariat, of "the workers." I believe that [107] every society alienates, even and above all a "socialist" society (in the West, in England or in France, the classes are leveled out or interpenetrate more freely) where the political leaders consider themselves an elite because they are enlightened and where they are absorbed as men by their function. Wherever one finds social functions, one finds alienation (society being an organization of functions), for once again man is not merely a social function.

When my lieutenant and my boss are back in their homes, alone in their rooms, they could, for example, just like me, being outside the social order, be afraid of death as I am, have the same dreams and nightmares, and having stripped off their social personality, suddenly find themselves naked, like a body stretched out on the sand, amazed to be there and amazed at their own amazement, amazed at their own awareness as they are confronted with the immense ocean of the infinite, alone in the brilliant, inconceivable and indisputable sunlight of existence. And it is then that my general or my boss can be identified with me. It is in our solitude that we can all be reunited. And that is why true society transcends our social machinery.

But that has nothing to do with the theatre. *Je m'excuse.* I am sorry.[108]

NATHAN A. SCOTT, JR.

The Broken Center: A Definition of the Crisis of Values in Modern Literature

Things fall apart; the center cannot hold;
Mere anarchy is loosed upon the world;
. . . .
The best lack all conviction, while the worst
Are full of passionate intensity.
—WILLIAM BUTLER YEATS, "The Second Coming."

> We need a theme? then let that be our theme:
> that we, poor grovellers between faith and doubt,
> the sun and north star lost, and compass out,
> the heart's weak engine all but stopped, the time
> timeless in this chaos of our wills—
> that we must ask a theme, something to think,
> something to say, between dawn and dark,
> something to hold to, something to love.
>
> —CONRAD AIKEN, *Time in the Rock.*

One of the characters in the dialogue on which Mr. Richard Chase has based his recent brilliant book *The Democratic Vista* gives me a kind of text for this essay when he remarks: "it seems that the greatest writers of the first half of the twentieth century lived in a high, tense world of strenuous and difficult metaphysics, moral doctrine, political ideology, and religious feeling. . . ." [1] The young [182] man who says this is a graduate student of literature who, together with his wife and two children, is spending a late summer weekend on the Massachusetts coast in the home of a professor at his university, and it is to his senior friend that he offers this observation. He is perhaps being characteristic of his generation when he argues that "it is no longer possible to share" the intellectual and spiritual preoccupations of the great heroes of the modern tradition, of people like Eliot and Joyce and Pound. But though this may be a foreclosure that is too narrow and too premature, he does, nevertheless, identify accurately what is the most important distinguishing feature of the great classic tradition of modern letters, for that is most certainly a tradition that posits "a high, tense world of strenuous and difficult metaphysics . . . and religious feeling."

When we think, for example, of Mann and Lawrence and Kafka and Faulkner, it becomes immediately apparent, of course, that these are writers not all of whom are easily to be sheltered under the same umbrella: their methods of practicing the arts of fiction and the various gestures that they make toward reality all represent

SOURCE: *Chicago Review*, Vol. XIII, No. 2 (Summer 1959). Reprinted by courtesy of *Chicago Review*. This essay also appears in the volume *Symbolism in Religion and Literature* (New York: George Braziller, 1961), ed. Rollo May. A brief portion of the present text is drawn from an earlier article ("The Meaning of the Incarnation for Modern Literature") and is used with the permission of the editor of *Christianity and Crisis*, in which it appeared.

[1] Richard Chase, *The Democratic Vista* (Garden City, N.Y.: Doubleday & Co., 1958), p. 16.

enormous diversity and the amazing differentiation of attitude and language that is a chief hallmark of literary art in our period. But, despite this multifariousness of creative technique and of fundamental point of view, they are writers whom we feel impelled to regard as constituting in some sense a genuine community and a unitary tradition. And this is, I believe, a view that we take because these are writers whose own most emphatic insistence has been upon the fact of their being unsustained by any vital and helpful traditions: the community which they have formed has been rooted, in other words, in their common awareness of their isolation. And this is an isolation which has not been primarily an affair of the artist's tenuous position in the polity of modern society: that, to be sure, has been something uncertain and problematic, and his social marginality has at times undoubtedly greatly added to his unease. But what has most fundamentally given life for him the aspect of crisis has been that recession of faith and that erosion of the religious terrain announced by Nietzsche in the nineteenth century, and, in our own time, by Sartre.

In such an age, when all is in doubt and when, as Yeats says, "Things fall apart" and "the center cannot hold"—in such an age, the philosopher may not be utterly crippled, if he is willing to have his vocation confined to the analysis of nothing more than the structure of sentences; and the social critic can always be kept busy [183] in notating the tics and the spasms that are the signs of our distress. And in similar reduced ways the other custodians of the cultural life may in some manner continue to function when overtaken by a late bad time. But when the traditional premises regarding the radical significance of things have collapsed and when, therefore, there is no longer any robust common faith to orient the imaginative faculties of men with respect to the ultimate mysteries of existence —when, in other words, the basic presuppositions of a culture have become just yawning question-marks, then the literary artist is thrust upon a most desolate frontier indeed. For, though his role is sometimes spoken of as though it involved presiding over an act of *communication,* this is a vulgar version of it which could pass muster only in an age of television and of what is called "the mass-audience." The writer may, to be sure, take his stand before a microphone and speak to a crowd in whose fate he is not at all implicated; and, when he does this, it may perhaps be that he plays a part in something that might be called a process of *communication.* But, when this is his position, surely it is impossible for anything to be "shared, in a new and illuminating intensity of awareness." [2] Indeed, as Mr. Allen Tate has reminded us, the very concept of literature as *communication* may well, in its currency, betoken a tragic victory of modern secularism over the human spirit. "Our unexamined theory of literature as communication could not," he says, "have appeared in an age in which communion was still possible for any appreciable majority of persons. The word communication presupposes the victory of the secularized society of means without ends. The poet, on the one hand, shouts to the public, on the other (some distance away), not the rediscovery of the common experience, but a certain pitch of sound to which the well-conditioned adrenals of humanity obligingly respond." [3]

No, says Mr. Tate, the language of *communication* may be the language of radio and television, but it is not the language which the artist seeks sensitively to supervise, for that is the language not of communication but of *communion:* it is a language, that is, into which an effort has been made to put a deep and authentic knowledge of what is involved in the life together of free men, and it is, therefore, a language which invites us to re-enter what Martin Buber calls "the world of *I* and *Thou.*" [184]

Which is, of course, to say that the language of imaginative literature is not the ethically and spiritually neutral jargon of any science: it is, rather, a language which, if it is to do its proper work, needs to be heavily weighted with the beliefs and sentiments and valuations that are the deep source in the culture of its "hum and buzz of implication" [4] and that bind the people together with ties that separate them from the people of other cultures. And it is only when the artist's language bears this kind of freight that it can be something more than a vehicle of *communication:* it is only then that it can become an instrument of *communion* and what all art is ultimately intended to be—namely, a servant of love.

But now we are brought back to that desolate frontier on which I have said the modern writer has found himself, for what has made his position as an artist so insecure has been precisely the very great difficulty he has had in making contact with any significant body of belief that, having vital authority in our period, might furnish his

[2] Allen Tate, *The Forlorn Demon* (Chicago: Henry Regnery Co., 1953), p. 13.

[3] Ibid., p. 12.

[4] Lionel Trilling, *The Liberal Imagination* (New York: The Viking Press, 1950), p. 206.

imagination with the premises of its functioning and facilitate the transaction between himself and his reader. "In the profoundest human sense," said Mr. Kenneth Burke in one of his early books, "one communicates in a *weighted* vocabulary in which the weightings are shared by [one's] group as a whole." [5] But it is just at this point that modern culture has represented great privation. There is, in fact, little of anything at all of profound significance that is widely shared by modern men. The dominant dispensation has, of course, been of a scientific character, but Max Planck tells us that "there is scarcely [even] a scientific axiom that is not now-a-days denied by somebody." [6] And, outside the realm of our scientific culture, the resistant pressure that has been offered to the relativizing tendencies of our time has been negligible indeed.

In his important book *Diagnosis of Our Time*, Dr. Karl Mannheim proposes the interesting and cogent hypothesis that the despiritualization of modern life is best understood in terms of the gradual evaporation in our period of authentic "paradigmatic experience" and of those great "primordial images or archetypes" which, being formed out of this kind of experience, have directed the human [185] enterprise in the most genuinely creative moments of cultural history. By "paradigmatic experience" Dr. Mannheim means those "basic experiences which carry more weight than others, and which are unforgettable in comparison with others that are merely passing sensations." [7] Without experience of this kind, he says, "no consistent conduct, no character formation and no real human coexistence and co-operation are possible. Without them our universe of discourse loses its articulation, conduct falls to pieces, and only disconnected bits of successful behaviour patterns and fragments of adjustment to an ever-changing environment remain." [8] And his contention is that "paradigmatic experience," in so far as it yields some conviction as to what is radically significant, does also, in effect, yield a kind of "ontological hierarchy," in accordance with which we say, "'This is bad, this is good, this is better.'" But, of course, the whole drive of the positivistically oriented secularism of modern culture has been towards such "a neutralization of that

[5] Quoted in Herbert Muller, *Modern Fiction* (New York: Funk and Wagnalls, 1937), p. 10.

[6] Quoted in Harry Slochower, *No Voice Is Wholly Lost* (New York: Creative Age Press, Inc., 1945), p. vii.

[7] Karl Mannheim, *Diagnosis of Our Time* (New York: Oxford University Press, 1944), p. 146.

[8] Ibid., pp. 147–148.

ontological hierarchy in the world of experience" as encourages the belief that "one experience is as important as any other" [9] and that the question of right or wrong is merely a question concerning the most efficient environmental adjustments. So the result has been the evaporation of those "primordial images" which objectify a people's faith and provide the moral imagination with its basic premises. And when there are no "paradigmatic experiences," then nothing is any longer revealed as having decisive importance, and men are ruled by a kind of "kaleidoscopic concept of life" [10] which, in giving an equal significance to everything, does, in effect, attribute radical significance to nothing at all. In such an age, the individual is condemned to the awful prison of his own individuality, since nothing means the same thing to any broad segment of people —and the primary fact about the human community is disclosed as being the complete collapse of anything at all resembling genuine community.

This is a fact which has been dramatized by much recent social criticism in its notation of the astonishing lack of drama in modern society. The life of the average megalopolitan today is ungraced by [186] any rituals which strengthen the ties of sympathy and fellow-feeling that bind him to his neighbors. Nor is the civic scene complicated and enlivened by any round of celebrations and festivities comparable to the religious liturgies or the secular rites which figured so largely in the common life of earlier times. In the great cities of our day we are cave-dwellers, scurrying about the urban wilderness from one vast compound to another, like "bits of paper, whirled by the cold wind" [11]; and, like the members of Captain Ahab's crew, we are, as Melville says, "nearly all Islanders," none "acknowledging the common continent of men, but each *Isolato* living on a separate continent of his own."

So this, then, is the intractable and unpromising reality which the modern writer has been up against. Mr. Burke says that it is the artist's task to supervise a *weighted* language whose weightings are shared by the commonalty. But it has been the fate of the modern artist to live in a time when the commonalty, as anything more than a statistical assemblage of unrelated atoms, is something only to be remembered by the historical imagination. And this is why it is,

[9] Ibid., p. 148.

[10] Ibid.

[11] T. S. Eliot, "Burnt Norton," *Four Quartets* (New York: Harcourt, Brace and Co., 1943), p. 6.

therefore, that the problem of understanding modern literature so largely involves the problem of understanding the stratagems that become inevitable for the artist, when history commits him to the practice of his vocation in such a vacuum.

What the modern artist has needed to find are "systems of reference, acceptable to the experience of our time, by means of which he [could] give order and unity to his work." [12] This is, indeed, what the artist has always needed, and, when the circumstances of his culture have afforded a good soil for art to grow in, the ethos of his community has provided him with co-ordinating analogies and key-metaphors and with myths and symbols which, in flowing out of the funded memories and experience of his people, could well serve him as instruments for the full evocation of the human communion. Surely it is no merely wilful or sentimental nostalgia that leads us, when we roam back through the tradition, to account in these terms for the greatness of the achievement of Sophocles and Dante, of Shakespeare and Racine, or, on a far less exalted level, of,[187] say, Madame de Lafayette or Jane Austen. In these older writers we feel a kind of freedom and a kind of security of reference that strike us as being a consequence of their having had the good fortune to live in cultures which, having a vital unity, could liberally provide them with those "primordial images" and "archetypes" which centralize and order the poetic imagination. These older writers were the lucky ones, for they did not have to invent for themselves ways of construing or of making sense of experience: they were lucky because the writer who has to expend energy on philosophical and theological enterprises before he can get his literary project under way will have squandered reserves of imaginative power that, in more favorable circumstances, would be used up in the practice of his art. And when one thinks, say, of Jane Austen in relation to the woman of our own time who wrote such a book as *Nightwood,* we cannot help but feel that the older writer was also lucky because, in receiving her ultimate terms of reference from her culture, she was relieved of any uncertainty about how to establish contact with her readers and was, therefore, enabled, so far as her fundamental terms of speech were concerned, to make the kinds of assumptions that facilitate the poetic transaction.

[12] Stanley R. Hopper, "The Problem of Moral Isolation in Contemporary Literature," in *Spiritual Problems in Contemporary Literature,* ed. by Stanley R. Hopper (New York: Harper & Brothers, 1952), p. 153.

But this is precisely the kind of luck that the writer in the modern period has not enjoyed. Inheriting no traditional and widely accepted frame of values from his culture, before his art could be steadied by some executive principle of valuation, it has been necessary for the artist to try to construct some viable system of belief for himself, by means of an effort of personal vision: he has had to be, in a sense, his own priest, his own guide, his own Virgil. He has been condemned by the cultural circumstances of his time to draw everything that forms and orders his art from himself. The deep waters in which he has swum have been the deep waters of his own individual mind into which he has descended in his search for a clue to the principles by means of which the anarchy of experience might be controlled and given a shape and a significance. And this is why we might say that the reigning law of the modern movement in the arts has been that of the *principium individuationis*.

Indeed, all the great literature of the modern period might be said to be a literature of metaphysical isolation, for the modern artist—and this is perhaps the fundamental truth about him—has experienced a great loneliness, the kind of loneliness that is known by the soul when it has to undertake, unaided by ministries either of Church or of culture, the adventure of discovering the fundamental principles [180] of meaning. And this is unquestionably the reason for the obscurity of so many great modern texts—of Rimbaud's *Une Saison en Enfer,* of Rilke's *Duino Elegies,* of Joyce's *Finnegans Wake,* of Malcolm Lowry's *Under the Volcano.* For, amidst the confusion of values of his age, the artist is attempting to invent a system of attitudes and beliefs for himself that will give meaning to his world. And it is this idiosyncrasy, this extreme individuality, of modern poetic vision that has often made our finest literature so difficult to penetrate. What has been most distinctive of the great heroes of the modern tradition is, as Stephen Spender says, that they assumed the task "of re-experiencing everything as though it had never been experienced before, and then expressing it not in terms with which traditions and education have made us familiar but in new ones minted out" [13] of their separate sensibilities. In a time when

So various
And multifoliate are our breeds of faith

[13] Stephen Spender, *The Creative Element* (London: Hamish Hamilton, 1953), p. 176.

That we could furnish a herbarium
With the American specimens alone [14]—

the writer has felt himself to be without a common background of reference by which his own imaginative faculties and those of his readers might be oriented and brought into a profound rapport with one another. So he has turned inward upon himself, pursuing a system of values or beliefs in the world of his own subjectivity. And, as Mr. Spender says, the result is that "it becomes increasingly more difficult for the reader to understand the significance of the writer's symbols and language, without his having experienced the process of the writer's experiencing. . . . Hence a vast literature explaining texts and the circumstances of each writer's life has grown up around the modern movement." [15] And this is a development that has tended to institutionalize the originally unique experimentations of the great pioneers and to make them, indeed, a staple of the new academic tradition—as is indicated, for example, by the notification we are given on the jacket of Professor William York Tindall's book on Joyce that, as the publisher says, Mr. Tindall "is a member of the [189] James Joyce Society, and has made the pilgrimage to Dublin." [16] Yet this is precisely what the appropriation of Joyce's work demands—membership in scholarly societies devoted to its study and foundation-sponsored tours to Dublin in search of scraps of information that may assist us in unravelling the bafflements of his incredibly complex art. For this writer "is in himself a culture and a country with myths and dialects derived from other ones." [17] And the necessity that we confront, when we tackle a book like *Finnegans Wake,* is that of trying to make some coherent sense out of a vast chaotic array of notes toward what its author heroically strove to make the great modern novel.

Indeed, the Joycean experiment, however stillborn it may in part have been, does at least, in a way, succeed in stating the significant questions and in drawing attention to what has been a fundamental dilemma of the artist in our period. We may say that the lesson of Joyce's career teaches us that, though the artist cannot by fiat produce adequate surrogates for traditions of faith and cul-

[14] Karl Shapiro, *Essay on Rime* (New York: Reynal & Hitchcock, 1945), p. 63.

[15] Stephen Spender, op. cit., pp. 176–177.

[16] William York Tindall, *James Joyce* (New York: Charles Scribner's Sons, 1950).

[17] Stephen Spender. op. cit., p. 177.

ture that are no longer available to him, he may, in attempting to do so, dramatize with an especial vividness the fact of the mythical vacuum in the modern period. And that is what Joyce succeeded in doing. As T. S. Eliot put the issue in his famous review of *Ulysses* in 1923: "In using the myth, in manipulating a continuous parallel between contemporaneity and antiquity, Mr. Joyce is pursuing a method which others must pursue after him. . . . It is simply a way of controlling, of ordering, of giving a shape and a significance to the immense panorama of futility and anarchy which is contemporary history." [18] And it is the radicalism of his effort to find this shape and this significance that makes him the great exemplar of the literary artist in the modern age: he gives the age away—by which I mean that he puts us in mind of how much "the greatest writers of the first half of the twentieth century lived in a high, tense world of strenuous and difficult metaphysics . . . and religious feeling." When we think not only of Joyce but of Proust and Kafka and Lawrence and Gide, we immediately remember how much these artists, amidst the disintegration and incoherence of our systems, had, in the quest [190] for a viable body of beliefs or "first principles," to expend energies that, in a more fortunate age, could have been directed into the labors of composition. These are all writers who, in various ways, were handicapped in not having been given by their culture an adequately objective framework of religious commitments and metaphysical beliefs. But these writers, like many other great artists of our period, are also notable by reason of the ardor with which they sought to compensate for this disability by religious and philosophic improvisations whose virtuosity is perhaps without previous parallel in literary history. And, indeed, the real religious power and greatness that we feel in the great classic tradition of modern literature is, I believe, the direct consequence of the immense courage with which the chief protagonists of this tradition have steered their lonely, separate courses through the spiritual void of our time. This is, of course, as Stanley Hopper says, a literature "the more austerely religious in that it is not prejudiced by religious belief" [19] of an orthodox sort, but we should not, even so, allow its heterodoxy to obscure for us the authenticity of its researches into the human condition.

[18] T. S. Eliot, "Ulysses, Order, and Myth," in *Critiques and Essays on Modern Fiction*, ed. by John W. Aldridge (New York: Ronald Press, 1952), p. 426. This review first appeared in the *Dial*, November, 1923.

[19] Stanley Hopper, op. cit., p. 155.

Now it is precisely the kind of extreme self-reliance in the quest for "first principles" that I have been positing as the inescapable necessity facing the modern writer—it is precisely this that makes evident his descendance from the great Romantics of the last century and makes evident also the fact that the literature of the age of Joyce and Kafka is essentially a late development of the Romantic movement. And, here, we must not be misled by the vigorous anti-Romanticism that informs so much of twentieth-century literature. It is true, of course, that men like Valéry and Eliot and Pound in poetry and Joyce and Proust in the novel have sponsored programs of one sort or another whose aim has been to encourage a rejection of the legacy of Romanticism—of its inspirationist aesthetic, of its cult of sincerity, of its artlessness, and of its confusions of art and religion. But, steady as this quarrel with the Romantic movement has been in our time, it is a family quarrel, and the fact remains that the great tradition of twentieth-century literature is, fundamentally, a product of the Romantic dispensation. As Professor Robert Langbaum has recently observed,

> Whatever the difference between the literary movements of the nineteenth and twentieth centuries, they are connected . . . by their response to the [191] same wilderness. That wilderness is the legacy of the Enlightenment, of the scientific and critical effort of the Enlightenment which, in its desire to separate fact from the values of a crumbling tradition, separated fact from all values—bequeathing a world in which fact is measurable quantity while value is man-made and illusory. Such a world offers no objective verification for just the perceptions by which men live, perceptions of beauty, goodness and spirit. It was as literature began in the latter eighteenth century to realize the dangerous implications of the scientific world-view that romanticism was born. It was born anew in at least three generations thereafter as men of genius arrived intellectually at the dead-end of the eighteenth century and then, often through a total crisis of personality, broke intellectually into the nineteenth. As literature's reaction to the eighteenth century's scientific world-view, romanticism connects the literary movement of the nineteenth and twentieth centuries.[20]

This recognition of the havoc wrought by Enlightenment iconoclasm did not, in the great English Romantics, lead to an exacerbation of spirit so extreme as that which is often noticeable in their French and German contemporaries, but we can, nevertheless, de-

[20] Robert Langbaum, *The Poetry of Experience* (New York: Random House, 1957), pp. 11–12.

tect the signs of this unrest in Coleridge and in Wordsworth and in Keats and Shelley. They all make us feel that for them the traditional archetypes and systems of faith had ceased any longer to be effective and that they, as a result, in their dealings with the world, were thrown back upon their own private resources. They had all felt what Keats called in *Lamia* "the touch of cold philosophy," and they knew themselves, as a consequence, to be deprived of that mythical machinery for the ordering of experience which writers in earlier periods of the tradition had been blessed in having: they knew themselves to be fated by the logic of their culture to bear, alone and unassisted, what Wordsworth called "the weight of all this unintelligible world." So, in works like *Tintern Abbey*, the *Immortality* ode, *The Rime of the Ancient Mariner*, *Adonais*, the *Ode to the West Wind*, and the *Ode to a Nightingale*, these men attempted to perform what Coleridge believed to be the poet's task, "of spreading the tone, the *atmosphere*, and with it the depth and height of the ideal world around forms, incidents, and situations, of which, for the common view, custom had bedimmed all the lustre, had dried up the sparkle and the dew drops." [21] [192]

When we turn, however, to Continental Romanticism, particularly in France, and here not to such relatively early figures as Rousseau and Chateaubriand and Lamartine but to such later writers as Baudelaire and Rimbaud and Lautréamont—when we turn to this French Romantic tradition, we leave the elegiac temper of the English school and come to a new kind of intensity and a new kind of violence that point directly towards the *Angst*-ridden literature of the twentieth century. It was with this tradition in mind that the distinguished French critic Jacques Rivière remarked in his essay on "La Crise du concept de littérature" that "with Romanticism. . . . the literary act began to be conceived as a kind of assault on the absolute, and its result as a revelation," the writer becoming a kind of "priest." Indeed, said Rivière, this whole literature is "a vast incantation toward the miracle." [22]

But not only does the artist working under the dispensation of Baudelaire and Lautréamont become a priest: he also becomes a kind of scientist, for, wanting to rescue himself from the metaphysical void of his culture, he is so much in the grip of a great pas-

[21] S. T. Coleridge, *Biographia Literaria*, ed. by J. Shawcross (London: Oxford University Press, 1907; Impression of 1954), Vol. I, Ch. IV, p. 59.

[22] Jacques Rivière, "La Crise du concept de littérature," *Nouvelle Revue Française*, February 1, 1924.

sion for knowledge till the poetic process itself becomes not primarily a process of the artist's *making* but rather a process of the artist's *discovering* the ultimate frontiers of human existence and of there staking out his claim to dominion. Listen, for example, to Rimbaud: he is writing to his friend Paul Demeny, and he says:

> The first study for a man who wants to be a poet is the knowledge of himself, entire. He looks for his soul, inspects it, learns it. As soon as he knows it, he cultivates it: it seems simple. . . . But the soul has to be made monstrous, that's the point. . . .
>
> One must, I say, be a *seer*, make oneself a *seer*.
>
> The poet makes himself a *seer* through a long, a prodigious and rational disordering of *all* the senses. Every form of love, of suffering, of madness; he searches himself, he consumes all the poisons in him, keeping only their quintessences. Ineffable torture in which he will need all his faith and superhuman strength, the great criminal, the great sickman, the utterly damned, and the supreme Savant! For he arrives at the unknown! Since he has cultivated his soul—richer to begin with than any other! He arrives at the unknown: and even if, half crazed in the end, he loses the understanding of his visions, he has seen them! Let him croak in his leap into those unutterable and innumerable things: there will come other horrible workers: they will begin at the horizons where he has succumbed.[23] [193]

Now here we have an inner dislocation which this particular poet called a sacred disorder, but it is clear to us that what is really signified was his having yielded to "an invasion of vertigo"[24] and lost his footing. So it is, therefore, not surprising that he abandoned poetry in 1873 at the age of nineteen to spend the rest of his brief life in exotic adventure and in angry defiance of bourgeois Philistinism. But, despite Rimbaud's abdication from literature, his prophecy was borne out, and other laborers did come after him, "who began," as Jacques Maritain says, "at the horizons where he had collapsed."[25] A horizon is, of course, the place where the extremes of earth and sky meet, and we may say that the particular horizon where Rimbaud collapsed was the point at which his own desperate need, as an artist and as a man, for metaphysical and re-

[23] Arthur Rimbaud, "Letters to Paul Demeny: 1871," *Prose Poems from the Illuminations, trans. by Louise Varèse* (New York: New Directions, 1946), pp. xxvi–xxvii.

[24] Jacques Maritain, *Creative Intuition in Art and Poetry* (New York: Pantheon Books, 1953), p. 188.

[25] Ibid.

ligious order collided with the spiritual void of the nineteenth century. And this is the precise horizon on which we may locate that great modern procession that includes, in addition to Baudelaire and Rimbaud and Lautréamont, such earlier writers as Hölderlin and Leopardi and Vigny and such later writers as Mallarmé and Valéry and Joyce and Hart Crane and André Gide and André Malraux and St. John Perse and many others. For all these, in the sense that I am claiming for the term, are Romantics: that is, they are writers bent upon *improvising* perspectives and principles in terms of which a shape and a significance may be given to "the immense panorama" of modern experience, thus making it accessible to art. This is their passion and their chosen task, and it is their dedication to this that makes them candidates for the special kind of sainthood that the *avant-garde* has tended to produce in the modern period. Which is to say that, in a way, they have been martyrized by the dislocations of the time, and, when we think of artists like Kafka and Hart Crane and Dylan Thomas and Malcolm Lowry, it does seem, indeed, that they have borne upon their own souls the stigmata of the bent and broken world to which they were committed by modern history.

So this, then, is, it seems to me, the first major observation to be made about the great classic tradition of contemporary letters: we must say that, in its tone and style and outlook, it is an incorrigibly Romantic tradition. And this is to be seen, for example, even in apparently so un-Romantic a figure as T. S. Eliot, who, to be sure, has made his way back to a classical tradition of religious faith and has [194] found in Christian history the deepest inspiration for his work of the past twenty-five years. But the particular tradition of Christian faith in which Mr. Eliot has chosen to live—the tradition, say, of Origen and Dame Julian of Norwich and Jacob Boehme and St. John of the Cross—is hardly one which strikes us as belonging to the great central tradition of Christian culture: it is very special and irregular, and its very reclamation by a contemporary Christian poet suggests that even his orthodoxy will, in its attainment, represent something of the same kind of improvisation that has tended generally to characterize the philosophic and religious stratagems of the modern artist.

But, now, a second major specification must be made of the modern tradition in literature, for we shall not fully comprehend it until we recognize that it is a tradition which represents that particular late development of the Romantic movement which is an outgrowth of what Professor Erich Kahler calls "the existentialist experience." [26] Not only, in other words, must we say that this is a Romantic literature: we must also say that it is an existentialist literature as well. And, of course, when I denominate the central tradition in our literature as existentialist, it must be apparent that I do not intend to refer merely to certain recent writers, particularly in France, who have found a theoretical sanction for their vision in the doctrines of existentialist philosophy. I use the term, rather, in a very much broader sense and intend it to define the literature of the last hundred years in which we find reflected an experience of existence as fundamentally and, perhaps even, essentially problematic.

This is an experience which it will doubtless be our first impulse to regard as having been occasioned by those ultimate exigencies in the history of the modern spirit which Nietzsche called our attention to in his announcement of "the death of God." But "the death of God," as a cultural fact of the modern age, is itself something whose fundamental cause, I believe, is to be sought in the "death of man" in our time, for this is the really primary fact in modern experience. What we confront, throughout the whole polity of modern society, is a tragic devitalization of the very concept of the person. The kind of life *en masse,* for example, that has been so distinctive of our period has been made possible by a system whose inner logic has necessitated a high degree of specialization in all fields of man's labor. And this, in turn, by a dreadful kind of inexorability,[195] has accomplished what might even be said to be a mutation in human nature itself, in so far as the habit of requiring a man to justify himself by his ability to perform a special task has weakened in us the capacity to make the crucial distinction between the function and the human being who performs it. And not only has the distinction become a difficult one to make, but the human act by which a man transcends his various social and economic functions has, under the pressures of a commercialized culture, become an act that it is increasingly more difficult to perform. Many of the most thoughtful observers of modern life have noticed how the logic of a technocratic culture tends to reduce the concrete particularity of the unique human individual to a purely abstract and functional identity; and they have also noticed the gray anonymity of life that this reduction accomplishes. What every reporter on the present human condition has, indeed, to take into account is the sense that men

[26] Erich Kahler, *The Tower and the Abyss* (New York: George Braziller Inc., 1957), pp. 168–175.

have today of being thrust into the nudity of their own isolated individual existence. Though "huddled together" in the great metropolises of the contemporary world "like dust in a heap,"[27] that which figures most prominently in their awareness is a sense of the world's vacancy, and the loss of which they are most acutely conscious is the loss of the real *proximity* of friends and neighbors. Life seems, as Karl Jaspers says, to have grown "indefinitely vast"[28]: it no longer has that "interlinkage"[29] which holds it together, "so that it is not frittered away" and disintegrated into "the brief perspective of the [immediate] present."[30] A man has the function that he performs for eight hours a day, and he has his bit of breathing-space somewhere in the urban or the suburban wilderness. But, as we are told in one of the choruses in Mr. Eliot's *The Rock:*

> The desert is squeezed in the tube-train next to you,
> The desert is in the heart of your brother.[31]

So, though all the time we live closer and closer together in our great urban compounds, we find it more and more difficult to recognize one another or even to retain a sense of our own identities.[196] And amidst this gray, dreary anonymity we know that we live in a world from which all the gracious marks of "presence" have been banished.

"Just as primitive man believed himself to stand face to face with demons and believed that could he but know their names he would become their master, so [too]," says Karl Jaspers, "contemporary man [is also] faced by . . . [something that is] incomprehensible, which disorders his calculations. . . . The nameless powers of Nothingness," he says, "are, in our world whence the gods have been driven forth, the analogy of the demons that confronted primitive man."[32] And this, I believe, is why men in the modern period have believed God to be silent and absent and even dead. This has been their conclusion, because they have not lived out their days in real nearness to one another, and, not having known the gracious reality of "presence" in their relations with their neighbors,

[27] Karl Jaspers, *Man in the Modern Age,* trans. by Eden and Cedar Paul (Garden City, N.Y.: Doubleday Anchor Books, 1957), p. 209.

[28] Ibid., p. 202.

[29] Ibid., p. 210.

[30] Ibid., p. 202.

[31] T. S. Eliot, "Choruses from 'The Rock,'" I, *Collected Poems: 1909–1935* (New York: Harcourt, Brace & Co., 1936), p. 182.

[32] Karl Jaspers, op. cit., p. 191.

their imaginations have been unable to grasp the possibility of the world itself being grounded in a transcendent "Presence."

In such a world, where the human communion has been destroyed and man's condemnation is to an empty and unfertile solitude, what Gabriel Marcel calls *Presence* [33] appears to be an obsolescent relic of the past: not only does it appear that God is dead, but so too does it appear that an obituary notice is to be written that will also memorialize the disappearance of man as well. In this "place of disaffection" (to use T. S. Eliot's phrase) the only available dispensation seems to be that of loneliness and exile, and it is the sober acceptance of this icy alienation as the inescapable ground of human existence that constitutes that special modern sensibility which I am calling (after Erich Kahler) "the existentialist experience."

This is not an experience that is the sole property of those contemporary theorists of it whose program goes under the name of existentialism. Their nineteenth-century predecessors were, to be sure, among the first to give emphatic definition to it, and it first became a public fact in the Berlin lectures of Schelling (*Die Philosophie der Mythologie und der Offenbarung*) during the winter of 1841–'42 and in the later writings of men like Kierkegaard and Marx and Feuerbach and Nietzsche and Max Weber. But this is also an experience whose beginning is to be dated from that morning when Baudelaire looked out upon the billboards of Paris—"that vast cemetery [197] that is called a great city"—and felt an immense disgust. And not only do we find it in writers like Baudelaire and Rimbaud and Dostoievski and Strindberg, but we also find it in artists like Cézanne and Van Gogh and the American Albert Pinkham Ryder. These were all men who belonged to that nineteenth-century vanguard of revolutionaries who were distinguished by the clarity and the courage with which they acknowledged the bitter facts of alienation and estrangement as the central facts of modern existence. And when, as Paul Tillich says, "the 19th century came to an end" on the thirty-first of July, 1914,[34] the existentialist experience ceased to be the experience of a sensitive minority and became the dominant experience of the age. In this century it has furnished the perspectives of the philosophic tradition that has been established

[33] Vide Gabriel Marcel, *The Mystery of Being* (Chicago: Henry Regnery Co., 1951), Vol. I, Chapters IX and X; Vol. II, Chapter I.

[34] Paul Tillich, *The Courage to Be* (New Haven: Yale University Press, 1952), p. 137.

by such thinkers as Berdyaev and Shestov and Heidegger and Jaspers and Sartre and Marcel; it is the experience that one feels in Stravinsky's *Pétrouchka,* in Schoenberg's *Pierrot Lunaire,* in Alban Berg's *Wozzeck,* in Bartok's second *Quartet,* and in much of the great music of our time; and it is also the experience that has been painted into many of the canvases of such classic moderns as Picasso and Rouault and the early de Chirico or of such recent artists as Willem de Kooning and Jackson Pollock and Hans Hofmann.

Now it is this strain of sensibility that is central in much of twentieth-century literature: it is what we recognize in such poets of verse as Rainer Maria Rilke and Hart Crane and Robert Penn Warren and Gottfried Benn and in such poets of the novel as Conrad and Kafka and Faulkner and Malraux. Indeed, as Lionel Trilling has remarked, "There is scarcely a great writer of our own day who has not addressed himself to the ontological crisis, who has not conceived of life as a struggle to be—not to live, but to be." [35] And what one feels to be formative in much of the representative literature of our period is a deep need for a deep restoration of confidence in the stoutness and reliability and essential healthiness of the things of earth. The trauma that has been suffered is the trauma that is inflicted upon the imagination when it appears that both God and man are dead.

So the narrative, then, that is at the center of our literature is a narrative of estrangement and alienation: the story that is told is a [198] story of our abandonment "in some blind lobby . . . or corridor of Time. . . . And in that dark," says Penn Warren, "no thread." [36] No thread. And we are given some measure of how emphatic is the insistence upon our lostness by the apocalypticism and the hyperaesthesia of the literary imagination in our day, "its feeling," as Richard Chase says, "that no thought is permissible except an extreme thought: that every idea must be directly emblematic of concentration camps, alienation, madness, hell . . . ; that every word must bristle and explode with the magic potency of our plight." [37]

In our own American tradition, the figure of William Dean Howells as a novelist has fallen into what is well-nigh a complete

[35] Lionel Trilling, *The Opposing Self* (New York: The Viking Press, 1955), p. 140.

[36] Robert Penn Warren, *Brother to Dragons* (London: Eyre & Spottiswoode, 1953), p. 7.

[37] Richard Chase, "Christian Ideologue" (a review of Basil Willey's *Nineteenth Century Studies*), *The Nation* (April 8, 1950), p. 330.

eclipse, and we may be helped to understand at least a part of the reason for the decline of his prestige by remembering the observation that was made many years ago by Henry James, when he said of Howells: "He is animated by a love of the common, the immediate, the familiar, and the vulgar elements of life, and holds that in proportion as we move into the rare and strange we become vague and arbitrary. . . ." [38] And, when we re-read today books like *The Rise and Fall of Silas Lapham* and *A Hazard of New Fortunes* and *A Modern Instance*, we realize that, with his customary acuteness, James put his finger exactly on what is one of Howells's primary qualities. So it is no wonder that the contemporary reader finds it so difficult to enter into a happy and reciprocal relation with his work, for, as Professor Trilling has reminded us in his essay on Howells, "we consent to the commonplace [only] as it verges upon and becomes the rare and the strange": we "want something that has affinity with the common, the immediate, the familiar. . . . [but] we like them represented in their extremity to serve as a sort of outer limit of the possibility of our daily lives, as a kind of mundane hell." [39]

All the great charismatic seers of modern literature from Baudelaire to Kafka and from Pirandello to Faulkner have, in one way or another, wanted us to understand that we are lost in a dark wood and that, in this maze, what is least trustworthy is the common, the [199] immediate, the familiar. So the motion that the modern artist has very often performed before the revolving universe has been a motion of recoil. Sometimes, like Rimbaud, he has fallen in love with what Jacques Maritain calls "the blind glitter of nothingness" [40] and made of his art a kind of incantatory magic. Or, like the author of *Finnegans Wake*, sometimes he has decided himself to be God and create *ex nihilo* a universe of his own. His retreat has, on occasion, like Mallarmé's, been into *la poésie pure*—or, like the early Hemingway or the Dos Passos of the *U.S.A.* trilogy, it has been into the neutral factuality of naturalistic documentation. The recoil may have been into the subjectivistic perspectives of a Proust or a Virginia Woolf, or it may have been into that distress which provokes the belch of disgust expressed, say, in Jean-Paul Sartre's *La Nausée*. But, various as the configurations are, it can, nevertheless, be said

[38] Henry James, "William Dean Howells," *The American Essays* (New York: Vintage Books, 1956), p. 152.

[39] Lionel Trilling, op. cit., p. 88.

[40] Jacques Maritain, op. cit., p. 189.

that many of the major literary artists of our time, whether they know it or not, have had as their patron saint not St. Athanasius but Dionysius the Areopagite, for, in their dealings with the body of this world, their Way has been not the Way of Affirmation but the Way of Rejection. Which is to say that they have not known the kind of confidence in the world and in temporal reality that was managed in happier moments in the literary tradition.

Those Roman Catholic apologists who explain this attrition in terms of the anti-sacramentalism of a Protestant ethos are doubtless right in part—but they are right only in part, for the authentic sacramentalism of the Christian faith has also been obscured by what has often been the theological and cultural obscurantism of post-Tridentine Romanism. Nor can we also forget the role that has been played in this development by the deep fears generated by the continual expansion of the universe mapped out by modern science and modern cosmology: back in the seventeenth century, Pascal was already conscious of the anxiety caused by contemplating "the infinite immensity of spaces" being revealed by the new science, and, in what is one of the great expressions of the modern consciousness, he said: "The eternal silence of these infinite spaces frightens me." [41] And of course, far more frightening even than the universes of modern physics have been the perils of historical existence itself which has tended increasingly in the modern period to involve a kind of global insecurity unexperienced in previous times. But by [200] far the deepest cause of the despondency and the sense of alienation in modern literature is to be found in the collapse of any real certainty that what is Radically and Ultimately Significant is not absolutely secluded from that which is only provisionally significant in nature and in history. To the men of our age God seems, as Heidegger says, to be "withholding" Himself: He seems to be absent and perhaps even dead. And, as a consequence, our journey through the world does itself seem to be a terribly uncertain and perilous journey: as Stanley Hopper puts it, "the familiar trails to reality are swallowed up in thickets of confusion: the spoors are thickly overlaid," [42] and the artist's motion of recoil before this dark and threatening wood is but type and example of the deep mistrust with which

[41] Blaise Pascal, *Pensées* (New York: E. P. Dutton & Co., Everyman's Library, 1943), Fragment 206, p. 61.

[42] Stanley R. Hopper, "On the Naming of the Gods in Hölderlin and Rilke," in *Christianity and the Existentialists,* ed. Carl Michalson (New York: Charles Scribner's Sons, 1956), p. 156.

modern man faces today the indigence and privation of the world of finite, historical existence.

W. H. Auden tells us that Kafka bears to our own age the kind of relation that Dante bore to his, and a part of what he means is, I am certain, that, whereas the hero of Dante's poem is a pilgrim and the movement of the poem is "from low to high . . . [or] from dark to light," [43] the hero of the Kafkan fable, on the other hand, is a man who, at the end of his journeying, is no nearer the Castle than he was at the beginning and who remains forever quavering in the dungeon of his dereliction. In the one case, we have the Christian drama of rebirth and redemption, and, in the other case, we have a story of the soul's exclusion from the Courts of the Most High and of the despair by which it is overtaken in its abandonment and isolation—the story, in other words, that forms the characteristic judgment of the human condition that is rendered by the existentialist imagination in modern literature.

Ours is, then, an "extreme" literature which plunges us into "extreme" situations. Conrad's Decoud, Kafka's K., Gide's Lafcadio, Malraux's Kyo, Faulkner's Joe Christmas, and Penn Warren's Jeremiah Beaumont are all men who have been "thrown into a world without [their] willing it and with no place prepared for [them]." [44] Their life has to be lived at a great distance from whatever are the [201] sources of ultimate meaning, and, as a consequence, the salient stigmata of the modern hero are to be seen in his scepticism and in his despondency and alienation. But the miracle that occurs in the existentialist universe of a Conrad or a Kafka or a Malraux or a Faulkner is that, through the grace of some power that is unnamed and perhaps unknown, this scepticism and this despondency are prevented from so completely encircling the hero as to undo his humanity. Which is to say that the modern hero, in his great moments, has had what Professor Tillich calls "the courage of despair" —the courage, that is, despite everything that is problematic and uncertain in his world, to affirm his humanity. And since, despite all the nihilism that is in modern literature, this is a courage which is an expression of a kind of faith—faith itself, as Dr. Tillich says, being simply "the state of being grasped by the power of being-itself" [45]—

[43] Mark Van Doren, "The Divine Comedy," *The Noble Voice* (New York: Henry Holt and Co., 1946), p. 213.

[44] Albert Votaw, "The Literature of Extreme Situations," *Horizon,* Vol. XX, No 117 (September, 1949), p. 155.

[45] Paul Tillich, op. cit., p. 172.

it is not surprising, therefore, that the redefinition in our time of classical traditions of faith has often been deeply informed by this whole body of testimony. The Orthodox thinker Nicolas Berdyaev, the Roman Catholics Romano Guardini and Jacques Maritain, and the Protestant theologian Paul Tillich are representative of many other leading strategists of contemporary religious thought who have been alert to the fact that, if the high forms of faith are once again to be made to appear at least *possible* for us, their interpretation must itself be informed by the kind of awareness that comes from facing the distresses of life without any of the supports and consolations of religious faith. And so, in the attentiveness with which the religious community today is often listening to our poets and novelists and dramatists, we may discern some earnest of the reconstructive role that may yet be played by modern negation and denial.[202]

STANLEY COOPERMAN

Kafka's "A Country Doctor": Microcosm of Symbolism

The work of Franz Kafka has been a boon to three great interpretive movements: the socio-materialist, the theological-mystic, and the psychological-rationalist. For the first of these groups Kafka is simply another manifestation of the social rot leading to fascism; he is, indeed, part of the fascist mentality itself. E. B. Burgum, for example, went so far as to equate the decay of Kafka as an individual with the decay of pre-fascist German society, adding the rather unkind note that readers who enjoy Kafka are likely to do so in ratio to their own neurosis.

Theological criticism, on the other hand, evolves a perverse *Divine Comedy* from the work of Kafka—the existential search for salvation and grace of a fictionalized Kierkegaard manipulating his

SOURCE: ***University of Kansas City Review*, Vol. XXIV (Autumn 1957). Reprinted with the permission of the *University of Kansas City Review* and the author.**

own guilt of reconciliation with the absolute. Kafka's religious critics, in brief, fashion his work into the Sacred (and neo-traditional) Wound of Despair—purposelessness, sin, and awareness of the essential absurdity of existence. It is the theology of crisis, which by its acceptance of negation, at last is saved.

Psychological criticism all too often attempts to make of Kafka a simple case history, usually of Oedipus, and seems far closer to the clinical study of neurotic personality than to the appreciation of art. The Freudians are, as usual, the worst offenders in this respect. There is the usual incantation—page after page of A means B and C means D; this is phallic and that is female; and whole catalogues from the Freudian dogma. Such criticism not only falls prey to the genetic fallacy, but more serious, attempts to set up mechanical and objective definitions of symbols.

Although we may classify certain areas of fiction as "psychological," it is vital to remember that here art remains the chief goal of our understanding. Psychology, both for an author and his readers, may be used for art or absorbed into it; exclusive concentration on psychiatric theorizing will be disastrous. This is the error made by many critics who, in a great effort to be scientific, treat symbols as though they were chemicals, or constant and quantitative data. Symbolic art is intensely rewarding precisely because there can be no balance-sheet, no bookkeeping method of excerpt and "meaning." Symbols are more than psychiatric short-hand for "complexes." As Albert Camus points out, no matter how exactly we translate a symbol (or believe we do), only the artist himself can restore movement to it. "There is no word-for-word correspondence . . . a symbol always goes beyond him who would use it." We might add that a symbol goes beyond those who would explain or describe it.

An essential factor in successful [75] symbolic art, then, is multi-level meaning which cannot be detached entirely from the work itself. The richer and greater the symbolism, the more complex will be the reader's response on several levels, each of which may be justified. The value of a sensitive eclecticism becomes especially apparent in discussing the work of Franz Kafka. Like other masters of the symbolic, Kafka may be approached from several directions; there is no one approach, and those who read Kafka (and comment on him) in order to grind a particular philosophical ax, run the risk of losing the work itself.

An examination of one of Kafka's shorter pieces—"A Country

Doctor"—will demonstrate symbolic method in all its multiplicity. This story is only eight pages long, but it is rewarding from several standpoints. As a microcosm of Kafka's thematic basis and stylistic approach it is invaluable. It is immensely suggestive on the symbolic level, setting up repeated echoes in the mind. Psychologically the story is powerful and rich in possible interpretations. Finally, the technique is superb, showing Kafka at his best.

A familiar characteristic of modern fiction—the absence of traditional plot or story-telling development—is found in "A Country Doctor." There is no precise beginning, middle or end. The primary concern is with the significance of events rather than with the events themselves. Narration is interior and vertical rather than exterior and horizontal. The reader is plunged immediately into the situation, and must make his way out as best he can; there are, if anything, more unanswered questions at the finish than at the start.

Because both development and conflict are enormously compact—with great symbolic association—any attempt to paraphrase or summarize will be watery; the impact of the prose, as highly charged as poetry, is non-transferable. Try, for example, to tell the story of *Ulysses* and you will of course find there is nothing much to tell. Joyce, of course, was a literary virtuoso, but aside from his word-performance the material of his art is dynamic largely on the psychic and psychological levels.

The unimportance of plotting is basic to "A Country Doctor"; we cannot "tell" the story and communicate more than a superficial orientation. Roughly, this is what occurs: a doctor, about to answer a call from the country, finds that his horse had died, and sends his servant girl to obtain another. She fails, but a groom and two great horses appear mysteriously from an old pigsty. The horses seem satisfactory, but the groom begins making sexual advances to the girl.

The groom ignores the doctor's objections, and the horses begin traveling with amazing speed, bringing him to his patient's house almost immediately. He finds his patient—a young country boy—suffering from a horrible wound which he cannot cure. This is resented by the family and friends, who undress the doctor and place him in bed with the boy, hoping for a cure. Preoccupied with the thought of the servant girl being assaulted by the groom, the doctor dresses and starts back home. The horses, however, travel with [76] agonizing slowness, and the doctor fears his home and place have been usurped.

One must admit that in paraphrase, the story line of "A Country Doctor" is hardly impressive. Yet from this rather loose construction, Kafka gives us an art at once disturbing and subtle, meaningful and elusive—apparently simple yet technically sophisticated.

Like most of Kafka's work, the story unfolds within a single consciousness—a single point of view, which is, moreover, largely passive. The doctor (just as Joseph K. in "The Trial"), is a logical little man bickering talmudically with the externals appearing to manipulate his fate. These externals are irrational, irreversible and fantastic, but despite his indignant posturing, the doctor is aware both of the inevitability of the process and his own role in creating it. As Claude-Edmonde Magny points out, there is "the idea of responsibility antedating the action . . . together with the theme of nightmare, the helplessness before the predestined event—the theme of gratuitous catastrophe for which we are nevertheless responsible."

"A Country Doctor" starts with a direct plunge into a situation of anxiety, and from the very first, introduces and confirms an impression of nightmare. The droning sentence structure, acceptance of the obviously impossible, distortions of time and space—in short, the entire nature as well as the contents of narration seem a description or reactivation of dream. "What was it about?" we may imagine a psychiatrist asking. The answer is, in part, given below:

> I was in great perplexity; I had to start an urgent journey; a seriously ill patient was waiting for me in a village ten miles off; a thick blizzard of snow filled all the wide spaces between him and me; I had a gig, a light gig with big wheels, exactly right for our country roads; muffled in furs, my bag of instruments in my hand, I was in the courtyard all ready for the journey; but there was no horse to be had, no horse . . .

Here is the combination which is to grow more striking as the story progresses: the monotone, the simple declarative clauses, the repetition. Then, from a "year-long uninhabited pigsty" come the man—a groom—and two magnificent horses, "their bodies steaming thickly." This is, certainly, fantastic; yet the sudden arrivals are accepted by the doctor-narrator and Rose, the servant-girl. When the groom turns abruptly to Rose, the doctor makes only feeble objection, for the girl has had a "justified presentiment that her fate was inescapable." From this point, the dream-narrative intensifies:

> I could just hear the door of my house splitting and bursting as the groom charged at it, and then I was deafened and blinded by a storm-

ing rush that steadily buffeted all my senses. But this only for a moment, since, as if my patient's farmyard had opened out before my courtyard gate, I was already there; the horses had come quietly to a standstill, the blizzard had stopped, and moonlight was all around.

The final effect, again, of realism and logic within sur-realism and illogic cannot be reproduced outside the story itself. Passages such as "guests . . . were coming in, through the moonlight at the open door, walking on tip-toe, keeping balance with their outstretched arms," or sequences such as the stripping of the doctor, the treadmill drifting of the horses on his return, the culmination [77] of impotency and frozen horror, lead us into a world where recognizable objects have become distorted beyond endurance. We arrive, finally, at an anguished sense of wakening from a dream which has become our own.

"A Country Doctor," like most dream literature, is rooted firmly in symbolism—so firmly, indeed, that any certain dichotomy between the literal and the symbolic vanishes. It is necessary to accept a simple dream narrative as the literal level of "A Country Doctor," since only a dream can give it any literal meaning whatsoever. On this basis, symbolic associations move within a psychological landscape and may be interpreted psychoanalytically. We are introduced to a situation of anxiety and impotence—the demands of duty cannot be fulfilled by the doctor. Into this situation comes a potency figure—the groom—offering what seems to be a solution. Notice the symbolism of birth permeating the entire "pigsty" sequence (the darkness, the smell, the groom crawling out on all fours calling "Brother" and "Sister"). This culminates in the arrival of the horses, "their legs tucked close to their bodies, each well-shaped head lowered like a camel's, by sheer strength of buttocking squeezed out through the door hole which they filled entirely."

The groom, then, is an ambivalent figure; on the one hand, he aids the doctor by providing "Brother and Sister" and the means for fulfilling duty; on the other, he is a "brute" who subjects Rose to her "inescapable fate"—sexual violation. Rose, later called "the pretty girl who had lived in my home for years almost without my noticing her," is a mother figure, domesticity, the love-object, and "servant." In a sudden and terrible insight, the doctor becomes aware of the violation of this mother figure ("I could just hear the door of my house splitting and bursting as the groom charged at it").

At that moment time is destroyed, the doctor is plunged back into the timelessness of the unconscious, and he meets himself as a youth—the boy with a wound. Here the atmosphere is one of disgust: "The air was almost unbreathable; I wanted to push open a window." This is a phase which appears in many of Kafka's works.

At first this aspect of himself—this youth—seems well, but the doctor is uncomfortable in his diagnosis. The family—especially the father—oppresses him. The situation finally becomes one with obvious Oedipus overtones, as well as self-defense of potency: "In the narrow confines of the old man's mind I felt ill; that was my only reason for refusing the drink. The mother stood by the bedside and cajoled me toward it." On his second examination the doctor discovers the boy's wound, the Oedipus fixation ("a fine wound is all I brought into the world, that was my sole endowment"), and he succumbs to an intense feeling of guilt and failure. He is guilty of the rape of Rose because he has left her to the groom's lust. And he is also guilty—a failure—because he is unable to effect a cure.

The doctor feels completely isolated as the family and friends stare at him: "The family and the village elders stripped my clothes off me; a school choir with the teacher at [78] the head of it stood before the house." Religion cannot help him, his sin is too great ("the parson sits at home and unravels his vestments"). He must get back to Rose and combat the groom; he must escape from the family and the nightmare of religious sanctions ("O be joyful, all you patients . . ."). The result, however, is impotence. He cannot return, or compete with the lustful tyranny of the groom: "Like old men we crawled through the snowy wastes . . . in my house the disgusting groom is raging; Rose is his victim; I do not want to think about it any more . . . I cannot reach it." The doctor's narration ends on a note of complete impotency, and the dream stops.

This—a slice of dream life—is one of many possible psychological interpretations. However, it by no means limits the meanings of "A Country Doctor," since the story is rich in associations operating through, but beyond the literal dream level. From another standpoint, the story need not be considered in terms of psychology, but rather as a poetic evocation of the individual buffeted by chaos in an age where all outlines are blurred, and faith has turned to frost. The basic conflict, as in "The Trial," may be considered that of evil breaking suddenly into a rational, well-ordered life (perhaps a life which is over-regulated: "I was the district doctor and did my duty to the uttermost") and finally paralyzing it. The doctor is impotent when faced with the Sacred Wound—which, as Herbert

Tauber points out, is the "awakened consciousness of the shattered condition of life."

Viewed in this light, the story becomes a symbolic restatement of the classic existential situation. On the one hand, we have a respectable and adjusted life; on the other, the swift insight, the crisis erupting within the placidly flowing sequence of "duties" and prosaic tasks. "I could see no way out," the doctor cries, and his words are an echo of the philosophers of crisis from Kierkegaard to Sartre.

Suddenly, without warning, the dark, irrational and diabolic forces represented by the beast-groom and the great horses take command. They drive the doctor deeply and instantaneously face to face with the insoluble—the "fear and trembling"—the moment when reasons fail, when "the center will not hold," when nothing is left but the scarlet wound—the beautiful wound—of awareness.

Rose's rape by the dark force of the groom represents the smashing of all that is near, protecting, feminine. But the guilt is strongly the doctor's in this violation; he has failed to realize the true value of Rose ("the pretty girl who had lived in my house for years without my noticing her"); everyday life has become formulistic, conventional, devoid of passion or awareness. As a result of this failure, the doctor is incapable of coping with the crisis when it comes—again, like the other isolated heroes (or victims) of existential literature. His failure delivers him to the disgusting wound and the bitter cold.

Faced with the wound (which represents his own ruined state and so cannot be cured) the doctor is isolated, completely alone before a [79] suddenly meaningless and hostile universe. The traditional answers are gone; they can no longer serve ("the parson sits at home and unravels his vestments"). Although the secular self must be relied upon ("the doctor is supposed to be omnipotent"), it provides neither meaning nor answer ("old country doctor that I am"), and, when the usual prosaic days and nights are shattered ("bereft of my servant girl"), there is nothing but sterility, the empty shell of what once were solutions ("strip his clothes off; then he'll heal us . . . O be joyful all you patients").

The nightmare ending is the doctor's chaotic spiritual state after meeting the wound: a wasteland of panicked effort and treadmill motion, a vain attempt to prevent the inevitable crisis. He is caught, now, between "neither—nor" in a ruined secularism ("earthly vehicle"), driven by a desperate necessity for something beyond himself ("unearthly horses"). But it is too late; he is incapable of making the choice made by those who meet the Wound but who arrive finally at acceptance through faith. And so he rides through the snowy wastes, the nightmare storm, an absurd and anguished figure ("I cannot reach it") in a shattered world ("It cannot be made good, not ever").

The two interpretations I have presented concern the same work, and in addition rely to a great extent on the same symbols. But they are not mutually exclusive; in the symbolic art of Kafka two methods of criticism may, and indeed must, occupy the same space at the same time. Kafka is ambiguous and difficult, but his material—the stuff of the human soul—would be violated if he presented a single dimension of meaning. The work has many truths, a weaving and reweaving of many themes, and it cannot be approached bluntly or singlemindedly. We must synthesize, separate and reform with every method at our disposal, without sneering at one method or completely discounting another. This may involve considerable difficulty. It has often been pointed out, however, that in the art of reading fiction, as in the art of living, our satisfactions increase as we are willing to hazard our resources.[80]

RICHARD SCHECHNER

The Inner and the Outer Reality

Ionesco is the closest thing we have to an abstract expressionist in the theatre. His plays are plainly autobiographical and confessional. "I try to project on stage an inner drama (incomprehensible even to myself) telling myself, nevertheless, that since the microcosm is the image of the macrocosm, it may happen that this torn up, disarticulated inner world is in some way the mirror or the symbol of universal contradictions." He discovers the astonishing in the banal, the unreal in the real, the new in the old, the fresh in the stale, and

SOURCE: First published in the *Tulane Drama Review*, Vol. VII, No. 3 (Spring 1963). Reprinted with permission of the *Tulane Drama Review* and the author.

the archtype in the stereotype. His work is romantic and subjective, mirroring his own anguish and inner struggles, translating them into symbols and patterns that have been empathetically embraced by audiences throughout the world. But this empathy should not confuse us. Ionesco's vision is private—as private as De Kooning's or Pollack's—and our warm response to it is not due to the fact that Ionesco has been watching us carefully; the truth is rather that our obsessions resemble his: the artist precedes his work into existence. Like Kafka's, Ionesco's most personal insights are public coin, at least for this moment in history.

But what is the exact relationship between the microcosm and the macrocosm, the inner and outer worlds, and what exactly are the universal contradictions? In the most simple terms the outer world is the setting and the inner world the action of Ionesco's plays. The heroes—Jack, Amédée, Choubert, Bérenger—are forced to undergo an action within a setting, and these two are never in harmony with each other. This is the most striking contradiction in Ionesco's work, one which is theatrical and visual as [187] well as dramatic and literary. The roots of his comedy (the angry humor of tragedy, as Peter Selz says) are set firmly in this dialectic. The corpse is growing in Amédée's *apartment;* the Pupil is murdered in the Professor's *study.* Both the corpse and the murder are bold externalizations of the inner reality—visualizations of the underlying anguish inherent in the human condition as Ionesco sees it. But the apartment and the study are there also; the banal setting silently affirms the existence of the external reality. The greater the gap between the action and the setting the more violent and comic the effect. Ionesco's comedy, we must not forget, is very primitive, springing from the chthonic, sado-masochistic sources of laughter itself. The hilarity of the first scene of *Jack,* for example, is an expression of the tension wrought from the triple disparity between the setting (bourgeois domesticity), the tone of voice (sentimental family love), and the action (sado-masochistic cruelty).

> MOTHER JACK: It was I, my son, who gave you your first spankings, not your father, standing here, who could have done it better than I, for he is stronger, no, it was I, for I loved you too much . . . Oh, ungrateful son, you do not even remember how I held you on my knees and pulled out your cute little baby teeth, and tore off your toenails so as to make you bawl like an adorable little calf.

This unresolved triple dialectic of setting, tone, and action persists even in the more "rational" Bérenger plays. The Killer is loose in the Radiant City, the rhinoceroses plague a small, provincial town in southern France, Bérenger takes a stroll in mid-air while the English town-folk chatter with their children. It is this coexistence of banal setting and outrageous action that makes us feel that Ionesco's world is our own. We live in an age where nuclear annihilation is a fine casual topic during a coffee break. Ionesco's settings are always "real" and, as in Kafka, each detail of the nightmare is "realistically" documented. The form—the virtual shape—of reality is left untouched, as are the tiniest details; it is in the middle ground—the vast range between minutiae and pattern—that Ionesco dislocates and disarticulates. It is the inclusion of phrases like "pulled out" and "tore off" in Mother Jack's speech that is disturbing—giving us a glimpse of what underlies her "love"—eliciting laughter and anguish at the same time.[188]

Ionesco uses this same device in his treatment of language where, for the most part, he leaves the word and sentence intact, while tampering with the choice and order of words within a sentence. A character in *The Bald Soprano* can say "I'd rather lay an egg than steal a cow" (*"J'aime mieux pondre un oeuf que voler un boeuf"*), and it will almost slip by our ears before we realize that it is complete nonsense. It looks and sounds like a sentence; its rhyme scheme disguises it as a proverb; it has all the grammatical necessities of a sentence. But it lacks the *intention* of a sentence.[1] In plays like *The Lesson* or *The Maid to Marry* this same device is amplified. Instead of tampering with the sentence, Ionesco vitiates entire sentences, thereby destroying the intention of paragraphs or even larger units.

PROFESSOR: That which distinguishes the neo-Spanish languages and their idioms from other linguistic groups, such as the group of languages called Austrian and neo-Austrian or Hapsburgian, as well as the Es-

[1] Sartre throws a strong light on this in *Being and Nothingness.* "It is within the sentence, in fact, that the word can receive a real function as a designation; outside of the sentence the word is just a propositional function . . . Entire sentences, commonplaces, do not, any more than words, preexist the use which is made of them . . . To understand the word in the light of the sentence is *very exactly* to understand any given whatsoever in terms of the situation and to understand the situation in the light of the original ends . . . In order for words to enter into relations with one another, in order for them to latch on to one another or repulse one another, it is necessary that they be united in a synthesis which does not come from them. Suppress this synthetic unity and the block which is called speech disintegrates; each word returns to its solitude and at the same time loses its unity, being parcelled out among various incommunicable meanings."

> peranto, Helvetian, Monacan, Swiss, Andorran, Basque, and jai alai groups, and also the groups of diplomatic and technical languages—that which distinguishes them, I repeat, is their striking resemblance which makes it so hard to distinguish them from each other. I'm speaking of the neo-Spanish languages which one is able to distinguish from each other, however, only thanks to their distinctive characteristics, absolutely indisputable proofs of their extraordinary resemblance, which renders indisputable their common origin, and which, at the same time, differentiates them profoundly—through the continuation of the distinctive traits which I've just cited.

This speech sounds erudite and yet it is hard to understand and murderous to memorize (ask any actor who has played the role).[189] It is impossible to *grasp* the Professor's idea; the speech as a whole is elusive and vaporous. The trick is simple. While preserving all the grammatical rules and using a scholarly vocabulary and tone, the speech pivots around a central contradiction: "That which distinguishes them, I repeat, is their striking resemblance which makes it so hard to distinguish them from each other." The Professor—and through him, language—is but another example of the universal contradictions; and the dialectic created between his scholarly, heavy tone and the weightlessness of what he says—its pivotal nonsense—is analogous to Mother Jack's opening speeches or the situation in which Amédée finds himself. Naturally I am citing only several examples of what saturates each play. Whereever we look in Ionesco's work—language, setting, characterization, action—we discover the same pattern of coexistent opposites; each dialectical pair adds texture to the whole scheme; we are thrown back and forth between irresolvable opposites, and we are trapped in this world of unresolved contradictions much in the same way as we are trapped among Genet's infinitely faceted characters.

To carry this point still further, the very ordinary appearances of Ionesco's heroes are contradicted by the nature of their acts. The timid Professor murders his pupil; Jack, the "poetic" and rebellious son, can hardly speak an intelligible sentence; hermetic Amédée floats away into the wide sky; irresponsible Bérenger defies the herd. It is as if, at last, the inner life of these characters forced its way to the surface, thrusting through the crust of banality. At this moment of "realization" (and the actor would do well to remember this), their very appearance changes and they look like what they are. The Professor stands taller, his voice deepens and he becomes more authoritative; Jack goes down on all fours, mumbling the single word "cat"; weak and immobile Amédée lugs the corpse outside; Choubert is reduced to a tortured infant; Bérenger accepts the skin of a man. After this "realization" only the setting remains to remind us of the outer reality.

What Ionesco gives us is an intricate pattern of contradictions, one transcending the next; but whatever dialectical pair is dominant at the moment, the unbearable tension between opposites remains constant—there is at least one contradiction between the [190] inner and the outer reality operating at all times in each of his plays. It is this dialectical tension which replaces plot. At each moment we are gripped by the dialectic, while at the same time the play moves forward rhythmatically, thrusting itself onward in a series of ever intensifying and tightening circular patterns or figures until a climactic, paroxysmal instant is achieved. Then the knot relaxes, the spasm is over, silence wins, and the curtain falls. But we must learn to watch his plays (particularly his work before the Bérenger plays) as the Greeks, we are told, watched dance. We must pay attention not only to the moment, the beat, but also to the completed figure—the trajectory traced by the rhythm. It is a difficult task, perhaps too difficult for our theatre and its audience, but we are asked to grasp the play as a *completed form*, as an action which is over, as an action in repose. If we will do this the contradictions will become more obvious and they will each fall into their own pattern, tracing their own musical line through the play.

The Bald Soprano as well as *The Lesson:* . . . abstract theatre, non-personality theatre . . . Thus to make the characters not characters. All intrigue, all particular action is stripped of interest. It is merely accessory. Everything is channelled into a dramatic tension . . . One must liberate the dramatic tension without the help of any real plot or particular goal. Everything will point to the revelation of something monstrous—it must be because theatre is, finally, the revelation of the monstrous, or of states of monstrosity, without characters or with the monstrous characters that we find within ourselves. To come to that exaltation or those revelations without the justification of motivation . . . Progression of a passion without object . . . Abstract theatre. Pure dream . . . Under a burlesque text, a dramatic motion. Under a dramatic text, a burlesque motion.

This selection from Ionesco's working notes (April, 1951) is an accurate statement of both his intention and achievement in his early work. It means simply that his plays are incremental without being culminant; the final moments may be more intense but they are not more important in terms of the completed figure than the early moments. In *The Lesson,* for example, the final "scalp dance" between the Professor and Pupil would be pointlessly shocking if it were not for the several analogous dances between them which precede the rape-murder. The little game they play [191] over taking seats, the more formal game of addition, the arguments they have over subtraction, the impasse they reach with multiplication, all cut the same pattern as the final dance. The earlier moments do not "prepare" us for the ultimate dance; they are early symphonic motifs which will finally be consummated and musically resolved in the rape-murder. The tension and contradictions so blatant at the end are subtly present at the beginning; there is no "development," but there is orchestration: variations on a theme, amplification, and then modal resolution.

To return now once again to Ionesco's characters. The gap between the inner and outer reality—that gap which informs Ionesco's entire technique—lays bare the alienation of his heroes from themselves and from the world. The Ionesco hero can neither reach and understand himself nor grasp the things of the world. Yet these things—his apartment, his wife, his coffee cups, his tables and chairs—are *his;* they are his only connection to the flow of life, to the abundance of life, and as the hero becomes conscious of his separation from these things he tries ever more desperately to unite himself to what is his. The Smiths and the Martins argue vehemently with each other over nonsense—then they rush across the stage looking for something—their own identities; the New Tenant tries to find peace and security amid his household furnishings; Madeleine, in *Victims of Duty,* fills the stage with numberless coffee cups while her husband Choubert is being tortured by the Detective. But each attempt at locating the self within things fails, and the characters can only try harder the next time. This next attempt is paced at an increased tempo, and the next still more rapidly, and so on, until the play reaches its climactic moment of realization and frustration. As Ionesco's heroes try to relate to the world around them they lose contact not only with that world, but also with themselves. Their very existence—or more exactly, the felt conviction that they exist—is threatened, and even the simple processes of life become dangerous. They substitute speed for substance, activity for act. The climax of this increasingly rapid acceleration which forms the penultimate moment in so many of Ionesco's plays reflects the utter inability of its heroes to resolve the living dialectic between the emptiness they *are* and the fullness which the world presents [192] teasingly to them. In the ecstatic paroxysm both the inner and the outer realities break apart, the multi-colored dome of their lives shatters, revealing the dark radiance and silence of nothingness. At this point only the memory of pure whirling motion remains—activity without substance, activity without reality—and the rest is fragmentary, chaotic, useless.

This alienation can best be understood if we adopt a term from existential psychoanalysis—ontological insecurity. According to R. D. Laing, who has explored this notion with brilliance and clarity,[2] the ontologically insecure person experiences the world in totally different terms than does "the individual whose sense of self is securely established in its health and validity. Relatedness to other persons will be seen to have a radically different significance and function . . . In the individual whose being is secure in this primary existential sense, relatedness with others is potentially gratifying; whereas the ontologically insecure person is preoccupied with preserving rather than gratifying himself; the ordinary circumstances of living threaten his low threshold of security." We have only to remember the Professor at the beginning of *The Lesson* or Amédée's encounter with the Postman to understand how well Laing's description fits Ionesco's characters. The ontologically insecure person "may lack the experience of his own temporal continuity. He may not possess an overriding sense of personal consistency or cohesiveness. He may feel more insubstantial than substantial, and unable to assume that the stuff he is made of is genuine, good, and valuable. And he may feel his self as partially divorced from his body." Ionesco puts the same experience in only slightly different words. "We are astounded to discover that we exist in this world that appears illusory, fictitious—where human behavior reveals its absurdity, and all history its absolute uselessness; all reality, all language seems to become disjointed, to fall apart, to empty itself of meaning so that, since all is devoid of importance, what else can one do but laugh at it?" Needless to say, this laughter expresses anguish, not joy.

During the early years of his public career as a playwright [193] (1950–1953), Ionesco felt most uneasy in the world. "I have never

[2] Ontological Insecurity," in *Psychoanalysis and Existential Philosophy,* a selection of essays edited by Hendrik M. Ruitenbeek.

succeeded in becoming completely used to existence, neither to that of the world, nor to that of others, nor above all to my own." The world itself seemed threatening, and it was in turn threatened. "Words are only noise stripped of all meaning. These houses, the sky, are only facades of nothingness; people seem to move automatically, without any reason; everything seems to evaporate, everything is threatened, including myself, by an imminent, silent sinking into I know not what abyss." The Ionesco hero, like Laing's patient, "feels that like a vaccum he is empty, but this emptiness is him." The nothingness which Ionesco's characters *are* may, at any time, annihilate the world of things by annihilating the consciousness which conceives this world. The noisy plays, the full stages, always stand on the brink of silence and emptiness. Remember that fine theatrical moment in *The Chairs* immediately after the suicide of the old couple when we realize that we have been fooled, that these chairs are not full, but utterly empty. Writing to Sylvain Dhomme, the first director of *The Chairs,* Ionesco made his intent clear. "The theme of the play is nothingness." At the moment of annihilation—the paroxysm, the climax, the point at which the intolerable tension between the inner and the outer reality can no longer be borne—the string snaps, both the inside and the outside disappear, and everything hurtles down the "black hole," so vividly named by the Old Woman in *The Chairs.* (Note how at the end of *The Future is in Eggs* the stage collapses and the characters "all unwittingly gently sink and disappear without interrupting their actions." Note also Ionesco's original plan for the end of *The Bald Soprano.* "In the first version the stage remained empty until the spectators began to rise from their seats. Then the director of the company came on stage with a machine gun and killed everyone.") The world is neither permanent nor substantial; the most routine processes are not to be depended on. The question debated with such vigor in *The Bald Soprano* is a real and indicative one: Is there someone at the door when the bell rings? [194]

. . . . .

What is the source of the *insolite* [3] world of the early plays? Ionesco tells us that as a young boy he lived near the Place de

[3] *Insolite* is one of Ionesco's favorite words; it is difficult to translate. An *insolite* world is one in which anything may happen, without cause, at any time; it is a world of simultaneously hilarious and horrendous caprice. The *insolite* lurks in the most everyday experiences; it surprises us, sometimes com-

Vaugirard, a working-class section of Paris, crowded with traffic.[195] One late fall evening—the street was already darkening—while walking home with his mother, a sudden fear gripped him. He took hold of his mother's hand. "On the sidewalks dark silhouettes were moving, people hurrying past—hallucinatory, phantom-like shadows." The memory of that evening's walk home haunted Ionesco obsessively, and each time he recalled it one question came to his mind: How many of those people were still alive? (We are reminded of the beginning of the final scene in *The Killer*, where the stage at first is crowded with traffic; and then, "as though by magic the trucks move back, the whole set at the back of the stage is movable, and so comes apart . . . Bérenger is now quite alone on stage . . . It is up to the director, the designer, and the electrician to bring out Bérenger's utter loneliness, the emptiness around him, and the deserted avenue somewhere between town and country." Quite literally, the great oppressive crowd "evaporates," leaving Bérenger even more oppressively alone to face the dwarf Killer.) Later, when Ionesco returned to his native Rumania at the age of fourteen, he remembers watching a young man pummel an old man into unconsciousness. This incident fused with his earlier memory of the Place de Vaugirard, and together they form the key image of Ionesco's first world view, one which informs his work through *The Chairs*, and in a slightly modified aspect, in *Amédée* and *The Killer*. "I have no images of the world aside from those expressing evanescence and hardness, vanity and anger, nothingness or hideous, useless hatred . . . Everything has tended to confirm what I had seen, what I had understood in my childhood: vain and sordid fury, sudden shrieks stifled by silence, shadows swallowed forever in the night." It is difficult, of course, to estimate the impact of the childhood experience on his mature mind. Were these truly obsessive, unpurged memories, or were they convenient metaphors firmly lodged in Ionesco's mind waiting for the call, ample and already formed symbols for the isolation and despair he felt between 1948 and 1956? It is impossible to resolve this question. But

---

ically, sometimes tragically, sometimes in both ways at once. The Professor's rape-murder of the Pupil is *insolite,* as is Mrs. Martin's description of a man tying his shoelace. But the *insolite* is not limited to phenomena—it pervades the entire structure of the plays. The sudden changes in character, the electric introduction of startling images, and the violent wrenches in the course of the action—these are all *insolite*. In short, the *insolite* is an attitude, a way of looking at the world.

whichever point of view we take, this tension between evanescence and presence—between the over-full and the utterly empty—forms the core of his early work. In this respect we must remember that Ionesco sees language—words—as fully [196] analogous to things. A stage full of empty yet "heavy" (tangible) noise is certainly *full,* in the literal sense of the word. The shouting of the Martins and the Smiths, the Jacks and the Roberts is in no way different than Madeleine's coffee cups, the New Tenant's furniture, or Roberta's eggs. In fact, words and things are both full and empty at the same time. They "fill" space and time, and yet they signify nothingness, they represent an emptiness. The coexistence of overabundance and utter emptiness is perhaps most perfectly achieved in *The Chairs.* The chairs themselves are heavy and full. (Recall that Ionesco has the Old Man knock over the chair with the Invisible Lady in it. The effort he and the Old Woman spend on lifting the chair and its occupant is tremendous. The struggle is very effective theatre.) And yet the stage is empty and the guests are phantoms. Finally, immediately before the old couple jump to their deaths, they are separated from each other by the invisible crowd. At this very touching moment we can fully understand what Ionesco means by a *vide encombrant,* a "bulky emptiness."

OLD MAN: O my faithful helpmate! . . . you who have believed in me, unfailingly, during a whole century, and who have never left me, never . . . alas, today, at this supreme moment, the crowd pitilessly separates us . . .

> Above all I had hoped
> that together we might lie
> with all our bones together
> within the selfsame skin
> within the same sepulchre
> and that the same worms
> might share our old flesh
> that we might rot together . . .

But this, the culminating wish of a lifetime, is denied them—the "crowd" keeps them apart, and when they jump they "fall far from each other," and their separate corpses "rot in aquatic solitude." It is not until they have jumped that we realize that we have been fooled. The play is so cunningly written that we enter into the joint fantasy of the old couple and believe with them in the reality of the guests. Ionesco's trick in *The Chairs* is one of the finest theatrical strokes of our day. His achievement here is underlined by the utter sense of despair and loneliness we feel [197] after the old couple commit suicide. In *The Chairs* Ionesco shows us just how completely "nothingness" can fill a stage and our minds. When he takes away the consciousness that created the nothingness (that joint illusion of the old couple) *we* are thrown into the *trou noire* (black hole) that engulfs the Old Man and Old Woman, the same *trou noire* that the Old Woman spoke of during the play's first moments. "If the theme of *The Chairs* is ontological emptiness or absence," Ionesco wrote in 1952 before the play had been produced, "it is, I think, the expression of this absence which must constitute the last definitive moment of the play . . . At this moment the audience will have under their eyes, in a light once again pallid, as at the beginning of the play, the empty chairs in an empty set ornamented by streamers, full of useless confetti, which will leave them with a sadness like that of an empty ballroom after the ball . . . It is this ending I had in mind when I wrote the play, and it was for this ending that I wrote it, an ending that I saw was like the beginning." As J. S. Doubrovsky has pointed out in his remarkable essay on Ionesco [4] the "eternal return"—the end repeating the beginning, the reappearance of characters, a structure which marks *The Bald Soprano, The Lesson,* and *The Chairs*—is the denial of self and substance, and not, as is so often believed, the assertion of a "life force," or any such thing. Doubrovsky: "The comedy of proliferation on the level of things, is complementary to the comedy of circularity on the human level. The chairs in *The Chairs,* the cups in *Victims of Duty,* the pieces of furniture in *The New Tenant,* or the eggs in *The Future is in Eggs* are multiplied until they crowd and choke the stage, the corpse and mushrooms in *Amédée* keep growing until there is no more room for the characters . . . The eternal return is not an eternal assertion of the self, as it was for Nietzsche, but its perpetual negation. Moreover, to man's absence corresponds the all-pervading presence of things. In the same way as Sartre's Rouquentin experienced nausea in front of a pebble or a root, the spectator experiences the essential emptiness of man before the monstrous kingdom of objects." But the dialectic is not as simple as this. As I have indicated, "fulness" and "emptiness" [198] are not inherent in either man or things or words; at any moment a "full" room can become empty, as at the end of *The*

[4] "Ionesco and the Comedy of Absurdity," *Yale French Studies,* No. 23 (Summer, 1959).

New Tenant when the lights are turned out, or at the end of *The Chairs* when we realize that these countless chairs are unoccupied —mere echoes of the abundant life that plunged out the window. But we get caught in a whirlpool—for that "full life," which is rotting now in the sea, was at the same time a completely "empty" life, a life of total illusion, a life of solitude spent fruitlessly in a lighthouse absolutely separated from all humanity. Sartre talks about Genet's "whirligig" effect with characters. A similar whirligig in Ionesco's theatre dizzily spins us from the full to the empty.

This dizziness is Ionesco's unique specialty, the incarnation of the sense of the *insolite*—the shocking, surprising, and (comically) astounding nature of existence itself; an existence which carries intolerable contradictions in its very heart, just as in Sartre's terms, this same nothingness lies coiled in the heart of being. Ionesco has described for us his state of mind during the early fifties. "For me existence seems unimaginable; but on the inside of existence anything is conceivable. No personal frontier can separate for me the real from the unreal, the true from the false; I have no criterion, no preferences. I feel that I am there at the outermost limit of being, a stranger to the historical development, not at all 'in it,' dazed, immobilized in that primordial stupefaction. All doors are closed to me or perhaps they have all disappeared, as have all walls and all distinctions." These remarks were written in 1953, before Ionesco achieved any measurable success, and they reflect his professional frustrations as well as his deep felt convictions. This notion of the *insolite* runs through all his early work. His characters, like the Pupil in *The Lesson,* come to understand what the Professor means when he says, "As you will learn, one must be ready for anything." The unexpected is the hallmark of this early work. Even the sight of a man tying his shoelace can excite Mrs. Martin. The slightest crack in her banal existence threatens Ionesco's characters—but this crack occurs within them: his characters are always being threatened by extinction from the inside. It is in this light that we must understand the clichés of *The Bald Soprano, Jack,* or *The Future is in Eggs.* When existence itself is threatened, all that's left is existence's empty shell—fossilized language, for [199] example. Character after character seeks substantive reality within the *forms* of reality—notably language—but, unhappily, all meaning has been drained from these very forms; they are no longer "real," they cannot protect man from the onslaught of the universal contradictions.

This much is certain: the world had overwhelmed, violated, and shocked Ionesco; and his first and most intense period of creation represents his counterattack. These early plays all reflect an unwillingness to yield to the human condition, whatever it may be. The deep vein of anti-tyranny which runs through these plays—remember Jack's rebellion, the Pupil's resistance to the Professor, the scathing satire of *The Leader*—is a reaction against both political and metaphysical oppression. (*The Killer* isolates the metaphysical oppression and *Rhinoceros* the political oppression. Mother Peep's geese—episodic figures in *The Killer*—metamorphose into the rhinoceroses of the later play.) In the early plays the great oppressor is not man, but God—that God who made man what he is, helpless against supra-personal forces, even if these forces, like social conformity or language, seem to be of his own making. Only "seem to be," because Ionesco sees conformity and fossilized formulas as *independent* and *inherent* factors in man's existence.

But despite the doom of frustration, despair, or death which overtakes the characters of these early plays, the plays themselves—as total, poetic assertions—are insolent and rebellious. Striking out in the darkness against metaphysical tyranny, these plays laugh at those forces which have thrust man down into the black pit. This laughter may be ineffective, but it is consoling—a mockery aimed at the original Mocker. I have noted that the eternal return is a denial of the self, of the individual human being; this is certainly true in terms of the characters; and yet at the same time the creative spirit persists in terms of the plays as completed figures. In short, the plays are more than the sum of their parts. There is none of the elegaic surrender of Beckett in Ionesco's early work. (We have this only at the end of *The Chairs* and, later, during that strange and moving soliloquy at the end of *The Killer*.) The characters are uneasy within a world which they find *insolite*, and the plays themselves are *insolite* within our world, *the* world.[200] There is a shocking impertinence to the early plays. The Pupil finds death, the Martins discover that they are married, the old couple in *The Chairs* are able to maintain a "full life" throughout a century of isolation Only in *Jack* and *The Future is in Eggs* is humanity, finally, completely crushed and returned to its animal sources. In *Jack* the comedy is indeed despairing, and the ending is meant to "produce in the audience a feeling of embarrassment, awkwardness, and shame." The characters can no longer speak. "We hear only their moans, their sighs, then all fades away, all is extinguished. Again, a gray light comes on. All the characters have disappeared, except Roberta, who is lying down, or rather squatting down, buried beneath her gown. We see only her pale face, with its three noses quivering, and her nine fingers moving like snakes."

Underneath the noise, shock, and furor there is, as Jean Vannier points out, the silence of an empty world. After their horrendous climaxes these plays pause in utterly naked silence: the long moment before the Orator "speaks"; the empty stage before the next pupil rings the bell; the dark stage before the lights come up again on the suburban English home of the Smiths (or Martins as was the case after the hundredth performance); the eery half-light and moans of Roberta; the pantomimic collapse of the stage in *The Future is in Eggs.* The contradictions are there in the confrontation between the noise and the silence, in the full and empty stage, in the characters we *see* but know are only vacuums, absences.

Everyone and everything goes through the same ritual of denial, silence, and death. There is no "me" but an endless stream of Martins, Smiths, Pupils, Jacks. The charge of meaninglessness has been brought against these early plays, and with good reason. They are intentionally "meaningless." They exist on the frontier, as Ionesco sees it, where man's consciousness confronts his inability to order, pattern, and understand the universe. At this point, and at this distinct moment, man can no longer structure chaos and assimilate it into his experience. Everything evokes its own contradiction, but without the reassuring promise of a forthcoming synthesis.

Life on this frontier is extremely precarious and dangerous. It is [201] here that man realizes that the meaning of the universe inheres in himself; if the world of experience is to make any sense he must first understand himself. This understanding of self, in its turn, rests on the answer to that most basic of existential questions: Who am I? Once the individual can satisfactorily answer that question, finding in the answer an integral sense of selfhood, the chaotic universe will again take a meaningful shape. Who am I? is the central question of Ionesco's dramaturgy. It is most exhaustively explored in *Victims of Duty,* the play which begins Ionesco's middle period. Of course, the theme of identity runs through every play, but it is in *Victims* not merely a means but the very goal of the play. Ontological insecurity is the realization by the individual that he does not know who he is and, lacking this central firm sense of identity, the world around him crumbles, becomes *insolite,* and his relationship with others is only a means of survival, not gratification. The frantic search undertaken by the characters at the end of *The Bald Soprano*—"It's not there, it's here!"—is the search for self. They find nothing, and the play explodes. It would be possible to go back through all the early work and trace this axial theme in each of the plays. In every case the characters fail to find themselves (with the exception of the old couple in *The Chairs;* indeed they know who they are, but this knowledge is patently false, built on a life-long illusion). Ionesco felt he was working out a new concept of character, one based on the assertions of Stephane Lupasco in his book, *Logique et Contradiction.* "Identity cannot be—as was thought for a long time—something static. It is a dynamism, and a dynamism contradictory to the dynamism of diversity, which is better described as diversification, just as identity is better defined as identification." This is the creed Nicolas d'Eu puts forth in *Victims.* "We'll get rid of the principle of identity and unity of character and let movement and dynamic psychology take its place. We are not ourselves. Personality doesn't exist. Within us there are only forces that are either contradictory or not contradictory." Such a view of character carried Ionesco through *The Chairs.*[202]

. . . . .

PHILIP RAHV

The Legend of the Grand Inquisitor

Until recently Dostoevsky's western interpreters were open to the reproach of making far too little of his Legend of the Grand Inquisitor. The same, however, can hardly be said of his Russian critics, who repeatedly stressed its significance long before the onset of totalitarianism in our time brought on the widespread recognition, if not of the Legend's actual content and meaning, then surely of its close relevance to modern historical experience.

The late Nicolas Berdyaev, writing from a philosophical standpoint, maintained that in the Legend Dostoevsky reached the sum-

SOURCE: *Partisan Review,* Vol. XXI, No. 3. Reprinted with the permission of the author.

mit of his creation; and some five decades ago V. V. Rozanov, whose insight into Dostoevsky is unsurpassed among Russian commentators, declared it to be of exceptional profundity as a revelation of the structure of human destiny—"terrifying unbelief and the deepest and most ecstatic faith are inconceivably mingled in it." There is some evidence, too, that its author himself thought of it in such terms. In 1902 one witness (V. F. Putzikovitch) published an account of a conversation he had had with the novelist in the summer of 1879, while *The Brothers Karamazov* was still running serially in the *Russky Vestnik*, in which he speaks of the chapter on the Grand Inquisitor as the "culminating point" of his creative career; and when questioned as to his reasons for interpolating a devised legend of sixteenth-century Spain into a narrative of contemporary Russia, his reply was that its theme had haunted him since early youth and for fear that he might not live to complete another major work he had resolved to try his hand at it without delay and incorporate it in the novel he was then engaged in writing.

One need not agree with Berdyaev that the Legend of the Grand [249] Inquisitor represents the summit of Dostoevsky's creation in order to make out that as an excursus on the theme of man's historical fate, its terror, despair and absurdity, it is nearly without equal in world literature. It enriches the ideological content of the novel in which it is embedded, enabling us to understand more fully the far-ranging implications of Ivan Karamazov's "rebellion," but it is even more meaningful in terms of Dostoevsky's development as a whole; and the figure of the Grand Inquisitor is dramatically compelling enough to stay permanently in our minds as a symbolic character-image of the dialectic of power. Moreover, the Legend lends itself to analysis, quite apart from its local narrative setting, as a unique essay in the philosophy of history. Deceptively easy on the surface, it is at bottom one of the most difficult texts in the Dostoevskyean canon. By the same token, however, it is also one of the most rewarding. And the difficulty is not in its dramatic form but in the complexity of the ideas, their immense suggestiveness and scope, and the dissonances of belief and emotional discords that sound in them.

But the dramatic form is indispensable to Dostoevsky. That he would have been capable of making substantially the same statement without recourse to the dramatized consciousness of a fictional character is extremely doubtful. For the truth is that this most daring of novelists is apt to decline abruptly to lower levels of performance whenever he puts himself in the position of addressing the reader directly—a stance that rarely suits him, as is shown by the inferior quality of most of the articles included in his *Diary of a Writer*. Now a disjunction of this sort would scarcely surprise us in a novelist deficient in intellectual force and stamina. In Dostoevsky's case, however, the felt disjunction between the qualities of his direct discourse and those emerging through the sustained imaginative projection of his fiction is due, I think, to the fact that when writing in the first person—out in the open so to speak—he at once loses the advantages of complicity. For it is complicity above all which is the secret of his creative triumph over the propagandist in himself. It arises in the process of his identification as novelist with his characters, but it is necessary to distinguish between its genesis and the larger uses to which he puts it. It saves him from the one-sidedness, the fanaticism of commitment, and the casuistry to which as an embattled reactionary ideologue he was all too prone. There is an ambiguity of feeling [250] and attitude in him, a tension between sympathies and antipathies, finding its release in this complicity. He fully depends on it in the creation of his characters; and the few from whom he withholds it are reduced to stereotypes, as, for example, Grushenka's Polish suitor and the student-radical Rakitin in *The Brothers Karamazov*. Creatures of their author's political malice, they fall below the level of the world into which he injects them.

Ivan, on the other hand, it has frequently been observed, is the figure in the novel to whom as author he most readily gives himself in the process of identification.[1] This must be taken into account in examining the Legend recounted by Ivan to his brother Alyosha in the course of that prolonged dialogue which is perhaps the most audacious and masterful in the whole of Dostoevsky. Ivan calls the Legend "a poem in prose" that he had not written down but simply made up, as he says, and he tells it to Alyosha in order to support, in a manner at once dramatic and metaphysically provocative, his denial not so much of God as of His creation. The denial consists of a relentless scrutiny of man in general, and particularly Christian

[1] My impression is that the identification is more on the intellectual plane than on that of intimate subjectivity. But of course in Dostoevsky ideas are never divorced from feeling; in his critical statements he was wont to link them by inventing such new-fangled terms as "idea-forces" and "idea-feelings." In her memoirs Aimée Dostoevsky recalls the family tradition that her father, in looking back to his youth, "portrayed himself in the person of Ivan."

man, in the light of what he has made of history and history has made of him.

In his assault on God and the traditional faith Ivan proceeds in a way that transcends the rationalistic argumentation of the old-time atheists. For him it can no longer be a question of attempting to disprove God's existence logically. Ivan is not one to permit his intellectual faculties to linger in the modes of the past. He has made the essentially modern leap from the static framework of analytic thinking to thinking in terms of the historical process. But his leap is made in the typical Russian fashion of that epoch. That is to say, it lands him not in the somewhat placid "historicism" then prevailing in the consciousness of the West but in the eschatological frame of mind common to the Russian intelligentsia of the latter part of the past century. For whatever their outlook, whether revolutionary or not, inclined to nihilism or given to apocalyptic visions, in the main those people tended to see history as verging toward the ultimate and bringing forth a final solution compounded either of pure good [251] or pure evil. "The orientation toward the end," as Berdyaev calls it, mastered the most sensitive spirits among them, some predicting the approach of anti-Christ and others fervently awaiting the imminent erection of the City of Man; and in the intensity of their longing for an incontrovertible decision they transform the historical realm into the realm of prophecy and revelation. This is the mood that Ivan's "rebellion" exemplifies to perfection.

His version of atheism is all the more forceful in that it allows for God's existence, if need be, but not for the justifications of His world as revealed progressively *in* and *through* history. Ivan proclaims that no restitution is possible: that the ultimate harmony or reconciliation in the fullness of time could never expiate the suffering of even a single innocent child, let alone efface the innumerable horrors of injustice which humanity has endured through the ages. Hence he refuses God's creation ("returns his entrance ticket") thus proclaiming the right of indifference to the issue of His existence.

Nor does Ivan dispute the ideality and supreme goodness of Christian teaching. On the contrary, it is this very ideality and goodness that he turns into the motive of his dissent from it when he depicts the Grand Inquisitor upbraiding Christ for thinking much too highly of man in endeavoring to augment his freedom of choice between good and evil instead of heeding the counsel of the wise and dread spirit of the wilderness to strip man of his freedom so that he might at long last live in peace and brutish happiness. God, confronted by the radical proofs of the meanness of His world, the senseless suffering prevailing in it and man's congenital inability to enter the promised spiritual kingdom, is disposed of through His works.[2]

But if Ivan does not believe in God, neither does he believe in man. It is true that he loves man—there is no one else left to love and perhaps there has never actually been anyone else. Yet how can he believe in man's freedom in the face of the appalling testimony of history proving his incapacity to achieve it? And in what way [252] does Ivan envisage the future? If we take the Grand Inquisitor as his *persona,* then he thinks that just as historical Christianity has failed man, so socialism—the Tower of Babel of the coming centuries—will fail him and afterwards the authoritarian theocrats will resume command. And the fault, from first to last, is in man himself because he is an "impotent rebel," a slave even if rebellious by nature. Implicit here is the idea of freedom as the consummation of rebellion and of happiness as the total renunciation of it. The choice is between freedom and happiness. But so long as man is unable to carry his rebellion through to the end or, alternatively, renounce it once and for all, he will attain neither goal. Ivan torments himself with the question of what is to be done with man if you at once love and despise him. The ideology of the Grand Inquisitor, which repudiates freedom for the sake of happiness, is the means he devises for forcing a solution. Yet it also is a means of exposing it. The very manner in which Ivan develops this ideology expresses his loathing of it even as he despairingly accepts it.

This is but another way of saying that in the last analysis he is not really possessed by it, that his mind moves freely in and out of it. The Legend as a whole, in its interplay of drama and ideology, is to be taken, I think, as an experiment, one of those experiments in frightfulness with which modern literature has the deepest affinity. Dostoevsky stands at two removes from the Inquisitor, and Ivan at one remove; and this placing, or aesthetic "distancing," re-

[2] Dostoevsky appears to have been inordinately proud of Ivan's subversive intelligence. "Ivan is deep," he wrote in his private notebook; "he is not one of your present-day atheists whose unbelief demonstrates no more than the narrowness of their point of view and the obtuseness of their small minds." And again: "Those thickheads never dreamt of so powerful a negation of God as that embodied in the Inquisitor and in the preceding chapter, to which the entire novel serves as an answer. . . . Even in Europe there have never been atheistical expressions of such power."

flects precisely the degree of commitment we are entitled to assume. Therefore to identify Ivan wholly with the Inquisitor, as so many commentators have done, is an error, though a lesser one than that of wholly identifying Dostoevsky with him. The fact is that the Legend has not one but two protagonists, Jesus and the Inquisitor, and that Ivan makes no real choice between them. Jesus is freedom and transcendent truth, whereas the Inquisitor typifies the implacable logic of historical reality; but so stark a confrontation in itself demonstrates that Ivan's dilemma is absolute. After all, he has no God to whom he can appeal for a guaranty of his choice; Jesus is his hero but not his God. Ivan, like his creator, is split through and through, torn between love and contempt, pride and submission, reason and faith, teleology and the extremest pessimism. Inherently a stranger in the world of action, he is capable, however, of apprehending his thought with such urgency [253] and fearlessness that it comes almost to resemble an action. And in his rage of love he invokes with prophetic violence a totalitarian elite whose rule is justified by humanity's refusal of Christ's tragic gift of freedom.

The scene of Ivan's "poem in prose" is Seville at the time of the Inquisition. On a day when nearly a hundred heretics had been burnt *ad majorem gloriam Dei* by the cardinal, the Grand Inquisitor, in a splendid *auto da fé,* Christ reappears in His human shape, as He appeared fifteen centuries earlier. The people, recognizing their Savior, welcome Him with cries of love and faith, but at that moment the cardinal—"an old man, almost ninety, tall and erect, with a withered face and sunken eyes, in which there is still a gleam of light"—orders the guards to seize and lead Him away to the dungeon of the Holy Inquisition. At night the door of the cell is suddenly opened and the aged cardinal comes in alone to confront his prisoner. On the morrow, he announces, he will condemn and burn Him at the stake as the worst of heretics: "And the very people who have today kissed Thy feet, tomorrow at the faintest sign from me will rush to heap up the embers of Thy fire." Throughout the long scene that follows Christ is speechless. Only the Inquisitor speaks, and his speech is an astonishingly coherent and complete apology for the total power of man over man. It has grandeur, penetration and enormous audacity—thus would the Inquisitor's counterparts in real life speak if they had candor and were capable of making independent forays into the philosophy of history. The phenomenon of power has always been surrounded by taboos.

Power is in some sense the deepest of mysteries, hence taboo, for whatever is behind it is at once holy and unclean. But the Inquisitor breaks all taboos. It was the recommendation of Edmund Burke, that enemy of extremism and of theory, that a "sacred veil" should ever be drawn "over the beginnings of all governments." Now if by "beginnings" we understand the motive-force or inner principle of government, then the Inquisitor is bent on rending asunder the veil that shrouds it and letting us in on its secret. Not that he is not himself a firm believer in the beneficent uses of Burke's "politic, well-wrought veil." He is that above all, but in the séance with his speechless prisoner he is for once intent on putting all things plainly.[254]

What he puts most plainly to his prisoner is the enormity of the error of rejecting coercion and domination for the sake of man's free love. The three powers with which Satan had tempted Him in the wilderness are miracle, mystery and authority, the sole means of vanquishing the conscience of men forever and holding it captive for their own good. The churchly hierarchy has found it necessary to correct that error and to found its work on those powers. Never has anything truer been said than what was revealed by the wise and dread spirit of the wilderness in the three questions later recorded in the Gospels as "the temptation." For in those questions "the whole subsequent history of mankind is, as it were, brought together into one whole and foretold, and in them are united all the unsolved historical contradictions of human nature. . . ."

Man, hungering both for "earthly bread" and "common worship," and on no account wanting the one without the other, will gladly exchange his freedom for the promise that his double hunger will be appeased. He longs "to find someone quickly to whom he can hand over the gift of freedom with which the ill-fated creature was born"; and he prefers to worship the one who feeds him, the one performing the miracle rejected by Jesus, the miracle of turning stones into bread. Yet man is so constituted that he seeks to worship only that which he believes to be established beyond dispute:

For those pitiful creatures are concerned not only to find what one or the other can worship, but to find something that all would believe in and worship; what is essential is that all may be *together* in it. This craving for *community* of worship is the chief misery of every man individually and of all humanity from the beginning of time. For the sake of common worship they have slain each other with the sword. They have set up gods and challenged one another, "Put away your gods and come and worship ours, or we will kill you and your gods!" And so it will be to the end of the world, even when gods disappear from the earth; they will fall down before idols just the same.

Jesus' hope that man would cling to God and not crave miracles is futile. Man seeks not so much God as the miraculous, and when deprived of it he creates "new miracles of his own for himself, and will worship deeds of sorcery and witchcraft, though he might be a hundred times over a rebel, heretic and infidel." The Inquisitor foretells that the downfall of the Church will come about exactly through [255] such a deed of sorcery and witchcraft when men, declaring that there is no crime and no sin but only hunger, will erect the terrible Tower of Babel. But after a thousand years of suffering, of the confusion of free thought and of science ending in "cannibalism," the people will seek out the priestly elite hidden in their catacombs: "They will find us and cry to us, 'Feed us, for those who have promised the fire from heaven haven't given it!' And then we shall finish building their tower. . . . And we alone shall feed them in Thy name, declaring falsely that it is in Thy name. . . . And we shall sit upon the beast and raise the cup, and on it will be written, 'Mystery.' "

The Inquisitor sneers at the nihilists and socialists even while appropriating what he conceives to be their principal idea: materialism and technics, the miracle of turning stones into bread. In other words, ecclesiastical totalitarianism comes to terms with the socialist cause by absorbing it. Only then begins the reign of the universal state—"an harmonious antheap"—assuring peace for all. Its principle of organization is power. Jesus repudiated power, but not the theocrats of Rome, who have taken up the sword of Caesar, proclaiming themselves the lords of the earth. "We shall triumph and we shall be Caesars," the Inquisitor cries, "and then we shall plan the universal happiness of mankind." All will be happy except the members of the ruling caste, since it is they alone who are not absolved from the knowledge of good and evil. They keep that knowledge strictly to themselves, just as they keep the secret of their atheism. The millions whom they rule submit meekly to their commands and die peacefully believing in the rewards of heaven and eternity, as they have been told to believe, though of course beyond the grave nothing whatever awaits them.

The only answer the Inquisitor receives from his prisoner is a kiss on his withered lips. The old man shudders and, opening the door of the cell, exclaims: "Go, and come no more . . . come not at all, never, never!" [256]

. . . . .

It is interesting to compare his earlier and later handling of this theme of "the compulsory organization of human happiness." Let us begin, then, by putting the Grand Inquisitor into relation with another and quite as famous protagonist of Dostoevsky's, the hero-narrator of *Notes from Underground.* It is for the content of their thought that they are worth comparing, and not primarily as novelistic creations. The aged cardinal of Seville, lacking the dimension of subjectivity so conspicuous in the underground man, is not a character in the proper sense of the term but simply the personification of a *Weltanschauung*—that of Ivan Karamazov in its most heretical and negative aspects. The undergroundling, on the other hand, is very far from being merely the embodiment of an idea. Still, in linking him with the Inquisitor, our concern is not with the undergroundling's prostrate personality, with his nausea of consciousness and enjoyment of his own degradation, but rather with the theory of human nature he propounds, a theory in which the bold affirmation of freedom is combined with the equally bold negation of "reason, progress and enlightenment."

What this theory has in common with that of the Inquisitor is that both are centered on the question of freedom. Where they differ is in their answers to this question, the undergroundling's answer being as positive as the Inquisitor's is negative. Hence the contrast between the two theories gives us the measure of the growth and change of Dostoevsky's thought between the early 1860s, when he wrote *Notes from Underground,* and the period of his last and greatest novel. The earlier work is written from the perspective of the isolated and perversely recalcitrant individual, who, in his "moral obliquity," will never consent to join the "universal and happy antheap" projected by the ideologues of rational self-interest and progress toward an harmonious society. Through the figure of this unconsoled and unconsolable individual Dostoevsky pointed to the chaos and irrationality of human nature, thus mocking the utilitarian formulas of the radicals and liberals. "Man everywhere and at all times . . . has preferred to act as he chose and not in the least as his reason and advantage dictated. . . . One's own unfettered choice, one's own caprice . . . is that very 'most advantageous advantage' . . . against which all systems and theories are shattered to atoms. . . . What man wants is simply *independent* choice, whatever that independence may [267] cost and wherever it may lead." He readily admits that man "likes to make roads and to create," but this admission goes with the emphatic reminder that man also loves chaos and destruction. He is therefore convinced that the organization of a rational society—which, in his view, cannot but turn out to be a human antheap—will prove forever impossible.

Now this is a vision entirely at variance with that of the Inquisitor, whose idea it is that "independent choice" is exactly what men fear most; that is the source both of his contempt for them and his paradoxical determination to strip them of the useless gift of free choice so as to convert them into the childishly happy and ignorant members of a totalitarian collective. He proclaims the failure of historical Christianity to illuminate and sanctify human existence, but this failure he imputes not to the Church but to the falsity of Christ's message in the light of the proven inadequacy of human nature. Consequently the Church can have no function but that of an instrument of power in the hands of an elite that has taken up the sword of Caesar. Since man is feebler and baser than Christ believed him to be, it was senseless to bring him the gift of freedom. The weak soul is unable to benefit from such heady gifts. The Inquisitor is not a psychologist pure and simple, like the undergroundling. In his thought psychological insights are supported by historical facts. Another difference is that the primary object of his polemic is what he takes to be the illusion of human freedom, whereas the undergroundling makes reason the target of his devaluating analysis.

When it came to writing *The Brothers Karamazov* Dostoevsky had wholly surmounted the standpoint of defiant and obdurate individualism exhibited in *Notes from Underground.* He then thought that the Palace of Crystal (at that time his prime symbol of socialism, superseded later by the Tower of Babel, a more cheerless symbol) would never be built because men were too independent to permit its construction. This type of individualism, however, with its stress on the unfettered human will and the inexhaustible intransigence of self-pride, is not really consonant with the religious valuation of life. It is, in fact, a secular type of individualism which can be turned quite as effectively against Christian philosophies as against the philosophy of social progress; the recalcitrant individual may after all refuse to choose Christ in the same "irrational" way as he refuses [268] to submit to the dictates of reason and self-interest. "Moral obliquity" provides as insecure a foundation for the Kingdom of God as for the Kingdom of Man. It is only in later years, as his religious consciousness became fully engaged in his creative effort, that Dostoevsky developed a new idea of freedom, based not on "moral obliquity" but on Christian love and the unviolated conscience.

Also, it is important to note that so far as socialism is concerned it is mainly the conception of it dramatized in *The Possessed* which is epitomized in the Legend, and that, in a sense, the figure of the Inquisitor also derives from that novel, being an elaborated and historically enriched variant of the sketchy figure of Shigalov. It will be remembered that Shigalov, an eccentric ideologue, comes to the conclusion that unlimited freedom can be attained only through unlimited despotism, or, rather, that the extremes of freedom and despotism are in reality identical. Accordingly he proposes, as no less than "a final solution of the social question," that mankind be divided into two unequal parts, one-tenth enjoying "absolute liberty and unbounded power over the other nine-tenths. The others have given up all individuality and become, so to speak, a herd, and, through boundless submission, will by a series of regenerations achieve primeval innocence, something like the Garden of Eden. They'll have to work, however." The society envisaged by the Inquisitor is plainly a later edition of Shigalov's herd, and the latter's elite is even further reduced in numbers by the Inquisitor: "There will be thousands of millions of happy babes, and a hundred thousand sufferers who have taken upon themselves the curse of the knowledge of good and evil." The reign of the "sufferers" will be cruel, of course, for they believe that their cruelty will guarantee the happiness of the rest of mankind. Moreover, as Albert Camus has remarked, they excuse their cruelty by claiming, like the Satan of the Romantics, that it will be hard for them to bear.

Yet there is no denying that even this mordant reading of the historical past and future did not deter Dostoevsky from asserting his belief that freedom of choice in the knowledge of good and evil is the essence of man's humanity and the essence of Christ's teaching. The kind of faith or obedience that is bought with bread is evil, and so is any constraint on man's conscience, in whatever form, even if the constraint is exercised for ostensibly good ends. Freedom is not [269] to be confounded with goodness or happiness. Goodness festers if bred by constraint, and happiness turns into brutish contentment. Only when freely chosen do they acquire a human content. This is precisely what makes Dostoevsky a novelist of tragic freedom, his perception that genuine freedom, being open to the choice between good and evil, is unthinkable without suffering. That is the price of freedom, and he who refuses to pay it can only dream of freedom without experiencing it, without substantiating it within the actual process of living. It is a conception which on one side of it is close to existentialist thought. For Dostoevsky, as for the existentialists, it is above all through the experience of choice and decision, resolutely entered upon, that the individual comes to self-realization. But this grasp and possession of one's own being, which is the human creature's truest rapture, is at the same time inescapably associated with anxiety and suffering, and for this reason men are continually driven to shirk meaningful choices. However, the difference between some of the latter-day existentialists and Dostoevesky is that for him the act of choosing is wholly a moral if not always a religious act while for them it is an act unconditionally open to existence in all its sheerness and totality, not limited to any single sphere, ethical or otherwise.

Now in the Legend Dostoevsky so represents the truth of history—that is, the truth not of what ought to be but of what is and has been—that we see it as patently belonging to the Inquisitor, not to Christ. Dostoevsky none the less takes his stand with Christ. This should not surprise us; if we consider his biography in its temporal depth, so to speak, we find that he committed himself very early to this clinging to Christ in the face of all the malignant realities of history and man's nature. More than twenty-five years before composing the Legend he wrote in a letter from his place of exile in Siberia that if it were proven to him that Christ is "outside the truth, and if the truth really did exclude Christ, I should prefer to stay with Christ and not with the truth."

This paradoxical attitude is not to be taken as mere sentiment. It has its consequences. In the context of the Legend it means that if Dostoevsky rejects the wisdom of the Inquisitor, it is solely in the terms of the desperate paradox of his faith in Christ. Otherwise he apparently neither doubts nor denies that malign wisdom. What is to be observed, too, is that he thus indirectly fulfills his ideological [270] aim of excluding any middle ground between Christ and the Grand Inquisitor. And the starkness and ultimatism of the choice he offers, which has the effect of shrinking our sense of historical possibilities and reducing our resourcefulness in the face of extremes, reminds us of other great thinkers of the nineteenth century, like Kierkegaard and Marx, who likewise made war, though from other standpoints, on that century's liberal humanism—Kierkegaard with his either-or formula that is spiritually quite as terroristic as that of the Russian novelist, and Marx with his inexorable idea that if humanity fails to choose socialism it will inevitably fall back into barbarism.[271]

PHILOSOPHY AND THEOLOGY

Pensées

72

Man's disproportion.—Let man then contemplate the whole of nature in her full and grand majesty, and turn his vision from the low objects which surround him. Let him gaze on that brilliant light, set like an eternal lamp to illumine the universe; let the earth appear to him a point in comparison with the vast circle described by the sun; and let him wonder at the fact that this vast circle is itself but a very fine point in comparison with that described by the stars in their revolution round the firmament. But if our view be arrested there, let our imagination pass beyond; it will sooner exhaust the power of conception than nature that of supplying material for conception. The whole visible world is only an imperceptible atom in the ample bosom of nature. No idea approaches it. We may enlarge our conceptions beyond all imaginable space; we only produce atoms in comparison with the reality of things. It is an infinite sphere, the centre of which is everywhere, the circumference nowhere. In short it is the greatest sensible mark of the almighty power of God, that imagination loses itself in that thought.

Returning to himself, let man consider what he is in comparison with all existence; let him regard himself as lost in his remote corner of nature; and from the little cell in which he finds himself lodged, I mean the universe, let him estimate at their true value the earth, kingdoms, cities, and himself. What is a man in the Infinite?

But to show him another prodigy equally astonishing, let him examine the most delicate things he knows. Let a mite be given him, with its minute body and parts incomparably more minute, limbs with their joints, veins in the limbs, blood in the veins, humours in the blood, drops in the humours, vapours in the drops. Dividing these last things again, let him exhaust his powers of conception, and let the last object at which he can arrive be now that of

SOURCE: From *Pensées* by Blaise Pascal. Translated by W. F. Trotter. Dutton Paperback Series. Reprinted by permission of E. P. Dutton & Co., Inc.

NOTE TO THE STUDENT: In documenting any part of the *Pensées*, it is customary to cite the number of the *Pensée* rather than a page number.

our discourse. Perhaps he will think that here is the smallest point in nature. I will let him see therein a new abyss. I will paint for him not only the visible universe, but all that he can conceive of nature's immensity in the womb of this abridged atom. Let him see therein an infinity of universes, each of which has its firmament, its planets, its earth, in the same proportion as in the visible world; in each earth animals, and in the last mites, in which he will find again all that the first had, finding still in these others the same thing without end and without cessation. Let him lose himself in wonders as amazing in their littleness as the others in their vastness. For who will not be astounded at the fact that our body, which a little while ago was imperceptible in the universe, itself imperceptible in the bosom of the whole, is now a colossus, a world, or rather a whole, in respect of the nothingness which we cannot reach? He who regards himself in this light will be afraid of himself, and observing himself sustained in the body given him by nature between those two abysses of the Infinite and Nothing, will tremble at the sight of these marvels; and I think that, as his curiosity changes into admiration, he will be more disposed to contemplate them in silence than to examine them with presumption.

For in fact what is man in nature? A Nothing in comparison with the Infinite, an All in comparison with the Nothing, a mean between nothing and everything. Since he is infinitely removed from comprehending the extremes, the end of things and their beginning are hopelessly hidden from him in an impenetrable secret; he is equally incapable of seeing the Nothing from which he was made, and the Infinite in which he is swallowed up.

What will he do then, but perceive the appearance of the middle of things, in an eternal despair of knowing either their beginning or their end. All things proceed from the Nothing, and are borne towards the Infinite. Who will follow these marvellous processes? The Author of these wonders understands them. None other can do so.

Through failure to contemplate these Infinities, men have rashly rushed into the examination of nature, as though they bore some proportion to her. It is strange that they have wished to understand the beginnings of things, and thence to arrive at the knowledge of the whole, with a presumption as infinite as their object. For surely this design cannot be formed without presumption or without a capacity infinite like nature.

If we are well informed, we understand that, as nature has

graven her image and that of her Author on all things, they almost all partake of her double infinity. Thus we see that all the sciences are infinite in the extent of their researches. For who doubts that geometry, for instance, has an infinite infinity of problems to solve? They are also infinite in the multitude and fineness of their premises; for it is clear that those which are put forward as ultimate are not self-supporting, but are based on others which, again having others for their support, do not permit of finality. But we represent some as ultimate for reason, in the same way as in regard to material objects we call that an invisible point beyond which our senses can no longer perceive anything, although by its nature it is infinitely divisible.

Of these two Infinities of science, that of greatness is the most palpable, and hence a few persons have pretended to know all things. "I will speak of the whole," said Democritus.

But the infinitely little is the least obvious. Philosophers have much oftener claimed to have reached it, and it is here they have all stumbled. This has given rise to such common titles as *First Principles, Principles of Philosophy,* and the like, as ostentatious in fact, though not in appearance, as that one which blinds us, *De omni scibili.*

We naturally believe ourselves far more capable of reaching the centre of things than of embracing their circumference. The visible extent of the world visibly exceeds us; but as we exceed little things, we think ourselves more capable of knowing them. And yet we need no less capacity for attaining the Nothing than the All. Infinite capacity is required for both, and it seems to me that whoever shall have understood the ultimate principles of being might also attain to the knowledge of the Infinite. The one depends on the other, and one leads to the other. These extremes meet and reunite by force of distance, and find each other in God, and in God alone.

Let us then take our compass; we are something, and we are not everything. The nature of our existence hides from us the knowledge of first beginnings which are born of the Nothing; and the littleness of our being conceals from us the sight of the Infinite.

Our intellect holds the same position in the world of thought as our body occupies in the expanse of nature.

Limited as we are in every way, this state which holds the means between two extremes is present in all our impotence. Our senses perceive no extreme. Too much sound deafens us; too much light dazzles us; too great distance or proximity hinders our view.

Too great length and too great brevity of discourse tend to obscurity; too much truth is paralysing (I know some who cannot understand that to take four from nothing leaves nothing). First principles are too self-evident for us; too much pleasure disagrees with us. Too many concords are annoying in music; too many benefits irritate us; we wish to have the wherewithal to over-pay our debts. *Beneficia eo usque læta sunt dum videntur exsolvi posse; ubi multum antevenere, pro gratia odium redditur.* We feel neither extreme heat nor extreme cold. Excessive qualities are prejudicial to us and not perceptible by the senses; we do not feel but suffer them. Extreme youth and extreme age hinder the mind, as also too much and too little education. In short, extremes are for us as though they were not, and we are not within their notice. They escape us, or we them.

This is our true state; this is what makes us incapable of certain knowledge and of absolute ignorance. We sail within a vast sphere, ever drifting in uncertainty, driven from end to end. When we think to attach ourselves to any point and to fasten to it, it wavers and leaves us; and if we follow it, it eludes our grasp, slips past us, and vanishes for ever. Nothing stays for us. This is our natural condition, and yet most contrary to our inclination; we burn with desire to find solid ground and an ultimate sure foundation whereon to build a tower reaching to the Infinite. But our whole groundwork cracks, and the earth opens to abysses.

Let us therefore not look for certainty and stability. Our reason is always deceived by fickle shadows; nothing can fix the finite between the two Infinites, which both enclose and fly from it.

. . . . .

206

The eternal silence of these infinite spaces frightens me.

233

Infinite—Nothing . . . If there is a God, He is infinitely incomprehensible, since, having neither parts nor limits, He has no affinity to us. We are then incapable of knowing either what He is or if He is. This being so, who will dare to undertake the decision of the question? Not we, who have no affinity to Him.

Who then will blame Christians for not being able to give a reason for their belief, since they profess a religion for which they cannot give a reason? They declare, in expounding it to the world, that it is a foolishness, *stultitiam;* and then you complain that they do not prove it! If they proved it, they would not keep their word; it is in lacking proofs, that they are not lacking in sense. "Yes, but although this excuses those who offer it as such, and takes away from them the blame of putting it forward without reason, it does not excuse those who receive it." Let us then examine this point, and say, "God is, or He is not." But to which side shall we incline? Reason can decide nothing here. There is an infinite chaos which separates us. A game is being played at the extremity of this infinite distance where heads or tails will turn up. What will you wager? According to reason, you can do neither the one thing nor the other; according to reason, you can defend neither of the propositions.

Do not then reprove for error those who have made a choice; for you know nothing about it. "No, but I blame them for having made, not this choice, but a choice; for again both he who chooses heads and he who chooses tails are equally at fault, they are both in the wrong. The true course is not to wager at all."

Yes; but you must wager. It is not optional. You are embarked. Which will you choose then? . . .

280

The knowledge of God is very far from the love of Him.

347

Man is but a reed, the most feeble thing in nature; but he is a thinking reed. The entire universe need not arm itself to crush him. A vapour, a drop of water suffices to kill him. But, if the universe were to crush him, man would still be more noble than that which killed him, because he knows that he dies and the advantage which the universe has over him; the universe knows nothing of this.

All our dignity consists, then, in thought. By it we must elevate ourselves, and not by space and time which we cannot fill. Let us endeavour, then, to think well; this is the principle of morality.

FYODOR DOSTOEVSKY

Notes from Underground

VII

But these are all golden dreams. Oh, tell me, who first declared, who first proclaimed, that man only does nasty things because he does not know his own real interests; and that if he were enlightened, if his eyes were opened to his real normal interests, man would at once cease to do nasty things, would at once become good and noble because, being enlightened and understanding his real advantage, he would see his own advantage in the good and nothing else, and we all know that not a single man can knowingly act to his own disadvantage. Consequently, so to say, he would begin doing good through necessity. Oh, the babe! Oh, the pure, innocent child! Why, in the first place, when in all these thousands of years has there ever been a time when man has acted only for his own advantage? What is to be done with the millions of facts that bear witness that men, *knowingly,* that is, fully understanding their real advantages, have left them in the background and have rushed headlong on another path, to risk, to chance, compelled to this course by nobody and by nothing, but, as it were, precisely because they did not want the beaten track, and stubbornly, wilfully, went off on another difficult, absurd way seeking it almost in the darkness. After all, it means that this stubbornness and wilfulness were more pleasant to them than any advantage. Advantage! What is advantage? And will you take it upon yourself to define with perfect accuracy in exactly what the advantage of man consists of? And what if it so happens that a man's advantage *sometimes* not only may, but even must,

NOTE TO THE STUDENT: In documenting any part of *Notes from Underground,* cite the number of the "note" rather than a page number.

consist exactly in his desiring under certain conditions what is harmful to himself and not what is advantageous. And if so, if there can be such a condition then the whole principle becomes worthless. What do you think—are there such cases? You laugh; laugh away, gentlemen, so long as you answer me: have man's advantages been calculated with perfect certainty? Are there not some which not only have not been included but cannot possibly be included under any classification? After all, you, gentlemen, so far as I know, have taken your whole register of human advantages from the average of statistical figures and scientific-economic formulas. After all, your advantages are prosperity, wealth, freedom, peace—and so on, and so on. So that a man who, for instance, would openly and knowingly oppose that whole list would, to your thinking, and indeed to mine too, of course, be an obscurantist or an absolute madman, would he not? But, after all, here is something amazing: why does it happen that all these statisticians, sages and lovers of humanity, when they calculate human advantages invariably leave one out? They don't even take it into their calculation in the form in which it should be taken, and the whole reckoning depends upon that. There would be no great harm to take it, this advantage, and to add it to the list. But the trouble is, that this strange advantage does not fall under any classification and does not figure in any list. For instance, I have a friend. Bah, gentlemen! But after all he is your friend, too; and indeed there is no one, no one, to whom he is not a friend! When he prepares for any undertaking this gentleman immediately explains to you, pompously and clearly, exactly how he must act in accordance with the laws of reason and truth. What is more, he will talk to you with excitement and passion of the real normal interests of man; with irony he will reproach the short-sighted fools who do not understand their own advantage, nor the true significance of virtue; and, within a quarter of an hour, without any sudden outside provocation, but precisely through that something internal which is stronger than all his advantages, he will go off on quite a different tack—that is, act directly opposite to what he has just been saying himself, in opposition to the laws of reason, in opposition to his own advantage—in fact, in opposition to everything. I warn you that my friend is a compound personality, and therefore it is somehow difficult to blame him as an individual. The fact is, gentlemen, it seems that something that is dearer to almost every man than his greatest advantages must really exist, or (not to be illogical) there is one most advantageous advantage (the very one omitted of which we spoke just now) which is more important and more advantageous than all other advantages, for which, if necessary, a man is ready to act in opposition to all laws, that is, in opposition to reason, honor, peace, prosperity—in short, in opposition to all those wonderful and useful things if only he can attain that fundamental, most advantageous advantage which is dearer to him than all.

"Well, but it is still advantage just the same," you will retort. But excuse me, I'll make the point clear, and it is not a case of a play on words, but what really matters is that this advantage is remarkable from the very fact that it breaks down all our classifications, and continually shatters all the systems evolved by lovers of mankind for the happiness of mankind. In short, it interferes with everything. But before I mention this advantage to you, I want to compromise myself personally, and therefore I boldly declare that all these fine systems—all these theories for explaining to mankind its real normal interests, so that inevitably striving to obtain these interests, it may at once become good and noble—are, in my opinion, so far, mere logical exercises! Yes, logical exercises. After all, to maintain even this theory of the regeneration of mankind by means of its own advantage, is, after all, to my mind almost the same thing as—as to claim, for instance, with Buckle, that through civilization mankind becomes softer, and consequently less bloodthirsty, and less fitted for warfare. Logically it does not seem to follow from his arguments. But man is so fond of systems and abstract deductions that he is ready to distort the truth intentionally, he is ready to deny what he can see and hear just to justify his logic. I take this example because it is the most glaring instance of it. Only look about you: blood is being spilled in streams, and in the merriest way, as though it were champagne. Take the whole of the nineteenth century in which Buckle lived. Take Napoleon—both the Great and the present one. Take North America—the eternal union. Take farcical Schleswig-Holstein. And what is it that civilization softens in us? Civilization only produces a greater variety of sensations in man—and absolutely nothing more. And through the development of this variety, man may even come to find enjoyment in bloodshed. After all, it has already happened to him. Have you noticed that the subtlest slaughterers have almost always been the most civilized gentlemen, to whom the various Attilas and Stenka Razins could never hold a candle, and if they are not so conspicuous as the Attilas and Stenka Razins it is precisely because they are so often met with, are so ordinary and have become so familiar to us. In any case if civilization has not made man more bloodthirsty, it has at least made him more abominably, more loathsomely bloodthirsty than before. Formerly he saw justice in bloodshed and with his conscience at peace exterminated whomever he thought he should. And now while we consider bloodshed an abomination, we nevertheless engage in this abomination and even more than ever before. Which is worse? Decide that for yourselves. It is said that Cleopatra (pardon the example from Roman history) was fond of sticking gold pins into her slave-girls' breasts and derived enjoyment from their screams and writhing. You will say that that occurred in comparatively barbarous times; that these are barbarous times too, because (also comparatively speaking) pins are stuck in even now; that even though man has now learned to see more clearly occasionally than in barbarous times, he is still far from having *accustomed* himself to act as reason and science would dictate. But all the same you are fully convinced that he will inevitably accustom himself to it when he gets completely rid of certain old bad habits, and when common sense and science have completely re-educated human nature and turned it in a normal direction. You are confident that man will then refrain from erring *intentionally*, and will, so to say, willy-nilly, not want to set his will against his normal interests. More than that: then, you say, science itself will teach man (though to my mind that is a luxury) that he does not really have either caprice or will of his own and that he has never had it, and that he himself is something like a piano key or an organ stop, and that, moreover, laws of nature exist in this world, so that everything he does is not done by his will at all, but is done by itself, according to the laws of nature. Consequently we have only to discover these laws of nature, and man will no longer be responsible for his actions and life will become exceedingly easy for him. All human actions will then, of course, be tabulated according to these laws, mathematically, like tables of logarithms up to 108,000, and entered in a table; or, better still, there would be published certain edifying works like the present encyclopedic lexicons, in which everything will be so clearly calculated and designated that there will be no more incidents or adventures in the world.

Then—it is still you speaking—new economic relations will be established, all ready-made and computed with mathematical exactitude, so that every possible question will vanish in a twinkling, simply because every possible answer to it will be provided. Then the crystal palace will be built. Then—well, in short, those will be halcyon days. Of course there is no guaranteeing (this is my comment now) that it will not be, for instance, terribly boring then (for what will one have to do when everything is calculated according to the table?) but on the other hand everything will be extraordinarily rational. Of course boredom may lead you to anything. After all, boredom even sets one to sticking gold pins into people, but all that would not matter. What is bad (this is my comment again) is that for all I know people will be thankful for the gold pins then. After all, man is stupid, phenomenally stupid. Or rather he is not stupid at all, but he is so ungrateful that you could not find another like him in all creation. After all, it would not surprise me in the least, if, for instance, suddenly for no reason at all, a gentleman with an ignoble, or rather with a reactionary and ironical, countenance were to arise and, putting his arms akimbo, say to us all: "What do you think, gentlemen, hadn't we better kick over all that rationalism at one blow, scatter it to the winds, just to send these logarithms to the devil, and to let us live once more according to our own foolish will!" That again would not matter; but what is annoying is that after all he would be sure to find followers—such is the nature of man. And all that for the most foolish reason, which, one would think, was hardly worth mentioning: that is, that man everywhere and always, whoever he may be, has preferred to act as he wished and not in the least as his reason and advantage dictated. Why, one may choose what is contrary to one's own interests, and sometimes one *positively ought* (that is my idea). One's own free unfettered choice, one's own fancy, however wild it may be, one's own fancy worked up at times to frenzy—why that is that very "most advantageous advantage" which we have overlooked, which comes under no classification and through which all systems and theories are continually being sent to the devil. And how do these sages know that man must necessarily need a rationally advantageous choice? What man needs is simply *independent* choice, whatever that independence may cost and wherever it may lead. Well, choice, after all, the devil only knows . . .

VIII

"Ha! ha! ha! But after all, if you like, in reality, there is no such thing as choice," you will interrupt with a laugh. "Science has even now succeeded in analyzing man to such an extent that we know already that choice and what is called freedom of will are nothing other than—"

Wait, gentlemen, I meant to begin with that myself. I admit that I was even frightened. I was just going to shout that after all the devil only knows what choice depends on, and that perhaps that was a very good thing, but I remembered the teaching of science—and pulled myself up. And here you have begun to speak. After all, really, well, if some day they truly discover a formula for all our desires and caprices—that is, an explanation of what they depend upon, by what laws they arise, just how they develop, what they are aiming at in one case or another and so on, and so on, that is, a real mathematical formula—then, after all, man would most likely at once stop to feel desire, indeed, he will be certain to. For who would want to choose by rule? Besides, he will at once be transformed from a human being into an organ stop or something of the sort; for what is a man without desire, without free will and without choice, if not a stop in an organ? What do you think? Let us consider the probability—can such a thing happen or not?

"H'm!" you decide. "Our choice is usually mistaken through a mistaken notion of our advantage. We sometimes choose absolute nonsense because in our stupidity we see in that nonsense the easiest means for attaining an advantage assumed beforehand. But when all that is explained and worked out on paper (which is perfectly possible, for it is contemptible and senseless to assume in advance that man will never understand some laws of nature), then, of course, so-called desires will not exist. After all, if desire should at any time come to terms completely with reason, we shall then, of course, reason and not desire, simply because, after all, it will be impossible to retain reason and *desire* something senseless, and in that way knowingly act against reason and desire to injure ourselves. And as all choice and reasoning can really be calculated, because some day they will discover the laws of our so-called free will—so joking aside, there may one day probably be something like a table of desires so that we really shall choose in accordance with it. After all, if, for instance, some day they calculate and prove to me that I stuck my tongue out at someone because I could not help sticking my tongue out at him and that I had to do it in that particular way, what sort of *freedom* is left me, especially if I am a learned man and have taken my degree somewhere? After all, then I would be able to calculate my whole life for thirty years in advance. In short, if that comes about, then, after all, we could do nothing about it.

We would have to accept it just the same. And, in fact, we ought to repeat to ourselves incessantly that at such and such a time and under such and such circumstances, Nature does not ask our leave; that we must accept her as she is and not as we imagine her to be, and if we really aspire to tables and indices and well, even—well, let us say to the chemical retort, then it cannot be helped. We must accept the retort, too, or else it will be accepted without our consent."

Yes, but here I come to a stop! Gentlemen, you must excuse me for philosophizing; it's the result of forty years underground! Allow me to indulge my fancy for a minute. You see, gentlemen, reason, gentlemen, is an excellent thing, there is no disputing that, but reason is only reason and can only satisfy man's rational faculty, while will is a manifestation of all life, that is, of all human life including reason as well as all impulses. And although our life, in this manifestation of it, is often worthless, yet it is life nevertheless and not simply extracting square roots. After all, here I, for instance, quite naturally want to live, in order to satisfy all my faculties for life, and not simply my rational faculty, that is, not simply one-twentieth of all my faculties for life. What does reason know? Reason only knows what it has succeeded in learning (some things it will perhaps never learn; while this is nevertheless no comfort, why not say so frankly?) and human nature acts as a whole, with everything that is in it, consciously or unconsciously, and, even if it goes wrong, it lives. I suspect, gentlemen, that you are looking at me with compassion; you repeat to me that an enlightened and developed man, such, in short, as the future man will be, cannot knowingly desire anything disadvantageous to himself, that this can be proved mathematically. I thoroughly agree, it really can—by mathematics. But I repeat for the hundredth time, there is one case, one only, when man may purposely, consciously, desire what is injurious to himself, what is stupid, very stupid—simply in order *to have the right* to desire for himself even what is very stupid and not to be bound by an obligation to desire only what is rational. After all, this very stupid thing, after all, this caprice of ours, may really be more advantageous for us, gentlemen, than anything else on earth, especially in some cases. And in particular it may be more advantageous than any advantages even when it does us obvious harm, and contradicts the soundest conclusions of our reason about our advantage—because in any case it preserves for us what is most precious and most important—that is, our personality, our individuality. Some, you see, maintain that this really is the most precious thing for man; desire can, of course, if it desires, be in agreement with reason; particularly if it does not abuse this practice but does so in moderation, it is both useful and sometimes even praiseworthy. But very often, and even most often, desire completely and stubbornly opposes reason, and . . . and . . . and do you know that that, too, is useful and sometimes even praiseworthy? Gentlemen, let us suppose that man is not stupid. (Indeed, after all, one cannot say that about him anyway, if only for the one consideration that, if man is stupid, then, after all, who is wise?) But if he is not stupid, he is just the same monstrously ungrateful! Phenomenally ungrateful. I even believe that the best definition of man is—a creature that walks on two legs and is ungrateful. But that is not all, that is not his worst defect; his worst defect is his perpetual immorality, perpetual—from the days of the Flood to the Schleswig-Holstein period of human destiny. Immorality, and consequently lack of good sense; for it has long been accepted that lack of good sense is due to no other cause than immorality. Try it, and cast a look upon the history of mankind. Well, what will you see? Is it a grand spectacle? All right, grand, if you like. The Colossus of Rhodes, for instance, that is worth something. Mr. Anaevsky may well testify that some say it is the work of human hands, while others maintain that it was created by Nature herself. Is it variegated? Very well, it may be variegated too. If one only took the dress uniforms, military and civilian, of all peoples in all ages—that alone is worth something, and if you take the undress uniforms you will never get to the end of it; no historian could keep up with it. Is it monotonous? Very well. It may be monotonous, too; they fight and fight; they are fighting now, they fought first and they fought last—you will admit that it is almost too monotonous. In short, one may say anything about the history of the world—anything that might enter the most disordered imagination. The only thing one cannot say is that it is rational. The very word sticks in one's throat. And, indeed, this is even the kind of thing that continually happens. After all, there are continually turning up in life moral and rational people, sages, and lovers of humanity, who make it their goal for life to live as morally and rationally as possible, to be, so to speak, a light to their neighbors, simply in order to show them that it is really possible to live morally and rationally in this world. And so what? We all know that those very people sooner or later toward the end of their lives have been false to themselves, playing some trick, often a most indecent one. Now I ask you: What can one expect from man since he is a creature endowed with such strange qualities? Shower upon him every earthly blessing, drown him in bliss so that nothing but bubbles would dance on the surface of his bliss, as on a sea; give him such economic prosperity that he would have nothing else to do but sleep, eat cakes and busy himself with ensuring the continuation of world history and even then man, out of sheer ingratitude, sheer libel, would play you some loathsome trick. He would even risk his cakes and would deliberately desire the most fatal rubbish, the most uneconomical absurdity, simply to introduce into all this positive rationality his fatal fantastic element. It is just his fantastic dreams, his vulgar folly, that he will desire to retain, simply in order to prove to himself (as though that were so necessary) that men still are men and not piano keys, which even if played by the laws of nature themselves threaten to be controlled so completely that soon one will be able to desire nothing but by the calendar. And, after all, that is not all: even if man really were nothing but a piano key, even if this were proved to him by natural science and mathematics, even then he would not become reasonable, but would purposely do something perverse out of sheer ingratitude, simply to have his own way. And if he does not find any means he will devise destruction and chaos, will devise sufferings of all sorts, and will thereby have his own way. He will launch a curse upon the world, and, as only man can curse (it is his privilege, the primary distinction between him and other animals) then, after all, perhaps only by his curse will he attain his object, that is, really convince himself that he is a man and not a piano key! If you say that all this, too, can be calculated and tabulated, chaos and darkness and curses, so that the mere possibility of calculating it all beforehand would stop it all, and reason would reassert itself—then man would purposely go mad in order to be rid of reason and have his own way! I believe in that, I vouch for it, because, after all, the whole work of man seems really to consist in nothing but proving to himself continually that he is a man and not an organ stop. It may be at the cost of his skin! But he has proved it; he may become a caveman, but he will have proved it. And after that can one help sinning, rejoicing that it has not yet come, and that desire still depends on the devil knows what!

You will shout at me (that is, if you will still favor me with your shout) that, after all, no one is depriving me of my will, that all they are concerned with is that my will should somehow of itself, of its own free will, coincide with my own normal interests, with the laws of nature and arithmetic.

Bah, gentlemen, what sort of free will is left when we come to tables and arithmetic, when it will all be a case of two times two makes four? Two times two makes four even without my will. As if free will meant that!

IX

Gentlemen, I am joking, of course, and I know myself that I'm joking badly, but after all you know, one can't take everything as a joke. I am, perhaps, joking with a heavy heart. Gentlemen, I am tormented by questions; answer them for me. Now you, for instance, want to cure men of their old habits and reform their will in accordance with science and common sense. But how do you know, not only that it is possible, but also that it is *desirable*, to reform man in that way? And what leads you to the conclusion that it is so *necessary* to reform man's desires? In short, how do you know that such a reformation will really be advantageous to man? And to go to the heart of the matter, why are you *so sure* of your conviction that not to act against his real normal advantages guaranteed by the conclusions of reason and arithmetic is always advantageous for man and must be a law for all mankind? After all, up to now it is only your supposition. Let us assume it to be a law of logic, but perhaps not a law of humanity at all. You gentlemen perhaps think that I am mad? Allow me to defend myself. I agree that man is preeminently a creative animal, predestined to strive consciously toward a goal, and to engage in engineering; that is, eternally and incessantly, to build new roads, *wherever they may lead.* But the reason why he sometimes wants to swerve aside may be precisely that he is *forced* to make that road, and perhaps, too, because however stupid the straightforward practical man may be in general, the thought nevertheless will sometimes occur to him that the road, it would seem, almost always does lead *somewhere,* and that the destination it leads to is less important than the process of making it, and that the chief thing is to save the well-behaved child from despising engineering, and so giving way to the fatal idleness, which, as we all know, is the mother of all vices. Man likes to create and build roads, that is beyond dispute. But why does he also have such a passionate love for destruction and chaos? Now tell me that! But on that point I want to say a few special words myself. May it not be that he loves chaos and destruction (after all, he sometimes unquestionably likes it very much, that is surely so) because he is instinctively afraid of attaining his goal and completing the edifice he is constructing? How do you know, perhaps he only likes that edifice from a distance, and not at all at close range, perhaps he only likes to build it and does not want to live in it, but will leave it, when completed, *aux animaux domestiques*—such as the ants, the sheep, and so on, and so on. Now the ants have quite a different taste. They have an amazing edifice of that type, that endures forever—the anthill.

With the anthill, the respectable race of ants began and with the anthill they will probably end, which does the greatest credit to their perseverance and staidness. But man is a frivolous and incongruous creature, and perhaps, like a chessplayer, loves only the process of the game, not the end of it. And who knows (one cannot swear to it), perhaps the only goal on earth to which mankind is striving lies in this incessant process of attaining, or in other words, in life itself, and not particularly in the goal which of course must always be two times two makes four, that is a formula, and after all, two times two makes four is no longer life, gentlemen, but is the beginning of death. Anyway, man has always been somehow afraid of this two times two makes four, and I am afraid of it even now. Granted that man does nothing but seek that two times two makes four, that he sails the oceans, sacrifices his life in the quest, but to succeed, really to find it—he is somehow afraid, I assure you. He feels that as soon as he has found it there will be nothing for him to look for. When workmen have finished their work they at least receive their pay, they go to the tavern, then they wind up at the police station—and there is an occupation for a week. But where can man go? Anyway, one can observe a certain awkwardness about him every time he attains such goals. He likes the process of attaining, but does not quite like to have attained, and that, of course, is terribly funny. In short, man is a comical creature; there seems to be a kind of pun in it all. But two times two makes four is, after all, something insufferable. Two times two makes four seems to me simply a piece of insolence. Two times two makes four is a fop standing with arms akimbo barring your path and spitting. I admit that two times two makes four is an excellent thing, but if we are going to praise everything, two times two makes five is sometimes also a very charming little thing.

And why are you so firmly, so triumphantly convinced that only the normal and the positive—in short, only prosperity—is to the advantage of man? Is not reason mistaken about advantage? After all, perhaps man likes something besides prosperity? Perhaps he likes suffering just as much? Perhaps suffering is just as great an advantage to him as prosperity? Man is sometimes fearfully, passionately in love with suffering and that is a fact. There is no need to appeal to universal history to prove that; only ask yourself, if only you are a man and have lived at all. As far as my own personal opinion is concerned, to care only for prosperity seems to me somehow even ill-bred. Whether it's good or bad, it is sometimes very pleasant to smash things, too. After all, I do not really insist on suffering or on prosperity either. I insist on my caprice, and its being guaranteed to me when necessary. Suffering would be out of place in vaudevilles, for instance; I know that. In the crystal palace it is even unthinkable; suffering means doubt, means negation, and what would be the good of a crystal palace if there could be any doubt about it? And yet I am sure man will never renounce real suffering, that is, destruction and chaos. Why, after all, suffering is the sole origin of consciousness. Though I stated at the beginning that consciousness, in my opinion, is the greatest misfortune for man, yet I know man loves it and would not give it up for any satisfaction. Consciousness, for instance, is infinitely superior to two times two makes four. Once you have two times two makes four, there is nothing left to do or to understand. There will be nothing left but to bottle up your five senses and plunge into contemplation. While if you stick to consciousness, even though you attain the same result, you can at least flog yourself at times, and that will, at any rate, liven you up. It may be reactionary, but corporal punishment is still better than nothing.

SØREN KIERKEGAARD

Concerning the Dedication to "The Individual"

There is a view of life which conceives that where the crowd is, there also is the truth, and that in truth itself there is need of having the crowd on its side.[1] There is another view of life which conceives that wherever there is a crowd there is untruth, so that (to consider for a moment the extreme case), even if every individual, each for himself in private, were to be in possession of the truth, yet in case they were all to get together in a crowd—a crowd to which any sort of *decisive* significance is attributed, a voting, noisy, audible crowd—untruth would at once be in evidence.[2]

For a 'crowd' is the untruth. In a godly sense it is true, eternally, Christianly, as St. Paul says, that [110] 'only one attains the goal'—which is not meant in a comparative sense, for comparison takes others into account. It means that every man can be that one, God helping him therein—but only one attains the goal. And again this means that every man should be chary about having to do with 'the others', and essentially should talk only with God and with himself—for only one attains the goal. And again this means that man, or to be a man, is akin to deity.—In a worldly and temporal sense, it will be said by the man of bustle, sociability, and amicableness, 'How unreasonable that only one attains the goal; for it is far more likely that many, by the strength of united effort, should attain the goal; and when we are many success is more certain and it is easier for each man severally.' True enough, it is far more *likely;* and it is true also with respect to all earthly and material goods. If it is allowed to have its way, this becomes the only true point of view, for it does away with God and eternity and with man's kinship with deity. It does away with it or transforms it into a fable, and puts in its place the modern (or, we might rather say, the old pagan) notion that to be a man is to belong to a race endowed with reason, to belong to it as a specimen, so that the race or species is higher

[1] Perhaps it may be well to note here once for all a thing that goes without saying and which I never have denied, that in relation to all temporal, earthly, worldly matters the crowd may have competency, and even decisive competency as a court of last resort. But it is not of such matters I am speaking, nor have I ever concerned myself with such things. I am speaking about the ethical, about the ethico-religious, about 'the truth', and I am affirming the untruth of the crowd, ethico-religiously regarded, when it is treated as a criterion for what 'truth' is.

[2] Perhaps it may be well to note here, although it seems to me almost superfluous, that it naturally could not occur to me to object to the fact, for example, that preaching is done or that the truth is proclaimed, even though it were to an assemblage of hundreds of thousands. Not at all; but if there were an assemblage even of only ten—and if they should put the truth to the ballot, that is to say, if the assemblage should be regarded as the authority, if it is the crowd which turns the scale—then there *is* untruth.

than the individual, which is to say that there are no more individuals but only specimens. But eternity which arches over and high above the temporal, tranquil as the starry vault at night, and God in heaven who in the bliss of that sublime tranquillity holds in survey, without the least sense of dizziness at such a height, these countless multitudes of men and knows each [111] single individual by name—He, the great Examiner, says that only one attains the goal. That means, every one can and every one should be this *one*—but only one attains the goal. Hence where there is a multitude, a crowd, or where decisive significance is attached to the fact that there is a multitude, *there* it is sure that no one is working, living, striving for the highest aim, but only for one or another earthly aim; since to work for the eternal decisive aim is possible only where there is one, and to be this one which all can be is to let God be the helper—the 'crowd' is the untruth.

A crowd—not this crowd or that, the crowd now living or the crowd long deceased, a crowd of humble people or of superior people, of rich or of poor, &c.—a crowd in its very concept [3] is the untruth, by reason of the fact that it renders the individual completely impenitent and irresponsible, or at least weakens his sense of responsibility by reducing it to a fraction. Observe that there was not one single soldier that dared lay hands upon Caius Marius—this was an instance of truth. But given merely three or four women with the consciousness or the impression that they were a crowd, and with hope of a sort in the [112] possibility that no one could say definitely who was doing it or who began it—then they had courage for it. What a falsehood! The falsehood first of all is the notion that the crowd does what in fact only the *individual* in the crowd does, though it be every *individual*. For 'crowd' is an abstraction and has no hands: but each individual has ordinarily two hands, and so when an individual lays his two hands upon Caius Marius they are the two hands of the individual, certainly not those of his neighbour, and still less those of the . . . crowd which has no hands. In the next place, the falsehood is that the crowd had the 'courage' for it,

[3] The reader will also remember that here the word 'crowd' is understood in a purely formal sense, not in the sense one commonly attaches to 'the crowd' when it is meant as an invidious qualification, the distinction which human selfishness irreligiously erects between 'the crowd' and superior persons, &c. Good God! How could a religious man hit upon such an inhuman equality! No, 'crowd' stands for number, the numerical, a number of noblemen, millionaires, high dignitaries, &c.—as soon as the numerical is involved it is 'crowd', 'the crowd'.

for no one of the individuals was ever so cowardly as the crowd always is. For every individual who flees for refuge into the crowd, and so flees in cowardice from being an individual (who had not the courage to lay his hands upon Caius Marius, nor even to admit that he had it not), such a man contributes his share of cowardliness to the cowardliness which we know as the 'crowd'.—Take the highest example, think of Christ—and the whole human race, all the men that ever were born or are to be born. But let the situation be one that challenges the individual, requiring each one for himself to be alone with Him in a solitary place and as an individual to step up to Him and spit upon Him—the man never was born and never will be born with courage or insolence enough to do such a thing. This is untruth.

The crowd is untruth. Hence none has more contempt for what it is to be a man than they who make it their profession to lead the crowd. Let some one approach a person of this sort, some individual—[113] that is an affair far too small for his attention, and he proudly repels him. There must be hundreds at the least. And when there are thousands, he defers to the crowd, bowing and scraping to them. What untruth! No, when it is a question of a single individual man, then is the time to give expression to the truth by showing one's respect for what it is to be a man; and if perhaps it was, as it is cruelly said, a poor wretch of a man, then the thing to do is to invite him into the best room, and one who possesses several voices should use the kindest and most friendly. That is truth. If on the other hand there were an assemblage of thousands or more and the truth was to be decided by ballot, then this is what one should do (unless one were to prefer to utter silently the petition of the Lord's Prayer, 'Deliver us from evil'): one should in godly fear give expression to the fact that the crowd, regarded as a judge over ethical and religious matters, is untruth, whereas it is eternally true that every man can be the *one*. This is truth.

The crowd is untruth. Therefore was Christ crucified, because, although He addressed himself to all, He would have no dealings with the crowd, because He would not permit the crowd to aid him in any way, because in this regard He repelled people absolutely, would not found a party, did not permit balloting, but would be what He is, the Truth, which relates itself to the individual.—And hence every one who truly would serve the truth is *eo ipso*, in one way or another, a martyr. If it were possible for a person in his mother's womb to make the decision to will to serve the truth truly, then, whatever his martyrdom [114] turns out to be, he is *eo ipso* from his mother's womb a martyr. For it is not so great a trick to win the crowd. All that is needed is some talent, a certain dose of falsehood, and a little acquaintance with human passions. But no witness for the truth (ah! and that is what every man should be, including you and me)—no witness for the truth dare become engaged with the crowd. The witness for the truth—who naturally has nothing to do with politics and must above everything else be most vigilantly on the watch not to be confounded with the politician—the God-fearing work of the witness to the truth is to engage himself if possible with all, but always individually, talking to every one severally on the streets and lanes . . . in order to disintegrate the crowd, or to talk even to the crowd, though not with the intent of forming a crowd, but rather with the hope that one or another individual might return from this assemblage and become a single individual. On the other hand the 'crowd', when it is treated as an authority and its judgement regarded as the final judgement, is detested by the witness for the truth more heartily than a maiden of good morals detests the public dance-floor; and he who addresses the crowd as the supreme authority is regarded by him as the tool of the untruth. For (to repeat what I have said) that which in politics or in similar fields may be justifiable, wholly or in part, becomes untruth when it is transferred to the intellectual, the spiritual, the religious fields. And one thing more I would say, perhaps with a cautiousness which is exaggerated. By 'truth' I mean always 'eternal truth'. But politics, &c., have [115] nothing to do with 'eternal truth'. A policy which in the proper sense of 'eternal truth' were to make serious work of introducing 'eternal truth' into real life would show itself in that very same second to be in the most eminent degree the most 'impolitic' thing that can be imagined.

A crowd is untruth. And I could weep, or at least I could learn to long for eternity, at thinking of the misery of our age, in comparison even with the greatest misery of bygone ages, owing to the fact that the daily press with its anonymity makes the situation madder still with the help of the public, this abstraction which claims to be the judge in matters of 'truth'. For in reality assemblies which make this claim do not now take place. The fact that an anonymous author by the help of the press can day by day find occasion to say (even about intellectual, moral, and religious matters) whatever he pleases to say, and what perhaps he would be very far from having the courage to say as an individual; that every time he opens his mouth (or shall we say his abysmal gullet?) he at once is addressing thousands of thousands; that he can get ten thousand times ten thousand to repeat after him what he has said—and with all this nobody has any responsibility, so that it is not as in ancient times the relatively unrepentant crowd which possesses omnipotence, but the absolutely unrepentant thing, a nobody, an anonymity, who is the producer (*auctor*), and another anonymity, the public, sometimes even anonymous subscribers, and with all this, nobody, nobody! Good God! And yet our states call themselves Christian states! Let no one say that in this [116] case it is possible for 'truth' in its turn by the help of the press to get the better of lies and errors. O thou who speakest thus, dost thou venture to maintain that men regarded as a crowd are just as quick to seize upon truth which is not always palatable as upon falsehood which always is prepared delicately to give delight?—not to mention the fact that acceptance of the truth is made the more difficult by the necessity of admitting that one has been deceived! Or dost thou venture even to maintain that 'truth' can just as quickly be understood as falsehood, which requires no preliminary knowledge, no schooling, no discipline, no abstinence, no self-denial, no honest concern about oneself, no patient labour?

Nay, truth—which abhors also this untruth of aspiring after broad dissemination as the one aim—is not nimble on its feet. In the first place it cannot work by means of the fantastical means of the press, which is the untruth; the communicator of the truth can only be a single individual. And again the communication of it can only be addressed to the individual; for the truth consists precisely in that conception of life which is expressed by the individual. The truth can neither be communicated nor be received except as it were under God's eyes, not without God's help, not without God's being involved as the middle term, He himself being the Truth. It can therefore only be communicated by and received by 'the individual', which as a matter of fact can be every living man. The mark which distinguishes such a man is merely that of the truth, in contrast to the abstract, the fantastical, the impersonal, the [117] crowd—the public excludes God as the middle term (for the *personal* God cannot be a middle term in an *impersonal* relationship), and thereby excludes also the truth, for God is at once the Truth and the middle term which renders it intelligible.

And to honour every man, absolutely every man, is the truth, and this is what it is to fear God and love one's 'neighbor'. But from an ethico-religious point of view, to recognize the 'crowd' as the court of last resort is to deny God, and it cannot exactly mean to love the 'neighbor'. And the 'neighbor' is the absolutely true expression for human equality. In case every one were in truth to love his neighbour as himself, complete human equality would be attained. Every one who loves his neighbour in truth, expresses unconditionally human equality. Every one who, like me, admits that his effort is weak and imperfect, yet is aware that the task is to love one's neighbour, is also aware of what human equality is. But never have I read in Holy Scripture the comamndment, Thou shalt love the crowd—and still less, Thou shalt recognize, ethico-religiously, in the crowd the supreme authority in matters of 'truth'. But the thing is simple enough: this thing of loving one's neighbor is self-denial; that of loving the crowd, or of pretending to love it, of making it the authority in matters of truth, is the way to material power, the way to temporal and earthly advantages of all sorts—at the same time it is the untruth, for a crowd is the untruth.

But he who acknowledges the truth of this view, which is seldom presented (for it often happens that [118] a man thinks that the crowd is the untruth, but when it—the crowd—accepts his opinion *en masse*, everything is all right again), admits for himself that he is weak and impotent; for how could it be possible for an individual to make a stand against the crowd which possesses the power! And he could not wish to get the crowd on his side for the sake of ensuring that his view would prevail, the crowd, ethico-religiously regarded, being the untruth—that would be mocking himself. But although from the first this view involves an admission of weakness and impotence, and seems therefore far from inviting, and for this reason perhaps is so seldom heard, yet it has the good feature that it is even-handed, that it offends no one, not a single person, that it is no respecter of persons, not a single one. The crowd, in fact, is composed of individuals; it must therefore be in every man's power to become what he is, an individual. From becoming an individual no one, no one at all, is excluded, except he who excludes himself by becoming a crowd. To become a crowd, to collect a crowd about one, is on the contrary to affirm the distinctions of human life. The most well-meaning person who talks about these distinctions can easily offend an individual. But then it is not the crowd which possesses power, influence, repute, and mastery over men, but it is the invidious distinctions of human life which despotically ignore the single individual as the weak and impotent, which in a temporal and worldly interest ignore the eternal truth—the single individual. [119]

SØREN KIERKEGAARD

Is There Such a Thing As an Absolute Duty toward God?

In "Is There Such a Thing as a Teleological Suspension of the Ethical?" the chapter of Fear and Trembling *preceding the selection below, Kierkegaard explicates the nature of faith and its relationship to the absurd by contrasting the tragic hero (who represents the "ethical" stage) and "the knight of faith" (who represents the "religious" stage). The tragic hero, such as Agamemnon or Brutus, sacrifices his child for a higher ethical law than that of "thou shalt love your son," for example, to reconcile the angry deities or to fulfill his duty to the state. That is, he does, through the mediation of the ethical law, a reasonable and therefore understandable act. He does not teleologically suspend the ethical. But Abraham, the knight of faith, who is called upon to sacrifice his son Isaac, teleologically suspends the ethical. He acts, not by virtue of reason, but by "virtue of the absurd." He is confronted as a solitary individual by a voice that demands that he sacrifice Isaac. He cannot turn to universals, as the tragic hero can, to help him decide and to comfort him in his decision. He alone, in dread and anguish, must decide. And when he has acted, he does not know by virtue of reason that he has not perhaps committed a murder. When he acts, that is, he acts not by reason but by utter faith, that is, by virtue of the absurd. The individual thus becomes paradoxically superior to the universal.*

In the story of Abraham we find such a paradox. His relation to Isaac, ethically expressed, is this, that the father should love the

SOURCE: Reprinted from *Fear and Trembling* by Søren Kierkegaard, translated by Walter Lowrie, by permission of Princeton University Press. Copyright 1941, 1954, by Princeton University Press.

son. This ethical relation is reduced to a relative position in contrast with the absolute relation to God. To the question, "Why?" Abraham has no answer except that it is a trial, a temptation (*Fristelse*)—terms which, as was remarked above, express the unity of the two points of view: that it is for God's sake and for his own sake. In common usage these two ways of regarding the matter are mutually exclusive. Thus when we see a man do something which does not comport with the universal, we say that he scarcely can be doing it for God's sake, and by that we imply that he does it for his own sake. The paradox of faith has lost the intermediate term, i.e. the universal. On the one side it has the expression for the extremest egoism (doing the dreadful thing it does for one's own sake); on the other side the expression for the most absolute self-sacrifice (doing it for God's sake). Faith itself cannot be mediated into the universal, for it would thereby be destroyed. Faith is this paradox, and the individual absolutely cannot make himself intelligible to anybody. People imagine maybe that the individual can make himself intelligible to another individual in the same case. Such a notion would be unthinkable if in our time [81] people did not in so many ways seek to creep slyly into greatness. The one knight of faith can render no aid to the other. Either the individual becomes a knight of faith by assuming the burden of the paradox, or he never becomes one. In these regions partnership is unthinkable. Every more precise explication of what is to be understood by Isaac the individual can give only to himself. And even if one were able, generally speaking, to define ever so precisely what should be intended by Isaac (which moreover would be the most ludicrous self-contradiction, i.e. that the particular individual who definitely stands outside the universal is subsumed under universal categories precisely when he has to act as the individual who stands outside the universal), the individual nevertheless will never be able to assure himself by the aid of others that this application is appropriate, but he can do so only by himself as the individual. Hence even if a man were cowardly and paltry enough to wish to become a knight of faith on the responsibility of an outsider, he will never become one; for only the individual becomes a knight of faith as the particular individual, and this is the greatness of this knighthood, as I can well understand without entering the order, since I lack courage; but this is also its terror, as I can comprehend even better.

In Luke 14:26, as everybody knows, there is a striking doctrine taught about the absolute duty toward God: "If any man cometh unto me and hateth not his own father and mother and wife and children and brethren and sisters, yea, and his own life also, he cannot be my disciple." This is a hard saying, who can bear to hear it? For this reason it is heard very seldom. This silence, however, is only an evasion which is of no avail. Nevertheless, the student of theology learns to know that these words occur in the New Testament, and in one or another exegetical aid he finds the explanation that μισεῖν in this passage and a few others is used in the sense of μείσειν, signifying *minus diligo, posthabeo, non colo, nihili facio.* However, the context in which these words occur does not seem to strengthen this tasteful explanation. In the verse immediately following there is a story about a man who desired to build a tower but first sat down to calculate whether [82] he was capable of doing it, lest people might laugh at him afterwards. The close connection of this story with the verse here cited seems precisely to indicate that the words are to be taken in as terrible a sense as possible, to the end that everyone may examine himself as to whether he is able to erect the building.

In case this pious and kindly exegete, who by abating the price thought he could smuggle Christianity into the world, were fortunate enough to convince a man that grammatically, linguistically and κατ' ἀναλογίαν [analogically] this was the meaning of that passage, it is to be hoped that the same moment he will be fortunate enough to convince the same man that Christianity is one of the most pitiable things in the world. For the doctrine which in one of its most lyrical outbursts, where the consciousness of its eternal validity swells in it most strongly, has nothing else to say but a noisy word which means nothing but only signifies that one is to be less kindly, less attentive, more indifferent; the doctrine which at the moment when it makes as if it would give utterance to the terrible ends by driveling instead of terrifying—that doctrine is not worth taking off my hat to.

The words are terrible, yet I fully believe that one can understand them without implying that he who understands them has courage to do them. One must at all events be honest enough to acknowledge what stands written and to admit that it is great, even though one has not the courage for it. He who behaves thus will not find himself excluded from having part in that beautiful story which follows, for after all it contains consolation of a sort for the man who had not courage to begin the tower. But we must be honest, and not interpret this lack of courage as humility, since it is really pride, whereas the courage of faith is the only humble courage.

One can easily perceive that if there is to be any sense in this passage, it must be understood literally. God it is who requires absolute love. But he who in demanding a person's love thinks that this love should be proved also by becoming lukewarm to everything which hitherto was dear—that man is not only an egoist but stupid as well, and he who would demand such love signs at the same moment his own death-warrant,[83] supposing that his life was bound up with this coveted love. Thus a husband demands that his wife shall leave father and mother, but if he were to regard it as a proof of her extraordinary love for him that she for his sake became an indolent, lukewarm daughter etc., then he is the stupidest of the stupid. If he had any notion of what love is, he would wish to discover that as daughter and sister she was perfect in love, and would see therein the proof that she would love him more than anyone else in the realm. What therefore in the case of a man one would regard as a sign of egoism and stupidity, that one is to regard by the help of an exegete as a worthy conception of the Deity.

But how hate them? I will not recall here the human distinction between loving and hating—not because I have much to object to in it (for after all it is passionate), but because it is egoistic and is not in place here. However, if I regard the problem as a paradox, then I understand it, that is, I understand it in such a way as one can understand a paradox. The absolute duty may cause one to do what ethics would forbid, but by no means can it cause the knight of faith to cease to love. This is shown by Abraham. The instant he is ready to sacrifice Isaac the ethical expression for what he does is this: he hates Isaac. But if he really hates Isaac, he can be sure that God does not require this, for Cain and Abraham are not identical. Isaac he must love with his whole soul; when God requires Isaac he must love him if possible even more dearly, and only on this condition can he *sacrifice* him; for in fact it is this love for Isaac which, by its paradoxical opposition to his love for God, makes his act a sacrifice. But the distress and dread in this paradox is that, humanly speaking, he is entirely unable to make himself intelligible. Only at the moment when his act is in absolute contradiction to his feeling is his act a sacrifice, but the reality of his act is the factor by which he belongs to the universal, and in that aspect he is and remains a murderer.

Moreover, the passage in Luke must be understood in such a way as to make it clearly evident that the knight of faith has no higher expression of the universal (i.e. the ethical) by which he can save himself. Thus, for example, if we suppose that the Church requires such a sacrifice of one of its members,[84] we have in this case only a tragic hero. For the idea of the Church is not qualitatively different from that of the State, in so far as the individual comes into it by a simple mediation, and in so far as the individual comes into the paradox he does not reach the idea of the Church; he does not come out of the paradox, but in it he must find either his blessedness or his perdition. Such an ecclesiastical hero expresses in his act the universal, and there will be no one in the Church—not even his father and mother etc.—who fails to understand him. On the other hand, he is not a knight of faith, and he has also a different answer from that of Abraham: he does not say that it is a trial or a temptation in which he is tested.

People commonly refrain from quoting such a text as this in Luke. They are afraid of giving men a free rein, are afraid that the worst will happen as soon as the individual takes it into his head to comport himself as the individual. Moreover, they think that to exist as the individual is the easiest thing of all, and that therefore people have to be compelled to become the universal. I cannot share either this fear or this opinion, and both for the same reason. He who has learned that to exist as the individual is the most terrible thing of all will not be fearful of saying that it is great, but then too he will say this in such a way that his words will scarcely be a snare for the bewildered man, but rather will help him into the universal, even though his words do to some extent make room for the great. The man who does not dare to mention such texts will not dare to mention Abraham either, and his notion that it is easy enough to exist as the individual implies a very suspicious admission with regard to himself; for he who has a real respect for himself and concern for his soul is convinced that the man who lives under his own supervision, alone in the whole world, lives more strictly and more secluded than a maiden in her lady's bower. That there may be some who need compulsion, some who, if they were free-footed, would riot in selfish pleasures like unruly beasts, is doubtless true; but a man must prove precisely that he is not of this number by the fact that he knows how to speak with dread and trembling; and out of reverence for the great one is bound to speak, lest it be forgotten for fear of the ill effect, which surely will fail to eventuate [85] when a man talks in such a way that one knows it for the great, knows its terror—and apart from the terror one does not know the great at all.

Let us consider a little more closely the distress and dread in the paradox of faith. The tragic hero renounces himself in order to express the universal, the knight of faith renounces the universal in order to become the individual. As has been said, everything depends upon how one is placed. He who believes that it is easy enough to be the individual can always be sure that he is not a knight of faith, for vagabonds and roving geniuses are not men of faith. The knight of faith knows, on the other hand, that it is glorious to belong to the universal. He knows that it is beautiful and salutary to be the individual who translates himself into the universal, who edits as it were a pure and elegant edition of himself, as free from errors as possible and which everyone can read. He knows that it is refreshing to become intelligible to oneself in the universal so that he understands it and so that every individual who understands him understands through him in turn the universal, and both rejoice in the security of the universal. He knows that it is beautiful to be born as the individual who has the universal as his home, his friendly abiding-place, which at once welcomes him with open arms when he would tarry in it. But he knows also that higher than this there winds a solitary path, narrow and steep; he knows that it is terrible to be born outside the universal, to walk without meeting a single traveller. He knows very well where he is and how he is related to men. Humanly speaking, he is crazy and cannot make himself intelligible to anyone. And yet it is the mildest expression, to say that he is crazy. If he is not supposed to be that, then he is a hypocrite, and the higher he climbs on this path, the more dreadful a hypocrite he is.

The knight of faith knows that to give up oneself for the universal inspires enthusiasm, and that it requires courage, but he also knows that security is to be found in this, precisely because it is for the universal. He knows that it is glorious to be understood by every noble mind, so glorious that the beholder is ennobled by it, and he feels as if he were bound; he could wish it were this task that had been allotted to him.[86] Thus Abraham could surely have wished now and then that the task were to love Isaac as becomes a father, in a way intelligible to all, memorable throughout all ages; he could wish that the task were to sacrifice Isaac for the universal, that he might incite the fathers to illustrious deeds—and he is almost terrified by the thought that for him such wishes are only temptations and must be dealt with as such, for he knows that it is a solitary path he treads and that he accomplishes nothing for the universal but only himself is tried and examined. Or what did Abraham accomplish for the universal? Let me speak humanly about it, quite humanly. He spent seventy years in getting a son of his old age. What other men get quickly enough and enjoy for a long time he spent seventy years in accomplishing. And why? Because he was tried and put to the test. Is not that crazy? But Abraham believed, and Sarah wavered and got him to take Hagar as a concubine—but therefore he also had to drive her away. He gets Isaac, then he has to be tried again. He knew that it is glorious to express the universal, glorious to live with Isaac. But this is not the task. He knew that it is a kindly thing to sacrifice such a son for the universal, he himself would have found repose in that, and all would have reposed in the commendation of his deed, as a vowel reposes in its consonant, but that is not the task—he is tried. That Roman general who is celebrated by his name of Cunctator checked the foe by procrastination—but what a procrastinator Abraham is in comparison with him! . . . yet he did not save the state. This is the content of one hundred and thirty years. Who can bear it? Would not his contemporary age, if we can speak of such a thing, have said of him, "Abraham is eternally procrastinating. Finally he gets a son. That took long enough. Now he wants to sacrifice him. So is he not mad? And if at least he could explain why he wants to do it—but he always says that it is a trial." Nor could Abraham explain more, for his life is like a book placed under a divine attachment and which never becomes *publici juris*.

This is the terrible thing. He who does not see it can always be sure that he is no knight of faith, but he who sees it will not deny that even the most tried of tragic heroes walks with a dancing step compared with the knight of faith, who comes [87] slowly creeping forward. And if he has perceived this and assured himself that he has not courage to understand it, he will at least have a presentiment of the marvellous glory this knight attains in the fact that he becomes God's intimate acquaintance, the Lord's friend, and (to speak quite humanly) that he says "Thou" to God in heaven, whereas even the tragic hero only addresses Him in the third person.

The tragic hero is soon ready and has soon finished the fight, he makes the infinite movement and then is secure in the universal. The knight of faith, on the other hand, is kept sleepless, for he is constantly tried, and every instant there is the possibility of being able to return repentantly to the universal, and this possibility can just as well be a temptation as the truth. He can derive evidence from no man which it is, for with that query he is outside the paradox.

So the knight of faith has first and foremost the requisite passion to concentrate upon a single factor the whole of the ethical which he transgresses, so that he can give himself the assurance that he really loves Isaac with his whole soul.[1] If he cannot do that, he is in temptation (*Anfechtung*). In the next place, he has enough passion to make this assurance available in the twinkling of an eye and in such a way that it is as completely [88] valid as it was in the first instance. If he is unable to do this, he can never budge from the spot, for he constantly has to begin all over again. The tragic hero also concentrated in one factor the ethical which he teleologically surpassed, but in this respect he had support in the universal. The knight of faith has only himself alone, and this constitutes the dreadfulness of the situation. Most men live in such a way under an ethical obligation that they can let the sorrow be sufficient for the day, but they never reach this passionate concen-

[1] I would elucidate yet once more the difference between the collisions which are encountered by the tragic hero and by the knight of faith. The tragic hero assures himself that the ethical obligation [i.e., the lower ethical obligation, which he puts aside for the higher; in the present case, accordingly, it is the obligation to spare his daughter's life] is totally present in him by the fact that he transforms it into a wish. Thus Agamemnon can say, "The proof that I do not offend against my parental duty is that my duty is my only wish." So here we have wish and duty face to face with one another. The fortunate chance in life is that the two correspond, that my wish is my duty and vice versa, and the task of most men in life is precisely to remain within their duty and by their enthusiasm to transform it into their wish. The tragic hero gives up his wish in order to accomplish his duty. For the knight of faith wish and duty are also identical, but he is required to give up both. Therefore when he would resign himself to giving up his wish he does not find repose, for that is after all his duty. If he would remain within his duty and his wish, he is not a knight of faith, for the absolute duty requires precisely that he should give them up. The tragic hero apprehended a higher expression of duty but not an absolute duty.

tration, this energetic consciousness. The universal may in a certain sense help the tragic hero to attain this, but the knight of faith is left all to himself. The hero does the deed and finds repose in the universal, the knight of faith is kept in constant tension. Agamemnon gives up Iphigenia and thereby has found repose in the universal, then he takes the step of sacrificing her. If Agamemnon does not make the infinite movement, if his soul at the decisive instant, instead of having passionate concentration, is absorbed by the common twaddle that he had several daughters and *vielleicht* [perhaps] the *Ausserordentliche* [extraordinary] might occur—then he is of course not a hero but a hospital-case. The hero's concentration Abraham also has, even though in his case it is far more difficult, since he has no support in the universal; but he makes one more movement by which he concentrates his soul upon the miracle. If Abraham did not do that, he is only an Agamemnon—if in any way it is possible to explain how he can be justified in sacrificing Isaac when thereby no profit accrues to the universal.

Whether the individual is in temptation (*Anfechtung*) or is a knight of faith only the individual can decide. Nevertheless it is possible to construct from the paradox several criteria which he too can understand who is not within the paradox. The true knight of faith is always absolute isolation, the false knight is sectarian. This sectarianism is an attempt to leap away from the narrow path of the paradox and become a tragic hero at a cheap price. The tragic hero expresses the universal and sacrifices himself for it. The sectarian punchinello, instead of that, has a private theatre, i.e. several good friends and comrades who represent the universal just about as well as the [89] beadles in *The Golden Snuffbox* represent justice. The knight of faith, on the contrary, is the paradox, is the individual, absolutely nothing but the individual, without connections or pretensions. This is the terrible thing which the sectarian manikin cannot endure. For instead of learning from this terror that he is not capable of performing the great deed and then plainly admitting it (an act which I cannot but approve, because it is what I do) the manikin thinks that by uniting with several other manikins he will be able to do it. But that is quite out of the question. In the world of spirit no swindling is tolerated. A dozen sectaries join arms with one another, they know nothing whatever of the lonely temptations which await the knight of faith and which he dares not shun precisely because it would be still more dreadful if he were to press forward presumptuously. The sectaries deafen one another by their noise and racket, hold the dread off by their shrieks, and such a hallooing company of sportsmen think they are storming heaven and think they are on the same path as the knight of faith who in the solitude of the universe never hears any human voice but walks alone with his dreadful responsibility.

The knight of faith is obliged to rely upon himself alone, he feels the pain of not being able to make himself intelligible to others, but he feels no vain desire to guide others. The pain is his assurance that he is in the right way, this vain desire he does not know, he is too serious for that. The false knight of faith readily betrays himself by this proficiency in guiding which he has acquired in an instant. He does not comprehend what it is all about, that if another individual is to take the same path, he must become entirely in the same way the individual and have no need of any man's guidance, least of all the guidance of a man who would obtrude himself. At this point men leap aside, they cannot bear the martyrdom of being uncomprehended, and instead of this they choose conveniently enough the worldly admiration of their proficiency. The true knight of faith is a witness, never a teacher, and therein lies his deep humanity, which is worth a good deal more than this silly participation in others' weal and woe which is honored by the name of sympathy, whereas in fact it is nothing but vanity.[90] He who would only be a witness thereby avows that no man, not even the lowliest, needs another man's sympathy or should be abased that another may be exalted. But since he did not win what he won at a cheap price, neither does he sell it out at a cheap price, he is not petty enough to take men's admiration and give them in return his silent contempt, he knows that what is truly great is equally accessible to all.

Either there is an absolute duty toward God, and if so it is the paradox here described, that the individual as the individual is higher than the universal and as the individual stands in an absolute relation to the absolute/or else faith never existed, because it has always existed, or, to put it differently, Abraham is lost, or one must explain the passage in the fourteenth chapter of Luke as did that tasteful exegete, and explain in the same way the corresponding passages and similar ones.[91]

SØREN KIERKEGAARD

Dread As a Saving Experience by Means of Faith

In one of Grimm's Fairy Tales there is the story of a youth who went out in search of adventures for the sake of learning what it is to fear or be in dread. We will let that adventurer go his way without troubling ourselves to learn whether in the course of it he encountered the dreadful. On the other hand I would say that learning to know dread is an adventure which every man has to affront if he would not go to perdition either by not having known dread or by sinking under it. He therefore who has learned rightly to be in dread has learned the most important thing.

If a man were a beast or an angel, he would not be able to be in dread. Since he is a synthesis he can be in dread, and the greater the dread, the greater the man. This, however, is not affirmed in the sense in which men commonly understand dread, as related to something outside a man, but in the sense that man himself produces dread. Only in this sense can we interpret the passage where it is said of Christ that he was in dread [*ængstes*] even unto death, and the place also where he says to Judas, "What thou doest, do quickly." Not even the terrible word upon which even Luther dreaded to preach, "My God, my God, why hast thou forsaken me?"—not even this expresses suffering so strongly. For this word indicates a situation in which Christ actually is; the former sayings indicate a relation to a situation which is not yet actual.

Dread is the possibility of freedom. Only this dread is by the aid of faith absolutely educative, laying bare as it does all finite aims and discovering all their deceptions. And no Grand Inquisitor has in readiness such terrible tortures as has dread, and no spy knows how to attack more artfully the man he suspects, choosing the instant when he is weakest, nor knows how to lay traps where

SOURCE: Reprinted from *The Concept of Dread* by Søren Kierkegaard, translated by Walter Lowrie, by permission of Princeton University Press.

he will be caught and ensnared, as dread knows how, and no sharp-witted judge knows how to interrogate, to examine the accused, as dread does, which never lets him escape, neither by diversion nor by noise, neither at work nor at play, neither by day nor by night.

He who is educated by dread is educated by possibility, and only [239] the man who is educated by possibility is educated in accordance with his infinity. Possibility is therefore the heaviest of all categories. One often hears, it is true, the opposite affirmed, that possibility is so light but reality is heavy. But from whom does one hear such talk? From a lot of miserable men who never have known what possibility is, and who, since reality showed them that they were not fit for anything and never would be, mendaciously bedizened a possibility which was so beautiful, so enchanting; and the only foundation of this possibility was a little youthful tom-foolery of which they might rather have been ashamed. Therefore by this possibility which is said to be light one commonly understands the possibility of luck, good fortune, etc. But this is not possibility, it is a mendacious invention which human depravity falsely embellishes in order to have reason to complain of life, of providence, and as a pretext for being self-important. No, in possibility everything is possible, and he who truly was brought up by possibility has comprehended the dreadful as well as the smiling. When such a person, therefore, goes out from the school of possibility, and knows more thoroughly than a child knows the alphabet that he can demand of life absolutely nothing, and that terror, perdition, annihilation, dwell next door to every man, and has learned the profitable lesson that every dread which alarms [*ængste*] may the next instant become a fact, he will then interpret reality differently, he will extol reality, and even when it rests upon him heavily he will remember that after all it is far, far lighter than the possibility was. Only thus can possibility educate; for finiteness and the finite relationships in which the individual is assigned a place, whether it be small and commonplace or world-historical, educate only finitely, and one can always talk them around, always get a little more out of them, always chaffer, always escape a little way from them, always keep a little apart, always prevent oneself from learning absolutely from them; and if one is to learn absolutely, the individual must in turn have the possibility in himself and himself fashion that from which he is to learn, even though the next instant it does not recognize that it was fashioned by him, but absolutely takes the power from him.

But in order that the individual may thus absolutely and infinitely be educated by possibility, he must be honest towards possibility and must have faith. By faith I mean what Hegel in his fashion calls very rightly "the inward certainty which anticipates [140] infinity." When the discoveries of possibility are honestly administered, possibility will then disclose all finitudes and idealize them in the form of infinity in the individual who is overwhelmed by dread, until in turn he is victorious by the anticipation of faith.

What I say here appears perhaps to many an obscure and foolish saying, since they even boast of never having been in dread. To this I would reply that doubtless one should not be in dread of men, of finite things, but that only the man who has gone through the dread of possibility is educated to have no dread—not because he avoids the dreadful things of life, but because they always are weak in comparison with those of possibility. If on the other hand the speaker means that the great thing about him is that he has never been in dread, then I shall gladly initiate him into my explanation, that this comes from the fact that he is spirit-less.

If the individual cheats the possibility by which he is to be educated, he never reaches faith; his faith remains the shrewdness of finitude, as his school was that of finitude. But men cheat possibility in every way—if they did not, one has only to stick one's head out of the window, and one would see enough for possibility to begin its exercises forthwith. There is an engraving by Chodowiecki which represents the surrender of Calais as viewed by the four temperaments, and the theme of the artist was to let the various impressions appear mirrored in the faces which express the various temperaments. The most commonplace life has events enough, no doubt, but the question is whether the possibility in the individuality is honest towards itself. It is recounted of an Indian hermit who for two years had lived upon dew, that he came once to the city, tasted wine, and then become addicted to drink. This story, like every other of the sort, can be understood in many ways, one can make it comic, one can make it tragic; but the man who is educated by possibility has more than enough to occupy him in such a story. Instantly he is absolutely identified with that unfortunate man, he knows no finite evasion by which he might escape. Now the dread of possibility holds him as its prey, until it can deliver him saved into the hands of faith. In no other place does he find repose, for every other point of rest is mere nonsense, even though in men's eyes it is shrewdness. This is the reason why possibility is so absolutely educative. No man has ever become so unfortunate in reality that there was not some little residue left to him, and, as common sense observes quite truly, if a man is [141] canny, he will find a way. But he who went through the curriculum of misfortune offered by possibility lost everything, absolutely everything, in a way that no one has lost it in reality. If in this situation he did not behave falsely towards possibility, if he did not attempt to talk around the dread which would save him, then he received everything back again, as in reality no one ever did even if he received everything double, for the pupil of possibility received infinity, whereas the soul of the other expired in the finite. No one ever sank so deep in reality that he could not sink deeper, or that there might not be one or another sunk deeper than he. But he who sank in the possibility has an eye too dizzy to see the measuring rod which Tom, Dick, and Harry hold out as a straw to the drowning man; his ear is closed so that he cannot hear what the market price for men is in his day, cannot hear that he is just as good as most of them. He sank absolutely, but then in turn he floated up from the depth of the abyss, lighter now than all that is oppressive and dreadful in life. Only I do not deny that he who is educated by possibility is exposed—not to the danger of bad company and dissoluteness of various sorts, as are those who are educated by the finite, but—to one danger of downfall, and that is self-slaughter. If at the beginning of his education he misunderstands the anguish of dread, so that it does not lead him to faith but away from faith, then he is lost. On the other hand, he who is educated by possibility remains with dread, does not allow himself to be deceived by its countless counterfeits, he recalls the past precisely; then at last the attacks of dread, though they are fearful, are not such that he flees from them. For him dread becomes a serviceable spirit which against its will leads him whither he would go. Then when it announces itself, when it craftily insinuates that it has invented a new instrument of torture far more terrible than anything employed before, he does not recoil, still less does he attempt to hold it off with clamor and noise, but he bids it welcome, he hails it solemnly, as Socrates solemnly flourished the poisoned goblet, he shuts himself up with it, he says, as a patient says to the surgeon when a painful operation is about to begin, "Now I am ready." Then dread enters into his soul and searches it thoroughly, constraining out of him all the finite and the petty, and leading him hence whither he would go.

When one or another extraordinary event occurs in life, when a world-historical hero gathers heroes about him and accomplishes [142] heroic feats, when a crisis occurs and everything becomes significant, then men wish to be in it, for these are things which educate. Quite possibly. But there is a much simpler way of being educated much more fundamentally. Take the pupil of possibility, set him in the midst of the Jutland heath where nothing happens, where the greatest event is that a partridge flies up noisily, and he experiences everything more perfectly, more precisely, more profoundly, than the man who was applauded upon the stage of universal history, in case he was not educated by possibility. [143]

. . . . .

FRIEDRICH NIETZSCHE

Joyful Wisdom

125

THE MADMAN: Have you ever heard of the madman who on a bright morning lighted a lantern and ran to the market-place calling out unceasingly: "I seek God! I seek God!"—As there were many people standing about who did not believe in God, he caused a great deal of amusement. Why! is he lost? said one. Has he strayed away like a child? said another. Or does he keep himself hidden? Is he afraid of us? Has he taken a sea-voyage? Has he emigrated?—the people cried out laughingly, all in a hubbub. The insane man jumped into their midst and transfixed them with his glances. "Where is God gone?" he called out. "I mean to tell you! *We have killed him,*—you and I! We are all his murderers! But how have we done it? How were we able to drink up the sea? Who gave us the sponge to wipe away the whole horizon? What did we do when we loosened this earth from its sun?

SOURCE: *Joyful Wisdom* by Friedrich Nietzsche. Reprinted with permission of George Allen & Unwin Ltd.

NOTE TO THE STUDENT: In documenting any part of this work of Nietzsche, it is customary to cite the number of the section rather than a page number.

Whither does it now move? Whither do we move? Away from all suns? Do we not dash on unceasingly? Backwards, sideways, forewards, in all directions? Is there still an above and below? Do we not stray, as through infinite nothingness? Does not empty space breathe upon us? Has it not become colder? Does not night come on continually, darker and darker? Shall we not have to light lanterns in the morning? Do we not hear the noise of the grave-diggers who are burying God? Do we not smell the divine putrefaction?—for even Gods putrefy! God is dead! God remains dead! And we have killed him! How shall we console ourselves, the most murderous of all murderers? The holiest and the mightiest that the world has hitherto possessed, has bled to death under our knife,—who will wipe the blood from us? With what water could we cleanse ourselves? What lustrums, what sacred games shall we have to devise? Is not the magnitude of this deed too great for us? Shall we not ourselves have to become Gods, merely to seem worthy of it? There never was a greater event,—and on account of it, all who are born after us belong to a higher history than any history hitherto!"—Here the madman was silent and looked again at his hearers; they also were silent and looked at him in surprise. At last he threw his lantern on the ground, so that it broke in pieces and was extinguished. "I come too early," he then said, "I am not yet at the right time. This prodigious event is still on its way, and is travelling,—it has not yet reached men's ears. Lightning and thunder need time, the light of the stars needs time, deeds need time, even after they are done, to be seen and heard. This deed is as yet further from them than the furthest star,—*and yet they have done it!*"—It is further stated that the madman made his way into different churches on the same day, and there intoned his *Requiem aeternam deo.* When led out and called to account, he always gave the reply: "What are these churches now, if they are not the tombs and monuments of God?"—

283

PIONEERS: I greet all the signs indicating that a more manly and warlike age is commencing, which will, above all, bring heroism again into honour! For it has to prepare the way for a yet higher age, and gather the force which the latter will one day require,—the age which will carry heroism into knowledge, and *wage war* for the sake of ideas and their consequences. For that end many brave pioneers are now needed, who, however, cannot originate out of nothing,—and just as little out of the sand and slime of present-day civilisation and the culture of great cities: men silent, solitary and resolute, who know how to be content and persistent in invisible activity: men who with innate disposition seek in all things that which is *to be overcome* in them: men to whom cheerfulness, patience, simplicity, and contempt of the great vanities belong just as much as do magnanimity in victory and indulgence to the trivial vanities of all the vanquished: men with an acute and independent judgment regarding all victors, and concerning the part which chance has played in the winning of victory and fame: men with their own holidays, their own work-days, and their own periods of mourning; accustomed to command with perfect assurance, and equally ready, if need be, to obey, proud in the one case as in the other, equally serving their own interests: men more imperilled, more productive, more happy! For believe me!—the secret of realising the largest productivity and the greatest enjoyment of existence is *to live in danger!* Build your cities on the slope of Vesuvius! Send your ships into unexplored seas! Live in war with your equals and with yourselves! Be robbers and spoilers, ye knowing ones, as long as ye cannot be rulers and possessors! The time will soon pass when you can be satisfied to live like timorous deer concealed in the forests. Knowledge will finally stretch out her hand for that which belongs to her:—she means to *rule* and *possess,* and you with her!

296

A FIXED REPUTATION: A fixed reputation was formerly a matter of the very greatest utility; and wherever society continues to be ruled by the herd-instinct, it is still most suitable for every individual *to give* to his character and business *the appearance* of unalterableness,—even when they are not so in reality. "One can rely on him, he remains the same"—that is the praise which has most significance in all dangerous conditions of society. Society feels with satisfaction that it has a reliable *tool* ready at all times in the virtue of this one, in the ambition of that one, and in the reflection and passion of a third one,—it honours this *tool-like nature,* this self-constancy, this unchangeableness in opinions, efforts, and even in faults, with the highest honours. Such a valuation, which prevails and has prevailed everywhere simultaneously with the morality of custom, educates "characters," and brings all changing, re-learning, and self-transforming into *disrepute.* Be the advantage of this mode of thinking ever so great otherwise, it is in any case the mode of judging which is most injurious *to knowledge:* for precisely the good-will of the knowing one ever to declare himself unhesitatingly as *opposed* to his former opinions, and in general to be distrustful of all that wants to be fixed in him—is here condemned and brought into disrepute. The disposition of the thinker, as incompatible with a "fixed reputation," is regarded as *dishonourable,* while the petrifaction of opinions has all the honour to itself:—we have at present still to live under the interdict of such rules! How difficult it is to live when one feels that the judgment of many millenniums is around one and against one. It is probable that for many millenniums knowledge was afflicted with a bad conscience, and there must have been much self-contempt and secret misery in the history of the greatest intellects.

343

WHAT OUR CHEERFULNESS SIGNIFIES: The most important of more recent events—that "God is dead," that the belief in the Christian God has become unworthy of belief—already begins to cast its first shadows over Europe. To the few at least whose eye, whose *suspecting* glance, is strong enough and subtle enough for this drama, some sun seems to have set, some old, profound confidence seems to have changed into doubt: our old world must seem to them daily more darksome, distrustful, strange and "old." In the main, however, one may say that the event itself is far too great, too remote, too much beyond most people's power of apprehension, for one to suppose that so much as the report of it could have *reached* them; not to speak of many who already knew *what* had taken place, and what must all collapse now that this belief had been undermined,—because so much was built upon it, so much rested on it, and had become one with it: for example, our entire European morality. This lengthy, vast and uninterrupted process of crumbling, destruction, ruin and overthrow which is now imminent: who has realised it sufficiently to-day to have to stand up as the teacher and herald of such a tremendous logic of terror, as the prophet of a period of gloom and eclipse, the like of which has probably never taken place on earth before? . . . Even we, the born riddle-readers, who wait as it were on the mountains posted 'twixt to-day and to-morrow, and engirt by their contradiction, we, the firstlings and premature children of the coming century, into whose sight especially the shadows which must forthwith envelop Europe *should* already have come—how is it that even we, without genuine sympathy for this period of gloom, contemplate its advent without any *personal* solicitude or fear? Are we still, perhaps, too much under the *immediate effects* of the event—and are these effects, especially as regards *ourselves,* perhaps the reverse of what was to be expected—not at all sad and depressing, but rather like a new and indescribable variety of light, happiness, relief, enlivenment, encouragement, and dawning day? . . . In fact, we philosophers and "free spirits" feel ourselves irradiated as by a new dawn by the report that the "old God is dead"; our hearts overflow with gratitude, astonishment, presentiment and expectation. At last the horizon seems open once more, granting even that it is not bright; our ships can at last put out to sea in face of every danger; every hazard is again permitted to the discerner; the sea, *our* sea, again lies open before us; perhaps never before did such an "open sea" exist.—

MARTIN HEIDEGGER

What Is Metaphysics?

"What is metaphysics?" The question leads one to expect a discussion about metaphysics. Such is not our intention. Instead, we shall discuss a definite metaphysical question, thus, as it will appear, landing ourselves straight into metaphysics. Only in this way can we make it really possible for metaphysics to speak for itself.

Our project begins with the presentation of a metaphysical question, then goes on to its development and ends with its answer.

SOURCE: From *Existence and Being* by Martin Heidegger. Henry Regnery, Chicago. Gateway Ed., 1960.

THE PRESENTATION OF A METAPHYSICAL QUESTION

Seen from the point of view of sound common sense, Philosophy, according to Hegel, is the "world stood on its head." Hence the peculiar nature of our task calls for some preliminary definition. This arises out of the dual nature of metaphysical questioning.

Firstly, every metaphysical question always covers the whole range of metaphysical problems. In every case it is itself the whole. Secondly, every metaphysical question can only be put in such a way that the questioner as such is by his very questioning involved in the question.

From this we derive the following pointer: metaphysical questioning has to be put as a whole and has always to be based on the essential situation of existence, which puts the question. We question here and now, on our own account. Our existence—a community of scientists,[325] teachers and students—is ruled by science. What essential things are happening to us in the foundations of our existence, now that science has become our passion?

The fields of the sciences lie far apart. Their methodologies are fundamentally different. This disrupted multiplicity of disciplines is today only held together by the technical organisation of the Universities and their faculties, and maintained as a unit of meaning by the practical aims of those faculties. As against this, however, the root of the sciences in their essential ground has atrophied.

And yet—insofar as we follow their most specific intentions—in all the sciences we are related to what-is. Precisely from the point of view of the sciences no field takes precedence over another, neither Nature over History nor vice versa. No one methodology is superior to another. Mathematical knowledge is no stricter than philological or historical knowledge. It has merely the characteristic of "exactness," which is not to be identified with strictness. To demand exactitude of history would be to offend against the idea of the kind of strictness that pertains to the humanistic sciences. The world-relationship which runs through all the sciences as such constrains them to seek what-is *in itself*, with a view to rendering it, according to its quiddity (*Wasgehalt*) and its modality (*Seinsart*), an object of investigation and basic definition. What the sciences accomplish, ideally speaking, is an approximation to the essential nature of all things.[326]

This distinct world-relationship to what-is in itself is sustained and guided by a freely chosen attitude on the part of our human existence. It is true that the pre-scientific and extra-scientific activities of man also relate to what-is. But the distinction of science lies in the fact that, in an altogether specific manner, it and it alone explicitly allows the object itself the first and last word. In this objectivity of questioning, definition and proof there is a certain limited submission to what-is, so that this may reveal itself. This submissive attitude taken up by scientific theory becomes the basis of a possibility: the possibility of science acquiring a leadership of its own, albeit limited, in the whole field of human existence. The world-relationship of science and the attitude of man responsible for it can, of course, only be fully understood when we see and understand what is going on in the world-relationship so maintained. Man—one entity (*Seiendes*) among others—"pursues" science. In this "pursuit" what is happening is nothing less than the irruption of a particular entity called "Man" into the whole of what-is, in such a way that in and through this irruption what-is manifests itself *as* and *how* it is. The manner in which the revelatory irruption occurs is the chief thing that helps what-is to become what it is.

This triple process of world-relationship, attitude, and irruption—a radical unity—introduces something of the inspiring simplicity and intensity of *Da-sein* into scientific existence. If we now explicitly take possession of scientific *Da-sein* [327] as clarified by us, we must necessarily say:

That to which the world-relationship refers is what-is—and nothing else.

That by which every attitude is moulded is what-is—and nothing more.

That with which scientific exposition effects its "irruption" is what-is—and beyond that, nothing.

But is it not remarkable that precisely at that point where scientific man makes sure of his surest possession he should speak of something else? What is to be investigated is what-is—and nothing else; only what-is—and nothing more; simply and solely what-is—and beyond that, nothing.

But what about this "nothing"? Is it only an accident that we speak like that quite naturally? Is it only a manner of speaking—and nothing more?

But why worry about this Nothing? "Nothing" is absolutely rejected by science and abandoned as null and void (*das Nichtige*).

But if we abandon Nothing in this way are we not, by that act, really admitting it? Can we, though, speak of an admission when we admit Nothing? But perhaps this sort of cross-talk is already degenerating into an empty wrangling about words.

Science, on the other hand, has to assert its soberness and seriousness afresh and declare that it is concerned solely with what-is. Nothing—how can it be for science anything other than a horror and a phantasm? If science is right then one thing stands firm: science wishes to know nothing [328] of Nothing. Such is after all the strictly scientific approach to Nothing. We know it by wishing to know nothing of Nothing.

Science wishes to know nothing of Nothing. Even so the fact remains that at the very point where science tries to put its own essence in words it invokes the aid of Nothing. It has recourse to the very thing it rejects. What sort of schizophrenia is this?

A consideration of our momentary existence as one ruled by science has landed us in the thick of an argument. In the course of this argument a question has already presented itself. The question only requires putting specifically: What about Nothing?

THE DEVELOPMENT OF THE QUESTION

The development of our enquiry into Nothing is bound to lead us to a position where either the answer will prove possible or the impossibility of an answer will become evident. "Nothing" is admitted. Science, by adopting an attitude of superior indifference, abandons it as that which "is not."

All the same we shall endeavour to enquire into Nothing. What is Nothing? Even the initial approach to this question shows us something out of the ordinary. So questioning, we postulate Nothing as something that somehow or other "is"—as an entity (*Seiendes*). But it is nothing of the sort. The question as to the what and wherefore of Nothing turns the thing questioned into its [329] opposite. The question deprives itself of its own object.

Accordingly, every answer to this question is impossible from the start. For it necessarily moves in the form that Nothing "is" this, that or the other. Question and answer are equally nonsensical in themselves where Nothing is concerned.

Hence even the rejection by science is superfluous. The commonly cited basic rule of all thinking—the proposition that contradiction must be avoided—and common "logic" rule out the question. For thinking, which is essentially always thinking about something, would, in thinking of Nothing, be forced to act against its own nature.

Because we continually meet with failure as soon as we try to turn Nothing into a subject, our enquiry into Nothing is already at an end—always assuming, of course, that in this enquiry "logic" is the highest court of appeal, that reason is the means and thinking the way to an original comprehension of Nothing and its possible revelation.

But, it may be asked, can the law of "logic" be assailed? Is not reason indeed the master in this enquiry into Nothing? It is in fact only with reason's help that we can define Nothing in the first place and postulate it as a problem—though a problem that consumes only itself. For Nothing is the negation (*Verneinung*) of the totality of what-is: that which is absolutely not. But at this [330] point we bring Nothing into the higher category of the Negative (*Nichthaftes*) and therefore of what is negated. But according to the overriding and unassailable teachings of "logic" negation is a specific act of reason. How, then, in our enquiry into Nothing and into the very possibility of holding such an enquiry can we dismiss reason? Yet is it so sure just what we are postulating? Does the Not (*das Nicht*), the state of being negated (*die Verneintheit*) and hence negation itself (*Verneinung*), in fact represent that higher category under which Nothing takes its place as a special kind of thing negated? Does Nothing "exist" only because the Not, i.e. negation exists? Or is it the other way about? Does negation and the Not exist only because Nothing exists? This has not been decided—indeed, it has not even been explicitly asked. We assert: "Nothing" is more original than the Not and negation.

If this thesis is correct then the very possibility of negation as an act of reason, and consequently reason itself, are somehow dependent on Nothing. How, then, can reason attempt to decide this issue? May not the apparent nonsensicality of the question and answer where Nothing is concerned only rest, perhaps, on the blind obstinacy of the roving intellect?

If, however, we refuse to be led astray by the formal impossibility of enquiry into Nothing and still continue to enquire in the face of it, we must at least satisfy what remains the fundamental pre-requisite for the full pursuit of any [331] enquiry. If Nothing as such is still to be enquired into, it follows that it must be "given" in advance. We must be able to encounter it.

Where shall we seek Nothing? Where shall we find Nothing? In order to find something must we not know beforehand that it is there? Indeed we must! First and foremost we can only look if we have presupposed the presence of a thing to be looked for. But here the thing we are looking for is Nothing. Is there after all a seeking without pre-supposition, a seeking complemented by a pure finding?

However that may be, we do know "Nothing" if only as a term we bandy about every day. This ordinary hackneyed Nothing, so completely taken for granted and rolling off our tongue so casually—we can even give an off-hand "definition" of it:

Nothing is the complete negation of the totality of what-is.

Does not this characteristic of Nothing point, after all, in the direction from which alone it may meet us?

The totality of what-is must be given beforehand so as to succumb as such to the negation from which Nothing is then bound to emerge.

But, even apart from the questionableness of this relationship between negation and Nothing, how are we, as finite beings, to render the whole of what-is in its totality accessible *in itself*—let alone to ourselves? We can, at a pinch, think of the whole of what-is as an "idea" and then negate what we have thus imagined in our thoughts and [332] "think" it negated. In this way we arrive at the formal concept of an imaginary Nothing, but never Nothing itself. But Nothing is nothing, and between the imaginary and the "authentic" (*eigentlich*) Nothing no difference can obtain, if Nothing represents complete lack of differentiation. But the "authentic" Nothing—is this not once again that latent and nonsensical idea of a Nothing that "is"? Once again and for the last time rational objections have tried to hold up our search, whose legitimacy can only be attested by a searching experience of Nothing.

As certainly as we shall never comprehend absolutely the totality of what-is, it is equally certain that we find ourselves placed in the midst of what-is and that this is somehow revealed in totality. Ultimately there is an essential difference between comprehending the totality of what-is and finding ourselves in the midst of what-is-in-totality. The former is absolutely impossible. The latter is going on in existence all the time.

Naturally enough it looks as if, in our everyday activities, we were always holding on to this or that actuality (*Seiendes*), as if we were lost in this or that region of what-is. However fragmentary the daily round may appear it still maintains what-is, in however shadowy a fashion, within the unity of a "whole." Even when, or rather, precisely when we are not absorbed in things or in our own selves, this "wholeness" comes over us—for example, in real boredom. Real boredom is still far off when this book or that play, this [333] activity or that stretch of idleness merely bores us. Real boredom comes when "one is bored." This profound boredom, drifting hither and thither in the abysses of existence like a mute fog, draws all things, all men and oneself along with them, together in a queer kind of indifference. This boredom reveals what-is in totality.

There is another possibility of such revelation, and this is in the joy we feel in the presence of the being—not merely the person—of someone we love.

Because of these moods in which, as we say, we "are" this or that (i.e. bored, happy, etc.) we find ourselves (*befinden uns*) in the midst of what-is-in-totality, wholly pervaded by it. The affective state in which we find ourselves not only discloses, according to the mood we are in, what-is in totality, but this disclosure is at the same time far from being a mere chance occurrence and is the ground-phenomenon of our *Da-sein.*

Our "feelings," as we call them, are not just the fleeting concomitant of our mental or volitional behaviour, nor are they simply the cause and occasion of such behaviour, nor yet a state that is merely "there" and in which we come to some kind of understanding with ourselves.

Yet, at the very moment when our moods thus bring us face to face with what-is-in-totality they hide the Nothing we are seeking. We are now less than ever of the opinion that mere negation of what-is-in-totality as revealed by these moods of ours can in fact lead us to Nothing. This could only happen in the first place in a mood so peculiarly [334] revelatory in its import as to reveal Nothing itself.

Does there ever occur in human existence a mood of this kind, through which we are brought face to face with Nothing itself?

This may and actually does occur, albeit rather seldom and for moments only, in the key-mood of dread (*Angst*). By "dread" we do not mean "anxiety" (*Aengstlichkeit*), which is common enough and is akin to nervousness (*Furchtsamkeit*)—a mood that comes over us only too easily. Dread differs absolutely from fear (*Furcht*). We are always *afraid* of this or that definite thing, which threatens us in this or that definite way. "Fear of" is generally "fear about" something. Since fear has this characteristic limitation—"of" and "about"

—the man who is afraid, the nervous man, is always bound by the thing he is afraid of or by the state in which he finds himself. In his efforts to save himself from this "something" he becomes uncertain in relation to other things; in fact, he "loses his bearings" generally.

In dread no such confusion can occur. It would be truer to say that dread is pervaded by a peculiar kind of peace. And although dread is always "dread of," it is not dread of this or that. "Dread of" is always a dreadful feeling "about"—but not about this or that. The indefiniteness of *what* we dread is not just lack of definition: it represents the essential impossibility of defining the "what." The indefiniteness is brought out in an illustration familiar to everybody.[335]

In dread, as we say, "one feels something uncanny." What is this "something" (*es*) and this "one"? We are unable to say what gives "one" that uncanny feeling. "One" just feels it generally (*im Ganzen*). All things, and we with them, sink into a sort of indifference. But not in the sense that everything simply disappears; rather, in the very act of drawing away from us everything turns towards us. This withdrawal of what-is-in-totality, which then crowds round us in dread, this is what oppresses us. There is nothing to hold on to. The only thing that remains and overwhelms us whilst what-is slips away, is this "nothing."

Dread reveals Nothing.

In dread we are "in suspense" (*wir schweben*). Or, to put it more precisely, dread holds us in suspense because it makes what-is-in-totality slip away from us. Hence we too, as existents in the midst of what-is, slip away from ourselves along with it. For this reason it is not "you" or "I" that has the uncanny feeling, but "one." In the trepidation of this suspense where there is nothing to hold on to, pure *Da-sein* is all that remains.

Dread strikes us dumb. Because what-is-in-totality slips away and thus forces Nothing to the fore, all affirmation (lit. "Is"-saying: "*Ist*"-*Sagen*) fails in the face of it. The fact that when we are caught in the uncanniness of dread we often try to break the empty silence by words spoken at random, only proves the presence of Nothing. We ourselves confirm that dread reveals Nothing—when we have got over our dread. In the lucid [336] vision which supervenes while yet the experience is fresh in our memory we must needs say that what we were afraid of was "actually" (*eigentlich:* also "authentic") Nothing. And indeed Nothing itself, Nothing as such, was there.

With this key-mood of dread, therefore, we have reached that event in our *Da-sein* which reveals Nothing, and which must therefore be the starting-point of our enquiry.

What about Nothing?

THE ANSWER TO THE QUESTION

The answer which alone is important for our purpose has already been found if we take care to ensure that we really do keep to the problem of Nothing. This necessitates changing man into his *Da-sein* —a change always occasioned in us by dread—so that we may apprehend Nothing as and how it reveals itself in dread. At the same time we have finally to dismiss those characteristics of Nothing which have not emerged as a result of our enquiry.

"Nothing" is revealed in dread, but not as something that "is." Neither can it be taken as an object. Dread is not an apprehension of Nothing. All the same, Nothing is revealed in and through dread, yet not, again, in the sense that Nothing appears as if detached and apart from what-is-in-totality when we have that "uncanny" feeling. We would say rather: in dread Nothing functions as if *at one with* what-is-in-totality. What do we mean by "at one with"? [337]

In dread what-is-in-totality becomes untenable (*hinfällig*). How? What-is is not annihilated (*vernichtet*) by dread, so as to leave Nothing over. How could it, seeing that dread finds itself completely powerless in face of what-is-in-totality! What rather happens is that Nothing shows itself as essentially belonging to what-is while this is slipping away in totality.

In dread there is no annihilation of the whole of what-is in itself; but equally we cannot negate what-is-in-totality in order to reach Nothing. Apart from the fact that the explicitness of a negative statement is foreign to the nature of dread as such, we would always come too late with any such negation intended to demonstrate Nothing. For Nothing is anterior to it. As we said, Nothing is "at one with" what-is as this slips away in totality.

In dread there is a retreat from something, though it is not so much a flight as a spell-bound (*gebannt*) peace. This "retreat from" has its source in Nothing. The latter does not attract: its nature is to repel. This "repelling from itself" is essentially an "expelling into": a conscious gradual relegation to the vanishing what-is-in-totality (*das entgleitenlassende Verweisen auf das versinkende Seiende im Ganzen*). And this total relegation to the vanishing what-is-in-totality—such being the form in which Nothing crowds round us in dread—is the essence of Nothing: nihilation. Nihilation is neither an annihilation (*Vernichtung*) of what-is, nor does it spring from negation (*Verneinung*). Nihilation [338] cannot be reckoned in terms of annihilation or negation at all. Nothing "nihilates" (*nichtet*) of itself.

Nihilation is not a fortuitous event; but, understood as the relegation to the vanishing what-is-in-totality, it reveals the latter in all its till now undisclosed strangeness as the pure "Other"—contrasted with Nothing.

Only in the clear night of dread's Nothingness is what-is as such revealed in all its original overtness (*Offenheit*): that it "is" and is not Nothing. This verbal appendix "and not Nothing" is, however, not an *a posteriori* explanation but an *a priori* which alone makes possible any revelation of what-is. The essence of Nothing as original nihilation lies in this: that it alone brings *Da-sein* face to face with what-is as such.

Only on the basis of the original manifestness of Nothing can our human *Da-sein* advance towards and enter into what-is. But insofar as *Da-sein* naturally relates to what-is, as that which it is not and which itself is, Da-sein *qua Da-sein* always proceeds from Nothing as manifest.

Da-sein means *being projected into* Nothing (*Hineingehaltenheit in das Nichts*).

Projecting into Nothing, *Da-sein* is already beyond what-is-in-totality. This "being beyond" (*Hinaussein*) what-is we call Transcendence. Were *Da-sein* not, in its essential basis, transcendent, that is to say, were it not projected from the start into Nothing, it could never relate to what-is, hence could have no self-relationship.

Without the original manifest character of [339] Nothing there is no self-hood and no freedom.

Here we have the answer to our question about Nothing. Nothing is neither an object nor anything that "is" at all. Nothing occurs neither by itself nor "apart from" what-is, as a sort of adjunct. Nothing is that which makes the revelation of what-is as such possible for our human existence. Nothing not merely provides the conceptual opposite of what-is but is also an original part of essence (*Wesen*). It is in the Being (*Sein*) of what-is that the nihilation of Nothing (*das Nichten des Nichts*) occurs.

But now we must voice a suspicion which has been withheld far too long already. If it is only through "projecting into Nothing" that our *Da-sein* relates to what-is, in other words, has any existence, and if Nothing is only made manifest originally in dread, should we not have to be in a continual suspense of dread in order to exist at all? Have we not, however, ourselves admitted that this original dread is a rare thing? But above all, we all exist and are related to actualities which we ourselves are not and which we ourselves are—without this dread. Is not this dread, therefore, an arbitrary invention and the Nothing attributed to it an exaggeration?

Yet what do we mean when we say that this original dread only occurs in rare moments? Nothing but this: that as far as we are concerned and, indeed, generally speaking, Nothing is always distorted out of its original state. By what? By the fact that in one way or another we completely [340] lose ourselves in what-is. The more we turn to what-is in our dealings the less we allow it to slip away, and the more we turn aside from Nothing. But all the more certainly do we thrust ourselves into the open superficies of existence.

And yet this perpetual if ambiguous aversion from Nothing accords, within certain limits, with the essential meaning of Nothing. It—Nothing in the sense of nihilation—relegates us to what-is. Nothing "nihilates" unceasingly, without our really knowing what is happening—at least, not with our everyday knowledge.

What could provide more telling evidence of the perpetual, far-reaching and yet ever-dissimulated overtness of Nothing in our existence, than negation? This is supposed to belong to the very nature of human thought. But negation cannot by any stretch of imagination produce the Not out of itself as a means of distinguishing and contrasting given things, thrusting this Not between them, as it were. How indeed could negation produce the Not out of itself, seeing that it can only negate when something is there to be negated? But how can a thing that is or ought to be negated be seen as something negative (*nichthaft*) unless all thinking as such is on the look-out for the Not? But the Not can only manifest itself when its source—the nihilation of Nothing and hence Nothing itself—is drawn out of concealment. The Not does not come into being through negation, but negation is based on the Not, which derives from the nihilation of Nothing.[341] Nor is negation only a mode of nihilating behaviour, i.e. behaviour based *a priori* on the nihilation of Nothing.

Herewith we have proved the above thesis in all essentials: Nothing is the source of negation, not the other way about. If this breaks the sovereignty of reason in the field of enquiry into Nothing and Being, then the fate of the rule of "logic" in philosophy is also decided. The very idea of "logic" disintegrates in the vortex of a more original questioning.

However often and however variously negation—whether explicit or not—permeates all thinking, it cannot *of itself* be a completely valid witness to the manifestation of Nothing as an essential part of *Da-sein.* For negation cannot be cited either as the sole or even the chief mode of nihilation, with which, because of the nihilation of Nothing, *Da-sein* is saturated. More abysmal than the mere propriety of rational negation is the harshness of opposition and the violence of loathing. More responsible the pain of refusal and the mercilessness of an interdict. More oppressive the bitterness of renunciation.

These possible modes of nihilating behaviour, through which our *Da-sein* endures, even if it does not master, the fact of our being thrown upon the world are not modes of negation merely. That does not prevent them from expressing themselves in and through negation. Indeed, it is only then that the empty expanse of negation is really revealed. The permeation of [342] *Da-sein* by nihilating modes of behaviour points to the perpetual, ever-dissimulated manifestness of Nothing, which only dread reveals in all its originality. Here, of course, we have the reason why original dread is generally repressed in *Da-sein.* Dread is there, but sleeping. All *Da-sein* quivers with its breathing: the pulsation is slightest in beings that are timorous, and is imperceptible in the "Yea, yea!" and "Nay, nay!" of busy people; it is readiest in the reserved, and surest of all in the courageous. But this last pulsation only occurs for the sake of that for which it expends itself, so as to safeguard the supreme greatness of *Da-sein.*

The dread felt by the courageous cannot be contrasted with the joy or even the comfortable enjoyment of a peaceable life. It stands—on the hither side of all such contrasts—in secret union with the serenity and gentleness of creative longing.

Original dread can be awakened in *Da-sein* at any time. It need not be awakened by any unusual occurrence. Its action corresponds in depth to the shallowness of its possible cause. It is always on the brink, yet only seldom does it take the leap and drag us with it into the state of suspense.

Because our *Da-sein* projects into Nothing on this basis of hidden dread, man becomes the "stand-in" (*Platzhalter*) for Nothing. So finite are we that we cannot, of our own resolution and will, bring ourselves originally face to face with [343] Nothing. So bottomlessly does finalisation (*Verendlichung*) dig into existence that our freedom's peculiar and profoundest finality fails.

This projection into Nothing on the basis of hidden dread is the overcoming of what-is-in-totality: Transcendence.

Our enquiry into Nothing will, we said, lead us straight to metaphysics. The name "metaphysics" derives from the Greek *τὰ μετὰ τὰ φυσικά*. This quaint title was later interpreted as characterising the sort of enquiry which goes *μετά*—trans, beyond—what-is as such.

Metaphysics is an enquiry over and above what-is, with a view to winning it back again as such and in totality for our understanding.

In our quest for Nothing there is similar "going beyond" what-is, conceived as what-is-in-totality. It therefore turns out to be a "metaphysical" question. We said in the beginning that such questioning had a double characteristic: every metaphysical question at once embraces the whole of metaphysics, and in every question the being (*Da-sein*) that questions is himself caught up in the question.

To what extent does the question about Nothing span and pervade the whole of metaphysics?

Since ancient times metaphysics has expressed itself on the subject of Nothing in the highly ambiguous proposition: *ex nihilo nihil fit*—nothing comes from nothing. Even though the proposition as argued never made Nothing itself the real problem, it nevertheless brought out very explicitly, from the prevailing notions about [344] Nothing, the over-riding fundamental concept of what-is.

Classical metaphysics conceives Nothing as signifying Notbeing (*Nichtseiendes*), that is to say, unformed matter which is powerless to form itself into "being" and cannot therefore present an appearance (*εἶδος*). What has "being" is the self-creating product (*Gebilde*) which presents itself as such in an image (*Bild*), i.e. something seen (*Anblick*). The origin, law and limits of this ontological concept are discussed as little as Nothing itself.

Christian dogma, on the other hand, denies the truth of the proposition *ex nihilo nihil fit* and gives a twist to the meaning of Nothing, so that it now comes to mean the absolute absence of all "being" outside God: *ex nihilo fit—ens creatum:* the created being is made out of nothing. "Nothing" is now the conceptual opposite of what truly and authentically (*eigentlich*) "is"; it becomes the *summum ens,* God as *ens increatum.* Here, too, the interpretation of Nothing points to the fundamental concept of what-is. Metaphysical discussion of what-is, however, moves on the same plane as the enquiry into Nothing. In both cases the questions concerning Being (*Sein*) and Nothing as such remain unasked. Hence we need not be worried by the difficulty that if God creates "out of nothing" he above all must be able to relate himself to Nothing. But if God is God he cannot know Nothing, assuming that the "Absolute" excludes from itself all nullity (*Nichtigkeit*).[345]

This crude historical reminder shows Nothing as the conceptual opposite of what truly and authentically "is," i.e. as the negation of it. But once Nothing is somehow made a problem this contrast not only undergoes clearer definition but also arouses the true and authentic metaphysical question regarding the Being of what-is. Nothing ceases to be the vague opposite of what-is: it now reveals itself as integral to the Being of what-is.

"Pure Being and pure Nothing are thus one and the same." This proposition of Hegel's ("The Science of Logic," I, WW III, p. 74) is correct. Being and Nothing hang together, but not because the two things—from the point of view of the Hegelian concept of thought—are one in their indefiniteness and immediateness, but because Being itself is finite in essence and is only revealed in the Transcendence of *Da-sein* as projected into Nothing.

If indeed the question of Being as such is the all-embracing question of metaphysics, then the question of Nothing proves to be such as to span the whole metaphysical field. But at the same time the question of Nothing pervades the whole of metaphysics only because it forces us to face the problem of the origin of negation, that is to say, forces a decision about the legitimacy of the rule of "logic" in metaphysics.

The old proposition *ex nihilo nihil fit* will then acquire a different meaning, and one appropriate to the problem of Being itself, so as to run: *ex nihilo omne ens qua ens fit:* every being, so far as it is a being, is made out of nothing.[346] Only in the Nothingness of *Da-sein* can what-is-in-totality—and this in accordance with its peculiar possibilities, i.e. in a finite manner—come to itself. To what extent, then, has the enquiry into Nothing, if indeed it be a metaphysical one, included our own questing *Da-sein*?

Our *Da-sein* as experienced here and now is, we said, ruled by science. If our *Da-sein*, so ruled, is put into this question concerning Nothing, then it follows that it must itself have been put in question by this question.

The simplicity and intensity of scientific *Da-sein* consist in this:

that it relates in a special manner to what-is and to this alone. Science would like to abandon Nothing with a superior gesture. But now, in this question of Nothing, it becomes evident that scientific *Da-sein* is only possible when projected into Nothing at the outset. Science can only come to terms with itself when it does not abandon Nothing. The alleged soberness and superiority of science becomes ridiculous if it fails to take Nothing seriously. Only because Nothing is obvious can science turn what-is into an object of investigation. Only when science proceeds from metaphysics can it conquer its essential task ever afresh, which consists not in the accumulation and classification of knowledge but in the perpetual discovery of the whole realm of truth, whether of Nature or of History.

Only because Nothing is revealed in the very basis of our *Da-sein* is it possible for the utter strangeness of what-is to dawn on us. Only when [347] the strangeness of what-is forces itself upon us does it awaken and invite our wonder. Only because of wonder, that is to say, the revelation of Nothing, does the "Why?" spring to our lips. Only because this "Why?" is possible as such can we seek for reasons and proofs in a definite way. Only because we can ask and prove are we fated to become enquirers in this life.

The enquiry into Nothing puts us, the enquirers, ourselves in question. It is a metaphysical one.

Man's *Da-sein* can only relate to what-is by projecting into Nothing. Going beyond what-is is of the essence of *Da-sein*. But this "going beyond" is metaphysics itself. That is why metaphysics belongs to the nature of man. It is neither a department of scholastic philosophy nor a field of chance ideas. Metaphysics is the ground-phenomenon of *Da-sein*. It is *Da-sein* itself. Because the truth of metaphysics is so unfathomable there is always the lurking danger of profoundest error. Hence no scientific discipline can hope to equal the seriousness of metaphysics. Philosophy can never be measured with the yard-stick of the idea of science.

Once the question we have developed as to the nature of Nothing is really asked by and among our own selves, then we are not bringing in metaphysics from the outside. Nor are we simply "transporting" ourselves into it. It is completely out of our power to transport ourselves into metaphysics because, in so far as we exist, we are already there. *Φύσει γὰρ, ὦ φίλει, ἔνεστί τις* [348] *φιλοσοφία τῇ τοῦ ἀνδρὸς διανοίᾳ* (Plato: Phaedrus 279a). While man exists there will be philosophising of some sort. Philosophy, as we call it, is the setting in motion of metaphysics; and in metaphysics philosophy comes to itself and sets about its explicit tasks. Philosophy is only set in motion by leaping with all its being, as only it can, into the ground-possibilities of being as a whole. For this leap the following things are of crucial importance: firstly, leaving room for what-is-in-totality; secondly, letting oneself go into Nothing, that is to say, freeing oneself from the idols we all have and to which we are wont to go cringing; lastly, letting this "suspense" range where it will, so that it may continually swing back again to the ground-question of metaphysics, which is wrested from Nothing itself:

Why is there any Being at all—why not far rather Nothing? [349]

JEAN-PAUL SARTRE

Existentialism

I should like on this occasion to defend existentialism against some charges which have been brought against it.

First, it has been charged with inviting people to remain in a kind of desperate quietism because, since no solutions are possible, we should have to consider action in this world as quite impossible. We should then end up in a philosophy of contemplation; and since contemplation is a luxury, we come in the end to a bourgeois philosophy. The communists in particular have made these charges.

On the other hand, we have been charged with dwelling on human degradation, with pointing up everywhere the sordid, shady, and slimy, and neglecting the gracious and beautiful, the bright side of human nature; for example, according to Mlle. Mercier, a Catholic critic, with forgetting the smile of the child. Both sides charge us with having ignored human solidarity, with considering man as an isolated being. The communists say that the main reason for this is that we take pure subjectivity, the *Cartesian I* [11] *think*, as our starting point; in other words, the moment in which man becomes fully aware of what it means to him to be an isolated being; as a result, we are unable to return to a state of solidarity

SOURCE: From *Existentialism* by Jean-Paul Sartre, translated by Bernard Frechtman, Philosophical Library, New York, 1947. Reprinted with the permission of Philosophical Library. This essay first appeared under the title "Existentialism Is a Humanism."

with the men who are not ourselves, a state which we can never reach in the *cogito*.

From the Christian standpoint, we are charged with denying the reality and seriousness of human undertakings, since, if we reject God's commandments and the eternal verities, there no longer remains anything but pure caprice, with everyone permitted to do as he pleases and incapable, from his own point of view, of condemning the points of view and acts of others.

I shall try today to answer these different charges. Many people are going to be surprised at what is said here about humanism. We shall try to see in what sense it is to be understood. In any case, what can be said from the very beginning is that by existentialism we mean a doctrine which makes human life possible and, in addition, declares that every truth and every action implies a human setting and a human subjectivity.

As is generally known, the basic charge [12] against us is that we put the emphasis on the dark side of human life. Someone recently told me of a lady who, when she let slip a vulgar word in a moment of irritation, excused herself by saying, "I guess I'm becoming an existentialist." Consequently, existentialism is regarded as something ugly; that is why we are said to be naturalists; and if we are, it is rather surprising that in this day and age we cause so much more alarm and scandal than does naturalism, properly so called. The kind of person who can take in his stride such a novel as Zola's *The Earth* is disgusted as soon as he starts reading an existentialist novel; the kind of person who is resigned to the wisdom of the ages—which is pretty sad—finds us even sadder. Yet, what can be more disillusioning than saying "true charity begins at home" or "a scoundrel will always return evil for good?"

We know the commonplace remarks made when this subject comes up, remarks which always add up to the same thing: we shouldn't struggle against the powers-that-be; we shouldn't resist authority; we shouldn't try to rise above our station; any action which [13] doesn't conform to authority is romantic; any effort not based on past experience is doomed to failure; experience shows that man's bent is always toward trouble, that there must be a strong hand to hold him in check, if not, there will be anarchy. There are still people who go on mumbling these melancholy old saws, the people who say, "It's only human!" whenever a more or less repugnant act is pointed out to them, the people who glut themselves on *chansons réalistes*; these are the people who accuse existentialism of being too gloomy, and to such an extent that I wonder whether they are complaining about it, not for its pessimism, but much rather its optimism. Can it be that what really scares them in the doctrine I shall try to present here is that it leaves to man a possibility of choice? To answer this question, we must re-examine it on a strictly philosophical plane. What is meant by the term *existentialism?*

Most people who use the word would be rather embarrassed if they had to explain it, since, now that the word is all the rage, even the work of a musician or painter is being [14] called existentialist. A gossip columnist in *Clartés* signs himself *The Existentialist,* so that by this time the word has been so stretched and has taken on so broad a meaning, that it no longer means anything at all. It seems that for want of an advance-guard doctrine analogous to surrealism, the kind of people who are eager for scandal and flurry turn to this philosophy which in other respects does not at all serve their purposes in this sphere.

Actually, it is the least scandalous, the most austere of doctrines. It is intended strictly for specialists and philosophers. Yet it can be defined easily. What complicates matters is that there are two kinds of existentialist; first, those who are Christian, among whom I would include Jaspers and Gabriel Marcel, both Catholic; and on the other hand the atheistic existentialists, among whom I class Heidegger, and then the French existentialists and myself. What they have in common is that they think that existence precedes essence, or, if you prefer, that subjectivity must be the starting point.

Just what does that mean? Let us consider [15] some object that is manufactured, for example, a book or a paper-cutter: here is an object which has been made by an artisan whose inspiration came from a concept. He referred to the concept of what a paper-cutter is and likewise to a known method of production, which is part of the concept, something which is, by and large, a routine. Thus, the paper-cutter is at once an object produced in a certain way and, on the other hand, one having a specific use; and one can not postulate a man who produces a paper-cutter but does not know what it is used for. Therefore, let us say that, for the paper-cutter, essence—that is, the ensemble of both the production routines and the properties which enable it to be both produced and defined—precedes existence. Thus, the presence of the paper-cutter or book in front of me is determined. Therefore, we have here a technical view of the world whereby it can be said that production precedes existence.

When we conceive God as the Creator, He is generally thought of as a superior sort of artisan. Whatever doctrine we may be considering, whether one like that of Descartes or that [16] of Leibnitz, we always grant that will more or less follows understanding or, at the very least, accompanies it, and that when God creates He knows exactly what He is creating. Thus, the concept of man in the mind of God is comparable to the concept of paper-cutter in the mind of the manufacturer, and, following certain techniques and a conception, God produces man, just as the artisan, following a definition and a technique, makes a paper-cutter. Thus, the individual man is the realisation of a certain concept in the divine intelligence.

In the eighteenth century, the atheism of the *philosophes* discarded the idea of God, but not so much for the notion that essence precedes existence. To a certain extent, this idea is found everywhere; we find it in Diderot, in Voltaire, and even in Kant. Man has a human nature; this human nature, which is the concept of the human, is found in all men, which means that each man is a particular example of a universal concept, man. In Kant, the result of this universality is that the wild-man, the natural man, as well as the bourgeois, are circumscribed by the same definition and have [17] the same basic qualities. Thus, here too the essence of man precedes the historical existence that we find in nature.

Atheistic existentialism, which I represent, is more coherent. It states that if God does not exist, there is at least one being in whom existence precedes essence, a being who exists before he can be defined by any concept, and that this being is man, or, as Heidegger says, human reality. What is meant here by saying that existence precedes essence? It means that, first of all, man exists, turns up, appears on the scene, and, only afterwards, defines himself. If man, as the existentialist conceives him, is indefinable, it is because at first he is nothing. Only afterward will he be something, and he himself will have made what he will be. Thus, there is no human nature, since there is no God to conceive it. Not only is man what he conceives himself to be, but he is also only what he wills himself to be after this thrust toward existence.

Man is nothing else but what he makes of himself. Such is the first principle of existentialism. It is also what is called subjectivity, [18] the name we are labeled with when charges are brought against us. But what do we mean by this, if not that man has a greater dignity than a stone or table? For we mean that man first exists, that is, that man first of all is the being who hurls himself toward a future and who is conscious of imagining himself as being in the future. Man is at the start a plan which is aware of itself, rather than a patch of moss, a piece of garbage, or a cauliflower; nothing exists prior to this plan; there is nothing in heaven; man will be what he will have planned to be. Not what he will want to be. Because by the word "will" we generally mean a conscious decision, which is subsequent to what we have already made of ourselves. I may want to belong to a political party, write a book, get married; but all that is only a manifestation of an earlier, more spontaneous choice that is called "will." But if existence really does precede essence, man is responsible for what he is. Thus, existentialism's first move is to make every man aware of what he is and to make the full responsibility of his existence rest on him. And when we say that a man is responsible for himself, we do not only [19] mean that he is responsible for his own individuality, but that he is responsible for all men.

The word subjectivism has two meanings, and our opponents play on the two. Subjectivism means, on the one hand, that an individual chooses and makes himself; and, on the other, that it is impossible for man to transcend human subjectivity. The second of these is the essential meaning of existentialism. When we say that man chooses his own self, we mean that every one of us does likewise; but we also mean by that that in making this choice he also chooses all men. In fact, in creating the man that we want to be, there is not a single one of our acts which does not at the same time create an image of man as we think he ought to be. To choose to be this or that is to affirm at the same time the value of what we choose, because we can never choose evil. We always choose the good, and nothing can be good for us without being good for all.

If, on the other hand, existence precedes essence, and if we grant that we exist and fashion our image at one and the same time, the image is valid for everybody and for our whole [20] age. Thus, our responsibility is much greater than we might have supposed, because it involves all mankind. If I am a workingman and choose to join a Christian trade-union rather than be a communist, and if by being a member I want to show that the best thing for man is resignation, that the kingdom of man is not of this world, I am not only involving my own case—I want to be resigned for everyone. As a result, my action has involved all humanity. To take a more individual matter, if I want to marry, to have children; even if this marriage depends solely on my own circumstances or passion or wish, I am involving all humanity in monogamy and not merely myself. Therefore, I am responsible for myself and for everyone else. I am creating a certain image of man of my own choosing. In choosing myself, I choose man.

This helps us understand what the actual content is of such rather grandiloquent words as anguish, forlornness, despair. As you will see, it's all quite simple.

First, what is meant by anguish? The existentialists say at once that man is anguish. What [21] that means is this: the man who involves himself and who realizes that he is not only the person he chooses to be, but also a law-maker who is, at the same time, choosing all mankind as well as himself, can not help escape the feeling of his total and deep responsibility. Of course, there are many people who are not anxious; but we claim that they are hiding their anxiety, that they are fleeing from it. Certainly, many people believe that when they do something, they themselves are the only ones involved, and when someone says to them, "What if everyone acted that way?" they shrug their shoulders and answer, "Everyone doesn't act that way." But really, one should always ask himself, "What would happen if everybody looked at things that way?" There is no escaping this disturbing thought except by a kind of double-dealing. A man who lies and makes excuses for himself by saying "not everybody does that," is someone with an uneasy conscience, because the act of lying implies that a universal value is conferred upon the lie.

Anguish is evident even when it conceals itself. This is the anguish that Kierkegaard called [22] the anguish of Abraham. You know the story: an angel has ordered Abraham to sacrifice his son; if it really were an angel who has come and said, "You are Abraham, you shall sacrifice your son," everything would be all right. But everyone might first wonder, "Is it really an angel, and am I really Abraham? What proof do I have?"

There was a madwoman who had hallucinations; someone used to speak to her on the telephone and give her orders. Her doctor asked her, "Who is it who talks to you?" She answered, "He says it's God." What proof did she really have that it was God? If an angel comes to me, what proof is there that it's an angel? And if I hear voices, what proof is there that they come from heaven and not from hell, or from the subconscious, or a pathological condition? What proves that they are addressed to me? What proof is there that I have been appointed to impose my choice and my conception of man on humanity? I'll never find any proof or sign to convince me of that. If a voice addresses me, it is always for me to decide that this is the angel's voice; if I consider [23] that such an act is a good one, it is I who will choose to say that it is good rather than bad.

Now, I'm not being singled out as an Abraham, and yet at every moment I'm obliged to perform exemplary acts. For every man, everything happens as if all mankind had its eyes fixed on him and were guiding itself by what he does. And every man ought to say to himself, "Am I really the kind of man who has the right to act in such a way that humanity might guide itself by my actions?" And if he does not say that to himself, he is masking his anguish.

There is no question here of the kind of anguish which would lead to quietism, to inaction. It is a matter of a simple sort of anguish that anybody who has had responsibilities is familiar with. For example, when a military officer takes the responsibility for an attack and sends a certain number of men to death, he chooses to do so, and in the main he alone makes the choice. Doubtless, orders come from above, but they are too broad; he interprets them, and on this interpretation depend the [24] lives of ten or fourteen or twenty men. In making a decision he can not help having a certain anguish. All leaders know this anguish. That doesn't keep them from acting; on the contrary, it is the very condition of their action. For it implies that they envisage a number of possibilities, and when they choose one, they realize that it has value only because it is chosen. We shall see that this kind of anguish, which is the kind that existentialism describes, is explained, in addition, by a direct responsibility to the other men whom it involves. It is not a curtain separating us from action, but is part of action itself.

When we speak of forlornness, a term Heidegger was fond of, we mean only that God does not exist and that we have to face all the consequences of this. The existentialist is strongly opposed to a certain kind of secular ethics which would like to abolish God with the least possible expense. About 1880, some French teachers tried to set up a secular ethics which went something like this: God is a useless and costly hypothesis; we are discarding it; but, meanwhile, in order for there to be an [25] ethics, a society, a civilization, it is essential that certain values be taken seriously and that they be considered as having an *a priori* existence. It must be obligatory, *a priori*, to be honest, not to lie, not to beat your wife, to have children, etc., etc. So we're going to try a little device which will make it possible to show that values exist all the same, inscribed in a heaven of ideas, though otherwise God does not exist. In other words—and this, I believe, is the tendency of everything called reformism in France—nothing will be changed if God does not exist. We shall find ourselves with the same norms of honesty, progress, and humanism, and we shall have made of God an outdated hypothesis which will peacefully die off by itself.

The existentialist, on the contrary, thinks it very distressing that God does not exist, because all possibility of finding values in a heaven of ideas disappears along with Him; there can no longer be an *a priori* Good, since there is no infinite and perfect consciousness to think it. Nowhere is it written that the Good exists, that we must be honest, that we must not lie; because the fact is we are on a plane [26] where there are only men. Dostoevsky said, "If God didn't exist, everything would be possible." That is the very starting point of existentialism. Indeed, everything is permissible if God does not exist, and as a result man is forlorn, because neither within him nor without does he find anything to cling to. He can't start making excuses for himself.

If existence really does precede essence, there is no explaining things away by reference to a fixed and given human nature. In other words, there is no determinism, man is free, man is freedom. On the other hand, if God does not exist, we find no values or commands to turn to which legitimize our conduct. So, in the bright realm of values, we have no excuse behind us, nor justification before us. We are alone, with no excuses.

That is the idea I shall try to convey when I say that man is condemned to be free. Condemned, because he did not create himself, yet, in other respects is free; because, once thrown into the world, he is responsible for everything he does. The existentialist does not believe in the power of passion. He will never [27] agree that a sweeping passion is a ravaging torrent which fatally leads a man to certain acts and is therefore an excuse. He thinks that man is responsible for his passion.

The existentialist does not think that man is going to help himself by finding in the world some omen by which to orient himself. Because he thinks that man will interpret the omen to suit himself. Therefore, he thinks that man, with no support and no aid, is condemned every moment to invent man. Ponge, in a very fine article, has said, "Man is the future of man." That's exactly it. But if it is taken to mean that this future is recorded in heaven, that God sees it, then it is false, because it would really no longer be a future. If it is taken to mean that, whatever a man may be, there is a future to be forged, a virgin future before him, then this remark is sound. But then we are forlorn.

To give you an example which will enable you to understand forlornness better, I shall cite the case of one of my students who came to see me under the following circumstances: his father was on bad terms with his mother, and, moreover, was inclined to be a collaborationist; [28] his older brother had been killed in the German offensive of 1940, and the young man, with somewhat immature but generous feelings, wanted to avenge him. His mother lived alone with him, very much upset by the half-treason of her husband and the death of her older son; the boy was her only consolation.

The boy was faced with the choice of leaving for England and joining the Free French Forces—that is, leaving his mother behind —or remaining with his mother and helping her to carry on. He was fully aware that the woman lived only for him and that his going-off—and perhaps his death—would plunge her into despair. He was also aware that every act that he did for his mother's sake was a sure thing, in the sense that it was helping her to carry on, whereas every effort he made toward going off and fighting was an uncertain move which might run aground and prove completely useless; for example, on his way to England he might, while passing through Spain, be detained indefinitely in a Spanish camp; he might reach England or Algiers and be stuck in an office at a desk job. As a result, he was faced with two very different [29] kinds of action: one, concrete, immediate, but concerning only one individual; the other concerned an incomparably vaster group, a national collectivity, but for that very reason was dubious, and might be interrupted en route. And, at the same time, he was wavering between two kinds of ethics. On the one hand, an ethics of sympathy, of personal devotion; on the other, a broader ethics, but one whose efficacy was more dubious. He had to choose between the two.

Who could help him choose? Christian doctrine? No. Christian doctrine says, "Be charitable, love your neighbor, take the more rugged path, etc., etc." But which is the more rugged path? Whom should he love as a brother? The fighting man or his mother? Which does the greater good, the vague act of fighting in a group, or the concrete one of helping a particular human being to go on living? Who can decide *a priori*? Nobody. No book of ethics can tell him. The Kantian ethics says, "Never treat any person as a means, but as an end." Very well, if I stay with my mother, I'll treat her as an end and not as a means; but by virtue [30] of this very fact, I'm running the risk of treating the people around me who are fighting, as means; and, conversely, if I go to join those who are fighting, I'll be treating them as an end, and, by doing that, I run the risk of treating my mother as a means.

If values are vague, and if they are always too broad for the concrete and specific case that we are considering, the only thing left for us is to trust our instincts. That's what this young man tried to do; and when I saw him, he said, "In the end, feeling is what counts. I ought to choose whichever pushes me in one direction. If I feel that I love my mother enough to sacrifice everything else for her—my desire for vengeance, for action, for adventure—then I'll stay with her. If, on the contrary, I feel that my love for my mother isn't enough, I'll leave."

But how is the value of a feeling determined? What gives his feeling for his mother value? Precisely the fact that he remained with her. I may say that I like so-and-so well enough to sacrifice a certain amount of money for him, but I may say so only if I've done it. I may say "I love my mother well enough to remain [31] with her" if I have remained with her. The only way to determine the value of this affection is, precisely, to perform an act which confirms and defines it. But, since I require this affection to justify my act, I find myself caught in a vicious circle.

On the other hand, Gide has well said that a mock feeling and a true feeling are almost indistinguishable; to decide that I love my mother and will remain with her, or to remain with her by putting on an act, amount somewhat to the same thing. In other words, the feeling is formed by the acts one performs; so, I can not refer to it in order to act upon it. Which means that I can neither seek within myself the true condition which will impel me to act, nor apply to a system of ethics for concepts which will permit me to act. You will say, "At least, he did go to a teacher for advice." But if you seek advice from a priest, for example, you have chosen this priest; you already knew, more or less, just about what advice he was going to give you. In other words, choosing your adviser is involving yourself. The proof of this is that if you are a Christian, you will say, "Consult a priest." [32] But some priests are collaborating, some are just marking time, some are resisting. Which to choose? If the young man chooses a priest who is resisting or collaborating, he has already decided on the kind of advice he's going to get. Therefore, in coming to see me he knew the answer I was going to give him, and I had only one answer to give: "You're free, choose, that is, invent." No general ethics can show you what is to be done; there are no omens in the world. The Catholics will reply, "But there are." Granted—but, in any case, I myself choose the meaning they have.

When I was a prisoner, I knew a rather remarkable young man who was a Jesuit. He had entered the Jesuit order in the following way: he had had a number of very bad breaks; in childhood, his father died, leaving him in poverty, and he was a scholarship student at a religious institution where he was constantly made to feel that he was being kept out of charity; then, he failed to get any of the honors and distinctions that children like; later on, at about eighteen, he bungled a love affair; finally, at twenty-two, he failed in military training, a [33] childish enough matter, but it was the last straw.

This young fellow might well have felt that he had botched everything. It was a sign of something, but of what? He might have taken refuge in bitterness or despair. But he very wisely looked upon all this as a sign that he was not made for secular triumphs, and that only the triumphs of religion, holiness, and faith were open to him. He saw the hand of God in all this, and so he entered the order. Who can help seeing that he alone decided what the sign meant?

Some other interpretation might have been drawn from this series of setbacks; for example, that he might have done better to turn carpenter or revolutionist. Therefore, he is fully responsible for the interpretation. Forlornness implies that we ourselves choose our being. Forlornness and anguish go together.

As for despair, the term has a very simple meaning. It means that we shall confine ourselves to reckoning only with what depends upon our will, or on the ensemble of probabilities which make our action possible. When we [34] want something, we always have to reckon with probabilities. I may be counting on the arrival of a friend. The friend is coming by rail or street-car; this supposes that the train will arrive on schedule, or that the street-car will not jump the track. I am left in the realm of possibility; but possibilities are to be reckoned with only to the point where my action comports with the ensemble of these possibilities, and no further. The moment the possibilities I am considering are not rigorously involved by my action, I ought to disengage myself from them, because no God, no scheme, can adapt the world and its possibilities to my will. When Descartes said, "Conquer yourself rather than the world," he meant essentially the same thing.

The Marxists to whom I have spoken reply, "You can rely on the support of others in your action, which obviously has certain limits because you're not going to live forever. That means: rely on both what others are doing elsewhere to help you, in China, in Russia, and what they will do later on, after your death, to carry on the action and lead it to its fulfillment, which will be the revolution. You even *have* to [35] rely upon that, otherwise you're immoral." I reply at once that I will always rely on fellow-fighters insofar as these comrades are involved with me in a common struggle, in the unity of a party or a group in which I can more or less make my weight felt; that is, one whose ranks I am in as a fighter and whose movements I am aware of at every moment. In such a situation, relying on the unity and will of the party is exactly like counting on the fact that the train will arrive on time or that the car won't jump the track. But, given that man is free and that there is no human nature for me to depend on, I can not count on men whom I do not know by relying on human goodness or man's concern for the good of society. I don't know what will become of the Russian revolution; I may make an example of it to the extent that at the present time it is apparent that the proletariat plays a part in Russia that it plays in no other nation. But I can't swear that this will inevitably lead to a triumph of the proletariat. I've got to limit myself to what I see.

Given that men are free and that tomorrow they will freely decide what man will be, I [36] can not be sure that, after my death, fellow-fighters will carry on my work to bring it to its maximum perfection. Tomorrow, after my death, some men may decide to set up Fascism, and the others may be cowardly and muddled enough to let them do it. Fascism will then be the human reality, so much the worse for us.

Actually, things will be as man will have decided they are to be. Does that mean that I should abandon myself to quietism? No. First, I should involve myself; then, act on the old saw, "Nothing ventured, nothing gained." Nor does it mean that I shouldn't belong to a party, but rather that I shall have no illusions and shall do what I can. For example, suppose I ask myself, "Will socialization, as such, ever come about?" I know nothing about it. All I know is that I'm going to do everything in my power to bring it about. Beyond that, I can't count on anything. Quietism is the attitude of people who say, "Let others do what I can't do." The doctrine I am presenting is the very opposite of quietism, since it declares, "There is no reality except in action." Moreover, it goes further, since it adds, "Man is nothing else [37] than his plan; he exists only to the extent that he fulfills himself; he is therefore nothing else than the ensemble of his acts, nothing else than his life."

According to this, we can understand why our doctrine horrifies certain people. Because often the only way they can bear their wretchedness is to think, "Circumstances have been against me. What I've been and done doesn't show my true worth. To be sure, I've had no great love, no great friendship, but that's because I haven't met a man or woman who was worthy. The books I've written haven't been very good because I haven't had the proper leisure. I haven't had children to devote myself to because I didn't find a man with whom I could have spent my life. So there remains within me, unused and quite viable, a host of propensities, inclinations, possibilities, that one wouldn't guess from the mere series of things I've done."

Now, for the existentialist there is really no love other than one which manifests itself in a person's being in love. There is no genius other than one which is expressed in works of [38] art; the genius of Proust is the sum of Proust's works; the genius of Racine is his series of tragedies. Outside of that, there is nothing. Why say that Racine could have written another tragedy, when he didn't write it? A man is involved in life, leaves his impress on it, and outside of that there is nothing. To be sure, this may seem a harsh thought to someone whose life hasn't been a success. But, on the other hand, it prompts people to understand that reality alone is what counts, that dreams, expectations, and hopes warrant no more than to define a man as a disappointed dream, as miscarried hopes, as vain expectations. In other words, to define him negatively and not positively. However, when we say, "You are nothing else than your life," that does not imply that the artist will be judged solely on the basis of his works of art; a thousand other things will contribute toward summing him up. What we mean is that a man is nothing else than a series of undertakings, that he is the sum, the organization, the ensemble of the relationships which make up these undertakings.

When all is said and done, what we are accused [39] of, at bottom, is not our pessimism, but an optimistic toughness. If people throw up to us our works of fiction in which we write about people who are soft, weak, cowardly, and sometimes even downright bad, it's not because these people are soft, weak, cowardly, or bad; because if we were to say, as Zola did, that they are that way because of heredity, the workings of environment, society, because of biological or psychological determinism, people would be reassured. They would say, "Well, that's what we're like, no one can do anything about it." But when the existentialist writes about a coward, he says that this coward is responsible for his cowardice. He's not like that because he has a cowardly heart or lung or brain; he's not like that on account of his physiological make-up; but he's like that because he has made himself a coward by his acts. There's no such thing as a cowardly constitution; there are nervous constitutions; there is poor blood, as the common people say, or strong constitutions. But the man whose blood is poor is not a coward on that account, for what makes cowardice is the act of renouncing or yielding. A constitution [40] is not an act; the coward is defined on the basis of the acts he performs. People feel, in a vague sort of way, that this coward we're talking about is guilty of being a coward, and the thought frightens them. What people would like is that a coward or a hero be born that way.

One of the complaints most frequently made about *The Ways of Freedom* [1] can be summed up as follows: "After all, these people are so spineless, how are you going to make heroes out of them?" This objection almost makes me laugh, for it assumes that people are born heroes. That's what people really want to think. If you're born cowardly, you may set your mind perfectly at rest; there's nothing you can do about it; you'll be cowardly all your life, whatever you may do. If you're born a hero, you may set your mind just as much at rest; you'll be a hero all your life; you'll drink like a hero and eat like a hero. What the existentialist says is that the coward makes himself cowardly, that the hero makes himself heroic. There's always [41] a possibility for the coward not to be cowardly any more and for the hero to stop being heroic. What counts is total involvement; some one particular action or set of circumstances is not total involvement.

Thus, I think we have answered a number of the charges con-

[1] *Les Chemins de la Liberté,* M. Sartre's projected trilogy of novels, two of which, *L'Age de Raison* (*The Age of Reason*) and *Le Sursis* (*The Reprieve*) have already appeared.—Translator's note.

cerning existentialism. You see that it can not be taken for a philosophy of quietism, since it defines man in terms of action; nor for a pessimistic description of man—there is no doctrine more optimistic, since man's destiny is within himself; nor for an attempt to discourage man from acting, since it tells him that the only hope is in his acting and that action is the only thing that enables a man to live. Consequently, we are dealing here with an ethics of action and involvement.

Nevertheless, on the basis of a few notions like these, we are still charged with immuring man in his private subjectivity. There again we're very much misunderstood. Subjectivity of the individual is indeed our point of departure, and this for strictly philosophic reasons. Not because we are bourgeois, but because we want a doctrine based on truth and not a lot [42] of fine theories, full of hope but with no real basis. There can be no other truth to take off from than this: *I think; therefore, I exist.* There we have the absolute truth of consciousness becoming aware of itself. Every theory which takes man out of the moment in which he becomes aware of himself is, at its very beginning, a theory which confounds truth, for outside the Cartesian *cogito,* all views are only probable, and a doctrine of probability which is not bound to a truth dissolves into thin air. In order to describe the probable, you must have a firm hold on the true. Therefore, before there can be any truth whatsoever, there must be an absolute truth; and this one is simple and easily arrived at; it's on everyone's doorstep; it's a matter of grasping it directly.

Secondly, this theory is the only one which gives man dignity, the only one which does not reduce him to an object. The effect of all materialism is to treat all men, including the one philosophizing, as objects, that is, as an ensemble of determined reactions in no way distinguished from the ensemble of qualities and phenomena which constitute a table or a chair [43] or a stone. We definitely wish to establish the human realm as an ensemble of values distinct from the material realm. But the subjectivity that we have thus arrived at, and which we have claimed to be truth, is not a strictly individual subjectivity, for we have demonstrated that one discovers in the *cogito* not only himself, but others as well.

The philosophies of Descartes and Kant to the contrary, through the *I think* we reach our own self in the presence of others, and the others are just as real to us as our own self. Thus, the man who becomes aware of himself through the *cogito* also perceives all others, and he perceives them as the condition of his own existence. He realizes that he can not be anything (in the sense that we say that someone is witty or nasty or jealous) unless others recognize it as such. In order to get any truth about myself, I must have contact with another person. The other is indispensable to my own existence, as well as to my knowledge about myself. This being so, in discovering my inner being I discover the other person at the same time, like a freedom placed in front of me which [44] thinks and wills only for or against me. Hence, let us at once announce the discovery of a world which we shall call inter-subjectivity; this is the world in which man decides what he is and what others are.

Besides, if it is impossible to find in every man some universal essence which would be human nature, yet there does exist a universal human condition. It's not by chance that today's thinkers speak more readily of man's condition than of his nature. By condition they mean, more or less definitely, the *a priori* limits which outline man's fundamental situation in the universe. Historical situations vary; a man may be born a slave in a pagan society or a feudal lord or a proletarian. What does not vary is the necessity for him to exist in the world, to be at work there, to be there in the midst of other people, and to be mortal there. The limits are neither subjective or objective, or, rather, they have an objective and a subjective side. Objective because they are to be found everywhere and are recognizable everywhere; subjective because they are *lived* and are nothing if man does not live them, that is, [45] freely determine his existence with reference to them. And though the configurations may differ, at least none of them are completely strange to me, because they all appear as attempts either to pass beyond these limits or recede from them or deny them or adapt to them. Consequently, every configuration, however individual it may be, has a universal value.

Every configuration, even the Chinese, the Indian, or the Negro, can be understood by a Westerner. "Can be understood" means that by virtue of a situation that he can imagine, a European of 1945 can, in like manner, push himself to his limits and reconstitute within himself the configuration of the Chinese, the Indian, or the African. Every configuration has universality in the sense that every configuration can be understood by every man. This does not at all mean that this configuration defines man forever, but that it can be met with again. There is always a way to understand the idiot, the child, the savage, the foreigner, provided one has the necessary information.

In this sense we may say that there is a universality of man; but it is not given, it is perpetually [46] being made. I build the universal in choosing myself; I build it in understanding the configuration of every other man, whatever age he might have lived in. This absoluteness of choice does not do away with the relativeness of each epoch. At heart, what existentialism shows is the connection between the absolute character of free involvement, by virtue of which every man realizes himself in realizing a type of mankind, an involvement always comprehensible in any age whatsoever and by any person whosoever, and the relativeness of the cultural ensemble which may result from such a choice; it must be stressed that the relativity of Cartesianism and the absolute character of Cartesian involvement go together. In this sense, you may, if you like, say that each of us performs an absolute act in breathing, eating, sleeping, or behaving in any way whatever. There is no difference between being free, like a configuration, like an existence which chooses its essence, and being absolute. There is no difference between being an absolute temporarily localised, that is, localised in history, and being universally comprehensible. [47]

This does not entirely settle the objection to subjectivism. In fact, the objection still takes several forms. First, there is the following: we are told, "So you're able to do anything, no matter what!" This is expressed in various ways. First we are accused of anarchy; then they say, "You're unable to pass judgment on others, because there's no reason to prefer one configuration to another"; finally they tell us, "Everything is arbitrary in this choosing of yours. You take something from one pocket and pretend you're putting it into the other."

These three objections aren't very serious. Take the first objection. "You're able to do anything, no matter what" is not to the point. In one sense choice is possible, but what is not possible is not to choose. I can always choose, but I ought to know that if I do not choose, I am still choosing. Though this may seem purely formal, it is highly important for keeping fantasy and caprice within bounds. If it is true that in facing a situation, for example, one in which, as a person capable of having sexual relations, of having children, I am obliged to choose an attitude, and if I in any way assume [48] responsibility for a choice which, in involving myself, also involves all mankind, this has nothing to do with caprice, even if no *a priori* value determines my choice.

If anybody thinks that he recognizes here Gide's theory of the arbitrary act, he fails to see the enormous difference between this doctrine and Gide's. Gide does not know what a situation is. He acts out of pure caprice. For us, on the contrary, man is in an organized situation in which he himself is involved. Through his choice, he involves all mankind, and he can not avoid making a choice: either he will remain chaste, or he will marry without having children, or he will marry and have children; anyhow, whatever he may do, it is impossible for him not to take full responsibility for the way he handles this problem. Doubtless, he chooses without referring to pre-established values, but it is unfair to accuse him of caprice. Instead, let us say that moral choice is to be compared to the making of a work of art. And before going any further, let it be said at once that we are not dealing here with an aesthetic ethics, because our opponents are so dishonest [49] that they even accuse us of that. The example I've chosen is a comparison only.

Having said that, may I ask whether anyone has ever accused an artist who has painted a picture of not having drawn his inspiration from rules set up *a priori*? Has anyone ever asked, "What painting ought he to make?" It is clearly understood that there is no definite painting to be made, that the artist is engaged in the making of his painting, and that the painting to be made is precisely the painting he will have made. It is clearly understood that there are no *a priori* aesthetic values, but that there are values which appear subsequently in the coherence of the painting, in the correspondence between what the artist intended and the result. Nobody can tell what the painting of tomorrow will be like. Painting can be judged only after it has once been made. What connection does that have with ethics? We are in the same creative situation. We never say that a work of art is arbitrary. When we speak of a canvas of Picasso, we never say that it is arbitrary; we understand quite well that he was making himself what he is at the very time he [50] was painting, that the ensemble of his work is embodied in his life.

The same holds on the ethical plane. What art and ethics have in common is that we have creation and invention in both cases. We can not decide *a priori* what there is to be done. I think that I pointed that out quite sufficiently when I mentioned the case of the student who came to see me, and who might have applied to all the ethical systems, Kantian or otherwise, without getting any sort of guidance. He was obliged to devise his law himself. Never let it be said by us that this man—who, taking affection, individual action, and kind-heartedness toward a specific person as his ethical first principle, chooses to remain with his mother, or who, preferring to make a sacrifice, chooses to go to England—has made an arbitrary choice. Man makes himself. He isn't ready made at the start. In choosing his ethics, he makes himself, and force of circumstances is such that he can not abstain from choosing one. We define man only in relationship to involvement. It is therefore absurd to charge us with arbitrariness of choice.[51]

In the second place, it is said that we are unable to pass judgment on others. In a way this is true, and in another way, false. It is true in this sense, that, whenever a man sanely and sincerely involves himself and chooses his configuration, it is impossible for him to prefer another configuration, regardless of what his own may be in other respects. It is true in this sense, that we do not believe in progress. Progress is betterment. Man is always the same. The situation confronting him varies. Choice always remains a choice in a situation. The problem has not changed since the time one could choose between those for and those against slavery, for example, at the time of the Civil War, and the present time, when one can side with the Maquis Resistance Party, or with the Communists.

But, nevertheless, one can still pass judgment, for, as I have said, one makes a choice in relationship to others. First, one can judge (and this is perhaps not a judgment of value, but a logical judgment) that certain choices are based on error and others on truth. If we have defined man's situation as a free choice, with no [52] excuses and no recourse, every man who takes refuge behind the excuse of his passions, every man who sets up a determinism, is a dishonest man.

The objection may be raised, "But why mayn't he choose himself dishonestly?" I reply that I am not obliged to pass moral judgment on him, but that I do define his dishonesty as an error. One can not help considering the truth of the matter. Dishonesty is obviously a falsehood because it belies the complete freedom of involvement. On the same grounds, I maintain that there is also dishonesty if I choose to state that certain values exist prior to me; it is self-contradictory for me to want them and at the same state that they are imposed on me. Suppose someone says to me, "What if I want to be dishonest?" I'll answer, "There's no reason for you not to be, but I'm saying that that's what you are, and that the strictly coherent attitude is that of honesty."

Besides, I can bring moral judgment to bear. When I declare

that freedom in every concrete circumstance can have no other aim than to want itself, if man has once become aware that [53] in his forlornness he imposes values, he can no longer want but one thing, and that is freedom, as the basis of all values. That doesn't mean that he wants it in the abstract. It means simply that the ultimate meaning of the acts of honest men is the quest for freedom as such. A man who belongs to a communist or revolutionary union wants concrete goals; these goals imply an abstract desire for freedom; but this freedom is wanted in something concrete. We want freedom for freedom's sake and in every particular circumstance. And in wanting freedom we discover that it depends entirely on the freedom of others, and that the freedom of others depends on ours. Of course, freedom as the definition of man does not depend on others, but as soon as there is involvement, I am obliged to want others to have freedom at the same time that I want my own freedom. I can take freedom as my goal only if I take that of others as a goal as well. Consequently, when, in all honesty, I've recognized that man is a being in whom existence precedes essence, that he is a free being who, in various circumstances, can want only his freedom, I have at the same time [54] recognized that I can want only the freedom of others.

Therefore, in the name of this will for freedom, which freedom itself implies, I may pass judgment on those who seek to hide from themselves the complete arbitrariness and the complete freedom of their existence. Those who hide their complete freedom from themselves out of a spirit of seriousness or by means of deterministic excuses, I shall call cowards; those who try to show that their existence was necessary, when it is the very contingency of man's appearance on earth, I shall call stinkers. But cowards or stinkers can be judged only from a strictly unbiased point of view.

Therefore though the content of ethics is variable, a certain form of it is universal. Kant says that freedom desires both itself and the freedom of others. Granted. But he believes that the formal and the universal are enough to constitute an ethics. We, on the other hand, think that principles which are too abstract run aground in trying to decide action. Once again, take the case of the student. In the name of what, in the name of what great moral maxim [55] do you think he could have decided, in perfect peace of mind, to abandon his mother or to stay with her? There is no way of judging. The content is always concrete and thereby unforeseeable; there is always the element of invention. The one thing that counts is knowing whether the inventing that has been done, has been done in the name of freedom.

For cxample, let us look at the following two cases. You will see to what extent they correspond, yet differ. Take *The Mill on the Floss.* We find a certain young girl, Maggie Tulliver, who is an embodiment of the value of passion and who is aware of it. She is in love with a young man, Stephen, who is engaged to an insignificant young girl. This Maggie Tulliver, instead of heedlessly preferring her own happiness, chooses, in the name of human solidarity, to sacrifice herself and give up the man she loves. On the other hand, Sanseverina, in *The Charterhouse of Parma,* believing that passion is man's true value, would say that a great love deserves sacrifices; that it is to be preferred to the banality of the conjugal love that would tie Stephen to the young ninny he had to marry.[56] She would choose to sacrifice the girl and fulfill her happiness; and, as Stendhal shows, she is even ready to sacrifice herself for the sake of passion, if this life demands it. Here we are in the presence of two strictly opposed moralities. I claim that they are much the same thing; in both cases what has been set up as the goal is freedom.

You can imagine two highly similar attitudes: one girl prefers to renounce her love out of resignation; another prefers to disregard the prior attachment of the man she loves out of sexual desire. On the surface these two actions resemble those we've just described. However, they are completely different. Sanseverina's attitude is much nearer that of Maggie Tulliver, one of heedless rapacity.

Thus, you see that the second charge is true and, at the same time, false. One may choose anything if it is on the grounds of free involvement.

The third objection is the following: "You take something from one pocket and put it into the other. That is, fundamentally, values aren't serious, since you choose them." My answer to [57] this is that I'm quite vexed that that's the way it is; but if I've discarded God the Father, there has to be someone to invent values. You've got to take things as they are. Moreover, to say that we invent values means nothing else but this: life has no meaning *a priori.* Before you come alive, life is nothing; it's up to you to give it a meaning, and value is nothing else but the meaning that you choose. In that way, you see, there is a possibility of creating a human community.

I've been reproached for asking whether existentialism is humanistic. It's been said, "But you said in *Nausea* that the humanists were all wrong. You made fun of a certain kind of humanist. Why come back to it now?" Actually, the word humanism has two very different meanings. By humanism one can mean a theory which takes man as an end and as a higher value. Humanism in this sense can be found in Cocteau's tale *Around the World in Eighty Hours* when a character, because he is flying over some mountains in an airplane, declares, "Man is simply amazing." That means that I, who did not build the airplanes, shall personally [58] benefit from these particular inventions, and that I, as man, shall personally consider myself responsible for, and honored by, acts of a few particular men. This would imply that we ascribe a value to man on the basis of the highest deeds of certain men. This humanism is absurd, because only the dog or the horse would be able to make such an over-all judgment about man, which they are careful not to do, at least to my knowledge.

But it can not be granted that a man may make a judgment about man. Existentialism spares him from any such judgment. The existentialist will never consider man as an end because he is always in the making. Nor should we believe that there is a mankind to which we might set up a cult in the manner of Auguste Comte. The cult of mankind ends in the self-enclosed humanism of Comte, and, let it be said, of fascism. This kind of humanism we can do without.

But there is another meaning of humanism. Fundamentally it is this: man is constantly outside of himself; in projecting himself, in losing himself outside of himself, he makes for man's [59] existing; and, on the other hand, it is by pursuing transcendent goals that he is able to exist; man, being this state of passing-beyond, and seizing upon things only as they bear upon this passing-beyond, is at the heart, at the center of this passing-beyond. There is no universe other than a human universe, the universe of human subjectivity. This connection between transcendency, as a constituent element of man—not in the sense that God is transcendent, but in the sense of passing beyond—and subjectivity, in the sense that man is not closed in on himself but is always present in a human universe, is what we call existentialist humanism. Humanism, because we remind man that there is no law-maker other than himself, and that in his forlornness he will decide by himself; because we point out that man will fulfill himself as man, not in turning toward himself, but in seeking outside of himself a goal which is just this liberation, just this particular fulfillment.

From these few reflections it is evident that nothing is more unjust than the objections that have been raised against us. Existentialism is nothing else than an attempt to draw all the [60] consequences of a coherent atheistic position. It isn't trying to plunge man into despair at all. But if one calls every attitude of unbelief despair, like the Christians, then the word is not being used in its original sense. Existentialism isn't so atheistic that it wears itself out showing that God doesn't exist. Rather, it declares that even if God did exist, that would change nothing. There you've got our point of view. Not that we believe that God exists, but we think that the problem of His existence is not the issue. In this sense existentialism is optimistic, a doctrine of action, and it is plain dishonesty for Christians to make no distinction between their own despair and ours and then to call us despairing.[61]

ALBERT CAMUS

Absurd Freedom

Now the main thing is done, I hold certain facts from which I cannot separate. What I know, what is certain, what I cannot deny, what I cannot reject—this is what counts. I can negate everything of that part of me that lives on vague nostalgias, except this desire for unity, this longing to solve, this need for clarity and cohesion. I can refute everything in this world surrounding me that offends or enraptures me, except this chaos, this sovereign chance and this divine equivalence which springs from anarchy. I don't know whether this world has a meaning that transcends it. But I know that I do not know that meaning and that it is impossible for me just now to know it. What can a meaning outside my condition mean to me? I can understand only in human terms. What I touch, what resists me—that is what I understand. And these two certainties—my appetite for the absolute and for unity and the impossibility of reducing this world to a rational and reasonable principle—I also know that I cannot reconcile them. What other truth can I admit without lying, without bringing in a hope I lack and which means nothing within the limits of my condition?

If I were a tree among trees, a cat among animals, this life would have a meaning, or rather this problem would not arise, for I should belong to this world. I should *be* this world to which I am now opposed by my whole consciousness and my whole insistence upon familiarity. This ridiculous reason is what sets me in opposition to all creation. I cannot cross it out with a [51] stroke of the pen. What I believe to be true I must therefore preserve. What seems to me so obvious, even against me, I must support. And what constitutes the basis of that conflict, of that break between the world and my mind, but the awareness of it? If therefore I want to preserve it, I can through a constant awareness, ever revived, ever alert. This is what, for the moment, I must remember. At this moment the absurd, so obvious and yet so hard to win, returns to a man's life and finds its home there. At this moment, too, the mind can leave the arid, dried-up path of lucid effort. That path now emerges in daily life. It encounters the world of the anonymous impersonal pronoun "one," but henceforth man enters in with his revolt and his lucidity. He has forgotten how to hope. This hell of the present is his Kingdom at last. All problems recover their sharp edge. Abstract evidence retreats before the poetry of forms and colors. Spiritual conflicts become embodied and return to the abject and magnificent shelter of man's heart. None of them is settled. But all are transfigured. Is one going to die, escape by the leap, rebuild a mansion of ideas and forms to one's own scale? Is one, on the contrary, going to take up the heart-rending and marvelous wager of the absurd? Let's make a final effort in this regard and draw all our conclusions. The body, affection, creation, action, human nobility will then resume their places in this mad world. At last man will again find there the wine of the absurd and the bread of indifference on which he feeds his greatness.

Let us insist again on the method: it is a matter of persisting. At a certain point on his path the absurd [52] man is tempted. History is not lacking in either religions or prophets, even without gods. He is asked to leap. All he can reply is that he doesn't fully understand, that it is not obvious. Indeed, he does not want to do anything but what he fully understands. He is assured that this is the sin of pride, but he does not understand the notion of sin; that perhaps hell is in store, but he has not enough imagination to visualize that strange future; that he is losing immortal life, but that seems to him an idle consideration. An attempt is made to get him to admit his guilt. He feels innocent. To tell the truth, that is all he feels—his irreparable innocence. This is what allows him everything. Hence, what he demands of himself is to live *solely* with what he knows, to accommodate himself to what is, and to bring in nothing that is not certain. He is told that nothing is. But this at least is a certainty. And it is with this that he is concerned: he wants to find out if it is possible to live *without appeal.*

Now I can broach the notion of suicide. It has already been felt what solution might be given. At this point the problem is reversed. It was previously a question of finding out whether or not life had to have a meaning to be lived. It now becomes clear, on the contrary, that it will be lived all the better if it has no meaning. Living an experience, a particular fate, is accepting it fully. Now, no one will live this fate, knowing it to be absurd, unless he does everything to keep before him that absurd brought to light by consciousness. Negating one of the terms of the opposition on which he lives amounts to escaping it. To abolish conscious revolt is to [53] elude the problem. The theme of permanent revolution is thus carried into individual experience. Living is keeping the absurd alive. Keeping it alive is, above all, contemplating it. Unlike Eurydice, the absurd dies only when we turn away from it. One of the only coherent philosophical positions is thus revolt. It is a constant confrontation between man and his own obscurity. It is an insistence upon an impossible transparency. It challenges the world anew every second. Just as danger provided man the unique opportunity of seizing awareness, so metaphysical revolt extends awareness to the whole of experience. It is that constant presence of man in his own eyes. It is not aspiration, for it is devoid of hope. That revolt is the certainty of a crushing fate, without the resignation that ought to accompany it.

This is where it is seen to what a degree absurd experience is remote from suicide. It may be thought that suicide follows revolt —but wrongly. For it does not represent the logical outcome of revolt. It is just the contrary by the consent it presupposes. Suicide, like the leap, is acceptance at its extreme. Everything is over and man returns to his essential history. His future, his unique and dreadful future—he sees and rushes toward it. In its way, suicide settles the absurd. It engulfs the absurd in the same death. But I know that in order to keep alive, the absurd cannot be settled. It escapes suicide to the extent that it is simultaneously awareness and rejection of death. It is, at the extreme limit of the condemned man's last thought, that shoelace that despite everything he sees a few yards away, on the very [54] brink of his dizzying fall. The contrary of suicide, in fact, is the man condemned to death.

That revolt gives life its value. Spread out over the whole length of a life, it restores its majesty to that life. To a man devoid of blinders, there is no finer sight than that of the intelligence at grips with a reality that transcends it. The sight of human pride is unequaled. No disparagement is of any use. That discipline that the mind imposes on itself, that will conjured up out of nothing, that face-to-face struggle have something exceptional about them. To impoverish that reality whose inhumanity constitutes man's majesty is tantamount to impoverishing him himself. I understand then why the doctrines that explain everything to me also debilitate me at the same time. They relieve me of the weight of my own life, and yet I must carry it alone. At this juncture, I cannot conceive that a skeptical metaphysics can be joined to an ethics of renunciation.

Consciousness and revolt, these rejections are the contrary of renunciation. Everything that is indomitable and passionate in a human heart quickens them, on the contrary, with its own life. It is essential to die unreconciled and not of one's own free will. Suicide is a repudiation. The absurd man can only drain everything to the bitter end, and deplete himself. The absurd is his extreme tension, which he maintains constantly by solitary effort, for he knows that in that consciousness and in that day-to-day revolt he gives proof of his only truth, which is defiance. This is a first consequence.[55]

If I remain in that prearranged position which consists in drawing all the conclusions (and nothing else) involved in a newly discovered notion, I am faced with a second paradox. In order to remain faithful to that method, I have nothing to do with the problem of metaphysical liberty. Knowing whether or not man is free doesn't interest me. I can experience only my own freedom. As to it, I can have no general notions, but merely a few clear insights. The problem of "freedom as such" has no meaning. For it is linked in quite a different way with the problem of God. Knowing whether or not man is free involves knowing whether he can have a master. The absurdity peculiar to this problem comes from the fact that the very notion that makes the problem of freedom possible also takes away all its meaning. For in the presence of God there is less a problem of freedom than a problem of evil. You know the alternative: either we are not free and God the all-powerful is responsible for evil. Or we are free and responsible but God is not all-powerful. All the scholastic subtleties have neither added anything to nor substracted anything from the acuteness of this paradox.

This is why I cannot get lost in the glorification or the mere definition of a notion which eludes me and loses its meaning as soon as it goes beyond the frame of reference of my individual experience. I cannot understand what kind of freedom would be given me by a higher being. I have lost the sense of hierarchy. The only conception of freedom I can have is that of the prisoner or the individual in the midst of the State. The only one I know is freedom of thought and action. Now [56] if the absurd cancels all my chances of eternal freedom, it restores and magnifies, on the other hand, my freedom of action. That privation of hope and future means an increase in man's availability.

Before encountering the absurd, the everyday man lives with aims, a concern for the future or for justification (with regard to whom or what is not the question). He weighs his chances, he counts on "someday," his retirement or the labor of his sons. He still thinks that something in his life can be directed. In truth, he acts as if he were free, even if all the facts make a point of contradicting that liberty. But after the absurd, everything is upset. That idea that "I am," my way of acting as if everything has a meaning (even if, on occasion, I said that nothing has)—all that is given the lie in vertiginous fashion by the absurdity of a possible death. Thinking of the future, establishing aims for oneself, having preferences—all this presupposes a belief in freedom, even if one occasionally ascertains that one doesn't feel it. But at that moment I am well aware that that higher liberty, that freedom *to be*, which alone can serve as basis for a truth, does not exist. Death is there as the only reality. After death the chips are down. I am not even free, either, to perpetuate myself, but a slave, and, above all, a slave without hope of an eternal revolution, without recourse to contempt. And who without revolution and without contempt can remain a slave? What freedom can exist in the fullest sense without assurance of eternity?

But at the same time the absurd man realizes that hitherto he was bound to that postulate of freedom on [57] the illusion of which he was living. In a certain sense, that hampered him. To the extent to which he imagined a purpose to his life, he adapted himself to the demands of a purpose to be achieved and became the slave of his liberty. Thus I could not act otherwise than as the father (or the engineer or the leader of a nation, or the post-office sub-clerk) that I am preparing to be. I think I can choose to be that rather than something else. I think so unconsciously, to be sure. But at the same time I strengthen my postulate with the beliefs of those around me, with the presumptions of my human environment (others are so sure of being free, and that cheerful mood is so contagious!). However far one may remain from any presumption, moral or social, one is partly influenced by them and even, for the best among them (there are good and bad presumptions), one adapts one's life to them. Thus the absurd man realizes that he was not really free. To speak clearly, to the extent to which I hope, to which I worry about a truth that might be individual to me, about a way of being or creating, to the extent to which I arrange my life and prove thereby that I accept its having a meaning, I create for myself barriers between which I confine my life. I do like so many bureaucrats of the mind and heart who only fill me with disgust and whose only vice, I now see clearly, is to take man's freedom seriously.

The absurd enlightens me on this point: there is no future. Henceforth this is the reason for my inner freedom. I shall use two comparisons here. Mystics, to begin with, find freedom in giving themselves. By losing themselves in their god, by accepting his rules, they become [58] secretly free. In spontaneously accepted slavery they recover a deeper independence. But what does that freedom mean? It may be said, above all, that they *feel* free with regard to themselves, and not so much free as liberated. Likewise, completely turned toward death (taken here as the most obvious absurdity), the absurd man feels released from everything outside that passionate attention crystallizing in him. He enjoys a freedom with regard to common rules. It can be seen at this point that the initial themes of existential philosophy keep their entire value. The return to consciousness, the escape from everyday sleep represent the first steps of absurd freedom. But it is existential *preaching* that is alluded to, and with it that spiritual leap which basically escapes consciousness. In the same way (this is my second comparison) the slaves of antiquity did not belong to themselves. But they knew that freedom which consists in not feeling responsible.[1] Death, too, has patrician hands which, while crushing, also liberate.

Losing oneself in that bottomless certainty, feeling henceforth sufficiently remote from one's own life to increase it and take a broad view of it—this involves the principle of a liberation. Such new independence has a definite time limit, like any freedom of action. It does not write a check on eternity. But it takes the place of the illusions of *freedom*, which all stopped with death. The divine availability of the condemned man before whom the prison doors open in a certain early dawn, [59] that unbelievable disinterestedness with regard to everything except for the pure flame of life—it is clear that death and the absurd are here the principles of the only reasonable freedom: that which a human heart can experience and live. This is a second consequence. The absurd man thus catches sight of a burning and frigid, transparent and limited universe in which nothing is possible but everything is given, and beyond which all is collapse and nothingness. He can then decide to accept such a universe and draw from it his strength, his refusal to hope, and the unyielding evidence of a life without consolation.

But what does life mean in such a universe? Nothing else for the moment but indifference to the future and a desire to use up everything that is given. Belief in the meaning of life always implies a scale of values, a choice, our preferences. Belief in the absurd, according to our definitions, teaches the contrary. But this is worth examining.

Knowing whether or not one can live *without appeal* is all that interests me. I do not want to get out of my depth. This aspect of life being given me, can I adapt myself to it? Now, faced with this particular concern, belief in the absurd is tantamount to substituting the quantity of experiences for the quality. If I convince myself that this life has no other aspect than that of the absurd, if I feel that its whole equilibrium depends on that perpetual opposition between my conscious revolt and the darkness in which it struggles, if I admit that my freedom has no meaning except in relation to its [60] limited fate, then I must say that what counts is not the best living but the most living. It is not up to me to wonder if this is vulgar or revolting, elegant or deplorable. Once and for all, value

[1] I am concerned here with a factual comparison, not with an apology of humility. The absurd man is the contrary of the reconciled man.

judgments are discarded here in favor of factual judgments. I have merely to draw the conclusions from what I can see and to risk nothing that is hypothetical. Supposing that living in this way were not honorable, then true propriety would command me to be dishonorable.

The most living; in the broadest sense, that rule means nothing. It calls for definition. It seems to begin with the fact that the notion of quantity has not been sufficiently explored. For it can account for a large share of human experience. A man's rule of conduct and his scale of values have no meaning except through the quantity and variety of experiences he has been in a position to accumulate. Now, the conditions of modern life impose on the majority of men the same quantity of experiences and consequently the same profound experience. To be sure, there must also be taken into consideration the individual's spontaneous contribution, the "given" element in him. But I cannot judge of that, and let me repeat that my rule here is to get along with the immediate evidence. I see, then, that the individual character of a common code of ethics lies not so much in the ideal importance of its basic principles as in the norm of an experience that it is possible to measure. To stretch a point somewhat, the Greeks had the code of their leisure just as we have the code of our eight-hour day. But already many men among the most tragic cause us to foresee that a longer experience changes this table [61] of values. They make us imagine that adventurer of the everyday who through mere quantity of experiences would break all records (I am purposely using this sports expression) and would thus win his own code of ethics.[2] Yet let's avoid romanticism and just ask ourselves what such an attitude may mean to a man with his mind made up to take up his bet and to observe strictly what he takes to be the rules of the game.

Breaking all the records is first and foremost being faced with the world as often as possible. How can that be done without contradictions and without playing on words? For on the one hand the absurd teaches that all experiences are unimportant, and on the other it urges toward the greatest quantity of experiences. How,

[2] Quantity sometimes constitutes quality. If I can believe the latest restatements of scientific theory, all matter is constituted by centers of energy. Their greater or lesser quantity makes its specificity more or less remarkable. A billion ions and one ion differ not only in quantity but also in quality. It is easy to find an analogy in human experience.

then, can one fail to do as so many of those men I was speaking of earlier—choose the form of life that brings us the most possible of that human matter, thereby introducing a scale of values that on the other hand one claims to reject?

But again it is the absurd and its contradictory life that teaches us. For the mistake is thinking that that quantity of experiences depends on the circumstances of our life when it depends solely on us. Here we have to be over-simple. To two men living the same number of years, the world always provides the same sum of experiences. It is up to us to be conscious of them. Being [62] aware of one's life, one's revolt, one's freedom, and to the maximum, is living, and to the maximum. Where lucidity dominates, the scale of values becomes useless. Let's be even more simple. Let us say that the sole obstacle, the sole deficiency to be made good, is constituted by premature death. Thus it is that no depth, no emotion, no passion, and no sacrifice could render equal in the eyes of the absurd man (even if he wished it so) a conscious life of forty years and a lucidity spread over sixty years.[3] Madness and death are his irreparables. Man does not choose. The absurd and the extra life it involves *therefore do not depend on man's will*, but on its contrary, which is death.[4] Weighing words carefully, it is altogether a question of luck. One just has to be able to consent to this. There will never be any substitute for twenty years of life and experience.

By what is an odd inconsistency in such an alert race, the Greeks claimed that those who died young were beloved of the gods. And that is true only if you are willing to believe that entering the ridiculous world of the gods is forever losing the purest of joys, which is feeling, and feeling on this earth. The present and the succession of presents before a constantly conscious soul is the ideal [63] of the absurd man. But the word" ideal" rings false in this connection. It is not even his vocation, but merely the third consequence of his reasoning. Having started from an anguished awareness of the inhuman, the meditation on the absurd returns at the

[3] Same reflection on a notion as different as the idea of eternal nothingness. It neither adds anything to nor subtracts anything from reality. In psychological experience of nothingness, it is by the consideration of what will happen in two thousand years that our own nothingness truly takes on meaning. In one of its aspects, eternal nothingness is made up precisely of the sum of lives to come which will not be ours.

[4] The will is only the agent here: it tends to maintain consciousness. It provides a discipline of life, and that is appreciable.

end of its itinerary to the very heart of the passionate flames of human revolt.[5]

Thus I draw from the absurd three consequences, which are my revolt, my freedom, and my passion. By the mere activity of consciousness I transform into a rule of life what was an invitation to death—and I refuse suicide. I know, to be sure, the dull resonance that vibrates throughout these days. Yet I have but a word to say: that it is necessary. When Nietzsche writes: "It clearly seems that the chief thing in heaven and on earth is to *obey* at length and in a single direction: in the long run there results something for which it is worth the trouble of living on this earth as, for example, virtue, art, music, the dance, reason, the mind—something that transfigures, something delicate, mad, or divine," he elucidates the rule of a really distinguished code of ethics. But he also points the way of the absurd man. Obeying the flame is both the easiest and the [64] hardest thing to do. However, it is good for man to judge himself occasionally. He is alone in being able to do so.

"Prayer," says Alain, "is when night descends over thought." "But the mind must meet the night," reply the mystics and the existentials. Yes, indeed, but not that night that is born under closed eyelids and through the mere will of man—dark, impenetrable night that the mind calls up in order to plunge into it. If it must encounter a night, let it be rather that of despair, which remains lucid—polar night, vigil of the mind, whence will arise perhaps that white and virginal brightness which outlines every object in the light of the intelligence. At that degree, equivalence encounters passionate understanding. Then it is no longer even a question of judging the existential leap. It resumes its place amid the age-old fresco of human attitudes. For the spectator, if he is conscious, that leap is still absurd. In so far as it thinks it solves the paradox, it reinstates it intact. On this score, it is stirring. On this score, everything resumes its place and the absurd world is reborn in all its splendor and diversity.

[5] What matters is coherence. We start out here from acceptance of the world. But Oriental thought teaches that one can indulge in the same effort of logic by choosing *against* the world. That is just as legitimate and gives this essay its perspectives and its limits. But when the negation of the world is pursued just as rigorously, one often achieves (in certain Vedantic schools) similar results regarding, for instance, the indifference of works. In a book of great importance, *Le Choix,* Jean Grenier establishes in this way a veritable "philosophy of indifference."

But it is bad to stop, hard to be satisfied with a single way of seeing, to go without contradiction, perhaps the most subtle of all spiritual forces. The preceding merely defines a way of thinking. But the point is to live.[65]

KARL JASPERS

The Tension between Technical Mass-Order and Human Life

Limits are imposed upon the life-order by a specifically modern conflict. The mass-order brings into being [41] a universal life-apparatus, which proves destructive to the world of a truly human life.

Man lives as part of a social environment to which he is bound by remembered and prospective ties. Men do not exist as isolated units, but as members of a family in the home; as friends in a group; as parts of this, that, or the other "herd" with well-known historical origins. He has become what he is thanks to a tradition which enables him to look back into the obscurity of his beginnings and makes him responsible for his own future and that of his associates. Only in virtue of a long view before and after does he acquire a substantial tenure in that world which he constructs out of his heritage from the past. His daily life is permeated by the spirit of a perceptibly present world which, however small, is still something other than himself. His inviolable property is a narrow space, the ownership of which enables him to share in the totality of human history.

The technical life-order which came into being for the supply of the needs of the masses did at the outset preserve these real worlds of human creatures, by furnishing them with commodities. But when at length the time in which nothing in the individual's

SOURCE: From *Man in the Modern Age* by K. Jaspers. Translated by Eden and Cedar Paul.

immediate and real environing world was any longer made, shaped, or fashioned by that individual for his own purposes; when everything that came, came merely as the gratification of momentary need, to be used up and cast aside; when the very dwelling-place was machine-made, when the environment had become despiritualised, when the day's work grew sufficient to itself and ceased to be built up into a constituent of the worker's life—then man was, as it were, bereft of his world. Cast adrift in this way, lacking all sense of historical continuity with past or future, man cannot [42] remain man. The universalisation of the life-order threatens to reduce the life of the real man in a real world to a mere functioning in the void.

But man as individual refuses to allow himself to be absorbed into a life-order which would only leave him in being as a function for the maintenance of the whole. True, he can live in the apparatus with the aid of a thousand relationships on which he is dependent and in which he collaborates; but since he has become a mere replaceable cog in a wheelwork regardless of his individuality, he rebels if there is no other way in which he can manifest his selfhood.

If, however, he wants to "be himself", if he craves for self-expression, there promptly arises a tension between his self-preservative impulse, on the one hand, and his real selfhood, on the other. Immediate self-will is what primarily moves him, for he is animated by a blind desire for the advantages attendant on making good in the struggle for life. Yet the urge to self-expression drives him into incalculable hazards which may render his means of livelihood perilously insecure. Under stress of these two conflicting impulses he may act in ways which will interfere with the tranquil and stable functioning of the life-order. Consequently the disturbance of the life-order has its permanent antinomy in a twofold possibility. Inasmuch as self-will provides the space wherein selfhood can realise itself as existence, the former is as it were the body of the latter, and may drag the latter down to ruin or (in favourable circumstances) bring it to fruition.

If, then, self-will and existence both seek a world for themselves, they come into conflict with the universal life-order. But this, in its turn, strives to gain mastery over the powers which are threatening [43] its frontiers. It is, therefore, profoundly concerned about matters which are not directly contributory to the self-preservative impulse. This latter, which can be indifferently regarded as a vital need for obtaining the necessaries of life and as an existential absolute, may be termed the "non-rational". When thus negatively conceived, it is degraded to a being of the second order: but it is either promoted once more to the first rank within certain restricted provinces; or else, in contrast with purely rational aims, it may acquire a positive interest, as in love, adventure, sport, and play. Or, again, it may be resisted as undesirable, this being what we see in those who are affected with a dread of life or a lack of joy in work. Thus in one or other of these ways it is diverted into the decisively and exclusively vital field—to the denial of the claim to existence slumbering within it. The powers interested in the functioning of the apparatus, in the paralysing of the masses, in the individual mind, seek to further the demands of the self-preservative impulse as a non-committal gratification, and to deprive it of its possible absoluteness. By rationalising the non-rational, in order to re-establish it as a kind of gratification of elementary needs, the attempt is made to achieve that which is not genuinely possible. The result is that what was originally fostered as something other than it is, is destroyed by what seems to be an endeavour to care for it. A prey to technical dominance, it assumes a grey tint or a crude motley coloration, wherein man no longer recognises himself, being robbed of his individuality as a human creature. Yet, since it is uncontrollable, it rides rough-shod over the ordinances formulated to destroy it.

The claim to self-will and to existence [to self-expression] cannot be abrogated—any more than there [44] is a possibility, once the masses have come into being, of dispensing with the need for a universal apparatus as an essential condition for the life and welfare of every individual. Tension between the universal life-apparatus and a truly human world is therefore, inevitable. Each is endowed with its reality only in virtue of the other; and were one to effect a definitive conquest of the other, it would thereby instantly destroy itself. Attempted mastery and attempted revolt will continue their reciprocal strike, each misunderstanding the other, though each fruitfully stimulates the other. Mutual misunderstanding is unavoidable because of the conflict between the self-preservative impulse as a vital urge and existence [the craving for higher forms of self-expression] in its absoluteness.

The limits to the life-order will everywhere become manifest where man grows fully aware of himself.

What has made life as we now live it possible, and what is therefore indispensable, is nevertheless a danger to man's selfhood. The growth of knowledge during the era of advanced technique in conjunction with the spreading dominion of apparatus seem to narrow man's potentialities even while enriching him. It is obvious that he may founder if, as is possible, no efficient leaders appear upon the scene. A symbol of the world in which, somehow or other, so long as he remains man, he has to live, a symbol of the world which is his necessary historical environment, is the life of the home. The fact that he knows himself menaced is shown by his dread of life; the fact that he can secure self-expression in his daily achievement is shown by (when he has it) joy in work; and the way in which he realises his vital reality is disclosed in sport.[45]

CONSCIOUSNESS DURING THE ERA OF ADVANCED TECHNIQUE

The upshot of technical advances as far as everyday life is concerned has been that there is a trustworthy supply of necessaries, but in a way which makes us take less pleasure in them, because they come to us as a matter of course instead of with the relish given by a sense of positive fulfilment. Being mere materials obtainable at a moment's notice in exchange for money, they lack the aroma of that which is produced by personal effort. Articles of consumption are supplied in the mass and are used up, their refuse being thrown away; they are readily interchangeable, one specimen being as good as another. In manufactured articles turned out in large quantities, no attempt is made to achieve a unique and precious quality, to produce something whose individuality makes it transcend fashion, something that will be carefully cherished. An article which thus satisfies ordinary needs arouses no peculiar sense of affection, and is only felt to be important if it should chance to be unobtainable. In that last respect, certainly, a general security of provision, growing ever more extensive, intensifies the emotions of want and danger should anything go wrong with the supply.

Among articles of consumption we distinguish the well-adapted and substantially perfected kinds, the definitive forms whose manufacture has become thoroughly normalised. Such commodities have not sprung completely finished from one exceptional brain, but are the outcome of successive discoveries and improvements that have continued, perhaps, for more than a generation. The bicycle, for instance, took twenty years to pass through the various stages of its revolution (some of which now look to us more than a little comic) before attaining finality in a restricted [46] number of minor varieties. Although the majority of articles of consumption still repel in one way or another by inelegancies of form, by errors of excess or defect, by unpracticalness in matters of detail, by maladaptations in point of technique, or what not, the ideal shines forth, and in a fair number of instances has been attained. When perfectionment has gone as far as this, fondness for a particular specimen has become unmeaning. The general form is what matters to us, and, however artificial that may be, such things have a functional suitability which almost makes them seem like natural products rather than the creatures of man's activity.

Thanks to the technical conquest of time and space by the daily press, modern travel, the cinema, wireless, etc., a universalization of contact has become possible. No longer is anything remote, mysterious, wonderful. All can participate as witnesses of events accounted great or important. Persons who occupy leading positions are as well known to us as if we rubbed shoulders with them day by day.

The attitude of mind characteristic of this world of advanced technique has been termed positivism. The positivist does not want phrase-making, but knowledge; not ponderings about meaning, but dextrous action; not feelings, but objectivity; not a study of mysterious influences, but a clear ascertainment of facts. Reports of what has been observed must be given concisely, plastically, without sentimentalism. An aggregate of disjointed data, even sound ones, producing the effect of being the relics of earlier education, are worth nothing. Constructive thought is demanded, rather than the making of many words; simplicity and directness, rather than eloquence. Control and organization are supreme.[47] The matter-of-factness of the technical realm makes its familiars skilled in their dealings with all things; the ease with which ideas about such matters are communicated, standardizes knowledge; hygiene and comfort schematize bodily and erotic life. Daily affairs are carried on in conformity with fixed rules. The desire to act in accordance with general conventions, to avoid startling any one by the unusual, results in the establishment of a typical behaviour which reconstructs upon a new plane something akin to the rule of taboos in primitive times.

The individual is merged in the function. Being is objectified, for positivism would be violated if individuality remained conspicuous. The individual consciousness is absorbed into the social, so that, in exceptional instances, the individual has joy in work without any tinge of selfishness. It is the collectivity that matters; and what to the individual would be tedious, nay intolerable, becomes endurable to him as part of the collectivity, in which a new stimulus inspires him. He exists only as "we".

Essential humanity is reduced to the general; to vitality as a functional corporeality, to the triviality of enjoyment. The divorce of labour from pleasure deprives life of its possible gravity: public affairs become mere entertainment; private affairs, the alternation of stimulation and fatigue, and a craving for novelty whose inexhaustible current flows swiftly into the waters of oblivion. There is no continuity, only pastime. Positivism likewise encourages an unceasing activity of the impulses common to us all: an enthusiasm for the numberless and the vast, for the creations of modern technique, for huge crowds; sensational admiration for the achievements, fortunes, and abilities of outstanding individuals; the complication and [48] brutalization of the erotic; gambling, adventurousness, and even the hazarding on one's life. Lottery tickets are sold by the million; crossword puzzles become the chief occupation of people's leisure. This positive gratification of the mind without personal participation or effort promotes efficiency for the daily round, fatigue and recreation being regularized.

In becoming a mere function, life forfeits its historical particularity, to the extreme of a levelling of the various ages of life. Youth as the period of highest vital efficiency and of erotic exaltation becomes the desired type of life in general. Where the human being is regarded only as a function, he must be young; and if youth is over, he will still strive to show its semblance. Add to this that, for primary reasons, age no longer counts. The individual's life is experienced only momentarily, its temporal extension being a chance duration, not remembered and cherished as the upbuilding of irrevocable decisions upon the foundation of biological phases. Since a human being no longer has any specific age, he is always simultaneously at the beginning and the end; he can do now this, now that, and now the other; everything seems at any moment possible, and yet nothing truly real. The individual is no more than one instance among millions; why then should he think his doings of any importance? What happens, happens quickly and is soon forgotten. People therefore tend to behave as if they were all of the same age. Children become like grown-ups as soon as they possibly can, and join in grown-up conversations on their own initiative. When the old pretend to be young, of course the young have no reverence for their elders. These latter, instead of (as they should) keeping the young at a distance and setting them a standard,[49] assume the airs of an invincible vitality, such as beseems youth but is unbecoming to age. Genuine youth wants to maintain its disparity, and not to be mingled without distinction among elders. Age wants form and realization and the continuity of its destiny.

Since positivism makes a general demand for simplicity that shall render things universally comprehensible, it tends towards establishing a sort of "universal language" for the expression of all modes of human behaviour. Not merely fashions, but rules for social intercourse, gestures, phrases, methods of conveying information, incline towards uniformity. There is now a conventional ethic of association: courteous smiles, a tranquil manner, the avoidance of haste and jostle, the adoption of a humorous attitude in strained situations, helpfulness unless the cost be unreasonable, the feeling that "personal remarks" are in bad taste, self-discipline to promote order and easy relationships whenever people are assembled in large numbers. All these things are advantageous to a multifariously communal life, and are actually achieved.

DOMINION OF APPARATUS

Inasmuch as the titanic apparatus for the provision of the elementary necessaries of human life reduces the individual to a mere function, it releases him from the obligation to conform to the traditional standards which of old formed the cement of society. It has been said that in modern times men have been shuffled together like grains of sand. They are elements of an apparatus in which they occupy now one location, now another; not parts of a historical substance which they imbue with their selfhood. The number of those who lead this uprooted sort of life is continually on the increase. Driven from pillar to post, then perhaps out-of-work [50] for a lengthy period with nothing more than bare subsistence, they no longer have a definite place or status in the whole. The profound saying that every one ought to have his own niche, to fulfil his proper task in the scheme of creation, has for them become a lying phrase, used in the futile endeavour to console persons who feel themselves adrift and forsaken. What a man can do nowadays can only be done by one who takes short views. He has occupation, indeed, but his life has no continuity. What he does is done to good purpose, but is then finished once for all. The task may be repeated after the same fashion many times, but it cannot be repeated in such an intimate way as to become, one might say, part of the personality of the doer; it does not lead to an expansion of the selfhood. What has been done, no longer counts, but only that which is actually being done. Oblivion is the basis of such a life, whose outlooks upon past and present shrink so much that scarcely anything remains in the mind but the bald present. Thus life flows on its course devoid of memories and foresights, lacking the energy derivable from a purposive and abstract outlook upon the part played in the apparatus. Love for things and human beings wanes and disappears. The machine-made products vanish from sight as soon as made and consumed, all that remains in view being the machinery by which new commodities are being made. The worker at the machine, concentrating upon immediate aims, has no time or inclination left for the contemplation of life as a whole.

When the average functional capacity has become the standard of achievement, the individual is regarded with indifference. No one is indispensable. He is not himself, having no more genuine individuality [51] than one pin in a row, a mere object of general utility. Those most effectively predestined to such a life are persons without any serious desire to be themselves. Such have the preference. It seems as if the world must be given over to mediocrities, to persons without a destiny, without a rank or a difference, without genuinely human attributes.

It is as if the man thus deracinated and reduced to the level of a thing, had lost the essence of humanity. Nothing appeals to him with the verity of substantial being. Whether in enjoyment or discomfort, whether strenuous or fatigued, he is still nothing more than the function of his daily task. As he lives on from day to day, the only desire that may stir him beyond that of performing this task is the desire to occupy the best obtainable place in the apparatus. The mass of those who stay in their appointed situations becomes segregated from those who ruthlessly press forward. The former are passive, remain where they are, and amuse themselves in their leisure hours; the latter are active, being spurred on by ambition and the will to power, consumed as with fire by the thought of the chances of promotion, by the tensing of their utmost energies.

The whole apparatus is guided by a bureaucracy, which is itself likewise an apparatus—human beings reduced to apparatus, one upon which all those at work in the greater apparatus are dependent. The State, the municipality, manufacturing and business enterprises, are controlled by bureaucracies. To-day men are associated for labour in multitudes, and their work must be organised. Those who force a way into the front ranks have secured advancement and enjoy higher consideration; but essentially they, too, are the slaves of their functions, which merely demand [52] an alerter intelligence, a more specialized talent, and a more lively activity than those of the crowd.

The dominion of apparatus is favourable to persons equipped with the faculties which will thus bring them to the front: is advantageous to far-seeing and relentless individuals who are well-acquainted with the qualities of average human beings and are therefore able to manage them efficiently, who are ready and willing to acquire expertise in some department or other, who can strive unrestingly without concern for anything but the main chance, and who are sleeplessly possessed by the thought of getting on in the world.

There are further requisites. The would-be climber must be able to make himself liked. He must persuade, and at times even corrupt—be serviceable enough to make himself indispensable—be able to hold his tongue, to circumvent, to lie a little though not too much—be indefatigable in the discovery of reasons—ostensibly modest—have a readiness to appeal to sentiment on occasions—be capable of working in a manner that will please his superiors—avoid showing independence except in those matters wherein independence is expected of him by his chiefs.

Where scarcely any one is born to command and therefore educated to command, and where a high position in the apparatus has to be climbed up to by the aspirant, this acquirement of a leading situation is dependent upon behavior, instincts, valuations, which imperil true selfhood as a determinant of responsible leadership. Luck and chance may sometimes bring about advancement. Speaking generally, however, the winners in the race have qualities which disincline them to allow others to be their true selves. Hence the winners tend to snub all those who aim at adequate self-expression, speaking of them as pretentious, [53] eccentric, biased, unpractical, and measuring their achievements by insincere absolute standards; they are personally suspect, they are stigmatized as provocative, as disturbers of the peace, as people who kick over the traces. Because he only "arrives" who has sacrificed his selfhood, the arrivist will not tolerate self-expression in subordinates.

Consequently peculiar methods of advancement in the apparatus decide the choice among the candidates for high places. Because no one gets on who does not thrust himself forward, and yet to be "pushing" is considered bad form in any particular case, the convention is that the candidate must ostensibly wait till he is summoned; and the problem each has to solve is how to thrust himself into a position while seeming indifferent to promotion. A rumour is started inconspicuously, in casual conversation. Hypotheses are mooted with an air of indifference. The ball is opened by some such phrase as: "I am not really thinking of"; or, "it is hardly to be expected that", etc. If nothing comes of the suggestion, no harm has been done. If, on the other hand, it bears fruit, one can soon begin talking of a concrete proposal, declare that an offer has been made, and bruit it abroad that nothing was farther from one's mind than any such expectation. One can even feign reluctance. The aspirant accustoms himself to being double-faced and double-tongued. He will enter into as many promising relationships as possible, so that he may be able to turn some of them to useful account. Instead of the comradeship of persons all of whom are their genuine selves, we have the spurious friendship of a gang whose motto is "You scratch my back and I'll scratch yours." The important thing is not to be a spoil-sport when pleasure is afoot; to be outwardly respectful [54] to all; to show indignation when one is sure that others will do the same; to join in log-rolling to the common advantage—and so on.

NIKOLAI BERDYAEV

Dream and Reality

The other basic element in human existence of which I want to speak is anguish. All my life anguish never left me, although my awareness of it varied and was more or less intense at different stages of my inner development. It is necessary to distinguish between anguish, fear,[39] and tedium. Anguish points to the world above and is associated with the experience of the insignificance, precariousness and transitoriness of this world. Anguish bears witness to the transcendent and, at the same time, to the distance, the yawning gulf that exists between man and the transcendent. Anguish is also a longing for another world, for that which is beyond the boundaries of this finite world of ours. It spells solitude in face of the transcendent; it is the point of greatest conflict between my existence in the world and the transcendent. Anguish can awake my awareness of God, but it can also signify my God-forsakenness. It intervenes, as it were, between the transcendent and the abyss of non-being, of void.

Fear and tedium, on the other hand, consign me to the nether world. Fear is evidence of danger, coming from the lower world; and tedium denotes this world's triviality and emptiness. There is nothing more frightful and hopeless than the tedious and wearisome void of life. Anguish admits of hope, but tedium is devoid of hope. There is no issue out of tedium, unless it be in the act of creation. Fear is always associated with external danger and must be distinguished from terror, which is an experience in the depths of spirit and concerns the transcendent realities of being and non-being. Kierkegaard draws a distinction between *Angst* and *Furcht;* and for him *Angst* is a primordial religious phenomenon. Anguish and terror are related experiences; but the experience of terror is the more poignant, the more intense and overpowering, while anguish is the gentler, the more tranquil and untroubled. Terror may deliver man from tedium, and, when it turns to anguish, man's diseased condition ceases to be acute and becomes chronic.

It is easier to endure anguish and terror than sadness of heart and sorrow, and I always sought to escape from these as quickly as possible. I felt helpless in face of anything that stirred my emotions: I was too deeply sensitive and impressionable. Sadness, which is of the heart, looks towards the past. Terror, which is of the spirit, looks towards the eternal. Turgenyev is the artist of sadness *par excellence;* Dostoevsky is the artist of terror. Sadness has a poetical quality; terror is inherently dramatic. I knew anguish and terror and bore them with fortitude; but it seemed to me that if I were to surrender to sadness, I would pass away.[40] Sadness is often associated with the sensation of pity, which I have always feared, knowing the power that it is apt to acquire over my soul. I was driven to raise barriers against sadness and pity, as indeed I did against anything that moved my emotions. But I was powerless to resist anguish, and it had no such destructive effects on me. To use an old-fashioned and rather inaccurate distinction, I combined in myself two types of temperament, commonly considered incompatible: I am at once sanguine and melancholic; and the sanguine element in me was perhaps even more pronounced than the melancholic. I was very easily roused, and my quick reaction issued, amongst other things, in the irascibility of which I have already spoken. But melancholy in me had deeper roots. Sometimes I suffered agonies of nostalgia and was driven by pessimistic moods, even when I appeared outwardly cheerful and content.

It is interesting, perhaps, that at the time of my spiritual awakening it was the philosophy of Schopenhauer rather than the Bible which impressed me—a fact which may have had far-reaching consequences for my later life. I found it difficult to recognize the alleged 'goodness' of creation. It is strange that I should have suffered most acutely from anguish during the so-called happy moments of life, if indeed it is at all possible to speak of such moments. I have always been afraid of happy, joyful experiences, for they have always brought me the most vivid memories of the agony of life. On great feast-days I almost invariably felt anguish, perhaps because I was awaiting some miraculous transformation of ordinary, workaday life: but it never came. The tragedy is that I was unable to idealize and romanticize, as some succeeded in doing, the painful condition of man—his anguish, his despair, his doubts, his sufferings and conflicts. I often thought of this condition as a frightful betrayal of life.

There is anguish which is characteristic of adolescence. In my youth I have known greater anguish than in later and more mature years: this anguish springs from an abundance of unrealized powers, from doubts and uncertainty as to the possibility of realizing them. Youth lives in the hope of a life rich, colourful, momentous and eventful; but there is disparity and contrast between life as it presents itself to hope and life as actually lived, life distorted and betrayed by untold disappointments,[41] injustices, suffering and pain. It is a mistake to think that anguish is born of weakness: on the contrary, it is born of abundant strength. In life's very intensity there is contained an element of anguish. I believe that the young endure more of the anguish and longing of life than others are generally ready to admit. But different people experience this in different ways. I was myself particularly prone to anguish at moments which are commonly said to be joyful; for there is agony in the joy of the given moment when it is experienced against the background of life as a whole, pervaded as this is by tragedy and torment.

Anguish is always evidence of longing for eternity, of inability to come to terms with time. When we face the future we are moved not only by hope but also by anguish; for, in the end, the future carries death within itself and thus gives rise to anguish. Both future and past are hostile to eternity. I have often experienced a burning anguish under a wonderful starry or moonlit sky or on a glorious sunny day; in the quiet of a blossoming garden or in the silent immensity of the steppes; on looking into the face of a beautiful woman or at the moment of the awakening of love. Such moments called forth a vision of contrast between these and the darkness, decay and ugliness which fill the world to overflowing.

I was always struck by the unspeakable pain and destructiveness of time: I always foresaw the end in imagination and found no strength or desire to adapt myself to the process which led up to it. I was impatient. Love in particular seemed to me to carry within itself the seed of anguish, and I have frequently been amazed that people could experience the exultation of love as sheer joy and happiness. *Eros* is in anguish, for it is concerned with, and deeply rooted in, the mystery of time and eternity: it concerns time athirst for eternal fulfilment, and yet never attaining it. Likewise, there is anguish in sex, which does not merely denote a passion for satisfaction of desire, but also bears the signature of the fallen nature of man. It is impossible to quench the thirst of sex in the conditions of this fallen life, for this thirst gives rise to illusions which make man the tool of an inhuman, biological process. Dionysos, the god of dying and rising life, gives birth to tragedy, from which sex cannot ever extricate itself: Dionysos and Pluto are one. Sex shows man wounded, fallen apart and never able to attain true fulness [42] through union. It bids man go out into another; but he returns once more into himself and the anguish of his longing for unity continues unrelieved. The desire for wholeness inherent in men cannot be satisfied, least of all in sexual passion, which indeed only serves to deepen the wounds of disunity. Sex is, in its very nature, unwholesome, unchaste: it is evidence of the divided nature of man: only true love prevails over the division and attains wholeness and chastity. This is a profoundly tragic problem, on which I shall dwell at a later stage.

I have known anguish at unusual times and in unusual circumstances. Summer twilight in the streets of a big city, especially in Petersburg and Paris, with their drifting, half-formed images, has frequently inspired anguish in me. I have always found it hard to bear the hour of twilight. It is the hour of transition between life and darkness—a time when the fount of daylight is already spent, and when the other light, which springs from the starry mystery of night, or when the man-made artificial light, by which we try to protect ourselves against the power of darkness, has not as yet illumined human existence. Twilight intensifies the longing for eternity, for eternal life. It is also at the hour of twilight, in the ghostly atmosphere of a large town, that the veil over the nightmares and the evil of human life is drawn aside. But the anguish of twilight is different from the anguish of night: the latter has a depth, a transcendence unknown to the former. I have known both: I have known the anguish of misty twilight and the anguish of night which turns into terror and which no human language can convey or express. But this experience vanished in time. There were periods when I could not wake or sleep in darkness, and I was haunted by terrifying dreams and nightmares. Dreams have altogether been a source of torment to me, although I have sometimes had remarkable dreams of great illumination for me. Night conveyed to me some alien presence which terrified and pursued me into daylight. Thus we would go, four of us, for a walk in the country, into forests or fields; and I would suddenly have a sense of the presence of a fifth, come I know not whence, and I would forget how many of us there were. I can see no other source of these experiences but this mysterious and unaccountable anguish.

Modern psychoanalysis describes these phenomena as having their origin in the sub-conscious, but this explains little and elucidates [43] nothing. I am deeply convinced that the transcendent is present in human life: it allures man and acts in human existence. I have known the depth and power of the sub-conscious and the subterranean, but I have also known that other and greater deep which is transcendence. Anguish is present in the very fabric of so-called life (though it may be unknown to those who take this life for granted and ask no questions), and all living beings are imbued with its deadly poison.

It has been said that 'green is the tree of life and grey the theory of life'. Paradoxical though it may seem, I am inclined to think that the reverse is true: 'grey is the tree of life and green the theory thereof'. But I must explain, lest this should give rise to misunderstandings. Have I not always been a declared enemy of scholastic conceptualism and the desiccated theories of discursive reason? Have I not always been a Faust rather than a Wagner? What is known as 'life', however, is as often as not an embodiment of the commonplace and consists of nothing but the cares of workaday existence. 'Theory', on the other hand, may be understood as creative vision, as the Greek *theoria*, which raises us above the habits of daily life. Philosophy, the 'green theory of life', is free of anguish and boredom. I became a philosopher and a servant of 'theory' that I might renounce and be relieved of this unspeakable anguish. Philosophical thinking had always freed me from life's ugliness and corruption. To 'being' I have always opposed 'creativity', that is to say, not 'life', but the breaking through and flight from 'life' into 'existence', from the finite into the infinite and transcendent.

Anguish, then, takes its rise in 'life'—in the twilight and the mists of life—and drives man toward the transcendent; while creativity is that very movement towards transcendence and the evocation of the image of the wholly other in relation to this life. In the realm of creativity all things acquire depth, meaning, character and interest, in contrast to the shallowness, insignificance, fortuitousness and insipidity peculiar to the realm of tedious external fact. A world endowed with beauty, unknown to this objective world where ugliness reigns supreme, unfolded itself before me, and called upon my creative spirit.

Has tedium, which rises from the waste and vacant regions of being, ever filled my heart? I have hardly ever been bored, and time never seemed to suffice for the accomplishment of my life's work and the [44] fulfilment of my vocation; nor have I ever wasted time. And yet many, all too many, things have bored me. I have been bored by the views and opinions of the majority of men; by politics; by ideologies; by the affairs of state and nation. The commonplace in life, the repetitions and imitations, the fetters and repressions of life have produced in me a sense of tedium and drawn me into a void of nothingness. Indeed, when man submits, through weakness or through ignorance, to the pressure of these things, the world becomes flat and empty, devoid of depth and meaning, and tedium comes into its own, in anticipation of that kingdom of utter emptiness which is hell. The final and infernal limit of tedium is reached when man says to himself that nothing is. Suffering is, no doubt, a relief and a salvation in such a human condition, for it is a way of regaining the depth of life. Anguish too may bring salvation. There are people who feel happy in the midst of their own and the world's emptiness, and this state may well be the supreme instance of triviality and the commonplace.

Many people are, or say they are, in love with life. But I have never been able to feel or, indeed, to understand this. I could only be 'in love' with creativity and with the rapture of the creative act. I could never escape the feeling of anguish when confronted with life in its inexorable finality, and always believed that man's stature and significance is in proportion to that in him which breaks through to infinity. This issued in my inability ever to master the art of living and to profit by life. 'The misfortune of man', says Carlyle in *Sartor Resartus,* 'has its source in his greatness; for there is something infinite in him, and he cannot succeed in burying himself completely in the finite.' The 'objective' world and 'objective' life are indeed buried in the finite; and burial is the most fitting thing that can happen in the finite world. 'Life', then, is, as it were, the dying of the infinite into the finite, of the eternal into the temporal. There is in me a strong anarchist instinct: I revolt against the power of the finite, the circumscribed and the limitatively determined. The commonplace, which is the epitome of finiteness in the life of man and of the world, has either struck me by its utter insignificance, or it has roused me to revolt; and any attempt to ascribe a sacred character to finite things was repulsive to me.

Anguish can denote a religious experience. Religious anguish involves [45] longing for immortality and eternal life, for redemption of the finitude of existence. Similarly, art appeared to me as imbued with anguish and, therefore, as evidence of the longing for transcendence. The magic of art is its power to wrench out the roots of finitude and to turn man's gaze to the eternal, archetypal forms and images of existence.

Anguish has persistently weakened my activity in the world: I thought to withdraw, whilst life was there to be re-shaped and transformed. That is, perhaps, why happiness and the sense of satisfaction were denied to me. From time to time it seemed to me that I would have known joy and happiness, had the cause of some particular pain at a particular moment been removed. But when this did happen the sense of anguish would persist and intensify some new and hitherto unknown torment. Nothing gave me a feeling of complete satisfaction and sufficiency; indeed these very states betrayed to me their fundamentally sinful character.[46]

PAUL TILLICH

The Courage to Be

COURAGE AND DESPAIR

Existentialism as it appeared in the 20th century represents the most vivid and threatening meaning of "existential." In it the whole development comes to a point beyond which it cannot go. It has become a reality in all the countries of the Western world. It is expressed in all the realms of man's spiritual creativity, it penetrates all educated classes. It is not the invention of a Bohemian philosopher or of a neurotic novelist; it is not a sensational exaggeration made for the sake of profit and fame; it is not a morbid play with negativities. Elements of all these have entered it, but it itself is something else. It is the expression of the anxiety of meaninglessness and of the attempt to take this anxiety into the courage to be as oneself.

Recent Existentialism must be considered from these two points of view. It is not simply individualism of the rationalistic or romantic or naturalistic type. In distinction to these three preparatory movements it has experienced the universal breakdown of meaning. Twentieth-century man has lost a meaningful world and a self which lives in meanings out of a spiritual center. The man-created world of objects has drawn into itself him who created it and who now loses his subjectivity in it. He has sacrificed himself to his own productions. But man still is aware of what [139] he has lost or is continuously losing. He is still man enough to experience his dehumanization as despair. He does not know a way out but he tries to save his humanity by expressing the situation as without an "exit." He reacts with the courage of despair, the courage to take his despair upon himself and to resist the radical threat of nonbeing by the courage to be as oneself. Every analyst of present-day Existentialist philosophy, art, and literature can show their ambiguous

SOURCE: *The Courage to Be* by Paul Tillich (New Haven: Yale University Press, 1952). Reprinted with permission.

structure: the meaninglessness which drives to despair, a passionate denunciation of this situation, and the successful or unsuccessful attempt to take the anxiety of meaninglessness into the courage to be as oneself.

It is not astonishing that those who are unshaken in their courage to be as a part, either in its collectivist or in its conformist form, are disturbed by the expressions of the Existentialist courage of despair. They are unable to understand what is happening in our period. They are unable to distinguish the genuine from the neurotic anxiety in Existentialism. They attack as a morbid longing for negativity what in reality is courageous acceptance of the negative. They call decay what is actually the creative expression of decay. They reject as meaningless the meaningful attempt to reveal the meaninglessness of our situation. It is not the ordinary difficulty of understanding those who break new ways in thinking and artistic expression which produces the widespread resistance to recent Existentialism but the desire to protect a self-limiting [140] courage to be as a part. Somehow one feels that this is not a true safety; one has to suppress inclinations to accept the Existentialist visions, one even enjoys them if they appear in the theater or in novels, but one refuses to take them seriously, that is as revelations of one's own existential meaninglessness and hidden despair. The violent reactions against modern art in collectivist (Nazi, Communist) as well as conformist (American democratic) groups show that they feel seriously threatened by it. But one does not feel spiritually threatened by something which is not an element of oneself. And since it is a symptom of the neurotic character to resist nonbeing by reducing being, the Existentialist could reply to the frequent reproach that he is neurotic by showing the neurotic defense mechanisms of the anti-Existentialist desire for traditional safety.

There should be no question of what Christian theology has to do in this situation. It should decide for truth against safety, even if the safety is consecrated and supported by the churches. Certainly there is a Christian conformism from the beginning of the Church on, and there is a Christian collectivism—or at least semi-collectivism, in several periods of Church history. But this should not induce Christian theologians to identify Christian courage with the courage to be as a part. They should realize that the courage to be as oneself is the necessary corrective to the courage to be as a part—even if they rightly assume that neither of these forms of the courage to be gives the final solution.[141]

THE COURAGE OF DESPAIR IN CONTEMPORARY ART AND LITERATURE

The courage of despair, the experience of meaninglesssness, and the self-affirmation in spite of them are manifest in the Existentialists of the 20th century. Meaninglessness is the problem of all of them. The anxiety of doubt and meaninglessness is, as we have seen, the anxiety of our period. The anxiety of fate and death and the anxiety of guilt and condemnation are implied but they are not decisive. When Heidegger speaks about the anticipation of one's own death it is not the question of immortality which concerns him but the question of what the anticipation of death means for the human situation. When Kierkegaard deals with the problem of guilt it is not the theological question of sin and forgiveness that moves him but the question of what the possibility of personal existence is in the light of personal guilt. The problem of meaning troubles recent Existentialists even when they speak of finitude and guilt.

The decisive event which underlies the search for meaning and the despair of it in the 20th century is the loss of God in the 19th century. Feuerbach explained God away in terms of the infinite desire of the human heart; Marx explained him away in terms of an ideological attempt to rise above the given reality; Nietzsche as a weakening of the will to live. The result is the pronouncement "God is dead," and with him the whole system of values and meanings in which one lived. This is felt both as a [142] loss and as a liberation. It drives one either to nihilism or to the courage which takes non-being into itself. There is probably nobody who has influenced modern Existentialism as much as Nietzsche and there is probably nobody who has presented the will to be oneself more consistently and more absurdly. In him the feeling of meaninglessness became despairing and self-destructive.

On this basis Existentialism, that is the great art, literature, and philosophy of the 20th century, reveal the courage to face things as they are and to express the anxiety of meaninglessness. It is creative courage which appears in the creative expressions of despair. Sartre calls one of his most powerful plays *No Exit,* a classical formula for the situation of despair. But he himself has an exit: he can *say* "no exit," thus taking the situation of meaninglessness upon himself. T. S. Eliot called his first great poem "The Wasteland." He described the decomposition of civilization, the lack of conviction and direction, the poverty and hysteria of the modern consciousness (as one of his critics has analyzed it). But it is the beautifully cultivated garden of a great poem which describes the meaninglessness of the Wasteland and expresses the courage of despair.

In Kafka's novels *The Castle* and *The Trial* the unapproachable remoteness of the source of meaning and the obscurity of the source of justice and mercy are expressed in language which is pure and classical. The courage to take upon oneself the loneliness of such creativity and the horror of such visions is an outstanding expression of the [143] courage to be as oneself. Man is separated from the sources of courage—but not completely: he is still able to face and to accept his own separation. In Auden's *The Age of Anxiety* the courage to take upon oneself the anxiety in a world which has lost the meaning is as obvious as the profound experience of this loss: the two poles which are united in the phrase "courage of despair" receive equal emphasis. In Sartre's *The Age of Reason* the hero faces a situation in which his passionate desire to be himself drives him to the rejection of every human commitment. He refuses to accept anything which could limit his freedom. Nothing has ultimate meaning for him, neither love nor friendship nor politics. The only immovable point is the unlimited freedom to change, to preserve freedom without content. He represents one of the most extreme forms of the courage to be as oneself, the courage to be a self which is free from any bond and which pays the price of complete emptiness. In the invention of such a figure Sartre proves his courage of despair. From the opposite side, the same problem is faced in the novel *The Stranger* by Camus, who stands on the boundary line of Existentialism but who sees the problem of meaninglessness as sharply as the Existentialists. His hero is a man without subjectivity. He is not extraordinary in any respect. He acts as any ordinary official in a small position would act. He is a stranger because he nowhere achieves an existential relation to himself or to his world. Whatever happens to him has no reality and meaning to him: a love which is not a real love, a trial which is not a real trial, an execution [144] which has no justification in reality. There is neither guilt nor forgiveness, neither despair nor courage in him. He is described not as a person but as a psychological process which is completely conditioned, whether he works or loves or kills or eats or sleeps. He is an object among objects, without meaning for himself and therefore unable to find meaning in his world. He represents that destiny of absolute objectivation against which all Existentialists fight. He represents it in the most radical way, without reconciliation. The courage to create this figure equals the courage with which Kafka has created the figure of Mr. K.

A glimpse at the theater confirms this picture. The theater, especially in the United States, is full of images of meaninglessness and despair. In some plays nothing else is shown (as in Arthur Miller's *Death of a Salesman*); in others the negativity is less unconditional (as in Tennessee Williams' *A Streetcar Named Desire*). But it seldom becomes positivity: even comparatively positive solutions are undermined by doubt and by awareness of the ambiguity of all solutions. It is astonishing that these plays are attended by large crowds in a country whose prevailing courage is the courage to be as a part in a system of democratic conformity. What does this mean for the situation of America and with it of mankind as a whole? One can easily play down the importance of this phenomenon. One can point to the unquestionable fact that even the largest crowds of theatergoers are an infinitely small percentage of the American population. One can dismiss the [145] significance of the attraction the Existentialist theater has for many by calling it an imported fashion, doomed to disappear very soon. This is possibly but not necessarily so. It may be that the comparatively few (few even if one adds to them all the cynics and despairing ones in our institutions of higher learning) are a vanguard which precedes a great change in the spiritual and social-psychological situation. It may be that the limits of the courage to be as a part have become visible to more people than the increasing conformity shows. If this is the meaning of the appeal that Existentialism has on the stage, one should observe it carefully and prevent it from becoming the forerunner of collectivist forms of the courage to be as a part—a threat which history has abundantly proved to exist.

The combination of the experience of meaninglessness and of the courage to be as oneself is the key to the development of visual art since the turn of the century. In expressionism and surrealism the surface structures of reality are disrupted. The categories which constitute ordinary experience have lost their power. The category of substance is lost: solid objects are twisted like ropes; the causal interdependence of things is disregarded: things appear in a complete contingency; temporal sequences are without significance, it does not matter whether an event has happened before or after another event; the spatial dimensions are reduced or dissolved into a horrifying infinity. The organic structures of life are cut into pieces which are arbitrarily (from the biological, not the artistic,[146] point of view) recomposed: limbs are dispersed, colors are separated from their natural carriers. The psychological process (this refers to literature more than to art) is reversed: one lives from the future to the past, and this without rhythm or any kind of meaningful organization. The world of anxiety is a world in which the categories, the structures of reality, have lost their validity. Everybody would be dizzy if causality suddenly ceased to be valid. In Existentialist art (as I like to call it) causality has lost its validity.

Modern art has been attacked as a forerunner of totalitarian systems. The answer that all totalitarian systems have started their careers by attacking modern art is insufficient, for one could say that the totalitarian systems fought modern art just because they tried to resist the meaninglessness expressed in it. The real answer lies deeper. Modern art is not propaganda but revelation. It shows that the reality of our existence is as it is. It does not cover up the reality in which we are living. The question therefore is this: Is the revelation of a situation propaganda for it? If this were the case all art would have to become dishonest beautification. The art propagated by both totalitarianism and democratic conformism is dishonest beautification. It is an idealized naturalism which is preferred because it removes every danger of art becoming critical and revolutionary. The creators of modern art have been able to see the meaninglessness of our existence; they participated in its despair. At the same time they have had the courage to face it and to express it in [147] their pictures and sculptures. They had the courage to be as themselves.

THE COURAGE OF DESPAIR IN CONTEMPORARY PHILOSOPHY

Existential philosophy gives the theoretical formulation of what we have found as the courage of despair in art and literature. Heidegger in *Sein und Zeit* (which has its independent philosophical standing whatever Heidegger may say about it in criticism and retraction) describes the courage of despair in philosophically exact terms. He carefully elaborates the concepts of nonbeing, finitude, anxiety, care, having to die, guilt, conscience, self, participation, and so on. After this he analyses a phenomenon which he calls "resolve." The German word for it, *Entschlossenheit*, points to the symbol of unlocking what anxiety, subjection to conformity, and self-seclusion have locked. Once it is unlocked, one can act, but not according to norms given by anybody or anything. Nobody can give directions for the actions of the "resolute" individual—no God, no conventions, no laws of reason, no norms or principles. *We* must be ourselves, *we* must decide where to go. Our conscience is the call to ourselves. It does not tell anything concrete, it is neither the voice of God nor the awareness of eternal principles. It calls us to ourselves out of the behavior of the average man, out of daily talk, the daily routine, out of the adjustment which is the main principle of the conformist courage to be as a part. But if we follow this call [148] we become inescapably guilty, not through moral weakness but through our existential situation. Having the courage to be as ourselves we become guilty, and we are asked to take this existential guilt upon ourselves. Meaninglessness in all its aspects can be faced only by those who resolutely take the anxiety of finitude and guilt upon themselves. There is no norm, no criterion for what is right and wrong. Resoluteness makes right what shall be right. One of Heidegger's historical functions was to carry through the Existentialist analysis of the courage to be as oneself more fully than anyone else and, historically speaking, more destructively.

Sartre draws consequences from the earlier Heidegger which the later Heidegger did not accept. But it remains doubtful whether Sartre was historically right in drawing these consequences. It was easier for Sartre to draw them than for Heidegger, for in the background of Heidegger's ontology lies the mystical concept of being which is without significance for Sartre. Sartre carried through the consequences of Heidegger's Existentialist analyses without mystical restrictions. This is the reason he has become the symbol of present-day Existentialism, a position which is deserved not so much by the originality of his basic concepts as by the radicalism, consistency, and psychological adequacy with which he has carried them through. I refer above all to his proposition that "the essence of man is his existence." This sentence is like a flash of light which illuminates the whole Existentialist scene. One could call it the most despairing and the most [149] courageous sentence in all Existentialist literature. What it says is that there is no essential nature of man, except in the one point that he can make of himself what he wants. Man creates what he is. Nothing is given to him to determine his creativity. The essence of his being—the "should-be," "the ought-to-be,"—is not something which he finds; he makes it. Man is what he makes of himself. And the courage to be as oneself is the courage to make of oneself what one wants to be.

There are Existentialists of a less radical point of view. Karl Jaspers recommends a new conformity in terms of an all-embracing "philosophical faith"; others speak of a *philosophia perennis;* while Gabriel Marcel moves from an Existentialist radicalism to a position based on the semi-collectivism of medieval thought. Existentialism in philosophy is represented more by Heidegger and Sartre than by anybody else.

THE COURAGE OF DESPAIR IN THE NONCREATIVE EXISTENTIALIST ATTITUDE

I have dealt in the last sections with people whose creative courage enables them to express existential despair. Not many people are creative. But there is a noncreative Existentialist attitude called cynicism. A cynic today is not the same person the Greeks meant by the term. For the Greeks the cynic was a critic of contemporary culture on the basis of reason and natural law; he was a revolutionary rationalist, a follower of Socrates. Modern cynics are not ready to follow anybody. They have no belief in reason,[150] no criterion of truth, no set of values, no answer to the question of meaning. They try to undermine every norm put before them. Their courage is expressed not creatively but in their form of life. They courageously reject any solution which would deprive them of their freedom of rejecting whatever they want to reject. The cynics are lonely although they need company in order to show their loneliness. They are empty of both preliminary meanings and an ultimate meaning, and therefore easy victims of neurotic anxiety. Much compulsive self-affirmation and much fanatical self-surrender are expressions of the noncreative courage to be as oneself.

THE LIMITS OF THE COURAGE TO BE AS ONESELF

This leads to the question of the limits of the courage to be as oneself in its creative as well as its uncreative forms. Courage is self-affirmation "in spite of," and the courage to be as oneself is self-affirmation of the self as itself. But one must ask: What is this self that affirms itself? Radical Existentialism answers: What it makes of itself. This is all it can say, because anything more would restrict the absolute freedom of the self. The self, cut off from participation in its world, is an empty shell, a mere possibility. It must act because it lives, but it must redo every action because acting involves him who acts in that upon which he acts. It gives content and for this reason it restricts his freedom to make of himself what he wants. In classical theology, both Catholic and Protestant, only [151] God has this prerogative: He is *ā sē* (from himself) or absolute freedom. Nothing is in him which is not by him. Existentialism, on the basis of the message that God is dead, gives man the divine "a-se-ity." Nothing shall be in man which is not by man. But man is finite, he is given to himself as what he is. He has received his being and with it the structure of his being, including the structure of finite freedom. And finite freedom is not aseity. Man can affirm himself only if he affirms not an empty shell, a mere possibility, but the structure of being in which he finds himself before action and non-action. Finite freedom has a definite structure, and if the self tries to trespass on this structure it ends in the loss of itself. The non-participating hero in Sartre's *The Age of Reason* is caught in a net of contingencies, coming partly from the subconscious levels of his own self, partly from the environment from which he cannot withdraw. The assuredly empty self is filled with contents which enslave it just because it does not know or accept them as contents. This is true too of the cynic, as was said before. He cannot escape the forces of his self which may drive him into complete loss of the freedom that he wants to preserve.

This dialectical self-destruction of the radical forms of the courage to be as oneself has happened on a world-wide scale in the totalitarian reaction of the 20th century against the revolutionary Existentialism of the 19th century. The Existentialist protest against dehumanization and objectivation, together with its courage to be as oneself,[152] have turned into the most elaborate and oppressive forms of collectivism that have appeared in history. It is the great tragedy of our time that Marxism, which had been conceived as a movement for the liberation of everyone, has been transformed into a system of enslavement of everyone, even of those who enslave the others. It is hard to imagine the immensity of this tragedy in terms of psychological destruction, especially within the intelligentsia. The courage to be was undermined in innumerable people because it was the courage to be in the sense of the revolutionary movements of the 19th century. When it broke down, these people turned either to the neocollectivist system, in a fanatic-neurotic reaction against the cause of their tragic disappointment, or to a cynical-neurotic indifference to all systems and every content.

It is obvious that similar observations can be made on the transformation of the Nietzschean type of the courage to be as oneself into the Facist-Nazi forms of neocollectivism. The totalitarian machines which these movements produced embodied almost everything against which the courage to be as oneself stands. They used all possible means in order to make such courage impossible. Although, in distinction to communism, this system fell down, its aftermath is confusion, indifference, cynicism. And this is the soil on which the longing for authority and for a new collectivism grows.

The last two chapters, that on the courage to be as a part and that on the courage to be as oneself, have shown [153] that the former, if carried through radically, leads to the loss of the self in collectivism and the latter to the loss of the world in Existentialism. This brings us to the question of our last chapter: Is there a courage to be which unites both forms by transcending them? [154]

. . . . .

THE GOD ABOVE GOD AND THE COURAGE TO BE

The ultimate source of the courage to be is the "God above God"; this is the result of our demand to transcend theism. Only if the God of theism is transcended can the anxiety of doubt and meaninglessness be taken into the courage to be. The God above God is the object of all mystical longing, but mysticism also must be transcended in order to reach him. Mysticism does not take seriously the concrete and the doubt concerning the concrete. It plunges directly into the ground of being and meaning, and leaves the concrete, the world of finite values and meanings, behind. Therefore it does not solve the problem of meaninglessness. In terms of the present religious situation this means that Eastern mysticism is not the solution of the problems of Western Existentialism, although many people attempt this solution. The God above the God of theism is not the devaluation of the meanings which doubt has thrown into the abyss of meaninglessness; he is their potential restitution. Nevertheless absolute faith agrees with the faith implied in mysticism in that both transcend the theistic objectivation of a God who is a being. For mysticism such a God is not more real than any finite being, for the courage to be such a God [186] has disappeared in the abyss of meaninglessness with every other value and meaning.

The God above the God of theism is present, although hidden, in every divine-human encounter. Biblical religion as well as Protestant theology are aware of the paradoxical character of this encounter. They are aware that if God encounters man God is neither object nor subject and is therefore above the scheme into which theism has forced him. They are aware that personalism with respect to God is balanced by a transpersonal presence of the divine. They are aware that forgiveness can be accepted only if the power of acceptance is effective in man—biblically speaking, if the power of grace is effective in man. They are aware of the paradoxical character of every prayer, of speaking to somebody to whom you cannot speak because he is not "somebody," of asking somebody of whom you cannot ask anything because he gives or gives not before you ask, of saying "thou" to somebody who is nearer to the I than the I is to itself. Each of these paradoxes drives the religious consciousness toward a God above the God of theism.

The courage to be which is rooted in the experience of the God above the God of theism unites and transcends the courage to be as a part and the courage to be as oneself. It avoids both the loss of oneself by participation and the loss of one's world by individualization. The acceptance of the God above the God of theism makes us a part of that which is not also a part but is the ground of the whole.[187] Therefore our self is not lost in a larger whole, which submerges it in the life of a limited group. If the self participates in the power of being-itself it receives itself back. For the power of being acts through the power of the individual selves. It does not swallow them as every limited whole, every collectivism, and every conformism does. This is why the Church, which stands for the power of being-itself or for the God who transcends the God of the religions, claims to be the mediator of the courage to be. A church which is based on the authority of the God of theism cannot make such a claim. It inescapably develops into a collectivist or semicollectivist system itself.

But a church which raises itself in its message and its devotion to the God above the God of theism without sacrificing its concrete symbols can mediate a courage which takes doubt and meaninglessness into itself. It is the Church under the Cross which alone can do this, the Church which preaches the Crucified who cried to God who remained his God after the God of confidence had left him in the darkness of doubt and meaninglessness. To be as a part in such a church is to receive a courage to be in which one cannot lose one's self and in which one receives one's world.

Absolute faith, or the state of being grasped by the God beyond God, is not a state which appears beside other states of the mind. It never is something separated and definite, an event which could be isolated and described. It is always a movement in, with, and under other states of the mind. It is the situation on the boundary of [188] man's possibilities. It *is* this boundary. Therefore it is both the courage of despair and the courage in and above every courage. It is not a place where one can live, it is without the safety of words and concepts, it is without a name, a church, a cult, a theology. But it is moving in the depth of all of them. It is the power of being, in which they participate and of which they are fragmentary expressions.

One can become aware of it in the anxiety of fate and death when the traditional symbols, which enable men to stand the vicissitudes of fate and the horror of death have lost their power. When "providence" has become a superstition and "immortality" something imaginary that which once was the power in these symbols can still be present and create the courage to be in spite of the experience of a chaotic world and a finite existence. The Stoic courage returns but not as the faith in universal reason. It returns as the absolute faith which says Yes to being without seeing anything concrete which could conquer the nonbeing in fate and death.

And one can become aware of the God above the God of theism in the anxiety of guilt and condemnation when the traditional symbols that enable men to withstand the anxiety of guilt and condemnation have lost their power. When "divine judgment" is interpreted as a psychological complex and forgiveness as a remnant of the "father-image," what once was the power in those symbols can still be present and create the courage to be in spite of the experience of an infinite gap between what we are and what we ought to be. The Lutheran courage returns [189] but not supported by the faith in a judging and forgiving God. It returns in terms of the absolute faith which says Yes although there is no special power that conquers guilt. The courage to take the anxiety of meaninglessness upon oneself is the boundary line up to which the courage to be can go. Beyond it is mere non-being. Within it all forms of courage are re-established in the power of the God above the God of theism. *The courage to be is rooted in the God who appears when God has disappeared in the anxiety of doubt.*[190]

APPENDICES

TOPICS FOR WRITING PROJECTS

My purpose in this section has been to provide both instructors and students who use this book the freedom to make their own discoveries about the literature and thought of existentialism. Thus rather than dictating the direction that writing assignments should take by presenting topics in the form of questions with built-in theses, I have compiled two brief lists of topics that are intended merely to serve as points of departure for reflection. Needless to say, the lists do not exhaust the possibilities.

LITERARY TOPICS

1. The symbolism of pursuit and flight, i.e., of the Furies. (See, for example, Leo Tolstoy's "The Death of Ivan Ilych"; Jean-Paul Sartre's *The Flies;* T.S. Eliot's *The Family Reunion;* Albert Camus' *The Fall;* Charles Williams' *Cranmer of Canterbury.*)

2. The form and/or style of the Drama of the Absurd ("anti-drama").

3. The symbolism of the underground man. (See, for example, Fyodor Dostoevsky's *Notes from Underground;* Franz Kafka's *Metamorphosis;* Albert Camus' *The Fall;* Jack Kerouac's *The Subterraneans;* Ralph Ellison's *The Invisible Man.*)

4. Jean-Paul Sartre's concept of *la littérature engagée* (the literature of engagement).

5. The "London Controversy" between Kenneth Tynan and Eugène Ionesco.

6. The existential hero (or anti-hero).

7. Ionesco versus Sartre (form and/or content).

8. Anti-utopianism in existential literature. (See, for example, Fyodor Dostoevsky's "The Legend of the the Grand Inquisitor," from *The Brothers Karamazov;* W. H. Auden's "The Massacre of the Innocents"; Aldous Huxley's *Brave New World;* George Orwell's *1984;* Jean-Paul Sartre's *The Flies.*)

9. The Grand Inquisitor symbol in contemporary existential literature (see topic 8 for suggested readings).

10. Proliferation in Ionesco's drama.

11. The existential choice.
12. The symbol of the abyss.
13. The theme of the courage to be in the face of despair in humanistic existential literature.
14. The image of contemporary man in Sartre, Camus, Unamuno, and Auden.
15. The "existential" form and/or style of Kafka's "A Country Doctor."
16. The problem of whether or not Sartre's *The Flies* is literature or philosophy.
17. The concept of Nothingness in the form and content of Hemingway's "A Clean, Well-Lighted Place."
18. The symbol of the map of France in Camus' "The Guest."
19. The ambiguity of Dostoevsky's position in "The Legend of the Grand Inquisitor."
20. The contrast between Orestes and Electra in Sartre's *The Flies.*
21. Disintegration in form and content in Dürrenmatt's "The Tunnel."
22. The concrete-universal in Auden's portrait of Herod.
23. The relationship between the content and the formal use of myth in Eliot's *The Family Reunion* and Sartre's *The Flies.*
24. The use of paradox in existential literature.
25. The absurd in Unamuno's "Saint Emmanuel the Good, Martyr."

IDEOLOGICAL TOPICS

1. The Christian existential critique of atheistic (or humanistic) existentialism.
2. The atheistic or humanistic critique of Christianity.
3. The theme of death and/or Nothingness.
4. The theme of dread or anguish.
5. The theme of alienation.
6. The individual and the crowd.
7. The theme of the death of God.
8. Sartre's argument that existentialism is not a philosophy of despair.
9. The American university or college and the kingdom of anxiety.
10. Existentialism and the Incarnation.

11. Technology and the individual.
12. The I-Thou and the I-It.
13. Pascal and contemporary existential thought.
14. The absurd in humanistic (Camus and Sartre) and theistic (Kierkegaard and Auden) existential thought.
15. The existential critique of essentialist philosophies.
16. Existential ethics.
17. The Sartre-Camus controversy.
18. The nature of language in existential philosophical writing.
19. Literature as a form of philosophical discourse.
20. Kierkegaard and contemporary existential thought.
21. The subjective-objective dichotomy.
22. Analytic philosophy versus existentialism. See especially A. J. Ayer, "Novelist-Philosopher, Jean-Paul Sartre," *Horizon,* Vol. XII (1954), pp. 12–26, 101–10; and "Novelist-Philosopher, Albert Camus," *Horizon,* Vol. XIII (1946), pp. 155–68.
23. Bad faith (or self-deception) and authenticity.
24. Freedom in humanistic and Christian existentialism.
25. Kierkegaard's "leap of faith."
26. Pascal's "wager."

SELECTED BIBLIOGRAPHY

The existential works listed below, all of them significant, were not included in the text because of the exigencies of space. For works of criticism and commentary, consult (1) Kenneth Douglas, *A Critical Bibliography of Existentialism (The Paris School)*, Yale French Studies Monograph No. 1 (New Haven, 1950); (2) Richard Lehan, "French and American Philosophical and Literary Existentialism: A Selected Checklist," *Wisconsin Studies in Contemporary Literature*, Vol. I, No. 3 (Fall, 1960), pp. 74–88; and (3) the bibliography on Jean-Paul Sartre in *Yale French Studies*, No. 30 (New Haven, 1962), pp. 108–119. The student should also avail himself of the annual PMLA bibliographical supplements, and the annual indices and occasional bibliographical supplements of such periodicals as *The Partisan Review, Yale French Studies, Modern Drama, and Drama Survey.*

EXISTENTIAL LITERATURE

Some Antecedents

Drama: The Book of Job
GEORG BÜCHNER, *Woyzeck*
HENRIK IBSEN, *Hedda Gabler*
ALFRED JARRY, *Ubu Roi*
LUIGI PIRANDELLO, *Six Characters in Search of an Author*
WILLIAM SHAKESPEARE, *King Lear*
AUGUST STRINDBERG, *The Ghost Sonata*
CYRIL TOURNEUR, *The Revenger's Tragedy*

Novels: JOSEPH CONRAD, *The Heart of Darkness*
CHARLES DICKENS, *Great Expectations; Hard Times*
FYODOR DOSTOEVSKY, *Crime and Punishment; The Possessed*
LEO TOLSTOY, *Anna Karenina*

Short Stories: NATHANIEL HAWTHORNE, "Young Goodman Brown"; "Wakefield"
MARQUIS DE SADE, "Dialogue Between a Priest and a Dying Man"

LEO TOLSTOY, "The Death of Ivan Ilych"; "The Diary of a Lunatic"

Some Contemporary Works

Drama: EDWARD ALBEE, *The American Dream; Zoo Story*
SAMUEL BECKETT, *Endgame; Waiting for Godot*
ALBERT CAMUS, *Caligula*
FRIEDRICH DÜRRENMATT, *The Visit*
T. S. ELIOT, *The Family Reunion*
MAX FRISCH, *The Firebugs*
CHRISTOPHER FRY, *A Sleep of Prisoners*
JEAN GENÊT, *The Blacks; The Maids; The Balcony*
ROLF HOCCHUTH, *The Deputy*
EUGÈNE IONESCO, *The Bald Soprano; Jack, or the Submission; The Lesson; Rhinoceros*
JOHN OSBORNE, *Look Back in Anger*
HAROLD PINTER, *The Birthday Party; The Room*
ELMER RICE, *The Adding Machine*
JEAN-PAUL SARTRE, *The Devil and the Good Lord; Dirty Hands; No Exit*
CHARLES WILLIAMS, *Thomas Cranmer of Canterbury; Seed of Adam*

Novels: JAMES BALDWIN, *Another Country*
SIMONE DE BEAUVOIR, *The Blood of Others*
ALBERT CAMUS, *The Fall; The Plague; The Stranger*
JOHN DOS PASSOS, *1919*
RALPH ELLISON, *The Invisible Man*
WILLIAM FAULKNER, *The Sound and the Fury*
MAX FRISCH, *I'm Not Stiller*
GRAHAM GREENE, *Brighton Rock; The Power and the Glory*
ERNEST HEMINGWAY, *The Sun Also Rises*
HERMAN HESSE, *Steppenwolf*
ALDOUS HUXLEY, *Brave New World*
FRANZ KAFKA, *The Castle; The Trial*
JACK KEROUAC, *The Subterraneans*
ARTHUR KOESTLER, *Arrival and Departure*
ANDRÉ MALRAUX, *The Royal Way; The Walnut Tree of Altenburg*
FRANÇOIS MAURIAC, *Thérèse Desqueyroux*
IRIS MURDOCH, *Under the Net*

ROBERT MUSIL, *The Man Without Qualities*
GEORGE ORWELL, *1984*
ALAIN ROBBE-GRILLET, *In the Labyrinth; Last Year at Marienbad; The Voyeur*
ANTOINE DE SAINT-EXUPÉRY, *Night Flight*
J. D. SALINGER, *Catcher in the Rye*
NATHALIE SARRAUTE, *The Age of Suspicion*
JEAN-PAUL SARTRE, *Nausea; The Age of Reason; The Reprieve; Troubled Sleep*
WILLIAM STYRON, *Lie Down in Darkness; The Long March*
RICHARD WRIGHT, *The Outsider*
EUGENE ZAMIATIN, *We*

Short Stories: ILSE AICHINGER, "The Bound Man"
FRANZ KAFKA, "The Bucket Rider"; "The Great Wall of China"; "The Penal Colony"; "The Burrow"; "Metamorphosis"
CESARE PAVESE, "Suicides"
J. D. SALINGER, "For Esmé—With Love and Squalor"
JEAN-PAUL SARTRE, "The Childhood of a Leader"; "The Wall"

Poetry: W. H. AUDEN, "New Year Letter"; "Under Which Lyre"
T. S. ELIOT, "The Hollow Men"; "The Love Song of J. Alfred Prufrock"; "The Waste Land"
ALLEN GINSBERG, "Howl"
RAINER MARIA RILKE, *The Duino Elegies*

WORKS OF EXISTENTIAL PHILOSOPHERS NOT INCLUDED IN THE TEXT

DE BEAUVOIR, SIMONE. *The Ethics of Ambiguity,* trans. Bernard Frechtman. New York: Philosophical Library, 1948.

BERGSON, HENRI LOUIS. *Time and Free Will: An Essay on the Immediate Data of Consciousness,* trans. R. L. Pogson. New York: Macmillan, 1913.

BUBER, MARTIN. *I and Thou,* trans. Ronald Gregor Smith. 2nd edn. New York: Scribner's, 1958.

BULTMANN, RUDOLF. "New Testament and Mythology," trans. Reginald H. Fuller, *Kerygma and Myth: A Theological Debate,* ed. Hans Werner Bartsch. New York: Harper & Brothers, 1961.

HEIDEGGER, MARTIN. *Being and Time,* trans. John Macquarrie, ed. Edward Robinson. New York: Harper & Row, 1963.

HUSSERL, EDMUND. *Phenomenology and the Crisis of Philosophy,* trans. with Notes and Introduction by Quentin Lauer. New York: Harper & Row, 1965.

JAMES, WILLIAM. *The Varieties of Religious Experience: A Study in Human Nature.* New York: Longman's, Green, 1925.

MARCEL, GABRIEL. *The Mystery of Being: Reflection and Mystery, I,* trans. G. S. Fraser. Chicago: Henry Regnery, 1960.

———. *The Mystery of Being: Faith and Reality, II,* trans. René Hague. Chicago: Henry Regnery, 1960.

MARITAIN, JACQUES. *Existence and the Existent: An Essay on Christian Existentialism,* trans. Lewis Galantière and Gerald B. Phelan. Garden City: Doubleday, 1956.

MERLEAU-PONTY, MAURICE. *Phenomonology of Perception,* trans. Colin Smith. New York: The Humanities Press, 1962.

———. *Sense and Non-Sense,* trans. Hubert L. and Patricia Allen Dreyfus. Evanston: Northwestern University Press, 1964.

ORTEGA Y GASSET, JOSÉ. *Man and People,* trans. Willard R. Trask. New York: Norton, 1963.

DE UNAMUNO, MIGUEL. *Tragic Sense of Life,* trans. J. E. Crawford Flitch. New York: Dover, 1954.

HEIDEGGER, MARTIN. Being and Time, trans. John Macquarrie and Edward Robinson. New York: Harper & Row, 1962.

HUSSERL, EDMUND. Phenomenology and the Crisis of Philosophy, trans. with notes and introduction by Quentin Lauer. New York: Harper & Row, 1965.

JAMES, WILLIAM. The Principles of Psychology, 2 vols. [illegible] New York: [illegible], [illegible].

MARCEL, GABRIEL. The Mystery of Being: Reflection and Mystery, I, trans. G. S. Fraser. Chicago: Henry Regnery, 1951.

——— The Mystery of Being: Faith and Reality, II, trans. René Hague. Chicago: Henry Regnery, 1950.

MARITAIN, JACQUES. Existence and the Existent, trans. Lewis Galantière and Gerald B. Phelan. Garden City: Doubleday, 1956.

MERLEAU-PONTY, MAURICE. Phenomenology of Perception, trans. Colin Smith. New York: The Humanities Press, 1962.

——— Sense and Non-Sense, trans. Hubert L. and Patricia Allen Dreyfus. Evanston: Northwestern University Press, 1964.

ORTEGA Y GASSET, JOSÉ. Man and People, trans. Willard R. Trask. New York: Norton, 1957.

UNAMUNO, MIGUEL DE. Tragic Sense of Life, trans. J. E. Crawford Flitch. New York: Dover, 1954.